NO BELLS ON SUNDAY

*'Everyone has not only
a story, but a scream.'*

RACHEL ROBERTS

# NO
# BELLS
# ON
# SUNDAY

## The Rachel Roberts Journals

*edited with a documentary
biography by Alexander Walker*

*1817*

**HARPER & ROW, PUBLISHERS,** New York
Cambridge, Philadelphia, San Francisco, London
Mexico City, São Paulo, Singapore, Sydney

*Photographs follow pages 118 and 182.*

Photographs obtained from the following sources:

John Haynes; Keystone Press Agency; Kobal Collection;
London Express News & Features; National Film
Archives; Popperfoto; Rex Features; John Timbers;
Van Williams; Wessex Newspapers

FIRST U.S. EDITION

ISBN 0-06-015235-4

LIBRARY OF CONGRESS CATALOG CARD NUMBER 83-48379

84 85 86 87 88 10 9 8 7 6 5 4 3 2 1

# INTRODUCTION

'IF YOU'RE IN NEW YORK ANY TIME, I'll show them to you.' – 'I happen to be going there this week-end.' – 'Where are you staying?' – 'At the Berkshire Place on East 52nd Street.' – 'Why, that's literally at our back door, we're 53rd – I'll send them round.'

Thus began, in a manner which I sensed retrospectively had an ominous coincidence about it, the quest for Rachel Roberts that comprises the present book. Lawrence Ashmead, executive editor at Harper & Row, the New York publishers, had met me in London in the summer of 1982 after casually mentioning to my agent Carol Smith that he had come into possession of some diaries kept by Rachel Roberts, the film and stage actress who had committed suicide in Los Angeles two years earlier. He had dipped into them . . . and read on, intrigued by their extraordinarily vivid testimony to what seemed not one life, but the multitude of lives led by this enormously talented, passionate and self-destructive woman.

The range of experiences she had sought, suffered, frequently survived but ultimately succumbed to was, in its breadth and diversity, almost epic. But her narrative was confusing to a degree. Famous names were there in abundance, easily recognisable. Rex Harrison, who had been Rachel's husband for nearly ten years; filmmakers like Lindsay Anderson, John Schlesinger, Sidney Lumet and Karel Reisz with whom she had won applause and awards in such movies as *This Sporting Life, Yanks, Murder on the Orient Express* and *Saturday Night and Sunday Morning*; Hal Prince the Broadway director; stars like Albert Finney, Richard Gere, Jill Bennett, Peter Ustinov and Tony Randall; the playwright Athol Fugard; novelists and screenwriters like Edna O'Brien and Gavin Lambert; and a host of others, some of them Ashmead's personal friends, who plied their trades in and around the arts and media: agent Milton Goldman, photo-journalist Nancy Holmes, opinion-maker Pamela Mason . . .

But there were other names to whom the publisher couldn't assign a face or a talent, but whose part in Rachel Roberts's professional achievements or emotional anguish she had endowed with importance: doctors and psycho-analysts and PR men, convicts on parole and hustlers forever on the make, school chums from Wales and academics from Yale, ex-wives who changed names with the passage of time and husbands, girlfriends and lovers, Good Samaritans and bad influences, and many, many more whom some lightning flash of yearning memory had recalled as Rachel's *driven* handwriting roved back and forth in time and place, mood and event. Despite the manuscript's confusion, Ashmead felt a power in the narrative that derived from emotional compulsion as much as artistic self-expression: there was evidence of great happiness, great sorrow, great candour, great insight, great helplessness . . . 'Everyone has not only a story, but a scream' – one phrase that leaped off the page summed up the two dominant impressions that Rachel's writing made on even a casual perusal. This was the tale of a woman fighting to stay this side of life, but setting down her feelings and memories with the accumulating shock of someone recognising she was powerless to escape her own fate. The turbulence needed to be controlled without being tamed, directed without being distorted, conducted into the compassionate comprehension of readers without its own self-lacerating integrity being drained of the pain that validated the writer's struggle to preserve life and sanity.

In due course an attaché case was delivered to my New York hotel, along with a note asking me to advise on whether the material in it could – or should – be published. I soon saw the difficulty in both respects: one was a matter of professional judgment; the other, moral choice. The dozen or so yellow lined legal pads or spiral-bound notebooks had been discovered under flowering shrubs in the conservatory of the house in the Los Angeles canyon where Rachel Roberts ended her life, aged 53, on 26 November 1980. They had been left there, along with Rachel's purse, to be discovered, probably before her body was: though this in itself might have caused her lover, Darren Ramirez, alarm since she never let the notebooks pass from her possession while they were living together.

To judge from internal evidence, she had been writing them up for the last eighteen months of her life. This was the first difficulty. For these were not diaries in the conventional sense, where entries are contemporaneous with the day-to-day events. The strong (and mercifully legible) handwriting – without a single false start or revision that I can recall in the 500-odd pages – only turned into that sort of 'diary' in the last four months of Rachel's life. They were really 'journals', in which she wrote about almost every period of her life as the urge or association took her.

Some parts of it, especially her early family history and childhood, had a slightly literary self-consciousness which hinted at some earlier but absent draft; other parts had the feverish telegraphic notation of someone fearing that a tragic extinction would overtake her before she reached the end of the page. The pages were packed with incidents, opinions, judgments on others and herself. As the end approached, the plea for help and understanding became insistently pathetic, yet never incoherent. As I read and re-read them, another and more disconcerting pattern emerged that did nothing to allay my own concern for Rachel or suggest my literary task would be easier. For the shape of her reminiscences was 'circular'. That is to say, she would cover the events of one period in her life in detail and at length; then she would advance the story until some accidental associative curve of memory sent her right back to the start; whereupon she would recapitulate the events, maybe with variations and added 'colour', until she pulled level with the detour and went a few months further down the road of life until yet another affective signpost sent her circling back . . .

After I had sorted the events in the notebooks into rough chronological order – which took several months of cross-indexing – I realised that these circles were growing smaller and smaller as Rachel's mind grew ever more tormented. It was as if she were being sucked down, down, down into the convulsions of a whirlpool of her own making. Ultimately, she reached the bottom of this diminishing spiral – and found the only way out was self-extinction. To forge a narrative out of this, that would be comprehensible, readable and void of repetitious detail, I had to turn the circular neurosis into a linear story-line, I hope without losing any of its urgency. Rachel wrote well. But she was as impulsive in her thinking as her actions. There is no breathing space, one feels, between an emotion and its dashed down expression: yet neither is there any lack of focus. She always supplied the self-critical distance. There is a sanity in the writing that disconcertingly belies the anguish in the mind.

What has ultimately emerged is the story of an addiction and an obsession. The addiction was to alcohol: no less terrifying a trauma because sadly commonplace. The obsession was altogether more singular. Rachel never recovered from her expulsion from Paradise – Paradise, this time round, being represented by the world of wealth, talent and celebrity inhabited with such seeming ease and enviable enjoyment by her second husband, Rex Harrison. Rachel clearly loved sharing the world that Rex had made: she also despised herself for loving it, for her puritan Welsh instinct never felt guiltless unless she were mortifying the artistic spirit, not indulging in borrowed hedonism. Yet when she lost access to 'Rex's world', after their marriage was dissolved in 1971, she was utterly bereft. Her state of mind recalled to me the well-known painting by Claude – the one said to have inspired Keats's marvellous line about 'magic casements, opening on the foam/ Of perilous seas in faery lands forlorn', and reproduced in the endpapers of this book. In it Psyche sits alone in the shadows, expelled from the God Cupid's palace. 'Celebrity' was the spell which Rachel mistakenly hoped would help her regain the heights her superstar husband had scaled – heights as real as Rex's mountain-top Villa San Genesio that he had built above Portofino and to which she kept returning in reverie when she could no longer return in person. But celebrity, she found, was a drug which takes fatal possession of anyone who mistakes it for achievement – and Rachel, goodness knows, needed enough drugs of the other kind to sustain her. Nor did her final vain and deluded bid to regain Rex himself bring her any surcease – just the reverse. That she clearly recognised all this as she wrote up her journals – so clearly that it is hard to credit the writer is a desperately ailing woman – yet couldn't put the insight to use to steady her life and restore her talents was what gave the pages of her journals their pathos. Other gifted women have taken their life: none that I recall kept a record of her losing struggle right up to the day before she died.

When I finished editing the journals, I found myself wishing Rachel Roberts had sat down twenty years earlier and begun a career as a professional writer. Had she done so, I believe she would be alive today: less of a celebrity, perhaps, but a more fulfilled woman, perhaps a novelist in the tradition of Edna O'Brien. (I didn't realise *then* how curious a link existed between Rachel's life and Edna O'Brien's fiction.)

Among Rachel's journals I found half-a-dozen short stories she had attempted and three of these are interpolated in the narrative – not just as psychologically interesting evidence of how she fictionalised her current state of mind, but as evidence of a creative writer's talent which never had the chance to do more than bud. That Rachel had it in mind to publish her journals cannot be doubted – she made specific reference to the possibility, she even noted down a title. Certainly the journals wouldn't have been printed as she wrote them, nor as I have edited them: but I devoutly hope she would feel they still do her justice in this form, and approve of the title I gave them: *No Bells on Sunday*.

It was suggested by a passage in which she was trying to find a reason for the 'peace and sweetness' going out of her life and blaming it in part on Los Angeles. 'Los Angeles belies all that man and womankind have done to minimise the darkness and the inexplicable nature of our lives. No cockerels crow to announce the day. No cows moo. No reachable birds sing. No church bells ring on Sunday to remind us of our spirit. We rarely see a funeral procession – no reminder of our mortality is ever present. People don't walk, don't talk, don't really laugh, cry inside or refuse to, and falsity is everywhere. All want to take, not give, and life laughs coldly back.' I think that *No Bells on Sunday* expresses the dark heart of the matter for this child of the Welsh chapel-valleys.

Rachel's journals, however, required more than narrative continuity: they required a perspective to frame them and, occasionally, to fill in the blanks she inevitably left in her account. So I began to seek out and interview the people I imagined would know her best: I myself had met her about half-a-dozen times. I called a halt after I had transcribed interviews with some fifty of them: for it seemed *everyone* I met knew Rachel, or 'a Rachel' – for she did indeed contain multitudes!

The people I felt had known her most revealingly spoke so tellingly of her as gifted actress or flamboyant personality or good companion or generous but erratic lover or desperate patient or in dozens of other guises, happy and tragic, that I decided not to lose the forthrightness of their recall by tossing the grist of what they said into the usual biography mill, but to reproduce their words as freshly (and, I trust, accurately) as they spoke them to me (or, in two or three cases, wrote them down and sent them to me). To most of them, it came as a total surprise to know of the existence of Rachel's journals: and no one read a line of them before speaking to me, except for Darren Ramirez and the stage and film director Anthony Page whom chance had placed literally next-door to Rachel in her last days.

Only three of those approached declined to help: one, an analyst, did so on understandable professional grounds; the others, two of Rachel's closest women friends, still felt her absence too acutely to share their memories of her. Others who were at or near the centre of Rachel's life have already written about her in their own memoirs (or may intend to do) and were not approached.

To Mr Harrison, I submitted my edited version of the journals, as a voluntary courtesy, and also talked privately to him: no other approach to him was sought or offered. But I would like to put it on record that although a lot of Rachel's story must have made painful reading for him, he did not obstruct me in seeking interviews with mutual friends and acquaintances of him and his late wife, nor did he ask for any changes in the printed text other than those which concerned factual accuracy or a possibly misleading impression.

I have tried to avoid unnecessary or undue pain to others who figure in the book: thus I have used a biographer's judgment to delete a very small number of harrowing remarks, and changed the names (in each case specified in the text) of a few people whom it was not necessary to identify. I have also excised some remarks on grounds of taste or possible legal risk. I would say that Rachel's manuscript has been reduced by a third. Naturally, publishing such a bizarre first-person account of a life that ended violently, and including the free and sometimes startlingly candid comments of friends and associates, is a hazardous venture subject to all kinds of interpretations and suspicions. My own view is that the probity of the enterprise must depend on two things – taste and faith. I leave the first to the reader's judgment: but if anyone is in doubt about the morality of it, I beg them to read the last two pages of this book first. Gavin Lambert's recollections of Rachel were contained in the last letter I received before the book went to press and I shall always be grateful to him for expressing, with such grace and skill, something of the 'force for life' which Rachel personified and which, he felt, should not be allowed to die with her. This book, I hope, preserves that force.

I am also grateful to Darren Ramirez for allowing me an entirely free hand with her journals. In telling Rachel's story, I have also to thank the following (in their order of appearance in the narrative): David Lewin, Sybil Christopher, Darren Ramirez, Elizabeth James, Gwladys Standfast, Brian Evans, Mansell Prothero, Ronnie Cass, Eileen Jeffries, Lionel Jeffries, Bryan Mathew, Kenneth Williams, Eleanor Fazan, Lindsay Anderson, Karel Reisz, Albert Finney, Pamela Mason, Ned Sherrin, Jean Marsh, Nancy Holmes, Lionel Bart, Peter Bull, Anthony Page, Felix Barker, Jeffrey Lane, Milton Goldman, Hal Prince, Sidney Lumet, Michael York, Jill Bennett, Pat Lovell, Peter Weir, Richard Gere, Tony Randall, Tom Patchett, John Schlesinger, Amadeo Limentani, Douglas Fairbanks Jr, Ferruccio A. di Cori, Earle R. Gister, Athol Fugard, Clive Donner, Jocelyn Rickards, Peter Ustinov, Ann Leslie, Edna O'Brien and Gavin Lambert.

All biographies, I believe, should draw on the refracted coloration that a 'life' acquires from what is written about the subject of it in contemporary interviews and stage and film reviews. Rachel was an interviewee who too often played the blind side of journalists and too many of them, if indeed they suspected her, colluded in giving the impression she was after – when the copy was good, why look critical? But a few among the dozens of interviews I read catch her – and a *very* few catch her out – at important junctures of her life and career.

With the respect of a fellow writer, I thank those quoted: Shirley Lowe, Clive Hirschhorn, Barry Norman, Felix Barker, Penelope Gilliatt, Michael Leech, Earl Wilson, Winfred Blevins, Charles Faber, Dan Sullivan, Judy Klemesrud, Clive Barnes, Richard Watts Jr, John Simon, Rex Reed, Walter Kerr, Howard Kissel, Sydney Edwards, Gordon Burn, Charles Champlin, Stephen Farber, Tina Mallet, Michael Billington, Philip French and Sheila Benson. I have acknowledged in the text and I wish to thank the authors of the following works which have been of assistance: *Rex: An Autobiography,* by Rex Harrison (Macmillan, London, 1974);

*Change Lobsters and Dance: An Autobiography*, by Lilli Palmer (Macmillan Inc., New York, 1975); *Love, Honour and Dismay*, by Elizabeth Harrison (Weidenfeld, London, 1976).

I thank the producer and staff of BBC Wales's breakfast news programme for help in making contact with some of Rachel's childhood friends.

I am grateful for facilities made available by the head librarian and staff, and in particular Carol Epstein, at the Margaret Herrick Library of the Academy of Motion Picture Arts and Sciences, Beverly Hills; the curator and staff of the Billy Rose Collection at the New York Public Library; and the chief librarian and staff of the Information Library at the British Film Institute, London.

The debt I owe my American and British publishers is already well-known to them: to Lawrence P. Ashmead, executive editor, Harper & Row Inc., for introducing me to this labyrinthine project and showing uncommon patience while I threaded my way through it; and to Colin Webb, managing director, Pavilion Books Ltd, London, for a matching endurance and for helping me assemble a printer's jigsaw of a text: if there are any mismated pieces, the fault is mine.

Alexander Walker
New York 1982 – London 1984

# NO BELLS ON SUNDAY

SHE WAS A WELSH GIRL who was born in a valley and died in a canyon –
thousands of miles from home. How far our end is from our beginnings.

Let us start (as Hollywood, where she died, so often does) with the end.

To anyone who does not know Beverly Hills and its affluent out-reaches,
the name 'Hutton Drive' probably signifies some conventionally laid out
street of suburban homes: not one of the famous or glamorous names, not a
Wilshire, or a Rodeo, or a Doheny, perhaps, but a protectively zoned place,
neat and neighbourly . . .

Only it is nothing of the kind. Hutton Drive lies well north of Sunset
Boulevard and is, in fact, the winding bottom of an overgrown canyon,
where houses take advantage of the hillside's vegetation spilling down on
top of them to pull themselves under cover or out of sight. Many of them,
though comfortable, are not large: mortgages, alimony and other cash
transactions have bought a lot of them or maintain the rental payments
and though there are owners' names that seem familiar tucked away here
and there, they are usually the ones found on medical, dental and legal
name-plates or in among the technical credits rather than above the titles
of the movies. It is a quiet place, can be a lonely place and has been a
dangerous place: though in 1980 that could be said of quite a lot of what is
generically called 'Hollywood'.

Hutton Drive pulled in its quota of service workers: day-maids, baby-
sitters, pool-cleaners, gardeners, who had 'their' employers, 'their' numbers
in a road that manifested (in the eyes of more compact European dwellers)
that American sense of easy sprawl, with houses that often needed four or
even five digits to identify their location in the spacious scheme of things.
No. 2620 Hutton Drive was on the worklist of a Mexican jobbing gardener, a middle-aged man called Luis Escobar. He spoke little English. Not
that he needed much for his job; and certainly he got by with less at No.
2620, where his employer was a handsome Mexican in his thirties named
Darren Ramirez who had been a good few years in America, was divorced,
and worked in a variety of jobs, usually to do with clothes-designing and

1

hair-styling in Beverly Hills, which was just about twenty minutes away by the owner's sports car. Escobar came to him every Wednesday and Saturday. He trimmed the hedges, clipped the lawn, cut back the ground ivies: usually he did not see Darren Ramirez at all, for he was away at work when the gardener arrived, round about 3.30 pm, and he was not infrequently still at work, or play, by the time darkness had covered Escobar's work. The gardener brought his own tools and did not need access to the house.

The house was a ranch-type bungalow: it sat on a raised lawn approached by, well, hardly a drive, more of a ramp that raked an entering car at a forty-five-degree angle. Behind the house, above a small paved patio, the canyon sloped even more steeply up to the top ridge and someone had cut a flight of tiny, precipitous steps leading up into a copse of bramble bushes that gave a faint reminder of that natural disorder which English city-dwellers like to cultivate in their back gardens in a vestigial link with countryside. Escobar was excused from having to tend this patch with rake and shears. *Someone*, though he did not know exactly who, liked it as it was and wanted it left that way. Spindly shrubs with puny lemons on them, and more matronly grapefruit trees poked up out of this wilderness. In the summer, the brambles would throw up wild roses. It was a good place to come for privacy.

There was a front lawn where eucalyptus trees shaded a reclining garden chair. The house was white clapboard, and a pillared verandah and green shutters were pleasant additions to its conventional shape. There was that commonplace item of garden equipment in most of the homes which had any pretensions to good living in Southern California – an octagonal blue disc that said in stern white lettering, 'Security Warning'. That was one more reason why Escobar did not enter the house: anything he needed was brought with him or out of doors already.

He was usually through inside ninety minutes: which was just as well, for by the time he arrived on this day, Wednesday, November 26, the sun was off the south-east slope of the canyon – a fact that was to be quoted later in an effort to find a partial explanation for the unexpected and piteous sight that Escobar encountered a few minutes after he entered the garden.

He undid the stiff latch of the wicket gate at the side and went round to the rear, meaning to connect the hose-pipe. To his surprise, he saw the glass-paned door opening out from the living-room on to the patio was half-open. He heard a kettle on the boil in the kitchen. He went over to the open door, stood outside and looked in, not quite daring to enter lest he set off the security alarm. What was that on the floor? Glass – many splinters of broken glass! Perhaps there had been a burglary! Perhaps the burglar was still inside! These thoughts chased themselves across his mind in a few seconds, as the kettle boiled steamily on . . . Then as he craned forward, peering round the door-frame, Escobar saw the woman lying there.

She was inert on the kitchen floor amidst the debris of what had been an ornamental Victorian glass screen used to divide the breakfast den from the living-room. She seemed to have knocked it over in her fall – hence the shattered glass. The woman was blonde, middle-aged, wearing a thin negligée-type gown that was in a terrible state – rumpled and snagged and plucked in a dozen places. The woman's legs were badly scratched, too, and she had deeper wounds from the shattered glass screen.

Although there was a telephone in the house, Escobar knew enough about police procedure not to enter further in order to use it – or indeed to turn off the kettle whose steamy emission suggested that whatever had happened at 2620 Hutton Drive hadn't happened so long ago for it to boil itself dry.

The gardener ran back along the side path, out the front entrance, and made for the next-door neighbours, an elderly couple who were next on his rota after the Ramirez residence had received its twice-weekly jot of horticultural attention. The time was about 3.45 pm.

David Lewin and his wife Betty were looking forward to a relaxed evening with the English actor David Warner: they'd a table reserved at Oscar's, opposite the Château Marmont. They were bathing and dressing in their room at the Beverly Wilshire Hotel on Wilshire Boulevard, Beverly Hills, when the telephone rang.

Lewin is acknowledged to be one of the best-known and most professional of English newspapermen. He had a reputation that goes back over several decades of keeping close to the leading, or, at least, temporarily newsworthy, figures of show-business in Hollywood and London. He had worked on two leading national dailies, the *Express* and the *Mail*, and had been spending time in California collecting material and doing interviews for his freelance assignments. His thick address book, filled with the ex-directory numbers that are the lifeblood of journalists in his field, testified to the multitude of celebrities who trusted him enough to be considered friends. Getting messages for a journalist is almost as vital as getting numbers: which was why Lewin usually preferred the Beverly Wilshire as his base: the folk who lived in Beverly Hills, and changed minds and appointments so frequently, kept that hotel's excellent message operator busy. So when he picked up the phone, he half-expected just such a change in the upcoming schedule and hoped it wouldn't spoil his evening. But it wasn't the operator: it was a man's voice. It didn't at once identify itself, but, to Lewin's surprise, asked if the caller could speak to 'Bet' Lewin.

Now almost no one called Betty Lewin that. Puzzled by the oddness and intimacy of the unknown caller, Lewin passed the phone over to his wife, who was just out of the bath, with the quip, 'One of your American boy-friends.' Betty Lewin listened a second or two, then sat down on the bed behind her and looked as if she would pass out. Lewin grabbed the phone.

'I don't know who you are or why you're calling,' he said, now speaking angrily in his alarm, 'but what you've just said to my wife has upset her terribly.'

The man on the line identified himself. 'Detective Sack, of the Los Angeles Police Department.' He was investigating a death, he said. A woman called Rachel Roberts. It was now Lewin's turn to experience that jag of shock, bewilderment and professional quickening of adrenaline that penetrates the consciousness of a reporter who, by chance, has some personal involvement in the unexpected. He put the obvious question.

'Bet' Lewin's voice giving her name and hotel room number was the last one recorded by the telephone answering machine at 2620 Hutton Drive the detective replied.

Then Lewin understood. He remembered the last time he had talked to Rachel Roberts, at a party a few days previously, when she asked, 'Is Bet coming over?' Rachel had her Welsh countrymen's habit of shortening all first names down to a homely identity tab – her Welsh friends never called *her* anything but 'Ray'.

Rachel liked Betty Lewin: something in Betty's blunt Yorkshire nature corresponded to Rachel's direct Welsh approach: they had hit it off together from the first. When Betty had arrived in Beverly Hills, she telephoned Rachel about getting together, got the answering device, left the message. But that had been a day or two ago, and already David had the journalist's fretful sense of unease that he might have missed 'a story', for Rachel had told him she was shortly leaving for New York. Frank Dunlop, the English stage director, wanted her to audition for the mother's role he was trying to cast in Edward Albee's musical adaptation of *Lolita*.

'Audition? *You* audition?' David recalled saying, implying his surprise that an actress so tried and proven and distinguished as Rachel Roberts already was should have to undergo the nervous preliminaries about getting a role that were the lot of the hapless Broadway beginner. But Rachel had only said she didn't mind . . . she didn't mind at all.

Now the detective was saying he would put three questions to David. (Interrogation-room habits were hard to break.) David suddenly became suspicious. Perhaps it was the unpleasant unexpectedness of being questioned by a total stranger about an event whose terrible sadness was just sinking in. Anyhow, was it true, what he was being told? *He* now began questioning the detective, demanding his precinct-station, the number there, the number he was calling from. Detective Sack didn't seem surprised, or annoyed: he just said he'd wait while David checked him out.

Yes, they said at West Los Angeles precinct station, Detective Sack worked there. His whereabouts now? 'He is in the field, sir, investigating a homicide.' 'Homicide?' That word to English ears has a more ominous meaning than the neutral category called 'death'. David quickly called back: the phone was picked up instantly.

He confirmed he'd known Rachel Roberts for many years, interviewed her often, written many stories, seen her on the stage, gone to her films.

'The detective said, "Who are the relatives?" I said there was a sister. I believed she lived in Wales. "Wales? Where's Wales?" – I said it was a part of the United Kingdom – of Britain. – "Any other relatives?" – I said No, unless you counted her ex-husband. – "Who is that?" – "Rex Harrison."' The detective said 'Oh,' and there was a slight pause. Though David Lewin knew Rex Harrison was scheduled to open in Los Angeles in the *My Fair Lady* production he'd been touring across the United States that fall, he wasn't aware that Harrison was right at that moment no further than a mile away at the home of an English friend, the composer and lyricist Leslie Bricusse.

'So when the detective said to me, "I would like for you to make contact with Mr Harrison and tell him what's happened and ask him to call me," I said a bit testily, "Look here, the resources of the Los Angeles police department are greater than mine. Why don't *you* people call him?"' (David later learned it was routine procedure in such events to ask the friend of any foreign citizen who had suffered a mishap, fatal or otherwise, in the States to break the news first to the next of kin: presumably a familiar accent countered, to some extent, the shock of the unexpected.) Detective Sack persisted. 'I told him I'd do a deal. I'd have to do a story on

4

this. If I tried contacting Rex, would the detective call me back and tell me more about Rachel's death for the story I'd be phoning to London? Was it suicide, murder or death from natural causes? I asked. "I don't know yet. We won't know till the autopsy. But I'm not at the moment entertaining murder."'

Lewin called around, discovered Harrison's whereabouts, found the Bricusses' ex-directory number in his book. Harrison was out, so the message was left. Then as David didn't need to write his story for a few more hours, since it couldn't appear before the morning of November 28 by London time, he and a dreadfully shaken Betty went out to dinner with Warner and a girlfriend. They were a melancholy foursome.

'We got back. No message. But at 2.30 am – yes, it shows you the hours detectives keep – the detective rang to keep his promise. "She was found stretched out on the kitchen floor. It looks like she fell and choked to death on whatever she was eating, a sandwich or muffin or something – there's bread in her mouth. It's not murder and it doesn't look like suicide. But we can't be sure till we have the autopsy."'

And so David Lewin put his robe on and swiftly wrote up Rachel Roberts' death and telephoned it to the *Daily Mail* copytakers in London. It was the earliest news of an event that saddened and surprised many, to appear in the British press. David ended it: 'The detective who phoned me . . . wanted to know – as everybody did – whether [Rachel] was happy. Certainly at the party at which I met her a few nights before she was witty and joking and appeared without a care in the world.'

International Creative Management is a pretentious title for a company that doesn't need to pretend. ICM is one of America's biggest talent agencies, with offices in New York, Los Angeles and London. It makes deals for all kinds of talents – stage, screen and TV performers, producers, directors, writers and, even, other deal-makers. It numbers figureheads of the English acting Establishment like Olivier and Gielgud among its clients; it corrals people who show promise and actively enhances their careers (if all goes well) until they show profit, too.

Sybil Christopher was at her desk at ICM on the afternoon that Luis Escobar was discovering the tragedy at 2620 Hutton Drive. She had recently joined ICM to read and report on manuscripts. She had been an actress herself in England before she married Richard Burton in 1949: their marriage lasted till her husband was involved in that ominously star-crossed production of *Cleopatra*. It was dissolved in 1963: Burton had married Elizabeth Taylor, and Sybil, in 1965, became Mrs Jordan Christopher, the wife of the Hollywood actor. Sybil was Welsh: an affinity with Rachel Roberts that a sympathy of temperament between the two women only strengthened while both were acting minor Shakespearian roles at Stratford-upon-Avon in the early 1950s, the era when Burton was being hailed as the best and brightest of the new generation of actors.

Sybil Christopher was the sort of person whom friends called a 'stoic'. She survived, with regret, maybe, but without corroding acrimony, a fair number of the crises that celebrity marriages (and divorces) bring to the partners. Her Welsh resilience helped: though California was her physical home, the Wales of tough muscle and austere religion had annealed her spirit. She thrived on bringing up her family by Burton and Christopher: but now that they were old enough to have moved out of the home and on to campus or into careers, she felt able to leave her children and seek work to keep herself busy. When she joined ICM, she had said to Rachel Roberts, 'You know, Rachel, I'm deserting to the enemy. I'm becoming one of the nine-to-five people.' Rachel envied her. 'She envied me the security and order that a regular job brought into my life,' Sybil said later. 'Even when I told her it wasn't the solution, she envied me.'

Rachel had come to stay with the Christophers in their home at Thousand Oaks during one of her 'in and out of love' periods, when she was finding life at 2620 Hutton Drive with Darren Ramirez was closing in on her. 'She wanted to be mothered,' Sybil was to recall. 'She had our child Amy's little room and left notes thanking Amy for "beddy-byes". At the end, we were like twins.'

The shock to Sybil Christopher was intense when her desk phone rang and a child's voice asked for her – she recognised one of the family of Delphine and Stanley Mann, the film director. Delphine had a house almost opposite 2620 Hutton Drive. 'Isn't Rachel Roberts your friend?' asked the child – 'Yes, why?' – 'Well, she's dead.'

Any unexpected death, any 'homicide', provokes a routine pattern to form swiftly around it in Los Angeles: that in turn immediately alerts the neighbours in a land where the 'cop operas' on the TV networks are what formulate people's expectations of life (and death) in 'the neighbourhood'. Not one, but two police cars, had raced over to Hutton Drive on receipt of the telephone call which Luis Escobar initiated. As Detective Sack said later, 'In this country you don't take chances with a thing like this.' Their presence in the narrow road, roof-lights glowing in brilliance in the 'magic hour', as film-makers call the 'twilight zone' gained the neighbours' apprehensive attention.

'I immediately dialled Darren's home number,' Sybil Christopher said. 'A strange voice answered and said, "Who are you?" – "I'm a friend of Rachel Roberts and I'm told something's happened to her." – "Well, keep away. We don't need friends here."'

Alarmed and angered, Sybil responded as her Welsh instinct ordered: she jumped up, left her desk, and made for her car. She remembers she somehow got past the cop in the now taped-off entrance to 2620, and got into the house.

Darren Ramirez was at his job in I Magnin, the Wilshire Boulevard branch of the exclusive women's wear department store, when the police call came about 5.00 pm with the news from Hutton Drive. As he, too, rushed home, he felt perplexed and stunned. Only a few hours earlier, Rachel had called to say good-bye: she was catching the 4.00 pm flight to New York, she said, to see Frank Dunlop about the *Lolita* part. 'Don't do anything foolish, will you?' Darren said. He knew she'd been collecting Nembutals all that summer, going to different doctors so as not to excite suspicion, and now and then, when they'd had their periodic rows, she used to show Darren the bottle in a threatening way. He'd once pulled the bottle out of her hand, but she demanded – and got – it back. It was Darren's nature to yield, not hold out, and Rachel who loved him for it also played the stronger partner's role. There were nearly twenty years between them: it was like a son trying to wrestle with a wilful mother on occasions. Calm her first, reason with her afterwards, hold it together with affection.

It was sometimes exhausting on Darren: but the complex nature of a partnership that had lasted, in and out of love, for over ten years had deprived this young and attractive Mexican of any alternative, save going his separate way. That had been tried, too: but when Rachel, at some crisis-point, had called to him to come back, he had returned. If it had become increasingly hard to live together, it seemed impossible for them to live apart.

Cursing the clogging homeward-bound traffic, Darren raced towards the home that he and Rachel owned. She had come in on its purchase, using a lucky-break tax rebate to co-finance it, then contributing to the monthly mortgage charges. He felt a mixture of desperation, bewilderment and awful loss. A part of himself had been extinguished by the news: that part was the central place that Rachel had occupied.

When he got there and verified his identity, he was almost glad to find the Los Angeles police 'in charge' and himself with nothing to do. Police on such occasions unintentionally (sometimes) turn a lawful mission into an unsettling invasion. They invade the minds as well as the territory of the inhabitants. Darren sat there, watching them make and take calls and move around among familiar furnishings as they waited for the coroner's office to put in an appearance. Unnecessary to say how shocked he was to see the state Rachel was in, her flimsy nightwear snagged and her lower limbs scarred and scratched – he connected these injuries with the brambles on the hill above the back yard. He knew she was in the habit of climbing the steep little steps and sitting there in the sun. He wasn't asked about pills and he said nothing. He was glad when Sybil Burton suddenly arrived through the front door. The two embraced. They felt terribly self-conscious with the police present.

At this point in their investigation, the police did not believe Rachel had killed herself. For one thing, there was no suicide note. Correction: there *was* a note, but it referred to a repair that she wanted done to her car – she hoped it would be ready by the time she returned from New York. Planning for the future isn't, generally, a feature of suicide cases. Then again, the boiling kettle didn't suggest an anticipation of death: people who kill themselves are frequently scrupulous about leaving the world with everything neat and tidy, and not on the boil. Darren confirmed that the English muffin found in Rachel's throat, apparently having choked her, came from the small stock of household food meant to ease the hunger rather than provide regular meals for a couple whose life-style tended to be lived in restaurants or at other people's parties.

But Sybil Christopher was already half-doubting one conclusion, half-dreading the other. 'As Darren and I sat in the little den round the corner from the kitchen and the smashed glass screen, I spied a book that Rachel had bought lying on a low table. It was about women's problems. I opened it idly, then I saw Rachel had been annotating it heavily in pencil.'

When she returned to her own home that night, she took the book with her, partly out of curiosity, partly as a keepsake. There had also been a copy of that day's *Los Angeles Times*, with the words 'Call Syb' scribbled in a margin. When Sybil opened the book again, the same writing, easily legible, in a strong hand, on flyleaves and other partially blank pages seemed to be spelling out for her all too clearly the message that the autopsy would relay in dispassionate officialese a few days later.

The thick book was called *Unfinished Business*. It was written by Maggie Scarf and had been published by Doubleday earlier that same year, 1980. It bore the sub-title: 'Pressure Points in the Lives of Women'.

According to the jacket blurb, it covered six decades in the lives of women, and the physical and psychological pressures that characterise each. 'It is about the times in every woman's life that can stimulate personal growth – or stop it.'

On the back fly-leaf, Rachel had written: 'Given a break, given a supportive man and encouragement of my talent, someone to come home to, I might not be undergoing this morbid, self-hating agony.'

In the chapter entitled 'Turning Thirty', sub-headed 'A Matter of Timing', dealing with separation, Rachel had underscored sentences in the passage which began, 'In a way, the hardest thing *I* had to handle' – the narrator was a woman identified as 'Kath' – 'was the realisation that what I experienced as his coolness or meanness wasn't directed at me personally. *He wasn't trying to hurt me, but he couldn't live with it. He couldn't be intimate: not on a day to day basis, not at that point in his life . . .*' and Rachel had added in the margin '. . . or ever'.

In the 'Diagnosing of Despair' chapter, about the 'treatment of the soul', Rachel had also underscored words that, like many others throughout the book, seemed to Sybil ominously apposite to the woman whom she had known so closely over 30 years: '. . . what we call "depression" has to do with the "losing" side of the equation . . . the loss could occur at a purely symbolic level. *It might be the loss of a fantasy – about the success that one's talents would bring, or even the fantasy that one would stay young and attractive for ever.*'

On the fly-leaf facing the chapter-head 'In the Twenties', Rachel had written:

'I don't want to see Rex. It's not his fault. I just don't want involvement. I can't cope with it. I have a knowledge of people and I want to utilise it to act. I'm the one who made a huge mistake. Because of need and the partial (this word was illegible) in me, I chose Rex over my craft. It happened. Not much of a sin, but I suffer for it dreadfully. I gave away my birthright. Therefore I cannot survive. More's the pity. I wish before God, Baba, you said, I could. It is a *fait accompli* – tragically. I threw away my talent. I know now that "glamour" doesn't exist. I thought it did. I "bought" it and enjoyed it for a time. A mistake.'

The next day, Darren himself found the 'other books'. The ones he knew existed, but had seen only two or three times in Rachel's lifetime. They were her private journals.

DARREN RAMIREZ: 'I think she'd begun keeping them in the last eighteen months of her life, when she started looking into herself and realising where she might be heading. I never saw what was inside them while she was alive. She was like a cat with kittens, where those journals were concerned – once I sneaked them away from her and she threw such a fit of fury that I had to give them back there and then.

'I had been looking for her purse: it hadn't been found anywhere near where she'd been, in the house or back yard: it wasn't in her car, either. I was going through the little conservatory at the rear of the house when my eye caught sight of it placed under one of the flowering bushes – and beside it, in a big square bag like a make-up case which she used for keeping medication, I found the journals. About a dozen notebooks, all loose-leaf variety, some of them yellow legal pads, others small, spiral-bound exercise books like the kids use at school. I really felt what losing Rachel meant when I handled those books – they'd come to mean everything to her. But the odd thing was even though she was no longer there to stop me, I could hardly bring myself to open them. It would have been like a violation. Although I flipped through a few of them there and then, I simply couldn't settle down to read them till months and months had gone by. And when I did, I found it almost impossible to believe one woman had crammed so much into her life before and after I got to know her and, at times, to love her. It didn't seem that there was *one* Rachel – it seemed there were dozens of her.

'The journals weren't written in conventional diary form – they only seemed to turn into a diary form in the last year of her life. But she wrote as her mind worked, going back and forth over her life, over every period in her life . . . Even, it seemed to me, before her life began.'

T here were yellow curtains and a feeling of sunlight in Llanelli in the manse where I was born, although there was never much sunlight in the town or on the sands. It was a long time before the word 'beach' entered my vocabulary – beaches with all the associations of bronzed bodies, 'beautiful' people, cold drinks, smart holidays. Beaches were 'the sands' then. Ours in Llanelli were undeniably dirty, the small Welsh town's only identity being the tin-plate works. It also rained a lot, so where 'Mothi', as I learned to call that first human creature I became aware of, my Mother, learned to love the sun, I'll never know. She would recite *Lord Ullin's Daughter* to me when I was three sitting on her lap in the rocking-chair. How she was also able to grow flowers and know them by name, and how to look after them in the Valley of Coal, I'll never know either. They were not exactly prolific in Cwmparc where she was born, in the Rhondda Valley, the eldest of six, the youngest of whom, Uncle Albert, was crippled. Grandma Jones had fallen during that last pregnancy and her child was born mentally and physically defective. I remember seeing him, remember a sunny disposition, remember liking him. It must have been shortly before he died in Talgarth, an institution in Cardiff, South Wales, when he was thirty-five and I was seven or eight. Mother told me of carrying that little defective younger brother on her back, piggy-back fashion, up the coal tips in the Rhondda.

My Mother was fine-featured and pretty with fair hair and blue eyes – the only English strain in our family came from my maternal grandfather, John Jones, who left Shropshire when he was nineteen to work in the pits in South Wales. He was a timber-man down the colliery and, though he spent his life in Wales, still spoke with the Shropshire countryman's burr – very English to our Welsh ears.

I didn't know him very well, but heard tales of his strong will and political convictions – Socialist, of course. You could hardly be anything else, working underground for a pittance for absentee English mine-owners, especially with a wife and six children to support. He liked his pint. Sometimes my Mother, the eldest, was sent to fetch him home from the pubs, when his liking for pints got excessive. But little Rachel Ann Jones

loved him all his life and beyond his grave. She loved his good, if unedu-
cated brain, his gentleness, above all his appreciation of that bright little girl
who was my Mother.

How did Mother know and love Shakespeare and Dickens and the
Romantic poets? How had she ever got to hear about Flaubert and Baude-
laire? But she did. She also wrote poetry, which was published in the *Western
Mail*. This I still have and treasure.

What happened to me from then to now – from that impression of a sunlit
room and my delicate Mother reciting poetry to her three-year-old, waiting
for Richard Rhys [Rachel's Father] to come back for his tea after a deacon's
meeting or from visiting the sick, to this house in Beverly Hills, California, I
find extraordinary.

None of it was planned, some of it was marvellous, some of it despairing;
yet through it all, when I am at peace and still, and at the centre of myself, I
feel not much different from 'little Ray' after all.

Around about Christmas, 1926, I was conceived. No guns were fired. No
rockets went up. Maybe a bed creaked: I hope so. For reasons that are
beginning now to become clear to me, for a very long time I behaved as if the
Westminster chimes of Big Ben echoed the night through at my conception,
let alone at my birth. But I am quite sure I did not have these thoughts as my
Father's guilty sperm hurtled to my Mother's adamantly hostile egg. I know
she loved him, came to love me, but simply didn't want children. But have
me she did, and suffered for it. Mother didn't weigh very much and I was a
large baby. I was told that I was a very good one. It couldn't surely have been
that I was trying to please even then?

I don't remember my christening, but I was told my Mother wasn't there.
She took a long time to recover after having me. She had septic breasts and,
in adolescence, I remember unearthing a glass nipple shield from the chest
of drawers in Swansea. I think it was from that moment that the thought of
suckling any child that I might have filled me with fright.

My Mother's name was Rachel and it became mine. My parents had
wanted a son and my name was to have been Hugh – the favourite – or
Goronwry or David. When Mother was presented with the new-born me,
her quite justified comment was, 'Take her away. I don't want to see her.' I
believe the 'her' was actually 'it', but I feel foolish writing that down, as it
sounds too Dickensian for words, and it may sound as if I am intending to
malign the other Rachel, which I'm not. I loved my Mother, and am
absolutely on her side, and completely understand. But I am sure that Dad
felt guilty and miserable and alone. Loveable though he was, he was not
particularly imaginative and he loved my Mother. I've no idea whether not
having a son upset him. I never thought to discuss it with him and he's long
dead now, so it's too late. I know he loved me with a fervour and a passion;
but that day in 1928, when faced, alone, with the decision of what to name
his second daughter, no other female name than his wife's came to mind. So
Rachel pure and simple – well, no, Rachel, alas! not so pure and decidedly
not so simple – I became.

I'm setting this down on a grey day in Beverly Hills. The gas crisis has
temporarily stemmed the daunting flow and noise of cars. The sun doesn't
shine and for a moment the mood is gentle in this hard, concrete, soulless
place. I think I'm beginning to understand the horror now, can at last begin
to put it all together . . .

'*She's got eyes of blue* . . .' marching round the table in the kitchen, with the tea-cosy on my head, sitting on Dad's shoulders, led by my Mother and flanked by my elder sister Hazel! Not that there were that many carefree, happy moments. I can remember well the sense of apology, of inferiority, I felt. Whether or not my sister did drop me and I rolled downstairs, I'll never really know – although the memory clings. But perhaps a one-year-old girl doesn't yet take in the feeling of dislike: again, I don't know. You soon do, though. You soon learn to please. You soon learn to efface yourself. You soon learn to bottle up your anger. You then start to die, or try to. You close up your bronchial passages, so you can't breathe. They've called it asthma. You close up your fallopian passages, so you can't accept life. They call it spasm contraction. Then you get so stifled, so completely closed up, that you take a little drink, do a little dance, take all your clothes off, scream and laugh and vomit and the fear grows and grows and you're still closed tight.

Mother was intelligent and delicate. She had what they called an 'artistic temperament' in those days. She also had her moods. When one was on her, my grandmother would walk me to feed the chickens in her house. The atmosphere was less severe there. She wasn't strict and intimidating like my over-protective Mother who, I think, much as she leaned on Father, felt she'd married her inferior and 'wore the pants'. Ruled the household in fact. Nowadays the informed, and the not-so-informed, would dub her, easily, manic-depressive, and take her agonies away, temporarily perhaps, with Lithium.

My little sister was a pretty, flaxen-haired, perfect little girl. For nearly ten years before I arrived she'd been spruced and cleaned and taught to read and write and sew at home by the delicate mother who washed this first child's hair with fresh eggs. Mother had strange ideas for bringing up children, putting Hazel's doll or dolls away in a drawer, and teaching the little girl herself. Who knows what the atmosphere was like in the small, stone chapel-house for the clean little girl? I don't know. I wasn't there. I came to another place, another chapel-house, ten long years later. But I don't think my perfect little sister could have been very much loved. Cared for, yes, but loved? No, I don't think so.

Yet how could a Baptist clergyman and his wife, struggling with their own dreams and already into early middle age, possibly have guarded over me better than they did? And how could the perfect and proper and pretty ten-year-old analyse the bewilderment she must have felt seeing her Father's love for that uglier younger sister? And how could my Mother bother about any of it, nose-diving as she was into untreated, neurasthenic early menopause?

The grey day continues outside, and the streets are emptying and the harsh sounds of an American escape-town deadened, and I've had five days in which I've realised that I've become an alcoholic. Days of deep shock, rage, anger, terror, relief and hope.

I just have a general sense of the inferiority growing inside me in those childhood years.

It was a tight, self-contained atmosphere that I was born into. But there was happiness, too. The chapel didn't depress me unduly. My dolls and especially my teddy-bear I loved, and analysed. There was even some

11

playtime in Dad's redundant Morgan run-about. Very well, there weren't many little girls and boys to play with. That is a long-past fact. But I was loved, except, understandably, by Hazel who was irritable by nature. But the isolated moments of my childhood that remain vivid are solely those that seemed instinctively too damaging to dismiss from memory.

I went to Swansea, a nice little very shy girl. I've only recently connected what, for the five-year-old, remains the most humiliating experience in the one case and puzzling in the second.

It was a Friday. I'd only just started Infants School. We said the Lord's Prayer in Welsh and then in English. I put up my hand. I had to go. The teacher was cross that morning. I can't remember what she said. We joined hands for a jolly game of 'ring-a-ring-a-roses'. I deposited a small, warm pile of defecation in my knickers instead. I don't think the teacher could have been at all well that morning. She commented on a certain smell, brilliantly traced it to me, and, it seems to me, though I cannot really credit it, even though our home was only five minutes' walk away, told an older girl to take me home, turds intact – Friday was comics-day!

I was greeted with the stupefaction of a returning war-hero – perhaps because they genuinely loved their little girl, perhaps because she broke the routine (I was to do *that* a great deal later on!) by having just been got ready and taken to school, and now here she was back home again so instantly. I don't remember any more, except the long pause and the long stare before the burst of tears. Was it the first of many things that would warn me never to let go again, to hold in, to hold on?

We had an outside lavatory at 59, Tyshia Road, Swansea. My sister and I shared the feathered double-bed. Under the bed was the customary china po in which all good people did their business, if they had to, at night. Wales was a rainy place, the houses weren't heated, there was no electric light, the bedroom was up a flight of stairs, the lavatory at the back of a dark garden. (Writing now, in 1979, about a china po under the bed seems to make this explanation necessary.) Maybe what happened to me then happened to everyone else all the time, too, but it only happened to me once, round about the time of the teacher and the 'ring-a-ring-a-roses' and I remember it.

My sister and I got up one morning. Whether or not the fifteen-year-old – because that's all she was – resented my defecation mingling with hers (if, in the event, she could differentiate them), she grabbed my head and stuck it over our po, not *in* it, but over it. Because I am fifty-one now, it seems a very long time indeed since my head was hanging over that china po. Of course it wasn't particularly upsetting at the time, as I remember, just puzzling. Have I held on to it in memory because of its proximity to the other humiliation?

There are other remembered instances accompanied with the unsmiling, irritable, impatient look. The game of 'Who's you and me and us two?' for instance, and being held before a mildly hot coal fire this time, holding in the obvious answer, hoping to please. Then to tell or not to tell about the jam tarts burning in the oven in the scullery while my sister entertained one of her rare guests – our home never had many people in – and finally judging it best to make the comment and receiving the usual impatient rebuff. I have the memory of mild satisfaction when those jam tarts did burn and my sister ran in – with yet another opportunity to release the ten-year-old's distress at 'that new baby' and couldn't, because I had tried to rescue them from burning. At five, I couldn't take them out of the stove – or could I have?

My sister and I would go to the corner shop together, but it was never hand-in-hand fun. Once I remember making a fanatical effort to pinch my mouth and make it appear like a rose-bud, my sister having grumpily declared it to be too large. I didn't think it was. It isn't now, certainly. However, I have retained the skill of making it appear even smaller than it is – I used to amuse schoolfriends with my imitation of a goldfish.

I sang in my Father's chapel – *Emmanuel, All Things Bright and Beautiful* – while my sister played the piano. But I had a gruff voice and didn't keep in time. I got one of those looks. My sister was pretty and capable and had golden hair done up in thick braids and was in the school plays and fell in love with a tall shy boy that she married.

I soon retreated with fascination into my real family headed by Donald the teddy-bear and his best friend Jack the golliwog (with apologies to all anti-racists), Margaret the gracious wax doll, and Queenie who was *her* friend, but of a lower caste.

My great-grandmother died before we left that chapel-house. I'd seen her, been to her cottage in the Rhondda. Her name was Margaret Harris. She looked fierce. She was small and strong, and with deep regret I have to say that she did not like me – although I won her round. I got adept at that early on. She had nothing against me, other than adoration for my Mother whom she'd brought up.

Grandma Harris had come by train from the Rhondda to us in Llanelli: for a Christmas. Her case was stuffed with new sheets, a home-made Christmas pudding, a doll for me. The day she died I went with Dad and the telegram and a cup of tea upstairs to their bedroom. My Mother choked on her tea. Someone who'd loved her so much had gone. But you don't know things like that when you are seven.

Why did that 'call' from God – the description that the Baptist Church used for the transference of a clergyman from one chapel to another – come for Dad to leave Llanelli for Swansea? Economic necessity made it essential he accepted, of course. But my sister was seventeen by now. And while all those little seeds of inferiority had been well scattered around my seven-year-old self, none had really, as yet, taken root. I was chubby and thumb-sucking and fancied myself loved. My sister had grown out of me. She was soon to be replaced by a much fiercer foe.

I looked very nice in yellow that first day at school in the new town. I was nicely mannered, appropriately shy, and one of the girls in the class took me up. Quite why Violet [not her real name] turned into my personal and unrelenting tormentor for the next three years of my life is still totally beyond my comprehension. My sister was now a young woman in training college, aloof now, and not concerned with me, nor I with her. My foe was now more formidable than any sibling rival. Those little seeds of inferiority flourished and grew and were nourished and daily fed by flaxen-haired Violet who distorted my name, ridiculed my nose, yelled out in the street that my Mother was a nun. My Mother preached sometimes on Sundays – she was very good at it. Perhaps Violet was Irish and a Catholic. She didn't look Welsh. She didn't have a Father, I don't think, and her house was dirty and sloppy. Oh yes, I went to it, to Violet's birthday party. There were boys at the party. I didn't know anything at all about boys. Violet did. Violet knew boys liked girls to be pretty. At eight or nine, I wasn't too concerned about this. But Violet was quite open about it. She simply asked three little boys who was the prettiest of us four little girls. They selected Jean and Violet and Joan – in that order, I'm afraid, Violet.

And I *was* afraid, Violet, because I knew what you were going to do next – force the little boys to make their final choice. They didn't want to, Violet; you wanted them to. Theirs was a good instinct, not to kick the fledgling bird in the beak. The little boys bowed to the all-powerful Violet's will, and, shuffling with embarrassment, pink in the cheek, barred me from the harem. I was to be no concubine for them.

I didn't say anything. I went down the hill to my house, No. 59, went upstairs, and looked in the mirror and saw what they meant. I think I cried up there. When I came down to tea, I held it in. That night in bed, I held it in more and had a truly bad attack of asthma. I'd not breathed properly since we'd moved from the lazy little *sospan* (Welsh) town to this colder anglicised place and the colder anglicised chapel. (When my Father had another 'call' from God to go to Bognor Regis, and thought, in his conscience, he at least ought to give the present chapel a chance to keep him by secret vote of confidence, they outvoted him to a man, so that he stayed on there until his death from cancer, one suspects in a wild effort to please his detractors instead of annihilating them with an axe – but then it's his daughter who writes this many years later. Dear Dad!)

I had another fantasy world now. Teddy was naturally still around, but pubescence was beginning and while I had no conception whatsoever of the significance of menstruation, no idea at all of its biological implications, as my sexual instincts were aroused just before it, I found the whole thing highly pleasurable.

I invented an exotic and dramatic world with my Mother's flame-coloured buckle belt around my skinny thighs. I carried out in those early erotic fantasies all I'd experienced so far. The little boys chose me now, standing up on my pillow, being auctioned off to the handsomest bidder. But I wasn't an arrogant slave – that came later. There had to be some sadness, some humility in the transaction. I couldn't keep my sister and Violet out of my psyche after all. Is that what masochism is? The sister or the friend who resents you, who doesn't like you, much as you want them to, and whom you try so hard to please, and you constantly get rebuffed, and you constantly try again, so you get used to the feeling. Then the body of the child changes and wants its physical needs satisfied. You are used to being slapped down: now you can be slapped about. It fits. It also festers.

So there I was, blocked up before I was fourteen. Communicating with no one, turned in . . . I developed nervous asthma. Nervousness and I go together. Long-drawn-out nights in bed, wheezing away, were part and parcel of it. Of course, it made me a little girl for far too long. What I could do was read, and read well. And I could act. Even in Violet's face I saw caution when I read a story to the class. I was too good to monkey around with when I did that. The bully would look like a fool. I had a good voice. I inherited it from Dad's father, Goronwry Owen Rhys Roberts, my Grandfather, whom I adored and rather resembled, pug nose and all. He had a marvellous voice and preached rhetorically and masterfully in Welsh and English. I loved words. Mother had read to me when I was too young to comprehend and I could do so myself when I was three: and I'd had plenty of time to observe, if not to understand, some of the intricacies of people.

So another secret was hugged inside the growing pile of this odd person I was becoming. She didn't bear much resemblance to the plain schoolgirl wheezing her way to high school, satchel on her back whose strap was to transport her into ecstasies that night.

---

THE NONCONFORMIST RELIGIOUS OUTLOOK of the people whom the Roberts family settled among in Swansea in the early 1930s is still a force that shapes sharp minds and makes for blunt speech. Some of those who were children when Rachel was a child have memories of her that show how keenly the Rev. Richard Rees Roberts and his family were scrutinised (and judged) in the tight-knit community of Welsh co-religionists.

The Roberts, after all, were strangers in a way. They had come from comparatively tiny Llanelli and, more importantly, the husband and wife spoke Welsh to each other, though not to the majority of their parishioners. One of Rachel's childhood companions felt it a point worth making even fifty years later.

ELIZABETH JAMES: 'We in Swansea are Welsh by birth, but not Welsh-speaking or Welsh-thinking. Welsh was taught as a subject in our schools, but people (like the Roberts) from Welsh-speaking Wales have a different outlook on life from us. Here was a family living in Swansea with its shops, theatres, colleges, art galleries, etc., totally different from what they were used to. But Mr and Mrs Roberts stayed themselves. Rachel's mother was a wonderful "speaker" – far better than her husband, but in those days were no women preachers, worse luck! When we put on a play, Ray, as we called her, was the star. No one else had a look in, little Ray was it! At that time, her diction had a very pronounced Welsh accent. Her sister Hazel was very quiet and lady-like, a teacher-to-be, obviously. What else do we Welsh produce but chapel ministers, actors or teachers?

'Ray was a very self-willed child and I'm sorry to say became a snob of the first order when she got her scholarship to Swansea High School. She dropped all her York Place Baptist Chapel friends (working-class, you see) and hated going to chapel . . . My friendship continued, though, as I was different from the Jones, Evans, Williams, and so on – you see, my maiden name was Mountstephens, which sounded good, didn't it?

'Ray was always a "first" – first to wear a red coat. First (later on) to dye her hair (to smoke, too!) First to use make-up – and to chapel! Sorry I've no photos of her then – Ray wouldn't go in a group photo on our annual Sunday School trip!'

Another of Rachel's classmates sensed the tensions eddying through the minister's family.

GWLADYS STANDFAST: 'My family were founder members of York Place chapel. I remember Ray as a plain, small girl with an older, pretty sister. [Apparently Mrs Roberts made no secret of her preference for her elder child.] This used to upset my own mother very much and she made a fuss of young Ray and invited her to Sunday lunch regularly, so we watched her grow up. (Her ambition as a small girl was to be as tall as my mother.) We in our family felt that a lot of Rachel's insecurity came from her treatment by her mother. Her mother was smart, a good if unofficial preacher (very dramatic), but a very jealous woman. She was even jealous of the affection that my mother showed to Ray, and more than once tried to spoil the child's pleasure at being invited out to lunch. She and her mother and sister sat on one side of the chapel. My family sat on the opposite side. My mother used to look across the chapel at Ray and often mouthed "Come to lunch" at her. I feel that the complexity of Rachel's character was to a very great extent caused by her mother's treatment of her. In spite of it, she was later very good to her mother and father and looked after them.'

Along came school plays, my only real talent then, until nervous asthma got in the way again and one awful day I wasn't cast in one. When I asked why, I was told that, good though I was, before the play I had had an attack of nervous asthma. But my Scrooge was a triumph and the headmaster came and congratulated me, saying I'd become a very good actress one day and not to let it go to my head.

Nervous and wincing and frightened, though, I've always been. Frightened of being told off, and exaggerating any reproof – i.e., for being late for school. Daddy always defended me: took out his own repressed temperament on those who criticised his little girl.

Trying for high-school entrance, my pattern of over-reaction stuck. Convinced I'd failed, I came home in tears. Daddy again took care of that and walked me up to high-school, explaining to the gardener that this little girl would soon be joining the school. I did. Outfitted as lots of others have been – if they've been lucky enough to be outfitted at all – in clothes sizes too big. I'd beaten Violet in the exam and she stopped bullying me, but still looked at me with dislike when our paths crossed. In school, I did what I wanted to do – stared around at my classmates, sucking up to them all – 'manipulating', they call it now. I played the hypocrite well and smiled and smarmed. Some fell like sitting ducks. Some of the ones who were already more self-sufficient saw through me and let me know by indifference, or scathing looks, or outspoken remarks. Yes, they actually scoffed!

Ingratiating myself with such insincerity, not concentrating on educating myself . . . Back at home, I'd stare into two adjoining mirrors and see how I could improve my nose, which turned up. I'd pluck my eyebrows to copy my sister. Masochistic fantasies occupied my waking hours, when I should have been studying. I'd play with myself, sticking up the school ruler. I tried to fuck myself with the hoover handle, even though I didn't know the word. At nights, I'd auction myself off to imaginary slave-drivers who'd handle my breasts and tell me to stand with my legs wide apart. At school, I developed the usual crush on the older prefect, went home, and played 'Sally in Our Alley' in her absent honour. I'd hammer the piano tunelessly, singing at the top of my voice, until my Mother banged the sitting-room door, so noisy was I. Alone I was, alone with myself.

My studies started suffering, and no wonder! I wasn't concentrating on anything. The holidays loomed long and, inevitably, lonely. No one came round to our house to play. I couldn't ride a bike. I couldn't play tennis.

I couldn't catch a ball. My sister mesmerised me – I looked for her disapproval, rather than at the ball. I think the symptoms of duality were showing their sickness even then.

The smarminess didn't pay off until it was coupled with my acting gift. At fifteen, I was a magical Touchstone in *As You Like It* on the school lawn, outshining Rosalind and Celia and Orlando. I had carefully painted a child's billiard cue – I took a long time doing it at home – turning it into a court-jester's baton, and twirling it with a manic talent. A good Touchstone: yes, I was a riotous success; but it meant much, much more to me. To have some *power*, some *recognition*, some *respect*, some *love* to combat the already growing belief and fear that everyone else was who they were, and I was not. The junior school fell in love with me. Smiling and Touchstone worked for me the next year, when sixth-form arrived and time for school captains, or, rather, the house-heads, to be elected. At sixteen, I was unanimously elected the head-girl of my house. But since the senior head teacher thought my exterior asinine, she asked for a re-vote, saying that while 'Ray' was a very good actress, Valerie was an all-round student, Anne a scholar, the other Valerie an athlete. Your instincts were good, dear dead Miss Stuart, but not because Anne who went to Oxford was a better academician, which she was not, not because the two Valeries together were better at hockey and, later, at marrying husbands and making homes – but because Anne was Anne and the two Valeries were the two Valeries. They knew who *they* were with a certainty I had not and never would have. They took the vote again. I waited like the desperate little Napoleon I was, dressed up in gym-tunic, blouse and tie, for the result to be announced. Unanimously, me!

I went back to the sixth-form classroom. Good, healthy honest laughter greeted the news that I was head girl of St Bran. I clowned around, smiled a lot, went home, howled my eyes out, closed up, relapsed into asthma. The sickness inside me took a little positive twist, and I vowed to my God that St Bran would win everything that year. I think we nearly did.

The triumph took away the horrible memories of those days when we all had to be chosen to be on the school team for netball or hockey – and I was always the last to be chosen, because I was no good. Well, either me or a pretty girl called Joan who was academically brilliant but also a rabbit at games. Joan won a scholarship to Oxford and later had a major nervous breakdown from which I heard she never recovered.

By now I knew I could act, but, looking like I did, I kept it to myself. It must have leaked out, however, because one day I heard my Mother say to the lady next door – 'Ray wants to be an actress, but she'll grow out of it.' I prayed that day, 'Oh God, don't stop me wanting to act – that's all I ask.'

Boys entered my consciousness then and I was amazed to find that some of the nice-looking ones liked me. I was so convinced I was the ugliest creature on the face of the earth. My own sexual fantasies and rigid upbringing of course prevented the slightest contact. I dreamed of the little girl I'd have some day – somehow without a man – a little, plain girl that I would teach how to ride, to read, to learn music, to do all the things I couldn't.

I'd been assigned a task. To weave a scarf. Mine was awful, just awful. So my sister impatiently took it over and finished it off beautifully. So beautifully that I got an A-plus mark – the reason given was the immense improvement I'd shown! The improvement was hardly mine.

Otherwise, I don't remember very much about my sister in those days.

She went about her business – went to the teachers' training college on the hill. The war came. She became an auxiliary nurse. She remained pretty and efficient.

I used to stay in bed until the last possible minute. I was still there when Rita McCanley came to call for me to go to school. I was still there while she was in the sitting-room waiting for me. A bad habit was formed. It did get better: but erratically better. I was 'not amenable to correction'. I was 'slovenly'. I didn't concentrate. The truth was, I didn't have the slightest idea how to live. I don't think anyone ever told me. But now in these present days of pain and doubt, I wonder what chance there was of escaping what has come to pass. I must learn to forgive myself. I've drowned for days and nights in the seas of my past. My three-year idyll with Rex [Harrison, Rachel's second husband, 1962–71] in the Sixties was just that. I knew it then. It didn't grow into a rock bed of security. It couldn't. Had my child Anna [apparently a miscarriage: not referred to again] been born, it might have. But it was not to be. And now these last ten terrible days attending meetings of Alcoholics Anonymous, hating and fearing them and distrusting them, too. I don't think alcoholism's an illness, a physical illness. *I don't believe that any human being, not just alcoholics, feels really part of things.* I believe anyone, even gentle Darren [Ramirez] and stoic Sybil would be prey to fears and resentments and nightmares and terrors if they drank undiluted alcohol the way I have been doing. They control it, so that they scream inside. I cannot go to AA meetings every night. I cannot say the Lord's Prayer. I cannot wallow in my own past. I cannot voice my degradations to AA meetings to a gallery of strangers . . . And yet I cannot stop feeling 'special'.

It is pleasant in Los Angeles today. Hot. The new grass is growing on the lawn. I do feel part of things. The hope that I can write is an intoxication. Please God I can. That would save my life. I'd like a life of peace and continuity, a house by the sea, in Mexico, a recognition quite different from that of the actor, and less exposed.

Acting now fills me with horror, standing up there saying words not your own, talking to strangers, communicating with strangers, seeing fear in the eyes of a fellow performer, seeing age, seeing ambition, paying lip-service to a profession I no longer have pride in, resenting the arrogance of the director who assembles us all, organises us, then goes away leaving us half ourselves, unpitying, relying on the fancied and lunatic assumption that actors love being up there. Maybe once we did. Why do it if you don't have to? Oh, but we often do have to, we often have to go on paying for those youthful dreams and act when we're tired and old and sick and disillusioned. We have to earn our bread like a tired old circus bear, repeating the same old tired routine day in, day out, to new faces who hoot and howl afresh each day. It's the first time *they* have seen it. What fun that tired old bear must be having up there!

The director and his friend of many years' standing who has been appointed his assistant go to lunch, a pleasant, easy, simple one with pleasant, easy, simple people. It's a warm Saturday afternoon: they eat delicious avocado salad and a delicate leek quiche, hot bread and butter, cold wine. They can swim if they want to. Miles down-town, the actors do their first matinee in a theatre too large, too modern for the play. But they opened last night to good notices. They got through it well. There had been a party. Not a real party, a theatrical party. The actors could unwind a little, not very

18

much because of the tomorrow and two shows. They shouldn't drink, because acting with a hangover belongs to nightmare. Actors who drink get bad reputations. They get themselves talked about. Sometimes they stop getting work. Work perhaps they do not want: but there are wives now and children. Or mistresses or boys. They have authors' lines to memorise and articulate. They have directors' mandates to carry out. They have couturiers' quirks of fancy to wear. They have set-designers' obstacles to race around. And they are constantly watched. And I, whose life cannot be a happy one, lived moment to moment without thought of the dense past and the mysterious future, can miraculously find peace again by a day like today when he didn't go to work but held me, and the sun shone, and a fat bird stalked the grass and Rex spoke of me in New York, and I drank a little wine – that dreaded first drink – and I won't join sickness and I will accept my difference without horror and fright. I'll be proud of me and will control the enemy. Acting . . . it taught me a lot. What it taught me is that it is not for me.

---

IN 1946, RACHEL WENT UP to the University of Wales at Aberystwyth – a rural college on the sea coast, but the academic backbone of the 'real' Wales. It had originally been built as a hotel, largely without architectural advice, in the Gothic Perpendicular tradition of public buildings. It had been one of the first attempts in Wales at running 'package tours'. It had been financed by contributions from Welsh miners and steelworkers – a penny a week from each man. So it was close to the heart and soul of Wales, and good teaching nurtured the Welsh mind, too. In Rachel's time, it was still an intimate little place: about 800 students and nearly a third of them women. For Rachel, it was also a dangerous place. She had vaulted over the Baptist walls of domestic surveillance: now she found all the seminal urges already rooted in her nature responding to a forcing-ground where her own generation which had been tightly tied to its parents, home and chapel – and no apron strings came more tightly knotted than Nonconformist ones – was set at heady liberty to study and fraternise in digs, classrooms and campus clubs with young men already opened up to life by their service in the forces.

'A time of flux, stimulating and disturbing,' said one of the earliest friends Rachel made on the campus.

BRIAN EVANS: 'School-leavers like Rachel were suddenly exposed to direct, unchaperoned contact with men who had more worldly experience and sexual assurance. She absorbed it all directly, quickly and greedily.'

Evans, who later became a newspaperman and broadcaster and, finally, information officer at the government's Welsh Office, could recall the odd disjuncture in Rachel's 'good' and 'bad' points at that time.

BRIAN EVANS: 'She wasn't a noticeable "beauty". She had a *retroussé* nose: very self-conscious about it, she was. But her legs were good – she was proud of *them*! She once did the Highland fling, a sword dance, in the Union

19

wearing a kilt that she even seemed to have abbreviated just in order to display her limbs. She was always so open and flirtatious about her encounters with boys, very amusing and candid the next day about what had – or hadn't – happened. She was hungry for experience, you could tell. Whatever she happened to be doing, she'd be thinking, "What'll I do next?" She was always asking friends for suggestions – well, she could hardly call home and ask her dad the upright minister *that* sort of thing. Probably that got her into the habit later on of ringing up her friends at all hours just to ask for their advice. I never witnessed any religious side to her: *human* feelings were what she displayed, not religious ones.'

Another friend on campus, who later became professor of geography at the University of Liverpool, agreed that the young Rachel was, well . . . 'striking'.

MANSELL PROTHERO: 'What you could call a "character". Rather garish, in fact. She made up heavily. She went around with a girl, the adopted daughter of another minister who was the principal of a theological college, too. You know what's said about the vicar's son: in this case, it applied to the vicars' daughters. Both girls had "reputations".'

The talents that a third friend possessed, which were later to make him a successful composer and lyricist, were what brought him and Rachel together at 'Aber', as the students affectionately called the place.

RONNIE CASS: 'We were very close, though never sexually. I came from Llanelli, too, though, oddly enough, we never met until we were both at college. I was studying economics, though music was my first love. She called me "Cass", I called her "Ray", as everyone did. My generation were "veterans of life" to her: hers were "raw beginners" to me. She was fascinated by what she called my "experience": I was taken by her "vitality". I composed songs even then, the Union had a piano, it was always crowded, for "Aber" prided itself on its sing-songs and its more serious chorales . . . and we were always bursting into song, Rachel included, on each and every occasion, or indeed when we didn't have any occasion at all.'

BRIAN EVANS: 'It was a place where a girl with Rachel's nature took the constraints almost as cause for rebellion. She lived in a curious sorority house, Alexandra Hall, about half a mile from the college, at the end of the promenade. If she wanted to be out after 8.00 pm, she had to sign "the book", and be in again by 10 pm – 10.30 pm on Saturdays. You had to apply for a pass to be out later at least three days before. The hostel had an even more Victorian air – a pervasive and constant smell of disinfectant. Any boy calling for Rachel would be shown into a small waiting-room, like the ones on railway platforms, and he waited there, breathing in the un-erotic disinfectant odours, till she arrived. It didn't stimulate passion. Between lectures, an enormous crocodile would form in the quadrangle, people walking round and round in a ring sometimes ten minutes on end. I remember Rachel doing it. My mother, one of the first generation at the place, told me how the tradition started. In her day, females would walk round clockwise, males anticlockwise. Thus you only had fleeting contact with any girl you were fond of! Another ritual that persisted down to Rachel's day and mine happened in the evenings. We boys who lived in digs in the town were "freer" than the girls in their hostels and before we turned in we'd parade in groups along the promenade to Alexandra Hall where I remember Rachel hanging out of the window to be chatted up. We never failed to bang our boot against the bar that marked the end of the promenade: a sort of shibboleth! It amused Rachel. Herself, she always had a rage to be noticed and some of the other girls would imitate her dress and make-up; then their parents would come to campus and read the riot act to their lewd daughters. The time came when Rachel's parents arrived – and then it was a *very* different daughter, demure, soberly dressed, showing them around very quietly . . . I wondered if they ever guessed.

'Rachel was good at English, fair at French. She used to ask me to help her with her French exercises. When she got low marks, she felt aggrieved and discovered I'd been using rude and randy French army expressions not at all suitable for a young female student's compositions, though maybe in keeping with her own nature. Though she'd only a smattering of Welsh, she had lots of Welsh characteristics: she was always good at telling a story. She was always starting off with, "You'll never believe this . . ." She had a great feel for words. I always liked her. I never heard her say an unkind, spiteful or nasty thing about anyone. And she had the talent to make things happen around her – like a whirlpool. Exciting to be with.'

MANSELL PROTHERO: 'Rachel was popularly seen as someone intent on "making her mark". People in those days didn't look too deeply into themselves – or others. There wasn't much speculation why a girl with Rachel's background should be behaving so flamboyantly. She never altered. Years later, a college friend of all of us was standing in Woolworth's in Cardiff. He'd taken holy orders. He was in his clerical collar. Suddenly, a great, ebullient, Junoesque Rachel Roberts appeared out of nowhere and bore down on him. He hadn't laid eyes on her in years. "Darling," she bawled, "You'll never believe this . . ." That was Rachel all over.'

RONNIE CASS: 'Rachel even then wanted to prove to everyone she could sing. We'd sing my songs and tell each other how terrible we were – a sort of mutual defence mechanism. Brian Evans and I started writing revues at college for the local BBC Welsh radio – to supplement our County Council grants. *Soldiers into Gowns*, the first was called, and the producer was Philip Burton, later the foster-father of Richard Jenkins, better known as Richard Burton.'

BRIAN EVANS: 'Rachel wasn't in this first show, but Ronnie was looking after her already and said to me, "You ought to use this girl." She took to broadcasting immediately, acting in sketches and singing. I never thought much of her singing voice, but it was okay for our show. One song she did put over well was about the difficulties of being a shy girl – "Things aren't funny when you're seventeen", was a line. We did three or four shows in the year and there was even a variety show broadcast from college, with Rachel getting the producer worked up about having her in it – she knew how to put herself over, even then.'

MANSELL PROTHERO: 'She acted in college plays. She appeared in Ibsen's *Ghosts* at a National Union of Students drama festival in Bristol, and in my production of Shaw's *Arms and the Man* at the King's Hall, Aberystwyth. She played Luca. Her parents came to see her. The part suited her.'

BRIAN EVANS: 'She was into every opportunity the place offered for acting. But I think she first realised what considerable talents she possessed when she played in *Juno and the Paycock*, which was staged in the college examination hall by her English tutor, William Armstrong. Her Irish accent was impressively good. It really was a performance!'

RONNIE CASS: 'Her father had what the Welsh call "hwyl", a very evocative style of preaching. It explains where Rachel got her power, though not her subtlety. I never felt as moved by anything I saw her do in London as I was when she did *Juno and the Paycock* for us at college. I knew then she had great things in her. She had a wonderful face for portraying suffering. There are very few actresses who can show suffering in all three dimensions – with body, expression and feelings. Rachel was one of them. I could tell she was very introspective, despite the extrovert play she put on on campus to make herself the talk of the place. She couldn't have been the actress she was if she didn't possess the gift of looking into herself and letting us see what she saw, whatever it was like.'

BRIAN EVANS: 'I think it was my advice which confirmed Rachel in her desire to act. She said to me one day, "What am I going to do next? Take a Bachelor of Education degree, I suppose, and become a teacher." "What the hell for?" I said. "You'll be wasting your time. Acting is what you're cut out for. Acting is what you want to do. Apply to RADA." Of course, I was hardly qualified to hand out such advice! But soon after we'd all graduated and left college, we were swapping stories in a pub and someone said, "Have you heard what Ray Roberts is doing?" – "What?" – "She's got into the Royal Academy of Dramatic Art, in London." And she had. And there she was, acquiring all the long "As" of the English acting establishment.'

T ime came for leaving school. I didn't want to go to training college to be a teacher. That meant staying in our suffocating house, not being allowed to do anything, or go anywhere, not even to the cinema, and coming home every night to do the ironing or wash the dishes, as my sister had before me.

So I half-studied – history, French, English literature. The things I liked, I did with ease – I didn't concentrate at all on Latin or mathematics. I studied things that revolved around people. With other things, I was expedient. I hadn't studied Oliver Cromwell as I was supposed to: so when my University entrance paper came up asking about the qualities of a dictator, I thought of Adolf Hitler – the Second World War was on then – and pretended Hitler was Cromwell. I passed. I put that down to the fact that the examiners were so bored with facts and figures given by the more industrious students that, when it came to my paper, they'd read it with interest; and that they, in their turn, had given me the benefit of the doubt – that I'd taken it for granted they'd know I had knowledge of all the historical dates (of which I had none!) and therefore had not bothered to introduce them into my paper.

In truth, I got to University, and away from home, by dint of my personal interview with Professor Edward Jones, whom I charmed. I used my personality to 'con' him. I'd tried that approach some years earlier with an ugly, greasy little Latin mistress. I smiled ingratiatingly at her a lot – and she who, I realise in retrospect, was no doubt a lonely person lacking warmth and friends – she beamed at me, until I had to construe a Latin sentence. Since I had done no work at all, I naturally didn't have the first idea of how to do this. I saw her look of affection freeze into knowledge of what was standing up facing her – a fake. My con-trick failed. It failed years later, too, when, not having attended a single lecture, I failed educational psychology outright. Professor Jones, who'd passed me into University after my plausible personal interview, intervened with the outside examiner telling him I was exceptionally bright. The reply came sharp and accurate – 'Not judging by her paper.' I'd had to compare the respective intelligences of rats and some other animal, I can't remember which. It was meant to be a scientific study with figures and facts. I wrote an emotional and imaginative and humanised piece of rubbish. Who did I think I was kidding?

So where am I now after such a 'preparation' for life? After such a preposterous assumption that I could go through college and after like a mad, demented, unlearning, unlearned child using up my mature resources recklessly without feeding anything back into myself? Heedlessly thinking of my own needs only, leaning on others, relying on 'getting away with it'? 'Why should you be spared?' Lindsay Anderson [stage and film director] said to me. Until now, I somehow thought I always would be. Did I really think that others would constantly cater to my needs all the time, irrespective of their own? Yes, I did.

Rex stays at the British Embassy, does a year's tour in *My Fair Lady*. He does not wallow in a dusty, unkempt apartment in New York, once admired because I rented it from Sir John Gielgud – *he* made it work! – now despised because in it are all the pathetic and paltry evidences of my terrifyingly mixed-up life. When I am in New York, I won't look at the beautiful view over Central Park. I won't sit on the once pretty terrace. I won't ask people around. I won't cook. I won't shop. I can't read a newspaper. I can't listen to music. I don't even want to get a cat. Rex won't have me back, nor should he. I simply seek refuge from him. I have nothing to give. Escape is what I seek.

And yet if it was Italy again with Rex and walks through mimosa trees, and lighting fires, and cooking meals, and reading in bed, and choosing his clothes, and being easily friendly to people, and travelling, then I think I could be happy.

It wasn't always that way, either. At the University of Wales I was full of confidence and vitality. I was liked and thought colourful. Yes, I pretended to be a sophisticated, know-it-all, sexually experienced 'woman' when I was only a total, frightened virgin. Not unusual. I pretended I was an ex-Wren or Waaf [wartime member of Women's Royal Naval Service and Women's Auxiliary Air Force]. I put on rouge: I wore red. I discovered the opposite sex, however, found me attractive when I stopped these practices. I obviously had (as I still do, or did have) a false impression of what men want. When I looked like *me*, then they liked me. For example, I had pretty legs. But I stayed extraordinarily virginal.

I stayed in bed in Alexandra Hall, then did my hair and went to the refectory to eat Welsh rarebit and play my amateur seduction act. I liked talking, debating and acting – but was far too frightened to join the dramatic society in case I was found out. Found out as what? Answer: that I could do better than most of them the only thing I can do, which is act – with Welsh fervour and passion.

William Armstrong [Rachel's English tutor] persuaded me to play Juno in O'Casey's *Juno and the Paycock*. I was frightened. I knew I could handle Mrs Madigan (rather than Juno), though it is in fact the better part. Fortunately, I was over-ruled. The fervour and emotion shone through my performance and, like my Grandfather before me, I held my audience as I was to do in later, professional days – sometimes.

I was happy in college. The arrogance was there. I was 'different', of course, and mysteriously 'better' than my fellows, except for the 'snobby' crowd who had followed me from school, like Lynn and Valerie . . . less so, Valerie, because she had glasses. I wanted people to love me, warts and all. I am impatient with people. I dislike those who do not respond at once.

But to return to happy memories. I had freedom and friends. I blossomed. I took the initiative and auditioned both for the Royal Academy of Dramatic Art *and* the Central School of Speech and Drama, and got into both. There was no guidance, no home, no advice, no finance, but to support myself while waiting to get into RADA I found work as a waitress and in a hospital. I was sacked from the hospital for coming in drunk one night after drinking with a chap called Tom. I slept with Tom – frigidly – watched by his friends Ham and Ted. I let Ted's old father kiss my vagina because I felt sorry for him. He was old, and what did it matter to me? But none of this was as unusual as my punitive, puritanical, harsh and masochistic temperament later imagined it. It wasn't as good as it should have been.

---

ALONG WITH RACHEL at the Royal Academy of Dramatic Art in that same year, 1948, though not in the same class, was the future wife of Lionel Jeffries. Jeffries became one of the best-known English character actors in the 1950s and 1960s and, later, a screenwriter (*The Railway Children*) and director (*The Amazing Mr Blunden*). He, too, was a student at RADA when Eileen Jeffries had cause to be grateful to Rachel.

EILEEN JEFFRIES: 'One evening I was to go and have dinner with Lionel and Pat Hitchcock – Alfred Hitchcock's daughter – and *her* boyfriend. I hadn't a thing to wear to where we were going, which was a nightclub called The Gargoyle. I got desperate as the day wore on and I still hadn't a notion. I rushed into one of the girls' cloakrooms at RADA and appealed to anyone and everyone – "*Please*, has anyone anything you can wear in a nightclub?" A voice called back. "Come here, dear," and it was Rachel, whom I'd never really spoken to before. But she pulled out a beautiful black-and-white dress from her locker – I can't imagine what she was doing with an evening dress in a cloakroom locker! – and told me to try it on and "tie your hair back, dear, and you'll look a beauty". That was thirty-two years ago, yet I remember her kindness more clearly than getting up today. When we went along to the nightclub, I was in Rachel's dress – and that was the night Lionel proposed to me.'

LIONEL JEFFRIES: 'I don't remember Rachel doing any plays at RADA, but then we were always acting in *bits* of plays, never the whole thing. I thought there was a Welsh volcano inside her and she had the makings of a wonderful Shakespearian actress. Later on I regretted she let so many great plays get away from her.'

EILEEN JEFFRIES: 'I always thought she had what so few people at RADA had – energy. She was very outgoing, very vibrant, but had strange periods of flatness and moroseness. I remember once going over to a little flat she had and she introduced me to a boy she said was her brother. I never knew till recently that she had only a sister, so he must have been her boyfriend. Then I met her one day and she was dressed in mourning and down in the dumps because, she said, her brother had died. One of her fantasies, I suppose!'

Another of Rachel's contemporaries at RADA was Brian Matthew, actor, and later one of BBC radio's most successful and literate late-night interviewers.

BRIAN MATTHEW: 'The most vivid memory I have of her is seeing her come into class one day with her hair cropped almost down to the scalp – an early example of a hair-cut I wasn't to see until the London skinheads took to the streets in the 1970s. Rachel was the protopunk of those days. "What *have* you done, Rachel?" I asked. "Darling," she said in the thick Welsh accent she used when she wanted to put herself on, "it's revolt against my upbringing as the Baptist minister's daughter!"'

Rachel was a little older than most of the other RADA students, having already been to university. Living and studying in London brought out what she called her 'English thing'. She arrived in awe of the English, hating them a bit, too, for their 'long umbrella faces'. Looking back, she told the author and journalist Hunter Davies: 'I suppose, it's anti-racial really, the way I thought about the English ... There was something love-hate about it all. They attracted me, really. The John Betjeman way of speaking, I think it's fascinating, and Mr Macmillan, the Prime Minister. I suppose I thought they were some sort of blooming master race. Do all Celts feel and fear that?' One senses in this confession the tidal pull of love and hate that later turned her marriage to that quintessential Englishman, Rex Harrison, into such stormy straits. Racially, as well as temperamentally, Rachel was never going to 'belong' to the English acting establishment. Her Welshness would have made her an outsider, had nothing else about her done so.

She won two student prizes at RADA and a round of applause at the end-of-term matinée of theatrical excerpts which graduates performed at Her Majesty's Theatre. But no agents rushed forward to sign her on. 'Her face was too real and natural for the Fifties,' Davies concluded. 'She wasn't glossy and candy-box. One of nature's non-starlets.'

I didn't really study at RADA. I had enough natural temperament and emotion and so good a voice! . . . It sufficed. Acting was all I wanted to do, not *study*. Now I did it with confidence and bravado. I didn't go to see all the great Shakespearian shows at the New Theatre with Sir Ralph [Richardson], Sir John [Gielgud], Sir Laurence [Olivier] . . . It didn't interest me. Men didn't mean much, either, though I remained attracted to boys (*men* they weren't!) and had my fair share of them, but got to love none of them. I liked causing scenes with men. Didn't make a real friend out of one of them. I lived poorly but happily in Asylum Road.

During vacations I worked as an office cleaner, as a nude model, and dogsbody for the Compass Players – them and their costumes! With one boy, I went to Paris. It didn't work: I left him when I realised he was a phoney.

---

THE ROYAL ACADEMY OF DRAMATIC ART did not make any great impression on Rachel: nor she on it. As she says in her journals, 'Acting was all I wanted to do, not study.' Acting for her was *Living*, intense and capitalised. Discipline and theory irked her. She was growing increasingly volatile, too, dissatisfied with the moment, impatient for the future to arrive – instead of pondering 'What does it all mean?' she was discontentedly enquiring, 'Is this all there is?' and determining that, No, there must be more and more and more to life. She was glad to leave her studies uncompleted and join the impresario Clifford Evans and his repertory company in Swansea, where her parents were still living. This was in 1950. It was a sort of homecoming: but a markedly different girl who came home. 'I sensed a passion in her that was akin to desperation,' says Kenneth Williams, another member of the company which Evans was grooming, vainly as it turned out, as the embryo of the Welsh National Theatre. Richard Burton was in it. 'He'd just done *The Last Days of Dolwyn* film,' says Williams, 'and we all thought him dreadfully famous.' Their theatrical base was the Grand Theatre.

KENNETH WILLIAMS: 'When I met Rachel's father, the minister, we talked about the medieval Morality plays and the tradition of actors performing on the church steps. The next I knew, he'd invited all of us, the whole company, to Sunday service at the chapel and preached us a special sermon on the text, "In the beginning was the Word . . ." The congregation weren't too pleased, if you ask me, to have a lot of raffish actors sitting in their nice respectable pews.

'Rachel did plays with us like *Family Portrait*, the story of Jesus and his mother – I don't think she was assigned a big Bible role – and Sartre's *Crime Passionel*, where she played Olga. A very powerful performance. About her sense of comedy at the time, I wasn't too sure. She was in Terence Rattigan's *Harlequinade*, as the girl who keeps crying out to the romantic lead in the play-within-the-play, "You're my Dad . . . Hello, Dad!" She simply stood there . . . legs wide apart . . . crying out . . .

absolutely manic. I said to myself, "She's got no comic inflection in that voice." But her voice was a great instrument for putting over the quite intellectually complex themes of Shaw or Sartre *without losing the passion* of the words. Those times, she'd already a brilliant intensity and then I'd say to myself, "You're bloody good."

'She was very vital off stage, too: but very strident. You might want to talk quietly, but she'd have none of it. Very insistent, she was: it led to some strange scrapes. I remember she came to my digs one day – I had the front parlour, it overlooked Mumbles Sands, a very nice room that the landlady and her husband hadn't been too keen on letting out in the first place – I was their first "theatrical". Well, Rachel had a love scene to rehearse and she'd decided to enlist my help. I had to get on top of her on the settee. The landlord entered in the middle of the scene with a fresh supply of coal and dropped the scuttle when he saw us locked together. I was given a week's notice. Rachel's comment was, "Narrow-minded bigots!"'

In *Back Drops, Pages from a Private Diary*, published in 1983, Williams wrote: 'I always remember dining with Rachel Roberts at La Coupole when she argued against my asexual nature. "You shouldn't condemn promiscuity," she said. I said it led to wasted aims, but she argued, "No, it's better to experience *something*. Your life is lived entirely on a fantasy level. You've no real knowledge of people."

KENNETH WILLIAMS: 'To the end, for her, the heart would always rule the head. But some of her moral evaluations took odd forms. On one occasion she travelled up to London for a costume fitting with another male member of the company. Coming back, the man faked a breakdown and said they'd have to stay overnight at a hotel he knew nearby. They got connecting rooms. He ordered a delicious supper and made it plain there was more in the air than a night's lodgings. He was in the bathroom, when he heard room service entering Rachel's bedroom with the supper trolley and he walked in to tip the man – and found Rachel sitting in a chair stripped to the buff, completely naked. The venerable old waiter was very shocked. But Rachel gave a hearty bellow and cried out, "I'm a Welsh Baptist minister's daughter – you don't get me that easy!" She always flew in the face of convention. The actor chap confided to me afterwards, "I realised then she was a bit of a Bolshie." You really had to laugh at the way she went about *experiencing* things. Once she met a very young, very effete actor. "All men can perform," she told him, "you can be provoked into it." So she set herself to "provoke" him and by all accounts it was a most painful job. The poor lad came out of it very bruised and scratched. "I had to put Germolene all over my back," he told me – he was black and blue. But apparently he'd managed it. So she was right there!'

A year of Swansea was about as much as Rachel's restless disposition could take. She wanted to move on. For someone so passionate about acting, she behaved like a traveller who takes a pin, closes his eyes and sticks it in the map – and then heads for that destination. In this case, it was Stratford-upon-Avon and the Shakespeare Memorial Theatre which engaged companies by the season. It was there she met a woman who was to be one of her life-long and closest friends.

Sybil Williams, as she'd been born, was as Welsh as Rachel: she was now into the third year of marriage to Richard Burton. They had rented a house and shared it with Hugh Griffith and his wife: Rachel lived in actors' digs just around the corner. The two women immediately drew close to each other 'although', says Sybil Christopher (as she now is after her marriage to actor Jordan Christopher), 'there was quite a social gulf. I was Welsh working class: Rachel came from what we tended to think of as the Welsh gentility. Actually, she talked more about her grandfather than anyone and I got the impression it was in his generation and his work – he was a coal miner – that she felt her roots were, if anywhere.'

SYBIL CHRISTOPHER: 'She seemed incredibly glamorous in a rather vivid way, with dyed hair (black), sweaters that were somehow always slipping off her shoulder, jewellery dangling and bangles jangling. She could manage an awfully good English accent, which was more than I could, and even Richard at that time had the Welsh strain audible in his voice. Rachel and I weren't dedicated actresses. She understudied me; and when she achieved an independent role and played Ceres in *The Tempest*, the vista of parts it opened up didn't excite her: it just seemed likely to spoil our mutual good times in the Green Room by thrusting responsibilities on her. Anthony Quayle led the company and seemed to be forever reprimanding Rachel and me for our lackadaisical behaviour.

'At that time, Rachel was attracted to a handsome young actor who was homosexual. Tony Quayle used to say that if she liked sleeping with gays then it was in a spirit of charity, if not chastity. A mission to redeem gays: that's how he saw Rachel's attachments. You were always hearing something about Rachel – she was the kind of person people talked about when they met. Rachel liked me – yes, but there was a lot about me that her nature couldn't accept. Years after Richard and I broke up, she'd say to me, "Come on, Syb, in the middle of the night don't tell me you don't grieve about those days." "Absolutely not," I'd say, quite truthfully. I'd developed the sense of self-protection which comes from knowing who you are. Rachel simply couldn't comprehend that, then or later.'

It was hardly surprising that, at the end of the Stratford season in the early spring of 1952, Rachel wasn't retained on the company's strength for the upcoming productions in the autumn. She drifted back to London.

KENNETH WILLIAMS: 'She called me in London in desperation to say she hadn't got any work. "How are you living?" I asked. "I've got a temporary job at the Ideal Home Exhibition at Olympia. I wear a red velvet frock and walk about with a bunch of leaflets promoting electric fires and kitchen ovens." I said, "I'll put you in touch with my agent, Peter Eade, in Cork Street."

'She asked me what she should wear. Well, I mean, *I* know nothing about what *women* wear, so I said, "Wear what you wear at work." Afterwards Peter Eade said to me this strange woman came in wearing a red velvet dress on that hot day and sweating all through the interview. He thought she had tremendous potential and took her on right away. But she gave him a terrible time, forever changing her mind, withdrawing from a commitment, then ringing up as he was breaking the news to the other party and saying she'd had second thoughts, and then, when the deal was all but done, pulling out again. Peter said he'd never met anyone with so little self-confidence, considering all her talent.'

London at that time had a myriad little theatre clubs. Sometimes producing a play there was a way of getting round the 'thou-shalt-nots' which were still strictly enjoined on the publicly licensed theatres by the Lord Chamberlain, an anachronistic Court flunkey who censored plays and other live entertainments and whose dictatorial powers endured right into the 1960s. But other clubs were simply the venue of cabaret and intimate revues which made a virtue of being done by a small company by cramming their audience into a correspondingly small space. Rachel began getting work at places like the Irving Theatre Club, which was over an Indian restaurant, just off London's Leicester Square. Another member of the company was a young American who was trying to forget that he was Mary Martin's son and win fame for himself alone: years later, as 'J.R.', Larry Hagman succeeded in a way.

BRIAN EVANS: '"Intimate" was the word for these revues. There was one small dressing room at the Irving which served both male and female artists. It was under the stage. Just two tables placed together, one for males, one for females, everyone relying on the segregating row of mirrors down the centre to give them some sense of privacy.'

She went to West Germany to entertain the British troops in the touring production of *Intimacy at 8.30*, a witty and tuneful revue written by her old campus chum Ronnie Cass and his partner Peter Myers: then it was back to the round of theatre clubs in the West End.

But when the show ended for the company, the night was only beginning for Rachel Roberts. It was her tireless pursuit of experience in which she now engaged that probably whetted her appetite for what was commonly called 'the good life' – a restless search for pleasure which her God-fearing background in puritan Wales would certainly have stigmatised by reference to the spectacular damnations promised by the certitude of self-righteous prophets on such self-indulgent transgressors as herself. Rachel went along and worked the night-club circuit at places like the Embassy and Churchill's for pickings that may now seem ridiculously slim – though £11.00 a week in 1952 could pay the rent and still buy a good meal a day. But being Rachel, she found the thrill of a different experience wasn't simply to be assessed by her pay-packet.

'Her taste for the fast life was definitely built up then,' says Eleanor Fazan, who worked with Rachel in the clubs and later established herself as a leading stage director.

ELEANOR FAZAN: 'We would dance, sing, do point numbers, and announce the numbers. It was wonderful experience, if you could take the hours. Rachel wasn't, I thought, a terribly good performer: she didn't sing very well, she lacked the discipline of the dancer. But she had vitality and a quality I can only call "depth". There seemed to be more to her than she showed. She didn't seem terribly interested in working at her talent, but – and this isn't hindsight – I did sense something special there.

'Now there were artists like us and there were "the other girls" – the club hostesses, the girls who greeted the customers, persuaded them to part with their money and gave them "a good time". The two sorts of women were strictly separated. We even used different dressing rooms. But we soon noticed that Rachel, after dashing round from the theatre when the curtain came down and racing through her act at the nightclub, began mixing with the hostesses and making up to the "punters". Instead of catching the bus home at 1.00 am, she'd go off with them to dance the rest of the night away at the Savoy or the private clubs that kept open all night in Chelsea or the Fulham Road. She got to look more and more like a hostess, too and started streaking lighter tones into her blonde hair from a bottle of dye. A bit, well, tarty-looking. Considering she was rehearsing a new show in the morning, doing the current one in the evening, playing the club circuit, and *then* turning into a party-girl when midnight struck, where she found the energy for it all, I don't know. But then, she was always seeing herself in a role and acting the part accordingly – and I suppose that sustains you. Right from the word go, Rachel was a daredevil: right from the start, she was after the first-class ticket.'

T hen I got a job at the Grand Theatre, Swansea, which brought an odd personality called Kenneth Williams to act with us and an agent Peter Eade who advised me to 'lady-killer' my appearance! While at Swansea, I lived at home and listened to my Father telling his congregation that since the theatre grew out of the church he wanted to welcome the members of the Grand Theatre, Swansea, to the service. Guilt again, but pride, too, in Dad for his bravery in out-facing the disapproval of his deacons.

I auditioned for the Shakespeare Memorial Theatre, Stratford-upon-Avon, and got in – but wasn't keenly interested except in Michael Redgrave's *Richard II*. I got involved with one of the pretty Stratford actors – at that time I didn't know about gays. Hugh came over from Ireland to see me, but I drove him away by inviting him to beat me. I was glad to see him go. I re-read his love letters in the bath, trying to recapture the old illusion of love. Sybil Burton meanwhile was weeping about her husband Richard's telling her he hoped that one day someone would love her as she had loved him.

I wasn't considering my future at all and I had a rather unrealistic view of acting. It was something that came naturally to me. I didn't think I had anything to gain, I suppose, except from watching my peers. I even equated myself with them. The truth was, I was glad to leave Stratford, it was too Shakespearian and folksy for me. I liked the neon-lit coffee-bar at the end of the town where I could be immersed in my own emotions – with a gay boy. I thought it all very funny indeed.

When the season was over, I didn't get asked back to Stratford. I returned to London and lived with three girls in a bed-sitter and worked as a 'Sabu Souvenir' girl at Harringay Arena in Tom Arnold's circus – a glorified programme seller. A circus! My craving for attention, I guess. Then I sold pies for Saxby Bros at the Olympia Fair in Kensington. I borrowed money, reluctantly, from my sister, though I paid her back. I was completely out of hand, I realise now. It wasn't charming to go round the circus, saying *'Baisez-moi'* to all the French fire-eaters in sight. I worked at the Irving Club and other small theatres in London, and found a little bed-sitter in Maida Vale. I read in *Under Milk Wood* at the Old Vic on two consecutive Sundays for Michael Benthall [stage director] – Katharine Hepburn commented on my talent. Then I got invited to join the Old Vic company, some of whom thought it shameful that a 'revue' artist should now be in Shakespeare. It seems to me more and more that the seeds of self-destruction had always been there. I was at the Old Vic when I saw Alan Dobie. He was serious and steady and twenty-two and I thought beautiful to look at – and I went for Alan because, on my own, I was personally adrift and promiscuous and unstable and getting to be twenty-six.

---

RACHEL MADE NO SECRET of her intention. Kenneth Williams remembers her going around at this time, in the early 1950s, chanting, 'I'm going to marry my Alan . . . I'm going to marry my Alan.' She did so, in 1955, at the York Place chapel, Swansea, her father officiating. It was not a union, in their friends' opinion at the time, that was likely to last. Dobie, then, was justly regarded as a most promising young actor, but 'romance' and 'dash' and 'sex appeal', the qualities that furnish male leads, were not his by gift, or indeed choice. He took his career very seriously: perhaps, as he asked himself some years later, a little too seriously. For years, he reflected, he had been playing 'unsmiling, red-brick University intellectuals . . . I used to do a lot of comedy in the theatre, but then I got all those *Look Back in Anger* parts.' He worried about whether his habit of turning down parts till he found the one *worth* doing was evidence of how selective he was – or how prodigal, since the choice was usually made out of necessity, when he discovered the money had run done. And if the latter, was it a reaction against his Yorkshire working-class background? Rachel, too, as her journals show, would be incessantly pulled back to just the same sort of self-querying debate over *her* liking for the good things of life and her pleasure-denying background. But while she acted on impulse and suffered for it at once when the inevitable hangover came, her first husband was a person of forethought and temperance. She was volatile: he had gravitas: this, of course, was why Rachel had married him. But the rock doesn't always like being used as the foundation for the anchor. 'We were temperamentally so different,' Dobie said from the softening perspective of twenty-five years later, and a happier second marriage which had given him several children. 'I was the introvert. [Rachel] was the extrovert, always looking for fun and excitement. I've always envied that "live now, pay later" set . . . I'm a planner.'

He was more than that in the early years: he was a carpenter, furniture-maker, designer and decorator; and one can imagine how Rachel, who could not have hammered in a nail straight to save her life, doted on Dobie's skill at home-making. He literally built up the house from nothing at the very same time as both of them knew their marriage was falling down.

When they moved into a £7.7s. a week council-owned flat at Lancaster Gate, Bayswater, it was Alan who chose the colour scheme, laid the carpets, made the furniture. 'We came here,' Rachel proudly told Shirley Lowe when the journalist came to interview her, 'with a bed, an enormous old Victorian wardrobe, a small ugly three-piece suite, and absolutely no money. I was delighted when Alan got out the breadknife and started hacking up the old furniture to make new. The three-piece suite became a long white-leather sofa (plastic leather). Terribly clever, isn't it? He broke up the wardrobe, turned one of the doors into a coffee table, took out the mirror, framed it, hung it in the sitting-room, made a little bedroom unit out of the rest of the wardrobe with touch-open doors, used the other door as a dressing table, fitted an old kitchen cupboard underneath and painted it all white. Marvellous idea, don't you think? He made a dining table out of a plank of wood covered with black leather, fitted pelmets and Venetian blinds of reed grass and painted the pictures on the walls. I don't know how he does it.'

But the marriage was not holding together as well as the furniture. There were other reasons besides temperamental difference. Work often kept them apart. Dobie was playing in a repertory season at the Old Vic in Bristol – then over a couple of hours' rail journey from London – while Rachel went from job to job in the metropolis. In April 1956, she suddenly took over from Wendy Hiller, who had fallen ill, in *Othello* at the London Old Vic. Her Emilia was so good that she received a solo curtain call: she described the experience as 'numbing'. Dobie was then in Peter Ustinov's play *The Empty Chair* at Bristol and driving up to town in his twenty-year-old car to see his wife at weekends.

SYBIL CHRISTOPHER: 'When I heard Rachel had married Alan Dobie, I simply didn't believe she could have been so lucky. She had married someone I adored. Later on, when she used to brood about losing Rex Harrison, I'd say to her, "If you'd brooded about losing Alan, I'd have understood it." The two of them came to stay with Richard and me at a house we had at Céligny, in the south of France – we called it 'Pays des Galles', which is French for 'Wales'. We'd had a chalet built in the garden, which was later christened 'Camelot'. She was very happy, when things were going well: but when things went wrong and forced her to reflect on why they had gone wrong, I'm afraid she didn't always reach the right conclusions. She used to say, "If only I'd had a guy to come home to . . ." And I'd have to say, "Come off it, Rachel. After all, you had *two* guys to come home to, Alan and Rex . . ." But she'd envy "the go" that Alan made of his life after they'd broken up – the wife, the home, the children who called her "Aunty Rachel" whenever she went to see them, as she did when she and Alan were playing in *Who's Afraid of Virginia Woolf?* in Bath, at a time when she and Rex were still married. Two of her best friends were the actor Donald Houston and Brenda his wife.

'She loved going for a drink to Donald and Brenda Houston's flat, and envying them, and seeing the little pairs of children's shoes waiting to be cleaned outside the hotel suite where Alan and his second wife were staying. Not having a child by either of her husbands – of course that depressed her. But as for adopting one, I'm afraid she left it a bit late in spite of all her good intentions and talk about finding a little girl, a little Welsh girl with glasses – the glasses were important to Rachel, for it had to be a plain little thing so that she could turn the child's life around. There was a Pygmalion feeling sometimes to Rachel's fantasies of motherhood.

'When she was married to Alan, she was very, very protective of him and jealous for his career. If she read a mean remark about him, or a disparaging judgment on one of his performances, she'd sit down a few days later and write a letter of praise about him and his performance to the newspaper in question, signing it with a name she'd make up. Not telling Alan, of course. She always came out fighting for her man. A Welsh characteristic.

'I think her drinking habit began when she was married to Alan. Perhaps because their work kept them apart so much, and she was left on her own. I used to warn her. "Alan's a solid North Country boy, Rachel," I'd say. "He doesn't want to have a drunk for a wife." She didn't want to be one, of course, but she used to say she was at her best when she could let her hair down – which wasn't Alan's style at all. And unfortunately, Rex Harrison's and Rachel's drinking habits were out of synch, too. Rex liked a drink, yes, but he could handle the stuff and get up the next day and call for his breakfast and tuck into it as if he hadn't eaten for a week, while Rachel would be looking a ruin.

'A lot of what she did tended to have its addictive side, not just drinking. When she did one play of Chekhov's, she'd set out to read everything else he'd written. If she read one Somerset Maugham story, she'd work through the collection of his stories. I recall when times were pretty black for her she'd read the whole of the *Los Angeles Times* from front page to back and call her friends up and ask if they'd seen such and such a story in it – and who, for heaven's sake, does that!'

I knew Alan wasn't exactly the kind of man I wanted, but I also knew instinctively that I couldn't get or keep that other kind of man. So I pursued Alan for a year in an inept gauche way. He resisted. He said he didn't want affairs and, if he did, I wasn't the type of girl he'd want an affair with. So I ran up the Strand, crying. He stayed nights with me, we went to see old movies at the National Film Theatre with apples and oranges and chocolates and walked home after the show. Alan cooked rabbit stew and commented that I drank gin-and-tonics in the pub because I didn't know what else to do and that with my intelligence it was strange – or words to that effect. I would say 'Marry me' every night. He'd always say, 'Not until the end of the season.' Finally we went with the Old Vic to Ireland, to Belfast and Dublin. By now I'd lost my infatuation for that face that looked like an angel's. Alan's dourness was beginning to depress me. But I knew that if we parted, it would be for good. So I forged ahead, telephoned my Father from Ireland and told him to post the bans in the morning. Then I informed Alan.

I told Alan we were going to get married on the flimsy basis that if we didn't, we'd lose contact since I was staying on at the Old Vic and he was going to Bristol. I went to Swansea and arranged a simple wedding. I saw Alan the night before it was to happen. His hair needed cutting. I cut it. I thought he looked pallid and slightly greenish.

The morning of the wedding, I woke early to prepare sandwiches. I wasn't in love at all. I felt nothing, not hysteria, just a blank feeling. I didn't want to marry, but I went through with it. The same thing happened at the church. I felt no rapture, no love. My Father broke down when it came to the bit where he had to say, 'Do you take this woman to be your lawful wedded wife?' As we were being pronounced man and wife, a small kitten came into the church and walked up the aisle. I went to go to it. 'Wait for your husband,' admonished my sister Hazel, whose own wedding day had been a starry-eyed occasion for her. We went to Langland Bay along the coast for a grim little wedding lunch, then on to the train to London. Alan had bought us second-class tickets. In the corridor I got hysterical and ordered him to change them to first-class ones. I think he did.

So it was back to the bed-sitter, with the girl I shared with in the other room and, on our bed, the 'wedding present' from one of our actor friends – the loan of his cat.

We drove to France, to Avignon, hardly speaking, not making love. Alan painted while I just walked or hung about. One day, watching the fishes, he spat out his front cap – I felt annoyance more than anything else. We wired his bloke from the Avignon post office, bought fruit and cheese, set out for Paris – I snarling by this time that I wanted men. I've always tended to blame the entire failure of the honeymoon on myself, but there was Alan's side to it, too. I knew he was young and virginal and not too turned on to me – but that didn't help, or contribute to my happiness.

Alan made the bed-sitting room more comfortable while I was at the Edinburgh Festival – and drinking water. My Father and Jacky, my little niece, came to stay. But when I returned to London and the Old Vic I started to get infatuated with Tony White [actor], because he laughed and talked – whereas Alan's silences were depressing in the extreme. Tony and I spent a lot of time together – I remember us walking down Edgware Road eating our boiled beef sandwiches. Tyrone Guthrie who directed me was inspirational, but it was Benzedrine which enabled me to be a good Emilia in *Othello*.

I went on to the Bristol Old Vic. Rehearsing by day, acting leads in the evening, studying at night, trying to push Alan whose nose was put out of joint by Peter O'Toole. I was very self-assured on the stage, and strong, though I don't think I was one to win any popularity contests then. However, I loved it when Miles Malleson [actor, translator and stage director] came to do the Molière play and I was Celimère, and he'd take us to have gin-and-its in the hotel. That was *fun*!

We moved to Lancaster Gate, with nothing, and Alan's carpentry transformed the place. I cooked. I refused to have a television set or a fridge. I read the *Manchester Guardian* and the *New Statesman*. Strong shades of my Mother there!

Alan and I gradually parted . . . 'Damn togetherness, let there be a separateness.' We quarrelled daily and never completed one walk through Kensington Gardens together. I'd shop and take things to the launderette on Saturday morning and feed my cat. I'd cook on Sunday and watch Alan go to sleep on the settee after lunch and think, 'What will he be like when I'm forty?' It seemed so old – forty! We'd go to the pub and Alan wouldn't talk. On Christmas Day, he wouldn't baste the turkey – that was a woman's job. He read a book, not wanting to join in the party that Donald Houston and his wife gave, and when he did, it was awkward. I longed for marriage to a man who would eat me up, though I repressed the thought. But no such man sought me out – wouldn't have put up with my selfishness had he done so, I think.

Alan did bring steadiness into my life . . . I saw a photograph of Alan taken as a little boy and longed for a son just like him. I was examined by a gynaecologist, but he didn't seem to come up with any conclusion.

I blamed HIM for me not being happy. Well, Alan is morose by nature perhaps, but I demanded of him more, it seems, than anyone can demand – to give ME, ME, ME contentment. Nowadays when I see Alan, I remember that I was discontented, though not at first. I did love him and his solidity. I wanted him because he gave me a sense of direction at that time. Well, I belonged a bit – we parted. Alan may not be in a seventh heaven of happiness – but then who is today? – but he has home and hearth and children and a constructed life.

Alan said that acting for me was a means to an end. *IT DID NOT START THAT WAY.*

We started work at the Royal Court Theatre and Alan was wonderful in *Live Like Pigs* with Robert Shaw. The same Robert Shaw with whom, years later, I drank brandy after I'd disgraced myself on Russell Harty's TV show which had had to be cancelled due to my arrogance and rudeness. Head-strong and outspoken, I'd left the Bristol Old Vic because O'Toole was getting the attention – I should have played Eliza in *Pygmalion*. Extraordinary now to think that I refused! When I was at RADA, Sir Kenneth Barnes, the principal, said, 'You're going to be a very good actress, but your personality will get in the way.' I longed to be the sort of actress who could play Iduna, as opposed to the Aunts, and, lo and behold! I suddenly was. Paul Burchard [stage director] asked me to sing the songs of *O Mein Papa!* for him – I used port to bolster up my fears even then. I got the part. When John Justin [actor] got the sack, I naturally roared round to the producer Jack Hylton, demanding his re-instatement. I wanted to go to bed with John – he was 'beautiful'. I went out with him and his wife the night he got the sack and, oblivious to his wife's presence, ogled him until she announced that she wanted to dance with her husband. In the try-out at Brighton, I was a hedgehog with the wardrobe mistress who reprimanded me for going out in 'their' tights. I reminded her of her place and mine – that *I* was the leading lady. (And I *was* good as Iduna!) I think I refused to see Jack Hylton on the first night. When O'Toole got drunk and made the headlines the second night and started not pulling his weight – I went for him. Oh yes, I enjoyed being Iduna all right – and got terrific notices!

Now I believed I could be an opera-singer. Instead, I went straight into John Cranko's [choreographer and director] revue *Keep Your Hair On*. On the last night of that, I went to the piano and ripped up the score – as I'd ripped up Jack Hylton's first-night telegram for *O Mein Papa!* Temperamental, uncontrolled behaviour! I was ill in bed for a week after *Keep Your Hair On* ended – never wanted to act again. A pretty normal reaction for me.

Alan went to South Africa, much to my relief, to do *Look Back in Anger* – and I went to the Oxford Playhouse to do *Under Milk Wood* and was in my element, flirting with Joss Ackland [actor] and the good-looking Welsh actor *and* the old boy from Newport. Then I joined Alan in Rome, in a *pensione*. I didn't really want to go. I took in Alan's navy suit and 'Henry Higgins' hat with distaste. All I remember is the *cannelloni* we ate at Otello's at the foot of the Spanish Steps. There was more out-of-control behaviour when we returned to the Oxford Playhouse for Nigel Dennis's play *Cards of Identity*. I remember wanting to go to the market with Joss and, against Alan's wishes, going . . . locking myself in the lavatory in a tantrum . . . throwing my rings down it. I stood up to Alastair Sim [stage and screen actor] in *A Clean Kill*, but I was very good finally. I had affairs with two or three of the people at the Playhouse to give me energy at the matinées: on stage, however, I was completely confident. Of course, I got great drive from the quarrels I had with Alan. I wanted more and more from him. I envied the look on Brenda's face when she and Donald Houston, her husband, came to the door in answer to our knock, obviously having just made love. I loved the turmoil, too, at Joss Ackland's house, his kids, and his *joie de vivre*. Our flat was so clean and antiseptic by comparison, and Alan and I so silent.

Belligerent and noisy – yes, I am most of the time. But it gave me the zest to play my character parts, which was what I'd loved at the Old Vic. I didn't want to play Rosalind in *As You Like It*, but I loved the Audrey role. And, as I have said, I was marvellous as Emilia – a combination of raw emotion and Benzedrine. *A Clean Kill* – that play I enjoyed doing, too, for I 'fell in love' with another actor Peter Copley and drank Pernod and took Preludin before the matinées.

There was always 'good old Alan' to go home to, no matter where I had spent the night.

---

IT WAS 'GOOD OLD ALAN' who also gave Rachel her first taste of celebrity – by association. Lindsay Anderson, the stage and film director, who was to be her life-long friend, mentor and comforter, had not yet formed his professional and sympathetic bond with Rachel herself: but he had established himself at the Royal Court as one of the most talented theatre directors of his generation. He was directing *Serjeant Musgrave's Dance*, a new play by John Arden, at the end of October, 1959. Among the cast was Alan Dobie . . .

LINDSAY ANDERSON: 'As well as directing the play, I wrote the programme notes. I recall that I said, "Alan Dobie is married to the actress Rachel Roberts." Rachel was delighted by what I'd simply intended to be a straightforward career-note and went around repeating, ". . . the actress Rachel Roberts." She was pleased to find herself, so to speak, "well-known". It should have been a warning.'

It is a fact, not contradicted by its tragic termination, that Rachel's career was a 'lucky' one. Something always turned up when she needed it: and often, it was a play or a film that brought her good notices, artistic nominations and awards, and sometimes itself made history. Such was the film she made at the start of 1960. *Saturday Night and Sunday Morning* galvanised commentators and critics and altered the traditional face of the middle-class and 'respectable' British cinema. It was a key film of the British 'New Wave'. Adapted by the author Alan Sillitoe from his own novel, it split open for inspection by the mass of cinemagoers in several continents a whole hitherto unpictured stratum of British life and morals – those of the urban working class. By dwelling particularly on the sexual energies of ordinary working people, it relegated into nostalgic discard the polite, asexual bourgeois cinema represented by *Brief Encounter*.

It made an instant star out of Albert Finney who had up to then been a stage actor of enormous promise but restricted opportunity. His truculent, unrepentantly sexy working-class lad who seduces the wife of a workmate on night shift was a new sort of romantic anti-hero in Anglo-Saxon cinema.

Rachel played the wife who finds herself pregnant after a furtive liaison. She has to overcome her fear of the flesh before she can enjoy its pleasures. It ends for her, after an attempted abortion, with her fearful and hunted countenance in the grim, denuding light of pain and betrayal.

*Saturday Night and Sunday Morning* was the first feature to be directed by Karel Reisz, a Czech-born naturalised Briton, and one of the group of young post-graduates who wanted to get into films in the days before there were film schools and who cut their teeth on short documentaries committed to intimate and sometimes poetic exploration of ordinary people's life-styles in the changing society of the 1950s. Others in the group included Tony Richardson, who produced *Saturday Night and Sunday Morning*, and Lindsay Anderson, who was to be Rachel's director in plays and films that included her other major movie, *This Sporting Life*, a couple of years later.

KAREL REISZ: 'Odd, isn't it, that the two films which made this great-hearted, flamboyant woman best known were ones in which she played withdrawn, bleak, ungiving women?

'Rachel's great talent was to sink her personality in the part without losing access to her own sensuality. You felt the tension. Not that she "surrendered" herself, like a hysteric: it was always a *considered* performance. I think she was someone who was freed by acting. Inside herself, she felt at ease being allowed to harness her intelligence and feelings and sexuality. Qualities that in real life she got into a frightful muddle. That's why I think that in spite of her saying she shook with nerves at the audition, she was inwardly very self-possessed. She *knew* she could play the role. We tested her on two or three long scenes, reading and discussing, discussing and reading – with me, it's not a five-minute sizing-up job – and then shooting her in make-up on sixteen-mm film.

'We'd had a lot of trouble casting the part. There seemed just no one suitable in all of British theatre. We kept being sent West End actresses who could "do" lower-class parts in a light-comedy way, and when we'd tell the casting lady that we wanted a real, earthy, sensual person, she'd say that type didn't exist and anyway the ladies she'd sent us were really "as common as dirt". That's what it was like making a "real-life" British film in those days. It was another casting agent, Miriam Brickman, who mentioned Rachel's name. But at first Tony Richardson and Harry Saltzman (the executive producer) wanted Diana Dors. She'd recently done *Yield to the Night*, in a prison-cell part she hoped would change her from "Britain's sex-symbol" into a "serious" actress. I was horrified at the prospect. We went to see her film and I said, "I really don't want her," but Harry and Tony were keen enough and we'd no other bankable stars, Albert being an unknown quantity then as far as films were concerned – he hadn't yet made *Tom Jones*. Fortunately Diana Dors turned it down: she was a star already, she didn't want to do a "small role". And that's how Rachel got the chance.

'Rachel had this professionalism right from the start. She'd a lot of scenes in the film with, well, let's call her "another actress", who was difficult to play with. But you could see Rachel saying to herself, "This one's not going to throw me. I'll keep my cool, wait till *she* blows" – there was no question of tears or appeals to my authority.

'She was nervous about her looks, it's true. Without cause. We weren't being asked to admire the woman she played for her beauty, but for her hunger for love. I humoured Rachel's anxiety, but sometimes teased her by pretending I couldn't remember which was the "bad" side of her face – though, quite frankly, "good" or "bad" was pure fantasy. You'd see her looking in the mirror before the take and pulling a face, hoping the tip of her nose would stay down instead of turning up. It got to the point where Lindsay and I would pull the face for her. During shooting, she got pissed off because the part was so "dowdy". She was always half-joking about how she wanted to show herself in a really *risqué* cabaret. It got to the point where she'd appear on the set on the days she wasn't working wearing a leotard, high heels and fishnet stockings and ask the stills man to photograph her!

'She was going through a bad patch with her first husband and kept banging on about 'poor Alan' and how awful she was to him. It got rather tiresome. So eventually I said, "Rachel, you may feel this way: but has it ever occurred to you that "poor Alan" might be relieved to see *you* go?" It was a throw-away line, meant as a joke: but I think it made its point. The thing about Rachel, even when she was "down", was that she could push her head up above the surface, look around and see the funny side of things, even tragic things. That was her nature and why her friends often forgave her for the monstrous things she did.'

Before *Saturday Night and Sunday Morning* came along, Rachel had played small, inconsiderable parts in a number of British films, the sort that gave a few days' work to a rep actress: only *The Good Companions* and *Our Man in Havana* are likely to be remembered (and not for her). But the male star of Karel Reisz's film, Albert Finney, had even less screen experience: his debut had come in a small part in *Look Back in Anger*, though already his stage reputation had got him spoken of as a new Olivier. Each had, therefore, more to think about than simply the other: it wouldn't be until twelve years later, when *Alpha Beta* brought them together again on stage and screen, that, as Finney later put it, 'I knew the pleasure of relaxing with Rachel and fully stretching our performances against each other.'

ALBERT FINNEY: 'We were really strangers brought together by the film in rather instantaneously intimate circumstances. Don't forget, British film censorship was much stricter then than it became a few years later. Rachel and I had a big bedroom scene. It was the first time I'd ever played a scene with a woman in bed. Passion had to be simulated between us, but it was hard to work any up after all the discussions we had about what we should be shown *wearing*. Should Rachel have a slip on, for instance? It wasn't a question of concealing it: just the reverse, for the straps might provide a useful hint of modesty if the censor found it "too strong". Then, should I be wearing a singlet, or not . . . ? The love scene was an elaborately produced affair. But it looked right because, playing with each other, it *felt* right: it still does. At that time, Rachel and I were probably a bit more subjective about our performances: it was easier, later, to relax and take stock. I remember she and Rex came along to the film's London premiere – really the only occasion I saw them together.'

T hen came Karel Reisz's film *Saturday Night and Sunday Morning* . . . I remember going to audition for the role of the faithless wife and saying in the hallway to myself, 'Why shouldn't it be me?' It *was* me. I was very good, but got hysterical when Karel Reisz wanted to photograph me on the left side of my face because of the blob on my nose. Albert Finney was in the part that Harry Saltzman, the producer, had envisaged for Alan. But Alan to his credit wouldn't play the game with him or with Binkie Beaumont, the theatrical impresario. Very different, me! I remember vividly the gold lamé cocktail dress and the rented mink and walking up the stairs at the Dorchester Hotel wanting Binkie Beaumont to notice me. My temperament was used to good advantage in *Saturday Night and Sunday Morning*. That scene in the bedroom with Finney – I've gone over it so many times. Alan used to tell me he'd never liked me that way.

---

CRITICAL ACCLAIM FOR *Saturday Night and Sunday Morning* continued to spill out over the months after its release. By the start of the awards-winning season of 1961, it was the clear front-runner, at least in England. America had yet to discover it and its stars. *Tom Jones* would do that for Albert Finney soon enough. But for Rachel, there was a strange, unanticipated aftermath that actually reinforced her insecurities and deepened the division in her personality about how she looked and wanted to look, and which roles she should and could play.

She won the Best Actress award for *Saturday Night and Sunday Morning* from the British Film Academy in April, 1961: Finney took the Most Promising Newcomer Award and the picture itself was adjudged Best Film. Yet Rachel was soon complaining, 'For all the good this has done me, I might as well be dead.

'Since I made [the film] over a year ago, I've not had one – *not one* – offer to make another film. What's the matter with me? Do I have leprosy or something?' She was reminded how Yvonne Mitchell had been out of work for a year after winning the same award in 1954 for *The Divided Heart*: British film-makers were still decidedly timid about using women whose strength of character displaced conventional beauty from their faces. 'A nice blue Wedgwood plaque from the BFA and a trophy from Equity' – Rachel had also won the Clarence Derwent award for Best Supporting Actress in *Platonov* at the Royal Court Theatre – 'are all I have to show for it. But what about work? Doesn't anybody think I need this? . . . Maybe I'm not star material. I know I'm not a glamour girl. Sometimes I wish I were. It might help.'

A fter a holiday at Sitges, I went to the Royal Court Theatre in 1960 – the Court, where years earlier Bernard Shaw's plays had been tried out and, apparently, not too successfully received at first. A pretty, smallish, red-plush 'proper' theatre, proscenium arch and all, which had been turned into a 'writer's theatre' by George Devine [artistic director, English Stage Company, 1955–64] who for all the world looked like the Hollywood producer David O. Selznick, had the latter had a liberal arts education and been born English.

---

BY THE TIME *Saturday Night and Sunday Morning* was premiered in London, in November, 1960, Rachel's never very secure marriage was coming apart.

The English popular newspapers – most of them now declare their tabloid tastes in format as well as contents – have their noses constantly cocked in the air for any whiff of scandal surrounding a celebrity. And now they sniffed one. Rachel, of course, didn't yet have the stuff that gave stamina to the gossip columns. Nor did Alan Dobie. But Rachel now found herself professionally, and then intimately associated with a man whose recent past and unpredictable future were matters of almost daily comment and speculation in the gossip columns. He was Rex Harrison.

That two such apparently contradictory people as the scintillating Rex and the rough-hewed Rachel should meet and fall in love is perhaps less remarkable in some ways than the place where it happened.

Even today, the Royal Court in Sloane Square, Chelsea, looks like a bit of decaying Victoriana. But the English, who are masochists when it comes to taking their theatrical pleasures, like it this way. Seedy on the outside, a cramped maze of upstairs-downstairs corridors with a tiny auditorium inside, it was done over in French Renaissance style with pretentious trimmings and chandeliers that rattled as the subway trains passed. Yet at the start of the 1960s, this theatre was the most talked about place in London. Home of a revolution – and a vision.

Since 1956, when the English Stage Company moved in, with George Devine as artistic director, the Court had reverberated to a great deal more than commuter trains.

As the critic Richard Findlater wrote, in its official history, published in 1982, it was 'a cockpit of battling egos', the birthplace of the Angry Brigade of writers spearheaded by John Osborne, experimenters on the reactions of audiences as well as vituperative commentators on social and political issues, bent on subverting more than the polite, across-town conventions of London's West End – even using the power of the Court 'collective' to accelerate wider political change and social revolution. The backlash following Britain's humiliating mishandling of the Suez crisis coincided with one of those generational turning points that made the Court 'a catalyst of change, a centre of experiment, a nursery of excellence and the focus of a legend'.

Major acting talent forced its way through the crust of dead conventions: Alan Bates, Joan Plowright, Kenneth Haig, Mary Ure, Robert Stephens. Ensemble playing was rotated with seasons from stars like Olivier, Peggy Ashcroft . . . Writers and directors, always the Court's favourite children, if sometimes obstreperous brats, purveyed a dazzlingly eclectic range. Playwrights like Osborne, Arnold Wesker, Harold Pinter, Nigel Dennis – directors like Lindsay Anderson, Tony Richardson, John Dexter, William

Gaskill. *Roots, Serjeant Musgrave's Dance, Cards of Identity, The Enter-tainer* were among the early plays staged there. The company often crossed into foreign territory – plays unstaged in English by Beckett, Ionesco, Brecht and others, alien names among the musicals, farces and light comedies served up by stars and conservative managements in the West End.

What, then, was a star like Rex Harrison doing in this kind of company in October, 1960?

Rex belonged to a totally different scene. He was part – an essential, valued part, of course – of 'the theatre of comfort, the theatre of nostalgia and the theatre of classical revivalism'. He stood for the star system, the showcase production, the clappable scenery, the matinée audience, the nine-month run and, above all, the phenomenon he himself seemed to be – an apotheosis of the celebrity whose reputation, acquired as much off stage as in the wide world behind the footlights, courses through the veins of any performance he gives like blue blood.

At this time, he was fifty-two. For two years in New York, then for one in London, he had been known to the world as 'Henry Higgins'. *My Fair Lady* had made him rich: it had catapulted him from a man who was a leading player into the sphere of the superstar. It had enabled him to turn his acting talent into real worldly power: limousines, hotel suites, staterooms, jet-set company, the sense that he could brush life aside if it got in his way. All this was his.

In looks and temperament, Rex went back to the Elizabethans. They would have called him 'a man of passionate parts'. His physique and looks were far more striking now that middle age had literally stretched too smooth and callow a youthful face into a lean, long, saturnine physiognomy, whose hooded eyes and wide mouth had satyr-like associations for some people. What most people feared, though, was his tongue. Rex, when vexed, had a famous temper. Higgins's irascibility was also part of Harrison's power, but it pre-dated Shaw's portrait of the actor-manager as a dictator of diction. There was a new, hell-raising breed of West End star around in the 1960s – O'Toole, Burton, Harris and Nicol Williamson were the noisiest – who used their fists. But to administer a thrashing, Rex simply used his tongue. He had a reputation, too, for being demanding, though in fairness, so had most stars whose years of experience at the top have given them a low guile and an even lower level of tolerance for any incompetence that impairs their own uniqueness.

Rex had a chronic restiveness: he was incapable, said one of the women he married, of spending an evening by himself. In 1960, he had been married three times: to Collette Thomas, Lilli Palmer, Kay Kendall. He most admired zest in his partners, whether married to them or not. He once wrote about a woman, Carole Landis who was to play a tragic role in his earlier Hollywood life by committing suicide, that he was attracted by her freedom, the way she talked ('offhand and jolly'), the way she looked ('warm, attractive'). He liked companions who enjoyed all life offered. True partners, in short, were much like himself. His last wife, Kay Kendall, had died the year before. By all accounts, theirs was one of the strangest partnerships in show-business, which can offer some bizarre arrangements: it even formed the basis of a play by Rex's friend, play-wright Terence Rattigan, who had been privy to its terminal tragedy. Lilli Palmer, in her memoirs, *Change Lobsters and Dance*, recounted how, while she and Harrison were still married, they were told by the physician treating Kay Kendall – he was also *their* doctor – that Kay had the fatal disease of myeloid leukaemia and would be lucky to live three years. If this account is true, then it would seem that the Harrisons dissolved their own marriage to let Rex wed his mistress, on the understanding that after Kay Kendall's death he would re-wed Lilli Palmer. For two years, while 'her vitality and magical joy in living infected me as nothing had ever done before', he tended Kendall *and* concealed from her the cause of her increasing enfeeblement. But after Kendall died, in 1959, Lilli Palmer was married to her own lover, Carlos Thompson, and stayed that way.

Rex in 1960 was thus trying to cope (and failing) with the unwonted loneliness of widowerhood. A situation he wasn't likely to endure for long: as the gossip writers knew.

He had also reached an impasse in his career. The very size of his *My Fair Lady* stage success had made it hard to find any other role as satisfying to him, or, more important, his public. Kay Kendall's death, he admitted, had left his judgment and energy at a low ebb. He played a general (a satirical portrait of de Gaulle) in Anouilh's *The Fighting Cock*: but audiences in London were scant and houses remained half-empty in New York. A much worse aberration followed: a film with Doris Day.

Rex had over the years articulated his light-comedy style into a marvellous medium of artistic dexterity. The English critic C. A. Lejeune, reviewing his 1945 film *The Rake's Progress*, characterised him as a man whose 'sense of timing is so delicate, and his sense of showmanship so disciplined, that he can make the flattest line seem knowing, and give an illusion of soundness and even depth to a part that is as hollow as a rotten apple'. That description had not needed renewing: time has only refined it.

Rex's satisfactions, however, did need renewing – and badly. He was not the only acting Establishment figure to feel that life had become a bit deadly. Even Olivier was down in the dumps – and hadn't he in his time scaled the peaks of the classics and Shakespeare, and breathed air that Rex prudently considered a bit too rarefied? Olivier was resuscitated unexpectedly when John Osborne invited him to incarnate Archie Rice, the stand-up comic who is emblematic of run-down Britain, in *The Entertainer*, first performed at the Royal Court. 'I was instantly,' Olivier wrote, 'put in touch with a new, vitally changed, entirely unfamiliar *Me*.' Rex Harrison, depleted and in retreat from Doris Day's lectures in Christian Science on the set of *Midnight Lace*, wondered if the same miracle cure would work for *him*.

Thus in 1959 he accepted the title role of Platonov in Chekhov's first play, which only the Court, with an eye for the curious as well as the iconoclastic, would have dared produce.

'It was an invigorating place to find myself in suddenly,' Harrison recalled, 'though certainly strange and out of keeping with the rest of my life.' The role, though, might have been tailored for his measurements. Platonov is a high-tempered pedagogue with a talent for insulting and belittling what he feels to be a world of fools. Women are his means of revenge against the lesser sort of mankind and he has a hypnotic attraction for them – especially for Anna, a general's widow, who lusts after him physically.

The play staged before *Platonov* had been a new one, *The Happy Haven*, by Court playwright John Arden, which used masks to let the players explore their identities and those of the characters. Rachel had her first Royal Court role in this: her next was the fateful part of Anna Petrovna in *Platonov*, opposite a reinvigorated Rex.

LINDSAY ANDERSON: 'In an indirect way, I was responsible for Rachel meeting Rex. I was going to direct *Platonov*. I had already considered Ian Bannen for the title role and I'd cast Rachel as Platonov's lover Anna Petrovna. Then, unexpectedly, Christopher Logue sent in his play *Antigone* and Royal Court "politics" took me off *Platonov* and started me directing the Logue play [which followed *Platonov*]. George Devine took over *Platonov* and decided that because it was a virtually unknown Chekhov play, it needed a star. He settled on Rex Harrison – and he threw out all my cast except, as it happened, Rachel Roberts.'

I had been called to do two plays in sequence. One was *The Happy Haven* by John Arden; the other was Anton Chekhov's *Platonov*. I loved the idea of Mrs Letouzel, an octogenarian bitch in the Arden play – and was quite interested in Anna Petrovna, the leading lady in Chekhov. What excited me more was the fact that it was supposed that Paul Scofield would be playing Platonov. I didn't know him personally but for me he was the greatest actor in the world. Then, to my intense disappointment, Paul was not available. Next it was rumoured that Trevor Howard would be cast – then an odd silence, plus a sense of titillation from the management. I remember feeling profoundly irritated by all this and I went to Miriam Brickman, the casting director, demanding to know just *who* was going to play opposite me. Dear, sweet Miriam, with a look of near reverence, said, 'Rex Harrison'. My initial reaction was outrage.

What an unfair thing to do to me, I thought. To cast the internationally famous Rex Harrison, still fresh from the staggering stage triumph of *My Fair Lady*, opposite me! What chance would I have to do justice to the role of Anna Petrovna, overshadowed as I would be by Harrison? My second reaction was that of a woman – or should I rather say 'of a girl', for 'woman' I was not – it would take some years before I became one. I went over to Brenda Houston's place. Brenda had been my friend for years. I could confide in her. I told her the news and of my anxiety lest Rex Harrison would not find me attractive enough to be playing the role of his mistress in *Platonov*. Brenda's reassurance was based on the fact that Rex was reputed to like females with small noses like mine. Having hated its tilt all my life, I remained unsure. She then proceeded to play the record album of *My Fair Lady* which I had never heard. I thought Rex's skill tremendous.

I was not at my best rehearsing for *The Happy Haven*. I was arrogant and antagonistic, patronising and grandiose. But there were giggles and whisky-sours with Barrie Ingham on pay-day at the Royal Court, with me secretly rehearsing my lines with Frank Finlay.

And then came the bolt from the blue . . . *Rex*.

Rex crackled. He seemed charged with electricity. Tall and hooded-looking, dressed in blue dog's tooth tweeds and blue cashmere sweater, thin and suspicious, lithe as an electric eel. I was aware of his scrutiny that first morning we met. He gave me a guarded look of appraisal. I desperately wanted him to approve of the way I looked. Despite Brenda's firm insistence that my nose would see me through, I remained unsure of my off-beat face. It was not one to launch a thousand tug-boats. However, I was also aware that the now old-fashioned expression 'sex appeal' was what I had in abundance – or, more probably, the appearance of it. So I was glad when I sensed that I had passed that slowly scrutinised test if not with flying colours, then at least well enough.

Rex cut such a dash. There was something Edwardian about him, something silky and ruffled. He liked his luncheons to be at a now long-forgotten and pulled-down, but then well-established little French restaurant off Sloane Square. The Queen's restaurant, it was called. Waiters were *waiters* there – long experienced in the trade and the tooth. The food was good classic bourgeois fare, the napkins were white, the glasses polished, the *maitre d'* greatly impressed to have Rex as his customer.

That first lunch of ours together was interesting. All those English eyes stared – so impressive were the stares, and so *expressive*, that the people might just as well have been shouting out loud. English reserve is easily penetrated, if you look behind it. The few women lunching – this was 1960 *and* London – looked downright hungry at the sight of Rex. Their menfolk's reaction was curious. They looked at me with an almost 'Wonder what *she* does to him' gleam. Rex either was indifferent or affected indifference. We didn't talk very much. He seemed preoccupied. I, too. In some narrow compartment of my mind I was determined not to let him disrupt the pattern of my life. Acting was my goal, I told myself, and I was achieving it.

But Rex fascinated me. Underneath the glitter, I saw the widower making a brave attempt to carry on – Kay Kendall had died only a year before, so appallingly young – and I admired his guts for doing so. I know that, for Rex, I represented the 'new blood' of the London theatre. The Royal Court was at its zenith.

Our *Platonov* was eulogised by the critics, both the play and the actor. I looked very attractive as Anna Petrovna, playing a glamorous part. I began to feel justified. I began to feel finally not plain, but pretty. Rex was successful. He was acclaimed, looked up to. *And he had chosen me!* I didn't then know about his fears: he kept them to himself, 'acted as if . . .' His vitality energised me. I was swept off my feet, felt pampered (wasn't actually), got attention. It was heady. My career had blossomed.

Yes, with the surprise package called Rex came a lot of joy. That my passion for the boards, for the pub next door after the curtain was down, my innate Welsh need to express myself – that all this was to wane, well, it seemed one of the sacrifices that had to be made. That there was much unhappiness for both of us at the end of what became a stranglehold, not a marriage – this, too, is true. But oh! what fun we sometimes had.

---

PASSION THAT WAS LIVED out so intensely (and publicly) could not be long in drawing attention to itself. As yet, though, the press were reasonably discreet. But by mid-January, 1961, they were badgering Alan Dobie, by now living alone in his tenth-floor council flat in Bayswater. 'We agreed to separate three or four months ago,' he stated, adding (or having the reply attributed to him by some reporter anxious to draw the inference without levelling the finger), 'In fact, we agreed to separate before my wife was in *Platonov* with Mr Harrison.'

*Platonov* ran only an agreed forty-four performances at the Court: every one of them was virtually a sell-out house. It achieved 91 per cent capacity (and box-office takings of nearly £14,000: a record bettered only by Olivier in Ionesco's *Rhinoceros* that year, and a tremendous tribute to Rex's drawing-power which was acknowledged even in the Court's *ensemble*-conscious management, which had kept a sharp eye on him lest he turned the play into a star vehicle).

Immediately it closed, Rex invited Rachel down to the villa he owned at Portofino, near Rapallo, on the Italian Riviera. It was the first taste of a life that left its dangerously sweet aftertaste on Rachel's tongue for ever: nothing else was ever to seem so fulfilling a fantasy.

Rex had fallen in love with Portofino, seeing it from the sea for the first time in 1949. Rex, like Rachel, was a child reared amidst provincial ugliness from which he had escaped, leaving school at fifteen, and thriving by effort, maturing talent and opportunity from the unstable base in ever dingier theatrical digs. To him and Rachel, the Mediterranean latitude was forever the great comforter. He could rule there, feel expansive, and be cared for. One of his worst films, *The Long Dark Hall*, in which he played a suburban murderer, paid for the construction of the villa on a spectacularly sited cliff-top. It had a more breathtaking view even than that enjoyed by the Hotel Splendido down below – it took in the whole Ligurian coastline along to La Spezia, promontories, cypress trees, grottoes, the ever-changing colours of the sea. It was a two-storey red villa built on the site of a wartime German gun emplacement – Lilli Palmer herself lit the dynamite fuse that made way for the site of the house they called San Genesio. The name was suggested by Max Beerbohm. Genesio, a comic mime who used to do a take-off of the Holy Sacrament before a vision of Christ turned him into a true believer, is the patron saint of actors. Rex, perhaps to be on the safe side, was wont to hoist the white flag with the red cross of St George whenever he was in residence. In time, the gardens he planted curled luxuriantly up and over the villa, so that, from afar, it was hard to pick it out from the rock's natural vegetation.

There he found peace; there he insisted on order. For a man who often caused turbulence in his professional world, he loved the security of knowing where things were in his private life; and there he and his wife entertained the *Who's Who* of several intersecting worlds – the Windsors, Garbo, Coward, Sir John Gielgud, the Roland Culvers, the Jean-Pierre Aumonts, even, on one occasion, the fragile, nearly mythical Helen Keller.

There was only, as Lilli Palmer put it, one 'serpent in our paradise'. It was the path up the cliff to San Genesio's doorway. To get there, one started from the village by car and drove up a steeply winding, rocky road. But half-way up, the car had to be abandoned – it traversed the property of another villa-owner who did not care for motor traffic. So guests had to slog it on foot from there on, a five-minute climb, but feeling much, much more in hot, humid weather, until, gratefully, they re-embarked in an ex-US Army Jeep which Rex had bought, the only thing capable of bumping up the mule track to the front door.

Rachel, when married to Rex, put her name to a newspaper article in 1964 in which she said: 'Portofino is the best place for Rex to discuss new projects and relax. One of his favourite pastimes is to go down to La Gritta, the local inn, to chat with the fishermen and sailors. It's run by an ex-prisoner-of-war, now a sort of lawyer who has his hand in everything. Through him, we've come to know and love the local people.' There was perhaps an idealistic gloss on this: like all such enclosed communities, Portofino had its incestuous undercurrents – the numbers of terrace telescopes in the vicinity was a fair warning of how constantly the neighbours were on each other's minds, and perhaps in each other's sights.

After Rex and Lilli Palmer had dissolved their marriage, they took to sharing the villa in turns, a year each. Rex had it (with Kay Kendall and now with Rachel), then Lilli with Carlos Thompson. Rex eventually ended the arrangement by reaching a settlement with his ex-wife on the ownership.

Though San Genesio's powers to watch over the lives and compatibilities of the people under his protection were to be severely tested in the next few years, the impression made on Rachel by her first visit to the place stayed with her for the rest of her life like a waking dream.

When she was banished from the magical spot, she was like the Psyche figure in Claude's well-known painting that is said to have inspired Keats (and reproduced on the endpapers of this book). Shadowy and isolated, she sits immobilised by the crushing weight of her own remorse at the foot of the God Cupid's towering palatial edifice, with only the slenderest hope of ever regaining access to its enchanted interior.

For the moment, though, Portofino was paradise enough.

It is June here in Los Angeles nearly twenty years after that fatal encounter. I woke up today still lost, still so lonely. Going over to Emily's [colleague of Darren Ramirez] and seeing the normalcy of her life-filled home eased the tension. Oh how different from the deadly quiet and total lack of atmosphere in this house. I could eat and I could laugh with Emily's family. I felt warmth. Yes, I know they are innocent folk, but they are living their lives and not drifting in a purposeless chaos.

The horror of Sunday remains with me – waking up with Darren who is no longer able to ease my anguish. I don't in the least blame him for adding to this abyss I'm in – but I'm unable to accept him for what he gently is. So I wandered around in this deathly quietness, went over to Sybil's, couldn't stay there . . . So I came back and swallowed vodka until there was no more left, swallowed tequila until there was no more left, and went over to Christopher Isherwood [novelist and screenwriter] and Don Bachardy [portrait artist and Isherwood's companion], again feeling not like the others or, rather, not in the same world, on the same wavelength – agonised inside, floundering and alone and frightened.

I was told by Darren on Monday when we 'talked' that I can no longer 'cover', told that Gavin Lambert [novelist and screen writer] and Sybil had said, 'It was touch and go, but she calmed down.' Like Vivien Leigh, eh,

Gavin? Perhaps [Vivien Leigh, actress and second wife, 1940–61, of Laurence Olivier, subject to severe manic-depressive states]. Bereft and lonely – certainly.

My childless marriage to Alan led directly to Rex, of course: Kay's death led to his marriage. But when I first met him, it was so splendid and rompy.

I dreamed of Rex again. I was reading a book, 'Mr Harrison' was connected with red carpeting somehow, in the theatre. The other and more disturbed night that I dreamed of him, Rex made a choice – between me and Mercia [Tinker, Rex Harrison's sixth wife, 1978], his present wife. She looked as if she'd lost. He looked at me with fondness for that simplicity, that naïveté, that sweetness, that warmth (for which I'm famous!!) – the opposite of the 'society' world. I was afraid. Since the reality of Rex is the Hôtel de Paris in Monte Carlo and the world of snobbery, why then the tail-spin of despair I so often feel – and felt when I knew him, when he wasn't there? A simple, not particularly physically attractive Welsh provincial girl, in awe of all the English, and of restaurants, and of all that 'real' life she never knew, discontented with her young safe husband because he didn't know it either and he didn't substitute laughter and good talk and friends for it, and she couldn't substitute babies and the interest of seeing children growing up – the sense of fulfilment that children might have given – not unnaturally, if blindly, and perhaps even desperately, such a girl would grab at that worldly, sophisticated man who drank black velvets, listened to Ray Charles records, lived in Eaton Square, ordered chauffeur-driven cars, consumed her little body, praised her green eyes; loved her very naïveté, her little-girl excitement over cats. For her, to walk with a man through olive groves, to have him make love to her just like her adolescent fantasies – in the safe comfort of a fire-lit bedroom in a villa far away in Italy, a place where she could play at cooking, play at being a woman really . . . Now the chill of being over fifty grips and I return endlessly to those years. *They* cannot return again.

Rex's villa in Portofino has often been described. High up in the hills above the port, the graceful garden, the mimosa, the lemon trees, the vineyard, the Roman bath built with the marble from Carrara, one of those hills not so far away where Michelangelo went for *his* raw material. The most extravagantly luxurious memories I have of my days with Rex before our marriage include the actual journey from London to Italy. At Victoria Station in those days they ran the Golden Arrow, the *de luxe* train that had taken the rich English to the Continent for years. And *de luxe* it was! A *coupé* was reserved for us, mahogany and gleaming. The table was laid with white linen and crystal, attentive friendly stewards serving chilled Champagne and a perfect English breakfast. Oh! the 'Sirring' and 'Madaming' that went on and oh! didn't all the participants enjoy it. The Golden Arrow and attention. The Lancaster Hotel in Paris and luxury. The Gare du Nord (or de Lyon: I don't know which) and the Rome Express to Santa Margherita Ligure – the deference to 'Signor Harrison', the villa with Mario, Giuseppe and Pina waiting in the doorway, the woman starched and so polite. Rain later and fires and cats and Homer the dog and my little kitchen where I cooked *sole véronique* and softer pillows and books and walks and wine and renovations to the house – a softening of the Prussian discomfort and bad food and hard beds.

We were together all the time. Ease entered my life. Rex took all the decisions. I had nothing to do but live for him. My extravagant temperament didn't seem to matter so much. Rex's temperament was quite as difficult as mine. Oh yes, everything 'they've' said is true. Terence Rattigan's opinion, which he expressed later, that my excesses lacked the style of Katie Kendall's – true enough. Olivier's instinctive distrust of me – saying the marriage wouldn't last because I was like Vivien – true enough, especially since he's a friend of Rex's second wife, the indefatigable and gifted Lilli Palmer. Lilli-the-powerhouse who gets her books written, has plays on, who doesn't get drunk, who doesn't go berserk, but who also ran, with a touch of Bismarck, a Portofino villa where, I heard, the food was dreadful, the bedroom uncomfortable despite her pink frilly dressing-table.

I absolutely loved those days in Italy. I was very much not alone. The house was taken care of. My friends were envious. Rex's position elevated me in that little port and he loved me. I felt whole. I could be indolent, was protected, had fun, escaped – didn't have to face living, didn't have to fight. I felt confident at last as I basked in the sun and held on to my half-baked liberal ideas. I had at last an ear that listened, was amused by me. I prayed that the happiness would last.

---

REX AND RACHEL'S HAPPY SOJOURN in Portofino came to an end early in the new year, 1961. Rex had to fulfil a film commitment that could not have been less to his liking – despite the upbeat intimations of the title. *The Happy Thieves* had begun life as *The Oldest Confession*, a bad omen to begin with. It was a dreary affair; Rex played a gentleman thief involved in murder. The executive producer, James Hill, was married to its other star, Rita Hayworth. He was her fifth husband and by this time she was well past the prime of her health and career.

Not that Rex's own film career was thriving. He had 'weakly agreed' – his own words – when his agent suggested getting the money 'while he could', and instantly repented of his 'sloppy professional judgment' when he got to Madrid with Rachel and had to face up to a despondent film crew who knew it was bad material and would likely make a worse film.

Boredom, frustration, anger with his agent and gnawing insecurity: such conditions brought him and Rachel even closer; and though Kenneth Williams later said he could not see the 'mutuality' in the affair, and Brian Evans did not understand the 'chemistry', others were not surprised.

One was Mrs Pamela Mason, the former wife of James Mason, and destined to be one of Rachel's closest and most supportive friends.

Mrs Mason resides in Hollywood today in impressive style, with a multitude of free-range cats populating her mansion, the old Buster Keaton residence behind the Beverly Hills Hotel. Pamela Mason is more than a personality – she is a Presence, an outspoken one, listened to avidly at the 'A'-list parties and on her frequent TV appearances. She speaks her thoughts in rapid-fire order, with unrepentant, undeviating, withering aim. Her mind has been well disabused of most of life's softer illusions, especially those to do with men, love and marriage.

PAMELA MASON: 'Rex is Rex. He goes through life not feeling very emotional about it all. He doesn't stop working. He can't. He will always survive any set-back because he doesn't allow it to get on top of him for long. What he and Rachel found in each other is easy to see. They were even alike in looks, a bit marmoset-y, I'd say. Rachel was very energetic, free-living, could be a bundle of fun. And beautiful, in a strong, decisive way, not unlike Tammy Grimes – to whom Rex was also later attracted.

'It was one of those romances that are like unfinished business. Fate intervenes eventually and violently so the partners never have to worry about how their attractiveness to each other will wane and wither. Like Mike Todd and Elizabeth Taylor: Mike was killed in a plane crash early in the marriage. It was grand romance with Rex and Rachel, at first, anyhow. Later on, of course, it all broke out, because basically men like Rex don't want domineering women. In the same way, Richard Burton wouldn't have been a suitable match for Rachel, either. These men don't take to energy being turned against them. One of the partners, usually the woman, has to be the placid type to make it work: Rachel assumed a totally uncharacteristic placidness in the early year or two.

'They shared one special interest. They both loved cats. It was an abiding passion with Rachel: a bit less, I think, with Rex who had his beloved basset hound, Homer. Rachel once gave me a kitten she was mothering. I'd said I'd fourteen cats already – but she arrived at the door with the kitten on a little pillow like the tiny tiara, so of course I kept it.

'When she and Rex stayed in one of the Beverly Hills Hotel bungalows, she used to feed the stray cats, sneaking out to do it in the dark, for the hotel didn't like her maintaining this menagerie of strays setting up a yowling chorus at feeding time.'

'My idea of heaven,' Rachel said at one time, 'is to be surrounded by pussycats, a glass of wine in my hand, someone playing a piano and me singing.'

Rex beat an exhausted retreat back to Portofino to recover from *The Happy Thieves* and invited Rachel's parents down for a summer break. Once the Baptist minister was back in Swansea, he said with an endearing mix of tolerance (where religion was concerned) and naïveté (where the press was concerned), 'I would not be surprised if there was a match between them.'

Rex and Rachel returned to England at the start of July. Characteristically, they were delayed at Dover Customs by two kittens they were importing from Europe when the cats' home failed to collect them at the pier for quarantine. Rex and Rachel waited patiently till the kittens were cared for.

On July 19, Ned Sherrin, who, along with David Frost, was about to revolutionise TV satire in Britain with a show called *That Was the Week That Was*, spotted Rachel going down Bywater Street 'in a little brown Chanel number'. – 'Where are *you* off to?' – 'The divorce court.'

In those days, before the divorce laws were reformed, the law *separating* man and wife was a curious mixture of chivalry and hypocrisy, in which the wife (usually) was allowed to cite the man for adultery and the judge (generally) exercised discretion with regard to the wife's admitted adultery. Thus were Alan Dobie and Rachel Roberts eventually set at liberty.

NED SHERRIN: 'It was obvious a strong, ambitious actress like Rachel couldn't reconcile herself to life in a little flat with her husband, even though she regarded Alan as a totem figure. Rex was just too magnetic a force. Moreover, meeting at the Royal Court had a lot to do with it: that particular theatre released Rachel's energies and recharged Rex's.'

Rex's memoirs confirm this view, but give the event a curious political afterthought. Rachel felt more kindly towards him, he reflected, when he was playing at the Royal Court with the 'theatrical angry brigade', than when he began dedicating himself to such a-political activities as making big expensive Hollywood movies.

Oddly enough, when a restless Rex rushed to Scotland that August to star in a new Nigel Dennis play at the Edinburgh Festival, *August for the People*, he played a part that echoed such aristocratic sentiments: a titled misanthropist who tongue-lashes the era of the 'common man' and declares democracy to be 'a disgusting thing'. Rachel played his mistress. But the play was poorly received in Edinburgh and a disaster when it reached the Royal Court in September. Relief – and release from the play – came unexpectedly promptly and in the shape of that 'big expensive Hollywood film' that was to change quite a few people's lives. Rex was offered the role of Caesar in Twentieth Century-Fox's *Cleopatra*.

I t didn't last very long. Rex had to go to Spain to do a really awful film with Rita Hayworth – how awful I was too naïve to know. I felt great pity for Rita when she came to visit us in Portofino with her producer husband James Hill. She behaved in Portofino in ways that showed the strains that daily life now held for her. I didn't know the fear inside her, but tried to give her her self-respect back by inviting her to the apartment that Rex and I had rented in Old Madrid, making love almost before the estate agents were out of the place. Rex told me I gave him back his youth. I didn't know what being fifty-one meant then: I didn't realise his fears of failure. Loneliness started making me feel its twinges, but there was Rex's picnic lunch to prepare and take to the location where *The Happy Thieves* was being shot – it was a 'comedy' with Rita as the accomplice of an art thief who was played by Rex. I'd take along the two cats, Don Pedro and Don Paco, we had bought in Madrid and sit opposite Rex while he ate his food and looked at me. Rita and Jim came to dinner: she tired and despairing, he looking as if it was all up with his marriage. Desperation set in and I started to flounder in this atmosphere. Rex called me his beloved, but I felt the chill. He called me 'Kate' when we made love, and I felt the chill more keenly still.

I flew back to London to escape for a bit and, while there, I heard I had won two awards – the Clarence Derwent Award for best supporting actress in *Platonov*, and the British Film Academy's best actress award for *Saturday Night and Sunday Morning*.

Apologetically, I telephoned Rex to tell him I'd won *two* awards and what double attention I was getting from the press. More chill. I defended him against all the long-forgotten journalists who came to the Dorchester to interview me, then came back to rejoin him in Madrid, and had my face slapped. I understand why now. He was in a film with a disintegrating Rita, a disenchanted producer – all were desperate people, like I am now. His agent had told him to grab the film when it was offered, since his starring days were over. In contrast, I was young and optimistic, and took my success lightly. Why should I wonder at the rebuff I received?

When the film ended, Rita and Jim went to Seville. We didn't, for some reason, but went back to Portofino, but couldn't stay because it was the turn of Rex's ex-wife, Lilli Palmer, to have the villa – none of which I knew about when we had first arrived and I had found Carlos Thompson's jock-strap in the room. Carlos [Argentine-born actor and author] was Lilli's husband. Rex had laughed about that. I called Sybil and Richard Burton and we got to stay in 'Camelot', the chalet in their garden at Céligny – Rex and I and the two cats. My husband Alan came driving by, stopped and said he'd come to collect me and to get into the car and we'd drive to the South of France – there and then. I'd dressed myself dowdily to meet him. He looked young and bruised and handsome. We dined at a smart restaurant – Alan's social manner wasn't Rex's. What could poor lost Rex, depressed after his terrible film, have been feeling then? I sensed what he was feeling, and returned to him, to the chalet and the cats.

We wandered around – how could I have known then about his immense professional fears? In Lausanne, he bought me an otter coat. I argued about that coat. I didn't want it to be bought.

Back in England, I set out to do a play and get divorced at the same time. I went round to see my Alan. We met in a pub. He was with a pretty girl, Julie Christie. I collected Bimba my cat and burst into tears. Then to the Royal Court. Rex was in deep discussion with George Devine when I told him about the divorce being 'clear'. He seemed not to care. I stayed in a horrible basement flat that night, alone, with a frightened Bimba. I moved back later into Vivien Leigh's flat with Rex – but it was different. Edith, Rex's secretary, was around. Carey, his son, came to tea. We went to Scott's restaurant – or they did. The chauffeur of the hired car asked me if I was 'the new one' – meaning secretary.

Rex and I went to Edinburgh for the festival try-out of Nigel Dennis's play *August for the People* – the silence was growing between us even then. It was cold and chilly in Edinburgh, though it was supposed to be summer. I got off the train at the station, and there were reporters waiting for me. I ran down the station like a cat in a maze. Rex had a suite in a hotel, I had a little room with a mouse-hole in the wall. I felt him drifting away and my love-making became desperate and piteous – not to much avail. Then he developed a sore throat and came to my little room. I wrapped a sock around his neck and comforted him. Then his agent Laurie Evans came up to Edinburgh, bringing an offer for the *Cleopatra* film. Rex gleamed again. *August for the People* had gone well at the previous place we'd tried it out, the Theatre Royal, Newcastle, but in Edinburgh it failed. Nigel Dennis wouldn't speak to Rex.

We returned to London and Vivien Leigh's flat. Rex was to leave for Rome before me. I saw him off with his family. Then I went back to the apartment where it had all started, needing its reassurance, and wept and drank

Fernet-Branca all Sunday long. I spent the night there, but on awakening flew back to the flat on 'the right side of the Park'.

I dozed off on the sofa here in the house in Hutton Drive, Los Angeles, that Darren and I live in. Total nervous exhaustion. I tried to enjoy reading Margot Asquith's autobiography and have woken up to that dread again. The unbearable, paralysing agony that clutches at me, despite my prayers. In my mind, I keep going back to the pre-Rex years.

George Devine remarked that I was an up-and-coming actress and that Rex should leave me alone: was this really the case and, if so, what good does it do me now? Yet I am endlessly thinking about it. What if the answer is yes? I wouldn't be in this agony if I'd remained an actress, familiarising myself with my craft, knowing nothing else; bound to Britain and Alan; doing BBC plays and maybe belonging to the National Theatre; knowing only the inside of theatres and film studios (not many of *them*) – never having done anything much but work. Would I now be like Irene Worth [actress]? I'd still be enjoying the sound of my admittedly good voice, my oratorical sort of acting never having known the glamorous life. Would this present malaise have eaten into me? I really don't know. I think I must believe it would have.

I never played huge parts, wasn't suitable for the romantic heroines. I didn't take it all that seriously and was very ready to flirt and play around. I would never have been a great international star. My horizons would have been limited to Shaftesbury Avenue, the Royal Shakespeare Company, the Royal Court Theatre.

I *was* nervous before I met Rex, less so on the stage for some reason, but very much so on television. My parts in films were tacky until *Saturday Night and Sunday Morning*. Joan Plowright even then was the actress they heralded – she had a bright-eyed, brown-eyed skill as a comedienne. I used my personality and my emotion and my voice.

I still have emotional power, but it is locked up inside me, devastatingly, eating me alive.

Yes, of course I was bowled over by Rex and Italy and for a moment all my inferiorities and fears were swept away. When Alan came to collect me at Céligny that day, I didn't want to go – not back to the council flat and the ordinary life. It was too late then. But if I'd *not* met Rex, would I have carried on as contentedly getting better and better as an actress? It must be faced: I think I wouldn't.

Rex brought me such joy . . . and release. Perhaps the pain would have come anyhow: I know I'll never know for sure. But I do remember those deadly times before Rex appeared on the scene – the Xmas in the pubs at the Bristol Old Vic when Alan lit up a cigar and I wished he'd a bit more of my personality or Peter O'Toole's – visiting him in Bristol in the flat he shared with actor Eric Porter, hating it. I used him really as a shelter so that I could cavort about – going in my dressmaker dress to that first night with my borrowed stole, wanting to be noticed. Yes, yes, I wanted all that Rex could give. To meet all the famous people. To stay at the Grand Hotel in Rome and not at a *pensione*. My large personality needed his and his existence. His world was a different place – I was swept off my feet so completely. All right, it's all part of the past. It seems the canker *is* within me. Which means I'm not a victim of circumstances, but a victim of my own longing for excitement. I remember staring at Kay Kendall, reading about her, wondering why *she* should have 'him'. I always wanted to be the 'star'. Well, I am not – never was. Can the knowledge ease the present pain? It can, if I feel I didn't throw my life away. I think that Rex still needs me. But I must get much better before I can even consider it.

---

IN SEPTEMBER 1961, Rex joined the cast of *Cleopatra* at the Cinecittà Studios in Rome. It was really Twentieth Century-Fox's second desperate attempt to get their foredoomed epic under way. Already it had cost them between two and three million dollars. There had been endless delays when shooting began in England and supposedly sun-drenched Alexandria, constructed in the open air at Pinewood Studios, had to suffer the surly autumn weather and sudden Buckinghamshire fogs. There had been the running chronicle of Elizabeth Taylor's alarming proneness to infections and accidents. Now work had been moved to Rome. Joseph L. Mankiewicz had replaced Rouben Mamoulian as director; Richard Burton took over Antony from Stephen Boyd; Peter Finch had dropped out and now Rex was to be Caesar. Ironically, but not surprisingly in view of her resilient record of overcoming past calamities, only the fragile Elizabeth Taylor retained her original role.

By February 1962, Taylor and Burton were well into the affair that was to be described, vulgarly but accurately, as 'the most publicly conducted adultery in cinema history'. It eventually took up more space in the Italian and foreign press than any other story emanating from Rome, not excluding the death of a Pope.

Rachel arrived shortly before re-shooting began. She and Rex played little part in the brouhaha. For reasons Rachel states, she was overawed by it all. And she and Rex had their own passionate affair to conduct, and were probably grateful for the distraction provided by the more newsworthy couple of stars.

Throughout her life, Rachel viewed Burton with a cool eye – except when she was drunk, that is, whereupon her hot Welsh tongue let him have it. One action of Rex's at this time caused her particular distress:

SYBIL CHRISTOPHER: 'Rex lent his Portofino villa to Richard Burton and Elizabeth Taylor when shooting came to a halt on *Cleopatra* for some reason or other – as it frequently did. This was so that Richard – who was still married to me at the time – should have some place to shelter from the pursuit of Elizabeth and him by the press. But Rachel felt very bad about it, always. That "her" house should have been lent to "that man and his woman" who had broken up my marriage . . . ! She told me about the way she felt fifteen years later. It had been on her mind all that time.'

Whatever the trials and tribulations of *Cleopatra*, filming in Rome was for Rex and Rachel a happy extension of the Mediterranean idyll they had been enjoying in Portofino. Rex was glad to have Rachel there to comfort him when things went wrong, which was almost every day. In his memoirs he gives a funny but piteous account of his first day's labour on *Cleopatra*. After stepping into Caesar's toga and being acutely conscious of his bony knees, he had to make a speech in front of 6,000 extras and hundreds of horses, elephants and camels! So huge was the set-up that he had to wait for a rocket to be fired in the distance in order to know when to begin speaking. The speech was as majestic as Mankiewicz's imperial pen could make it. But its syntax was even more twisted than Rex's tongue was required to be in order to get round lines like, 'For each of our distinguished senators, a medal is inscribed with the name of him for whom it is intended.'

Rachel shunned the parties for reasons referred to in her journals, but made friends readily enough with some of the English players in the subordinate roles. In particular with Jean Marsh, who was playing Octavia. Jean's boyfriend, Kenneth Haig, who was Brutus, had known Rachel in their Royal Court days. Jean Marsh became an internationally known name some years later, both as actress in and author of the television series *Upstairs, Downstairs*. Once she and Rachel took to each other, she had visiting rights to Caesar's court.

JEAN MARSH: 'Kenneth and I felt rather grand, both of us being English working-class kids, mixing with the high and mighty and enjoying the Roman *dolce vita*. Rachel seldom came on the *Cleopatra* set; but we'd meet to eat in a restaurant called George's, after the Englishman who ran it; and sometimes Italian film people joined us and one would say to Rachel, "What a wonderfully witty face you've got." Trouble was, it was a woman who said it, not a man! She initiated our outings to places like Orvieto or into the Roman *campagna*. As Rex was the star, and rich, we did it in style, meeting at their villa early in the day, going up to the hill villages in his studio Mercedes, drinking the local wine, eating small chunks of rough sausage carved off a large one by a man with his pocket-knife. And olives, olives, olives . . . ! Rachel was really happy then. Occasionally, when I turned up at the villa, she'd ask me, "D'you want a vodka?" in the hope, maybe, that if I accepted a drink that early in the day, Rex couldn't object to her having one, too.

'Rachel and I were a bit alike: both of us had pug noses, both of us were a little radical. One night we had an argy-bargy over politics and Rex called us "a couple of Left-wing cunts". Whereupon Rachel whipped off her shoe and whacked Rex over the head with the heel of it – I was terrified the sharp end would dent him, or worse. Meals with Rachel were always unpredictable, especially when the wine got to her. I remember a few years later, when she and Rex were filming *A Flea in Her Ear*, together in Paris, she decided to learn French to kill time when her part was over – it was a small part – and after a few lessons, had a few too many drinks, and vanished for the whole evening. The next night she turned up, much the worse for wear, sat down among the guests at dinner, and was heard by someone practising her French and telling anyone who'd listen, *"Hier soir, j'ai fucké le chauffeur de mon mari."*

'Rachel reminded me of that line – I think it's from T. S. Eliot – "Distracted from distraction by distractions." '

Some time in February or early March, Rex asked Rachel to become his fourth wife.

'I was so overwhelmed by his charm, his elegance, his sheer bloody sophistication,' she recalled in an interview with an English journalist,

Clive Hirschhorn, in New York, 'that when he asked me to marry him, I couldn't get over the shock – especially as his former wives had numbered Lilli Palmer and Kay Kendall. Now before I married Rex, if God had said to me, "Rachel what would you like to be, apart from a great actress?" I would have said a dazzling courtesan. Not a whore, not a hooker, you understand, but a lovely lady whom men adored. But after meeting Rex, all I wanted to be was the best, the most brilliant *wife* in the world.'

Such feelings probably contributed to the nervous hesitation Rachel experienced when an offer came to her before her marriage at the start of 1962 to make a film in England.

It wasn't just the unexpected that excited and unnerved her: it was the nature of the film.

Lindsay Anderson, having established his reputation as a stage director, now wanted to follow his co-revolutionaries Karel Reisz and Tony Richardson into the film studios. Tony Richardson had agreed to produce *This Sporting Life*, if Anderson directed. Though it was about a North Country rugby footballer, David Storey's novel (and screenplay) were only superficially in the *Saturday Night and Sunday Morning* tradition of working-class reality. This story had a hard, bleak, intransigent, ruthless quality that was to send people away from it feeling pained, not cheered. The 'affair' between the aggressively inarticulate footballer, who was to be played by Richard Harris, and his widowed landlady, who was to be Rachel, had no room for charm or proletarian sentiment. It was a story of self-punishment, of masochistically 'missed connections' in which the male partner cannot embody his love in any expression of tenderness and the female will not accept the pleasure of releasing her own repressed sexuality.

After one or two available actresses had been considered, including Mary Ure, Rachel was approached.

KAREL REISZ: 'She had great doubts about her ability to play Mrs Hammond, because she's a very held-back, undemonstrative woman. A passionate person, certainly, but someone who's turned puritanical through so much constant repression of her feelings. Rachel was afraid of this: she simply didn't know out of which part of herself to play the role.'

LINDSAY ANDERSON: 'Karel was very keen on her. To tell you the truth, I wasn't so sure at the time we were casting the film. She didn't appear to me to be the "Mrs Hammond" character in any immediately recognisable way – Rachel was anything but a repressed, closed-up, North Country widow. Yet I'd seen what she could do at the Royal Court and in *Saturday Night and Sunday Morning*. So I said, "Let's test her," willingly enough.

'She arrived early to read the part for Karel and me. Half an hour later, Rex turned up unexpectedly in his Rolls-Royce, clearly not impressed at the sort of role Rachel was being offered by these two . . . I recall us talking about the very savage rugby football sequences we were planning for the film. Of course, said Rex, we'd use doubles. No, I said, the actors would be required to pitch in, however rough or mucky it got. I think he interpreted this as a kind of threat to a professional way of life which he'd spent years mastering. Rachel kept quiet, but before she left with Rex she agreed to test for the part. We set it up at Beaconsfield Studios and were waiting with lighting photographer, sound recordist, make-up artist, everything and everyone ready – and she never showed up. The news came that she'd gone back to Italy with Rex. It was pretty plain that she wasn't being encouraged to do it.

'Well, as it happened, we couldn't begin filming for six months because our male star, Richard Harris, was committed to returning to Hollywood for re-takes on *Mutiny on the Bounty*. In the meantime, we did tests with four other actresses. But none of them made us think they'd be as good as we now were convinced Rachel could be. Eventually, she agreed, though still telling us, "I'm too emotional . . . I'm too Welsh." I'd tell her, "Rachel, I want all the emotions you have, but I want you to keep them bottled up inside you and make us feel the force that this woman uses to suppress all that's natural in life." Which she did: brilliantly.

'Richard Harris was a bit awed by Rachel. You see, she lacked self-confidence *until* she began to act the part. Then she was totally secure in it. She could acquit herself with a first-rate reading in just a couple of takes. Richard took a few more to feel that he had got it right. Rachel's security as an actress made him feel respectful towards her.'

SYBIL CHRISTOPHER: 'Once she'd made her mind up about a part, she was relentless. I remember going into her dressing room during *This Sporting Life*. She wasn't there, but the script was on a table. I picked it up to have a look, and out dropped a whole sheaf of notes that Rachel had written about the Mrs Hammond character she seemed to be playing so intuitively. She was a tenaciously academic actress, despite appearances. She had obviously talked to herself about "this woman I'm playing", figuring her out, and not pushing herself in front of the role lest she obscured it, and then she'd written an essay about the woman's "life".'

Even so, the glamour by association that was penetrating her relationship with Rex showed its earliest signs at this time, though, typically, Rachel could still kid herself about it. The time of recrimination was still far off.

KAREL REISZ: 'She was starting to be intoxicated by the starry feeling that came with Rex. She did feel she was in the slip-stream of some great meteor. When we were filming *This Sporting Life* we had, well, one of those evenings when we all got a bit pissed and then a bit passionate when we went back on the floor to rehearse the next day's scenes and discuss them. Lindsay and Richard [Harris] got locked into argument. Rachel said, "Look, when you bloody kids have finished, let me know," and took herself off to her dressing room. We went on arguing and forgot about her. When I remembered and went to find her, she was gone. The next day, I said, "What happened to you?" And she said with her typical bawdy directness, "Oh, I went into my room and locked the door and sat on the lavatory and my arse got cold and I said to myself, They're not going to treat the future Mrs Rex Harrison like this! and I pulled up my knickers and went home."'

During a few days' unexpected break in the production schedule, she flew back to Italy to become the *current* Mrs Rex Harrison.

Getting married often catches celebrities at their most vulnerable and unintentionally comical. The ordinary legal obligations that simple folk fulfil are seldom waived for famous faces who, in any case, seek to escape attention by complying with the rules.

When Rex Harrison applied to get married in the British consulate in Rome, he had a stencilled form thrust into his hand, was told to fill it in, pay the equivalent of £3.00 and come back to take his turn in line with glum Brits assembled at the consulate because they had lost passports or purses or suffered other mishaps. Rex wanted to get married in Portofino, but was told his marriage would be better solemnised at Genoa, which was in the same province of Liguria. Despite the use of their full but slightly unfamiliar names, 'Reginald Carey Harrison' and 'Rachel Dobie', the banns posted on March 11, 1962, on a green baize board, beside the impending wedlock of an English typist, alerted the international press – all of whom seemed to be trying to get into Genoa City Hall on March 21. (Actually, Rex and Rachel had erred in arriving there twenty-one hours too soon for a marriage that had been set for 9.00 am, on the morrow. A case of certainly getting to the church on time.)

One appalled, angry glance at the melee of media people, and Rex threatened to call the whole thing off, Rachel burst into tears and one Dr Machiavelli, who appositely combined the duties of city registrar and budget assessor, declared a 'state of necessity' which enabled the doors to be closed – which was contrary to established Italian practice and became the subject of a law suit by the disappointed *paparazzi*. The groom (in grey check and carrying a 'Henry Higgins' hat) clutched his bride (in tailored chocolate) and Dr Machiavelli reminded them that under Italian law Rex was head of the family, but Rachel was obliged to contribute to her husband's maintenance 'should he lack sufficient means'.

Then it was a race back to Portofino and a scramble into the wedding 'limousine', otherwise Rex's battered US Army Jeep, for the last trek up the mountain by foot and into the relative peace and security of San Genesio.

I bought some clothes at Simpson's and travelled to Rome by boat and train to be with Rex while he was filming *Cleopatra*.

Rex met me at the station. I ran towards him – he looked furtively to left and right before embracing me when I hurried into his arms. Again he had a hotel suite, at the Grand this time: again, I had another little room. I drank vodka and screamed *for Alan*! Finally the concierge had to come and knock on my door. The start of the film was delayed and Rex and I hung around the beaches playing ball games. Finally *Cleopatra* got under way and I went to see Rex in his Julius Caesar costume. It was all wrong. He was dressed in red velvet, his face was taped up, he had on a curly wig. I told him to tell Irene Sharaff [noted Hollywood costume designer, responsible for Elizabeth Taylor's wardrobe in *Cleopatra*] to look at the statues of Caesar in Rome. It was a hot country. They used Persian dyes which were purple. Finally, Rex looked wonderful in the film. We took a rented house on the Appia Antica, owned by a jeweller. Our cats came to stay. Rex disapproved of the country couple who were to be our servants. Elizabeth Taylor gave a big party. I *couldn't* go. I was too ashamed of my looks to attend – I wasn't pretty enough. Rex (or 'Reg', as I called him) and Ray (as he called me) had turned into Rex Harrison and me, and I felt the world was not finding me up to it. The miserable inferiority complex was turning its talons inwards again.

On Rex's first day of filming he called me to say he'd 'blobbed' – forgotten his lines. We went to dine at a smart restaurant and Rex was rude to Spyros Skouras, the head of Twentieth Century-Fox who were producing the picture. Rex told me how all the English actors had looked pleased – and they were! – when he'd made a fool of himself. I wouldn't go near the set. I'd been to Rex's small dressing room and tried to recapture the old days by suggesting making love. He looked surprised – said he'd got work to do.

I don't quite know what I did with my time in Rome, but then a call came from Lindsay Anderson for me to be in his film *This Sporting Life*. I'd read the David Storey book. Rex said the part was exactly like that in *Saturday Night and Sunday Morning* – another North Country girl. But it wasn't, and I forgot to add, when I told him so, that I'd won the Best Actress award for *Saturday Night and Sunday Morning* – so even if it was, what did it matter? Lindsay persisted. I was now too unsure of myself to do anything, so I called for a screen-test. I said No again, and went into the lavatory with the script and howled my eyes out. Lindsay called a third time and I said Yes, thereby saving a bit of my life. It has stood me in good stead. I left for England to do the film. Rex came over during one of the interminable breaks in *Cleopatra* and saw the scene with me reverently, obsessively, fetishistically polishing the boots belonging to my late husband Eric. Rex said he wished he was in 'Eric's boots', rather than in 'Reggie's Triumphal Entry into Rome' – an indifferent, paltry piece of filming. He didn't like the bruise on my arm, caused by Richard Harris squeezing the Mrs Hammond character a bit too brutally – something of no importance to me. Round about this time, he or I or we decided to get married.

Rex went and did all the necessary things in the British Consulate in Rome. I had a few unexpected days off from filming *This Sporting Life* and flew back to Rome from London with just my hand luggage. Rex was at the airport to meet me. I rushed out to see him, but was stopped by a Customs official. I called this man *'stupido'*, a bad thing to do apparently, for we were taken into custody. I had to appear before a civil judge. Bystanders had accused me of saying *'merde'*. Twentieth Century-Fox got us off, but what exactly had I done, I asked myself. Now, of course, I know. Puffed up with the pride of thinking I'll soon be Mrs Rex Harrison, I was – someone protected, someone above the law.

The film finished, we went to Portofino for Christmas, then to Almeria, then to Madrid. Rex wasn't allowed to stay at the Ritz by the management because they didn't take actors. He'd booked in his real name, Reginald Carey Harrison, but the manager recognised him. So we stayed across the street. We went to see a horror movie and walked back. A sign said in Spanish: 'Pedestrians Don't Cross'. I knew what it meant. Rex didn't. We crossed. This resulted in us being taken into custody and held till four in the morning! The next morning, fruit and sherry were sent by the manager of the hotel who had seen Rex in *My Fair Lady* in New York and an apology was offered by the mayor. Rex said he would never set foot in Spain again – and home we went.

'THIS SPORTING LIFE' had a huge critical success in Britain and America. Its box-office fell far short of the acclaim; but this is understandable, given its 'difficult' flashback narrative, the pain at the consuming centre of it, and the Lawrence-like passions of puritan denial eating, worm-like, throughout it. Ironically, too, it was the last of the English neo-realistic movies, dubbed 'the kitchen-sink drama' by their detractors; for *Tom Jones*, which won the Best Picture Oscar in 1963, and James Bond, who introduced himself in *Dr No* at the end of 1962, diverted British filmmaking energies away from the proletarian look-at-life genre and into what Christopher Booker in *The Neophiliacs* called the 'vitality fantasy' of the Swinging Sixties.

The film proved to be Rachel's graduation piece. Her 'deathhead beauty', as Felix Barker called it in London's *Evening News*, and 'marvellously unstressed tragic quality' were new notes, visually and emotionally striking, profoundly vibrating, in that small repertory company of British talents who could measure up to the sheer physicality of American players or match the radar wavelengths of the best performers in European cinema. '[She] manages to project oceans of suppressed passion,' *Newsweek* wrote.

Penelope Gilliatt, then the best film critic in England, wrote at length and with strength of passion about the epic capacity for pain and violence expressed by the suffocating tension of desire and denial in the performances of Richard Harris and Rachel:

'The first time you see him with his landlady . . . you wonder what on earth the pressure is between them. This is the way it happens in life (and in Ibsen's plays), but hardly ever in the cinema . . . There is something about her put-upon Englishwoman's silences that makes him behave like a pig, and he could boot her for the way she droops over the memory of her dead husband: but at the same time there is a kind of purity about her withdrawal that somehow consoles him, although he does everything to wreck it . . . The relationship thickens with hostility. Sometimes love-making works, but she generally manages to make him feel that he has assaulted her. They begin to have a gruelling power over each other, but it is a power only to give pain; they make demands of each other that are cruel because they can't be met, can't be communicated, can't even be defined in themselves.'

There hadn't been before – and there hasn't been since – such a piece of tragic playing as Rachel's in English cinema. It brought her a Best Actress nomination in the 1963 Oscars. That she lost to Patricia Neal, in *Hud*, scarcely matters.

Rex Harrison was nominated as Best Actor in the same listings, for Caesar in *Cleopatra*. (He lost to Sidney Poitier in *Lilies of the Field*). The coincidence of husband and wife both receiving nominations was rare enough: it suggested the irresistible question, which *Time* magazine was first on the doorstep with: Who would Rachel like to win, Rex or her?

She told Clive Hirschhorn the answer she gave, and her words catch nicely (and sadly) what her marriage was about to do to her.

'. . . in all honesty, I said "Rex". The very fact that he was able, in that circus of a film, to maintain his cool and keep his *superb* craftsmanship intact, was, as far as I was concerned, worthy of some sort of general recognition. And for that alone he certainly deserved the Oscar more than I did. I was beautifully, quietly nurtured into giving a good performance by Lindsay Anderson in a small studio in Twickenham, away from the madding crowd and the publicity and all the palaver that made *Cleopatra* such an impossibly difficult film to work on. So for me it was easy.

'Believe me, darling, I'm not telling you all of this to wave a Welsh banner and say how fantastically generous a spirit I am. I'm only telling you this to illustrate my point that I do *understand* the problems actors have to face. And *because* I appreciated what went into Rex's performance, I wanted him to win the Oscar. I respect craftsmanship, wherever I see it.'

Rachel elaborated on the theme of putting Rex before herself in interviews which cause the heart to sink in retrospect. It was as if love were just one of the drugs, an aphrodisiac, though, rather than a tranquilliser, on which she was to become so tragically dependent. Barry Norman spoke to her shortly after *This Sporting Life* was finished. It did not seem to be the same woman on whom Penelope Gilliatt would soon be lavishing her praise: a tribute, maybe, to Rachel's power to transform her nature by her acting, but also a disconcerting omen of how she was trying to damp herself down for life with Rex in order to radiate a cosy domestic warmth instead of stoking herself up on the artistry that fed her in the prime of her life and career:

'I suppose the main thing is that I'm not ambitious any more. I don't want to be a great success, to be a star, to have an acting career and be a public figure for fifty-two weeks of the year . . . With Rex, I have the perfect life. If I get an offer that seems worth taking, I accept it with his full blessing . . . Being with [him] is much more important than rushing around, working madly and generally playing the career woman. I'm not that kind of woman, in any case. As an actress, I am quite fulfilled . . . Things are much more satisfactory as they are. I can take a role, and then go quietly back to my husband and private life. I'm always glad to get back to him. He's a much misunderstood man, you know. We are both happiest when we are sitting in the sun, talking and reading and away from the crowds. I am happy to be an actress, but I know now that what I want most is children and a family life somewhere, the kind of things women used to want before it became fashionable for us all to have a career.'

There is no doubt: the Rachel who spoke this meant every word of it, at the time. But in retrospect, it sounds like a woman determinedly talking herself into a role that she knows, in her heart of hearts, is not the right one for her to be playing.

Portofino and fiestas and I suppose – though I don't remember too well – the drinking began. One afternoon the gardener's dog barked. I yelled down at the gardener – took a bottle of wine down later as a peace-offering – was yelled at in return. Rex's son Noel and Sara, his daughter-in-law, came to stay.

Noel and Sara, especially Sara, brought back the past – Kay and Rex. Walking through the Port, I heard the tourists talking of Rex and his ex-wife Lilli Palmer, a marvellous actress. Reggio, the bartender at La Quitta said, 'Sorry, madam, the most beautiful woman in the world, with the exception of Ava Gardner, was Kay Kendall.' Rex took him outside and slapped his face. It came upon me with full force that I wasn't 'glamorous Kate' – my idea of glamorous Kate, anyhow. I remember going into a bookshop to buy some Somerset Maugham stories and coming across Dirk Bogarde's autobiography. I instantly looked up 'Kendall, Kay' and read avidly about her and him. It all came rushing back. My envy of her having 'him', thinking she wouldn't want what I had, which was Alan, thinking about the tragedy of her and Rex, after her death, when I was in the London Clinic having cartilage removed from my nose, thinking about her in the place where she died. Despite her beauty, she was probably as insecure as I was – and dying. The truth was, I was still living in my mind and groping for an idealised form of life and riddled with self-doubts – the old ones now simply reinforced.

---

KAREL REISZ: 'Rachel afterwards gave one the feeling that Rex put her into a double bind, that really he didn't want her to act. But that wasn't true. It's nearer the mark to say that Rex was contemptuous of non-star acting.

'Rex *is* a star. He absorbs everything and puts it out again through his own personality. Whereas Rachel is a very good character actress. So really, he was applying irrelevant strictures to the sort of performances she was brilliantly equipped to give and the sort of career *he* thought one should have. Rachel was made to feel that she was being exploited by people who sought her services, that she should be far more "difficult" and hold out for star billing. The truth of the matter was that Rachel wasn't technically the kind of beauty made to play female leads. She could have had a good career, playing damn good interesting roles, during her marriage: but she was made to feel that it was, sort of, *beneath* her – which I don't think she felt naturally. Rex had an ambivalent attitude towards those films she appeared in. He admired her performances, but he would think of the films as 'unglamorous'. They weren't what show-business stars did, appearing in dirty clothes as the working classes. It ran counter to his notion of stardom.'

PAMELA MASON: 'When she was acting, Rachel showed great self-respect. She was a great achiever. She had a wide range – comedy and tragedy. She was like a ball of fire: the only trouble, so often she had no material worthy of setting alight with her combustible energy.'

KAREL REISZ: 'She once told me that when Rex was making *Dr Dolittle* in Hollywood, and she was sitting at home doing nothing, he suggested that when they came to post-syncing the film she should do the voice of Polynesia the parrot. Rachel said a few years later that she suddenly realised the whole thing had gone completely crazy, that night after night they were discussing whether she, who had played in the West End and taken leading roles in movies and had been nominated for the Oscar and won British stage and screen awards, should or should not post-sync the voice of a parrot.'

W̲e had to go to Paris for Rex to re-record some of his lines in *Cleopatra*. No sooner had we arrived at the Lancaster than I read an article by Roddy Mann in the *Sunday Express* – the story that Peter O'Toole was going to play Professor Higgins in the film of *My Fair Lady*. I kept the article away from Rex and prayed that he would get the *Fair Lady* part. I actually asked God that He would let Rex do it – for my sake, too, of course. For my hideous, greedy, inept, childlike self. I *had* to be important. Rex couldn't let me down.

We returned to Portofino. Rex had bought a Polaroid camera to take pictures. One day he was swimming around the boat and I'd taken some silly snaps of him – thin, balding, naked. I pasted them in an album. Then George Cukor, who was to direct *My Fair Lady*, asked Rex to come over to Hollywood and do a screen test: Warners were worried that by now he would look too old for the role on the screen. I suggested he send the Polaroids to Cukor. Rex did. Cukor wired back that the part was his.

We went to Paris. We were going to Cherbourg, to sail from there to New York and thence to California, when among some newspaper clippings that Edith had sent us I found one that froze me – it said that my Father had had a stroke. I left for Wales at once, alone of course. My mother and sister were next door with Mrs Johns when the hired car I was in drew up at our house. We went to the hospital. My Father was in the general ward, unable to speak, looking up at me with frightened eyes. I was aggressive with the matron, telling her of all the good, hard work my Father had done in the hospital and to please give him a private ward. I asked Dad if he wanted to come to America. I insisted he answered and he spoke and said 'Yes'. And his eyes filled with tears.

Rex and I sailed on the *Queen Elizabeth*. He'd done that many times before. My feelings of inadequacy grew. Rex's favourite photograph of me was the one he took on that voyage. I was sitting in a corner of the deck – looking like I felt – and he laughed and said I looked like an early immigrant. I suppose I was.

---

ALONG WITH REX AND RACHEL on the *Queen Elizabeth* went – Rex's Rolls-Royce. He had it driven across America; when he and his wife arrived in Los Angeles, after a stop-over in New York, its resplendent comfort met them at the airport. A perfect example of Rex's effortless ability, so envied by Rachel, to order the creature comforts of his life. On bad days on the set of *My Fair Lady*, the luxurious car that took him to studio and home was a substantial solace.

In other respects, he was not so fortunate. 'Home' was a pretentious little house – everything about it a bit bogus – that he and Rachel had rented from two male decorators after a spell in the Bel Air Hotel. It depressed Rachel, too, who had to stay in it most of the time since she herself did not drive a car. But there were more subtle afflictions than being immobilised in Los Angeles. She was turning into a 'Hollywood wife', experiencing the new and increasingly dreaded sensation of being excluded from the larger myth that was made flesh in the shape of the 'Hollywood stars', in whose company Rex now indubitably belonged – perhaps for the first time in his off-and-on career in Hollywood, which has a habit of taking to its heart (wherever that may be located) only the talents on whom the money is riding. A great deal of money was riding on Rex in *My Fair Lady*: he earned his comforts.

Besides the Rolls-Royce, he was soon joined by another companion: Homer, the famous basset hound which so took his fancy (and Rachel's, though to a lesser extent) was acquired from a litter in the San Fernando valley. No one knows if Professor Henry Higgins ever had a dog about the house: but as he was used to ordering Eliza to bring him his slippers, it is unlikely. Thus Rex improved on the original.

The tensions now working their way to the surface of Rachel's marriage are evident in her account of those 'locust' months that ate away at her flourishing artistry. One friend who witnessed the deterioration over the years was Nancy Holmes, the internationally known photo-journalist. She had made the acquaintance of Rex and Rachel in 1963, in circumstances that were characteristically wary.

NANCY HOLMES: '*Look* magazine, which I was working for then, told me to go without delay to Portofino and do a picture story on Rex. He was up for the part in *My Fair Lady*, but wasn't sure if he'd got it yet. The directions I got were to wait in Reggio's bar, *not* go up to the villa. So I'm waiting . . . And in comes, not Rex, but this blonde in a bright red coat who falls on me with a shriek of, "You must be Nancy Holmes – how *can* you be so bloody beautiful?" Rachel, of course . . . Rex wanted the *Look* story badly, but he was nervous, so he'd sent Rachel out to look me over and see whether he could put up with a woman photographer!

'Rachel at that time appeared to me like a little girl lost amidst all that sophistication. In Rex's world, she was a Welsh waif. But when it came to looking after her man, she was in her element. She comforted and cosseted Rex, and cooked those solid English dishes he loved, like roasts and Yorkshire pudding and sausage-and-mash and shepherd's pie. Drinking wasn't yet a big problem for her. She used to say, "Rex, you know, is bad at making friends – I have to make the friends for him." She found contact with people easier than he did: even going into a restaurant made Rex feel nervous, since he thought actors shouldn't mix with the audience.

'Obviously, they were devoted to each other, then. One problem area I could sense, though, had to do with work. If Rachel was anything, it was a *working* actress. But she couldn't work *and* live with Rex at this time. For the simple reason that although *she* could work freely in England, *he* couldn't do so for tax reasons. That was the reality of things, whatever she said.

'But they certainly were very affectionate. I remember going on a yacht to Corsica with them in a party that included their friends the "Pip" Roystons. We all went ashore. Rex was in a good humour, Rachel a bit tiddly. Rex said he was going to bed, and turned in. On the waterfront, a stray cat crossed Rachel's path and before it could dodge out of the way, she'd scooped it up and was cooing, "Oh, you poor dear, have you been abandoned?" It was angry enough to kill us all. "I'll put the poor thing into the cabin," said Rachel, ignoring the way it was lashing out at her. We could hear Rex's stertorous breathing as she opened the cabin door and tossed the mangy tabby on to the bed. It let out an ear-splitting yowl. Rex half-woke up and said in his sweetest tones, "Is that you, Rachel?"'

Nancy Holmes joined the Harrisons the following March, 1964, for part of the winter season at the fashionable Swiss resort of Gstaad. 'Rachel was in her element: not so, Rex. He would do anything on earth not to have to appear on the *pistes*. But Rachel adored the snow and the *après-ski* wear, especially the furs. She had this lifelong "thing" about furs – of course, well before Animals Lib began making people feel guilty about the pelts on their backs.'

Among the visitors that Rex and Rachel invited to stay with them in California while he was shooting *My Fair Lady* through much of 1964 were her parents.

Rex was deeply touched by the plight of the Rev. Rees Roberts. The old man was now seventy. He had been operated on for a stomach cancer, with temporary remission, the previous year in London. 'Reverend,' said Rex to him when he arrived, 'you've just got to make a comeback.' It was as if the 'actors' in both men had met.

NANCY HOLMES: 'Rex was as devoted as Rachel to her frail father. He had such a simple trusting attitude to life, I think he reminded them both of their roots in less fraught times. Rex took him to a very grand Hollywood party where the Rev. Roberts, at the end of dinner, was offered his choice of *espresso* or *capuccino*. He'd never heard of either so, much to Rex's affectionate amusement, he said he'd have a little of both, thank you!'

When Rachel's father returned to Swansea, he was able to preach a few final sermons, full of his old fiery 'hwyl', before he died, aged seventy-one, in the following June 1965. This, too, was to add to Rachel's sense of emotional severance from family and work.

When we went to America there was still a togetherness. I loved Rex and all the fun he stood for. (I'd never had much.) The Ray Charles records and black velvets and *my* 'sexy Rex' looking warm and woolly and being written about . . . Portofino: there was no one else there when he was around, and he was around all the time and we walked and talked and made love in front of open fires and Pina kept the place so clean, the pasta was delicious, the wine better. Oh! if only all my present existence were a nightmare I'd wake up from tomorrow, full of vitality and hope and pride and joy and able to cope – and with my beloved Rex by my side. But lack of experience made me make a mess of it – or was it that I was not (am not) up to *their* life?

Hollywood and the terrible little faggot house we rented in Hidden Valley

Road in Coldwater Canyon really started to take the idyll away from us. I began to be alone and I floundered more and more. There was no repose in me when I was Rex's wife. I felt apologetic for my own inferiority and so got noisy and 'outrageous'. Had I been able to learn to drive – not much of a feat, really. Had I driven to Jorgensen's and done the shopping – after all, we had the money! Had I seen to it that Rex had an excellent dinner when he came back from work at Warner Bros. Had I gone to the hairdresser in order to look as pretty as I *can*. Had I arranged the household, so that Rex had had breakfast in bed. Had I changed in the evening. Had I thought more about his comfort. All could have been so much better . . .

But no, I sweated as Rex rode off in his Rolls-Royce each morning. I drank. I was afraid of the servants. I was me, in short. Had I been the talented person I've described above, I wouldn't be here now.

Word went round that I'd 'made him (Rex) human'. But I hadn't. Homer the dog was brought over and I rented a little beach house on the proceeds of a television play I was in. (Doing that play with Richard Kiley frightened me near to death. Rex didn't have that kind of fear, or else he didn't understand it.) But the week-ends at the beach didn't work. Rex just drank and mumbled into his corn-on-the-cob pipe. We no longer made love. I wept and woke up to emptiness and the dog on Monday mornings at the beach. Rex would leap up at the bidding of Romy Schneider while I, half-heartedly, fought in 'the enemy camp' – part of me despising the enemy, part of me longing to belong. I took futile tennis lessons, piano lessons, singing lessons – 'Bewitched, Bothered and Bewildered' probably helped later when I did the London musical *Maggie May*. Sybil Burton came to stay, and Lindsay Anderson, and my parents. I rallied. I got to know David O. Selznick, and week-ends at the Selznicks' house were a form of reprieve. We went to all the parties then; but although we had a house with a pool and a tennis court, I didn't entertain. When we went out, I didn't 'return' much. I just 'pushed in'.

I had money to dress well – but I didn't even know how to go about it!

All I could do was make noisy friends with the people we met at the Selznicks' and we had drunken week-ends – I again bright and breezy, but not in control. I was still getting parts offered me, the part of Dylan Thomas's wife in the play *Dylan*, for instance, with Alec Guinness. I ignored it loftily. I wanted the easy life, I suppose.

Meanwhile, elegant and guarded, sophisticated and famous, Rex drove his Rolls-Royce to Warner Bros. to star in the film of the play that made him world-famous. Rex lived up to his myth – and the myth shut me out.

---

ALL THE TIME she was in Hollywood, Rachel concealed her discontent. It is doubtful if she admitted it even to herself. To have done so would have been to expel herself from the material enchantment that a great deal of 'Rex's world' held for her, and would continue to do for years even when she was no longer a pampered part of it.

To have said publicly that she was fed up with not working would have exposed their marriage to embarrassing scrutiny, and been unfair to Rex in the middle of a film that was physically taxing and vital for his career. Not till a long time later was Rachel able to admit, publicly and privately, to the depth of deprivation that a gifted woman could experience in circumstances of apparent plenty.

When they returned to Europe in mid-1964, Rex was what is known as 'hot'. Advance news of his performance in *My Fair Lady* – premiered in November – was sensational. This news, plus Warner's multi-million-dollar stake in what was then the most expensive movie musical ever made, exposed its star to urgent entreaties from producers eager for a little (or, preferably, a lot) of his spoken-for success to rub off on their film plans. With more urgency than he usually gave them leave to apply to his film and stage commitments, Rex's agents signed him to appear in several expensive (and rewarding) productions. He was to be Jeanne Moreau's husband in *The Yellow Rolls-Royce*. Besides the name, it was very much a 'vehicle' to his taste. It had quality coachwork, polished to a gloss by three old friends: Anatol De Grunwald (producer), Anthony Asquith (director), Terence Rattigan (writer). Rex was, in his words, 'on top of the world'. The film was a joyride.

Rachel might have realistically hoped for a role in its multiple stories all linked to the fate of the prestige vehicle. After all, she was an 'Oscar' nominee and she wanted to work *when Rex worked*, and, if possible *with* him, and so extend her reach beyond her grasp to encompass something of his glamour. It was not to be. She had no hope at all of a role in the other film which Rex committed himself to: *The Agony and the Ecstasy* was an early example of male bonding (ecclesiastical division), in which Rex played the Pontiff Julius and Charlton Heston was Michelangelo. It turned out a laborious 'Pope opera'.

In fact, up to now, Rachel had scored only a minor and not-much-remarked-on success in performing with Rex, and this in circumstances in which neither of them was seen, only heard.

Rex had not made his name in the theatre's Classics: a fact he may sometimes regret, since his formidable technical talents and personality surely equipped him for them. Rachel's experience at Stratford was limited – even lax – but her attitude to Shakespeare was fearless. She expressed it some years later to Michael Leech, of the London *Times*: ' "Come on, girl," I said to myself, "get a little Welsh backbone," and whether I turn out good, bad or indifferent – at least its been *fas-cin-a-ting*.' But now Rex was persuaded by her into a three-disc recording of *Much Ado About Nothing*, released as he was starting the film of *My Fair Lady*. He played Benedict to Rachel's Beatrice. Both remained justly proud of their accomplishment. Ironically, the play's theme is one of marital bondage.

Perhaps it was seeing Rex signed up, as far as filming was concerned, for the best part of the next six months that contributed to Rachel's increasing restiveness and intemperance. It also made a breach in her vow to be the 'ideal wife' when she was offered the star part in Lionel Bart's new London musical, *Maggie May*, in September, 1964.

LIONEL BART: 'I wrote *Maggie May* as an up-dated, lay version of Christ and the Magdalene. It was inspired by the Kozantzakis story *He Who Must Die*, which tried the same thing, but set the story in Greece. My musical was set in Liverpool's dockland.

'I'd Georgia Brown in mind from the start, after her great hit as Nancy in *Oliver!* But when I offered it to her in New York, she turned it down – didn't want to play second fiddle to Christ, I suppose! Then Albert Finney said No to the Jesus role. It had all just happened for Albert – *Tom Jones* the film hit of New York and himself starring in *Luther* on Broadway. He hadn't had a break in eighteen years, he said. He was going to lose himself in the Far East for a year. And he did – so well that his accountants rang me up in a panic and said there was ten per cent of *Tom Jones* piling up daily in Albert's bank account and they *had* to know what to do with it and had I his address.

'So Rachel and Kenneth Haig played the roles. I went down to Portofino. She was having intensive voice training from Signor Tutti-Frutti, or someone.

'We had our battles during the try-out. I gave her a hard time. "Look, dolly, it's not a hymn-singing class, you know," I remember bawling her out. She was good – but she was difficult. Sean Kenny was designing the show. Rachel had to appear high up on one of his mobile sets. "She might fall," I said. He gave me a wink – "We'll risk it."

'Her contract was for a limited run, six months, I think. She opened big in London: but she got tired. She also started drinking. She got pissed out of her mind one night, forgot to put her girdle on, and came in from the wrong side for one of her duets. Afterwards we all met, Bernard Delfont (he wasn't then a "Sir", much less a "Lord") who was presenting it, Ted Kotcheff who directed it, and Alun Owen who wrote it though I'd lost him half-way through when he rushed off to do *A Hard Day's Night* for the Beatles' first film. None of them dared face a tigress like Rachel to tell her what they thought of her bloody awful conduct. I was pushed forward.

'I knocked on her dressing-room door, very nervous. "Come in," she said – you could hear how pissed she was. I told her I thought her conduct was disgraceful. "Do you think I'm drunk?" she said. "Darling, I've tripped over the empties outside," I said. I'd a huge bundle of money with me, from the box-office, or somewhere. I shoved it at her. "If I were you, Rachel, I'd take this and catch the folk while they're still outside and offer them their money back – for you were fucking *awful!*'

'Well, home I go, very choked, and get into bed, and about 2.00 am the phone rings. It's Rex. Blazing angry. "I hear you've been bloody rude to my wife. What did you say to her, you little homosexual runt?" Well, I got really angry at that. "Here," I shouted at him down the phone, "who the hell are you calling *little*?"'

NED SHERRIN: 'An actress called Julia McKenzie understudied Rachel in *Maggie May*, but when Rachel met her again, years later, she was in my production of *Side by Side by Sondheim*. Rachel came to hear the show. Afterwards, she went up to Julia and said very humbly, "To think that *you* should have been understudying me!"'

LIONEL BART: 'Rachel had a break clause in her contract and could walk out when she wanted to after giving notice. A few weeks later, that's what she did – walk.'

When the curtain rose on the evening performance of *Maggie May*, on February 18, 1965, a shock of surprise rippled through the audience. They had been expecting Rachel: but what was this . . . ? *Georgia Brown?* The actress-singer whom Bart had originally seen in the role when he wrote the show was half-way across her long, slow, initial walk across the stage when people woke up to the fact that it was not the advertised Rachel Roberts. She was given an ovation.

The management was taken by surprise by the suddenness of Rachel's exit. There had been no official notification: even Bernard Delfont's office did not seem to be sure of anything until shortly before curtain-up. 'We gather (sic) Miss Brown played in the matinée,' said an Adelphi Theatre spokesman, 'and will continue to play all performances from now on.'

We crossed back to the Old World on the *Leonardo da Vinci* with Homer the dog and Alice the cat – Bimba, my other cat, died on the day President Kennedy was assassinated. We stopped off first and briefly at New York and stayed at the St Regis. Homer had a fan club. A little bit of the idyll came back. We stopped at Naples. Homer loved the smells. I loved the old men with their morning Fernet-Brancas. We were met at Genoa by Reggio – and then it was up the mule track and home. Was that the Christmas of the tree with the blue balloons? I'm not sure. It's the American toys that I remember.

It seems extraordinary now, that group of circumstances when I was Rex's glamorous leading lady and then his consort – when I could not bear it if he wasn't in the room. Today I came, in tears, to the public library in Los Angeles where I am writing this and there – opposite me, on the shelf – was *Platonov*. Today my concentration is blurred. It was all nineteen years ago and I feel I shall go mad. I fear my ability or, worse, my desire to stand on my own two feet. I don't want to act, to write, to do anything really. What if I really did love Rex? What if he is essential to my happiness? He's gone now. Marriage has seen to that. I no longer know him. I don't know their friends. I can't imagine their relationship. I knew about Rex when he got re-married – to Elizabeth [Harrison, Rex's fifth wife, 1971–76, previously married to actor Richard Harris and subsequently to financier Peter Aitken] – after our divorce. He wasn't lost to me then. And he came back to me. Would I have secured him then – and could I have? He was bereft, vulnerable again. I was 'cavalier' about the situation. I didn't think. Oh Rex and *Platonov* and Rachel, where did it all go so wrong that I feel unbearably alone and empty and hopeless?

I saw him on the Dick Cavett Show – nineteen years later – an old man now, someone I didn't know, never probably did. He looked like a Victoria plum. But his graceful body was still attractive. He talked about 'listening' on the stage – admitted he was thinking should it be white wine or Champagne after the show, and what would he eat for supper.

From early on with Rex – in Madrid – the feeling of being stifled started. Empty days got emptier and pussy-cats and fires and booze and sex began to pall. Before that, I had a firm grip on myself, I think. I was interested in the world. I read and thought about things in the *Observer* and the *Guardian*. I was hotly liberal. I disliked unfairness. I fought with optimism. And yet that other side was there – wanting to be in a position of power, wanting the unreachable 'good' life exemplified by going into the bar at the Dorchester and being catered to – but too frightened ever to do so. I wanted attention. I wanted to penetrate that world of English 'class'. How amazing that Rex should come along and open up not just the bar at the Dorchester and 'those' restaurants where 'they' dined, but also undreamed of worlds of prestige and apparent power. How awkward I felt – there under false pretences and unable to cope. I know all about 'that world' now. It's a dying world, too. Do I still hanker after it and its illusions? Well, I don't quite know what to put in its place. I think I and Darren are making a pathetic, half-cock attempt to emulate it here in Los Angeles and New York and London, without the prerequisites of money and prestige, and making unhappy fools of ourselves in the process.

After *My Fair Lady*, Rex was offered *The Yellow Rolls-Royce* and *The Agony and the Ecstasy* and I went into Lionel Bart's stage musical *Maggie May* – that was in the autumn of 1964, I think. I felt frightened and lost. Rex wasn't 'my' Rex – he was an aloof Rex in the rented house with his manservant. It was cold and chill. Then came Rex's Oscar award for Professor Higgins – he was grumpy about it, nervousness I suppose. But it meant so much to him. There is no point in recording what I saw as his ungraciousness, no point in recalling the advice I used to give him about his filming – to care about Pompey's death in *Cleopatra*, or not to pre-record the songs from *My Fair Lady*. No point, either, in recalling the efforts I made to see him well-fed, or make his home more comfortable. It was selfishness and masochism, I think. No more were my green eyes praised. I started to feel even plainer than before. My achievements seemed to mean little. Yet I loved him, irascible though he was.

---

AFTER 'MAGGIE MAY', Rachel went to Portofino with Rex to resume her role as 'a proper full-time wife'. She spoke of adopting a 'Welsh baby . . . a boy who will come and live with us in our villa here'. Adoption was constantly in her head – and her interviews – over the next few years: but nothing ever came of it. Reunion with Rex did not help her compose herself, as she may have hoped. Her reiterated loyalty to him had now a desperate edge to it – though she was not yet turning the edge against herself. It is this one senses in the remarks she made when she went with Rex to Hollywood in April 1965 – and saw him win the Best Actor Oscar for *My Fair Lady*.

Rachel was interviewed by one of her most dogged press friends, the columnist Earl Wilson. Wilson's breezy, self-referral style fed his many readers' mythic expectations of the movie world: at the same time, his calculated emphasis insinuated that perhaps all was not quite as it should be.

'The fourth Mrs Sexy Rexy,' he began, using an expression that always set Rex's teeth on edge, 'is tossing her own booming acting career into the jolly old Thames to become a dutiful housewife. She'll patter along after her Oscar-winning master like a terrier barking a soft "Yes, Love . . ." to all . . . or practically all . . . of his requirements. "I know I'll sound like a real square, but, rather than be an actress, I prefer being a housewife to Rex," she said. I can't say she told me exclusively, because people all round the table heard her raving about him. In fact, she lectured me about his qualities with such violence that in about three more hours I'd have hated him . . .' '. . . and I love him,' Earl Wilson added, for Rex's reassurance, no doubt.

If public statements at this time convey the feeling that the lady 'doth protest too much' about her acceptance of a life-without-art, except through the surrogate talents of her husband, home-life employed fewer subterfuges. Even the funniest of Rachel's unconventional bouts of behaviour had their disturbing note.

PAMELA MASON: 'I remember Rex and Rachel being invited to a fund-raising dinner honouring George Cukor on one of the University of California campuses. They'd both been having a dinner of their own earlier in the evening and felt a bit tired and decided not to go on to the function. They ordered their limo to stop somewhere where they could call George and apologise; but when they tried, they couldn't discover where *exactly* they should call. So they drove on to the campus and Rex told Rachel to go and tell George they couldn't come. So Rachel sashays into the big room where the dinner is being held and there's a U-shaped top table with George Cukor right in the middle. And of course, as Rachel's in her ridiculously short mini-skirt – for she hadn't changed – she catches everyone's eye, and as she wends her way unsteadily through the tables, everyone's eyebrows are going up, except George's – he hasn't seen her. So to catch his attention, she goes "*Woof! Woof!*" Just like a dog. And when George looks up in surprise, she says, 'We've come to tell you we can't come to dinner," which no doubt seems a bit odd, since she's there. "But before I go," she says, "I just want to say something to the company. I want to say one big Woof." And turns to everyone and goes "*WOOF!*"'

Though she adored cats, Rachel had a peculiarity about dogs and imitated one whenever she felt compelled to draw attention to herself. Her journals suggest a rather pathetic origin for behaviour that amused some – like the time at another Hollywood function, when she crawled under a table and 'worried' at Robert Mitchum's trouser leg. 'It was all in fun,' she explained, 'I was pretending to be a Welsh corgi.' Breed of dog apart, public misconduct was apt to upset her husband. Rex was quite capable of 'upsetting the table' on occasions and showing considerable panache in his choice of language as he did so. But such anecdotes that are part and parcel of his mythology have usually one thing in common: they take place amidst friends. There was the *contretemps* one night in Hollywood when he and Rachel, after drinks at the Daisy, a favourite watering-hole of the British colony, took their friends back to their house and Rex was impelled by the disorderly jesting to tell a few home truths to each member of the company – whereupon Rachel put a Welsh curse on *him*. It was presumably lifted in the morning: whereupon *she* was asked to apologise to the guests for her behaviour. When Rachel broke the public decorum that her husband valued, and exposed him and his fellow guests to *public* embarrassment, it was not at all amusing to him. It could become quite pathetic.

NANCY HOLMES: 'We used to put to sea in the motor vessel that Rex kept at Portofino – a 'Riva' class Chriscraft. We'd fish from it, using tiny crabs as bait. Rachel didn't fish. She sat on deck in the sun, drinking white wine.

Suddenly we heard her growl, "Fish murderers," followed by, "Crab murderers." When I heard that spoiling-for-a-fight sound coming from her, I knew it was time to get the hell out of the way.'

Rex, however, professed amusement at Rachel's sympathies for marine life: *Look* magazine, in a November, 1965, article, quoted him as saying that, 'My real key to trying to understand women is to imagine back to what they must have been like when they were pigtailed little girls.' Rachel's concern at killing anything was mentioned. Rex, according to *Look*, commented: 'All this goes back to my little-girl theory.'

But an example of how such a private joke – if that is what it was – could turn into acute public embarrassment was provided not many months later.

NANCY HOLMES: 'Rex and Rachel and myself and a Texas beau of mine were having dinner at "21". Rex said to me, "What are you eating?" I decided on soft-shell crabs, a *salade verte* and white wine. Rachel was wearing a beautiful white dress with a scooped out neckline. She was also lowering the Pouilly Fuissé that we'd ordered, really knocking it back.

'When she heard what we were having, she started to cry out, "Fish murderers, crab murderers . . . I'm not having anything like that." To the waiter, she commanded, "Bring me an uncooked egg." One was brought. Rachel took it, cracked one end and tried to suck the raw yolk out of the shell – and of course the sticky, messy stuff ran down her chin, down her bosom, and on to her white dress. Rex ordered her to stop it, but she shouted at the waiter, "Bring me another egg." Eventually we jollied her out of it. When the time came to pay for the meal, Rachel demanded a separate cheque. "I want to see what '21' charges for a raw egg," she said, and screamed with laughter. Rachel never lost her sense of the ridiculous especially when she was contributing to it. It put her in a good mood. The egg stains, though, never came off her dress.'

Rachel had a rare experience when she and Rex attended the Moscow Film Festival in July, 1965. Here, at last, was one place in the world where she was better known than her husband! *My Fair Lady* was due to be shown in Moscow (but not competing): but *Saturday Night and Sunday Morning* and *This Sporting Life*, being films about 'the workers', had already played in Russia. Rachel's performances in both had earned her praise – though not, as it turned out, when she arrived, immediate recognition.

NANCY HOLMES: 'The Russians rushed up to the plane when we landed and came down the steps, with me first to take pictures of Rex and Rachel. Suddenly I had this huge bouquet of flowers thrust into my arms – they were meant for Rachel! But as she was behind Rex, they'd mistaken her for my maid. Before I could explain, Rachel flounced in between me and the bowing and scraping Russians and cried out in mock indignation: "How dare you give flowers to the woman who is living with my husband!" Rex hissed, "Rachel, this is Russia – you'll get us all shot." '

Moscow had an extraordinary effect on Rachel. It incited her to break the rules if only to vary the monotony. The restraints on guests, even celebrities in 'official' hotels like the National, immediately brought out the rebel in Rachel. Other stimulants played their part. She was particularly incensed at a city devoid of domestic pets. Suddenly she took off . . .

NANCY HOLMES: 'She screamed, "Nancy, I've found a cat in Moscow!" and rushed away. Rex gave up: "Let her take care of herself." Which wasn't exactly what happened. She was later found in the hotel bar with two Englishmen we'd never seen before. Rex went to bed. But at 5.00 am, the telephone rang. "Nancy, is Rachel with you?" She wasn't. She didn't get back till after breakfast-time, and then she discovered her wedding ring wasn't on her finger. It was found, by one of the Englishmen. Physical fidelity didn't count for very much with Rachel when the urge was in her. We left with Rex – who was by then "famous", as about 30,000 Russians had seen *My Fair Lady* – thrusting bundles of photos of himself as Henry Higgins into the Moscow fans outside the hotel: it was maybe as well that they couldn't understand what he was saying.'

After Rex had detoured to Taormina, Sicily, to receive a Davide di Donatello award, Italy's Oscar, at the August film festival for *My Fair Lady* and *The Yellow Rolls-Royce*, they arrived in Rome where Joseph L. Mankiewicz was to film *The Honey Pot*. Rex rented a house on the Via Appia Antica, a place whose proximity to the sites of pagan massacres and Christian martyrdom throughout the ages turned an already gloomy habitation into a positively spooky one.

It was in this place that Rachel made the first attempt to take her own life.

Rex fortunately arrived in time to have her rushed to hospital. While she recovered, he was rushed into *The Honey Pot*, a modernised version of Ben Jonson's *Volpone*. He played a mountebank – even his *palazzo*'s resplendent furnishings are merely on hire from Cinecitta – who gulls the rich as they run to his supposed deathbed in search of the fortune he has promised to leave each.

The film can be 'read' as Joseph L. Mankiewicz's own acerbic judgment on a fantasy industry like film-making that feeds on false promises, illusory hopes, terminal deceits – as well as a form of cathartic revenge on the kinds of female stars (Rex's mistresses in the film) whom Mankiewicz had had to put up with in a long career.

Rex gave one of his deftest performances: alas, one of his least appreciated, since the film failed to find its audience and was withdrawn for a time and drastically re-cut.

W e went back to Rome where Rex was to play a Pope in *The Agony and the Ecstasy*. The house we rented on the Via Appia Antica, belonging to Carlo Ponti's first wife, was dismal. The ceiling was covered with mosquitoes. Rex was considering the film of *Volpone*, re-done by Joe Mankiewicz as an up-dated comedy entitled *The Honey Pot*. The agent Kurt Frings wanted to represent me – and there was a role I could have played in *The Honey Pot*. Instead, Maggie Smith got it – quite rightly probably.

Rex was being asked to do *Dr Dolittle*. One minute he wanted to do it, the next he didn't, so it went to Christopher Plummer. Then Rex wanted it back. Days were spent shouting over the phone to Aaron Frosch, Rex's lawyer, or Laurie Evans, his agent in London. Even Jolie, the little girl with the squint who washed the clothes, was yelled at. I sacked the Roman servants. The man sneered at me, contemptuously referring to me as 'La Signora'. We dined out that Saturday in Rome with two agents. Rex was in a temper. Abuse flowed. I drank brandy. I came home to emptiness and ice and swallowed Seconal. I came to, shouting 'Alan! Alan! Alan!'

---

'DR DOLITTLE' TRAPPED REX for months on end. Like *Cleopatra* and *My Fair Lady*, it was a film with huge logistic problems. Shooting seemed endless. Many times Rex paused in the middle of some bit of 'insanity' taxing the infinite patience he needed to play and re-play scenes with the 'stars' of a menagerie of two hundred animals and birds and asked himself why in hell he was there. The basic reason, he concluded, was 'the gold' that he observed had been first discovered in California, right there on one of the locations they were using.

According to producer Arthur P. Jacobs, Rex was 'getting more money than God'. In mortal terms, this probably meant $750,000 plus overages (moneys disbursed for every day of shooting that went over schedule) plus *per diems* (moneys used to soothe the stars' temperaments by paying for their daily 'necessities').

Filming had actually begun at the Wiltshire village of Castle Combe in August, 1966. But as the English summer ushered in the same monsoon season that had driven Twentieth Century-Fox's *Cleopatra* to take flight to Mediterranean latitudes, the unit eventually shipped itself over to the Walt Disney ranch in California.

If it was a nightmare for Rex, playing the eponymous country physician of Hugh Loftus's children's story, who has the gift of holding man-to-mammal conversations with the furred and feathered co-stars, the lengthy schedule was disastrous for Rachel. Sometimes, though, her by now gravely erratic behaviour had its amusing side.

NANCY HOLMES: 'The *Dr Dolittle* production eventually shifted to Santa Lucia which is one of the Windward Islands in the Caribbean. Rachel joined us. [She had been in New York, trying to regain her emotional bearings by recording a TV version of Coward's *Blithe Spirit*.] Rachel, you know, couldn't do many of the things that most people do naturally, or learn to do out of necessity very quickly – such as swimming. But we taught her in the bay. No sooner could she breaststroke, than she swam out to where *Dr Dolittle*'s trained seals were penned up until they were needed for a scene. Before we realised what she was up to, she had nearly succeeded in undoing the net and letting them escape! Arthur Jacobs nearly had a heart attack. He said to Rex, "We should have taken out an insurance policy against your wife setting all our animals free!"'

The house that Rex and Rachel rented on North Bedford Drive had belonged to Greta Garbo and was now owned by Jean Negulesco. Rachel made feverish efforts to 'fit in', but this in itself was not a reassuring symptom to her friends.

NANCY HOLMES: 'She tended to overwhelm people with just too big a show of hospitality and affection. It was a sign of how desperate she was to be liked – she, who had such a genuinely warm and likeable nature when all was well with her. Richard Harris was in Hollywood at the same time, making *Camelot*, and he and his wife Elizabeth threw a big party for Rex and Rachel. Rachel showed up in a long black dress, looking already very much the worse for wear. As soon as she'd looked the guests over rather unsteadily, she saw Richard's much prized pet, a Chinese mocking bird. It was in an ornamental cage: it was a very valuable bird – if it had been in a safe, you wouldn't have been surprised. Rachel was heard to say, "Don't you think birds should be free?" and before anyone could stop her, she'd flung open the cage door, the bird got out, hopped through the open window and was off into the night. Well, it just had to be one dead bird before long! Richard cut up very rough over that.'

Rachel said later in her own defence (as well as the bird's): 'I don't like to see *any* kind of creature caged up. I wasn't to know that Richard had a very special feeling for the bird, or he believed it contained a part of his soul, or something. Elizabeth replaced it with a parakeet – but it was never the same for him, he said.'

She was growing ever more depressed at the lack of opportunity to act. She had been off the cinema screen for three years; yet, oddly and occasionally reassuringly, she would find that she had a very special place in people's memories, short though these were in a city like Hollywood where time is measurable by the span between your last hit and your current flop. Her name was frequently mentioned by young people who recognised a style in her acting, an intensity of explored emotion, that had the instinctual integrity of the Method school.

SYBIL CHRISTOPHER: 'I recall my present husband Jordan saying to me at a time when he had no notion that Rachel and I were so intimate: "Do you know one actress I'm mad about? Rachel Roberts." One 4 July, we all went to an Independence Day party that Sal Mineo was throwing – Roddy MacDowall, Margot Fonteyn, Nureyev, Rex Harrison, Rachel and a lot of people of that calibre. There was this young actor, a friend of Sal's, who'd seen them all, but he singled out Rachel, dashed up to her and said, "Rachel Roberts! How I love your work." She stood there and did one of her barks – "WOOF!" She was the one who'd made that boy sit up and pay attention – one actor recognising the sort of "call sign" another had for him.'

But the prismatic pleasure of seeing herself refracted through someone else's unsolicited admiration was as fleeting as the rainbow. More often in 1966–67, the emotional weather was threatening or stormy. Rachel's now widowed mother came to stay at their Santa Monica beach house. Even Mother had worrisome habits, as one of the co-stars in *Dr Dolittle* recalled:

PETER BULL: 'Mrs Roberts would start off paddling in the water along the beach; then she'd turn and face the horizon and start to walk out to sea.

Rachel had to retrieve her parent from the waves several times and was getting a bit tired of it all. She would stand on the terrace of their house with a drink in her hand, eyeing her mother and speculating to me, "Will she do it this time?"'

In his memoirs, Rex Harrison spoke of his 'private troubles' around this time, suppressing the alarming dimension they had now assumed.

PAMELA MASON: 'One night I was going over to their house on North Bedford. Just as I got there, the front door flew open and Rachel rushed out, down the path, down the steps, and into a cab she had called. "What's happening?" I asked Rex. He said she was going to kill herself. She was going to the beach. She'd threatened to throw herself off a rock. He'd done his best: he could do no more. "Oh, Rex," said Rachel's mother limply. Well, I thought I knew where she was headed for. It was a rocky promontory and Jennifer Jones had an apartment opposite it and I knew the people who lived nearby. So I called them, told them what Rachel had threatened to do and begged them to intercept her. They did. But they had to talk to her all night before she calmed down and came back. Laurie Evans, who was Rex's agent, said to me, "I think she's very seriously ill, mentally."'

But Rachel wouldn't hear of the possibility: even her closest friends could make no impression on her. A desperately worried Rex Harrison now felt that perhaps work was the best remedy in the circumstances. He himself had always found it effective, when his spirits were low, though there was a crucial difference between him and his wife.

PAMELA MASON: 'Rachel never had enough on which to work off her energy. Considering what she was going through then, and later on particularly, she did an incredible amount of work. Now Rex was – and is – a professional, a *total* professional. But he's not a *driven* performer the way Rachel was. He keeps his distance, whereas she used herself up – consumed herself. To him, it wasn't death's door if the theatre was half-empty or the people stayed away from his new movie. If you're Rex, you may feel sad for a bit, but you ultimately don't give a damn. If folk like it, good: if not, we close Saturday night. But Rachel, she was *driven*: she just *had* to display herself and have an audience at all costs. Like when she'd decide to bake a pie: she'd bake six, then call up everyone to come round and sample them, so what had been a solitary pursuit became a block party. To her, work was like that.'

So in the hope of taking the pressure off, it was decided that Rachel was 'available' for offers. Paul Kohner, a respected agent, was appointed to represent her. And *Variety*, the show-business weekly, announced this in a large display advertisement in October, 1966. It listed Rachel's screen awards and nominations, her *Blithe Spirit* special for NBC TV and her performance as Lady Hamilton in a TV play, *Nelson*, she had squeezed in during a brief trip to England that summer. There was a picture of Rachel in the urchin cut she had adopted when she went brunette that same summer, hiding her nose and mouth (the features she was sensitive about) in one cupped hand, sitting on a chair in a light summer-length skirt that displayed her legs (the features she was proudest of). She looked younger than her thirty-eight years: she looked as if she would be fun.

An offer came. Richard Zanuck, production chief at Twentieth Century-Fox, had already a commitment from Rex to star in a film of the Feydeau farce *A Flea in Her Ear*: now he decided (or was persuaded) that Rachel would be the perfect foil as the 'best friend' who colludes with Rex's wife in trying to cure her husband's temporary impotence. One of Rachel's closest friends, Rosemary Harris, was to play the wife.

The Harrisons sailed for Europe: but it was not the happiest of voyages.

LIONEL JEFFRIES: 'My wife and I were aboard the *Queen Elizabeth* when suddenly we saw Rex and Rachel. They looked terribly depressed, both of them. I was a bit dubious about keeping them company on a rough voyage when they were in that mood, but a note arrived asking us to join them in the Verandah restaurant. Rachel had already had a bit to drink and immediately took against a few of the American women there, one of whom was wearing a fur that Rachel, to Rex's embarrassment, called a "terrible piece of old tat" in her high Welsh-y voice. Then she announced she was fed up with the bloody ship's cabaret which, to tell the truth, was none too hot, and up she climbed on to a piano and began singing the dirtiest Welsh rugby songs you could imagine. She really gave a performance! But you should have seen the place empty. I reckon about thirty per cent of the people left, mostly women. The men, I noticed, stayed on and applauded her and even joined in.'

Such excess energies, Rex hoped, would burn themselves out in work and so, as he wrote later, 'be a help to our marriage'. As for Rachel, she could hardly contain her enthusiasm – working again! And working with Rex!!

There was a pre-production lightning trip to Paris in May, 1967, using the private plane of their friends the Guinnesses, to arrange their four-month stay there. Jacques Charon, of the Comédie Française, who had directed the play in London was to do the film version. Rachel was now bubbling with enthusiasm: 'I'm sick of playing the North Country sad sack. This is a turn-of-the-century uncorseted comedy. I play a rather practical girl who falls into impractical situations, and I play one scene with Rex whom I mistake for the porter in a brothel. It should suit us. We once set out to see the Sacre Coeur, lost our way and found ourselves in a nightclub.'

Rex did all in his nature to keep Rachel in this mood. To aid the impression of normality, they even gave a press interview – something he scarcely ever agreed to do.

' "If *My Fair Lady* had never happened," ' he told Clive Hirschhorn, ' "I'd be the same Rex Harrison as I am today, only fewer people in the world would have heard of me. What *does* make a difference is whether one is emotionally happy or not. And I'm an ecstatically happy man. I say this quite unequivocally.

' "I prefer Rachel to work. She *needs* to work. You see, she's got all this Welsh energy. And, of course, I need hardly tell you she's a very fine actress and I love her very much."

' "He says the nicest things," Rachel said, and winked.

'The Harrisons have been made honorary citizens of Portofino. Only three other people have been so honoured, one of them being Marconi.

' "It doesn't give us additional privileges. If anything, it means we have to behave ourselves better than anyone else – and set an example." '

The real disintegration followed. We sailed back in the *Queen Elizabeth* for *Dr Dolittle*. I don't remember how we got to Hollywood, except that when we got there we found that Arthur Jacobs, who was to produce the film, had jazzed up the bungalow in the Beverly Hills Hotel with stuffed animals! I took art lessons. I went house-hunting and found 904 North Bedford Drive. I was determined to try to be like a Hollywood wife. I gave a good party in the garden. Rex said to Pamela Mason 'What a terrible party! Whose is it?'

At Christmas, I fixed up a magnificent white tree. Rex gave me a handful of unwrapped diamond rings procured from a Beverly Hills store by a friend. I didn't want them. I tried taking driving lessons, and couldn't do it. I tried to learn how to ride a horse at Mike Manesco's riding stables. The horse was called Red and was fifteen years old. I couldn't do it. I got a parakeet from Jungleland and tried to teach it to be Polynesia in *Dr Dolittle*. The afternoons in Los Angeles were hot and empty, leaving one feeling like Emil Jannings in *The Blue Angel*. We used to eat with James Hill on Fridays. Rex was no company. No one from the film world came to my Christmas party. We moved from our Jean Negulesco house to another smaller, more dreadful one, taking with us Ruby and the other black maid.

One day I had to be taken home from the Bistro by Mary Scott, drunk. Rex was furious. We left eventually, in the *Queen Elizabeth* – now I complained it was fuddy-duddy. Gavin Lambert, the writer, had sent us a case of tequila. I stayed in the state-room and drank it.

Now Paul Kohner asked to represent me. But all confidence had gone. Standing by the orange tree, I told him I couldn't act. But I got a part in Rex's new picture, the Feydeau farce *A Flea in Her Ear*. We went to Paris, but antagonised Jacques Charon [stage and film director] and André Levasseur [costume designer] instantly. We rented a house at Malmaison and Ruby the maid flew over from Los Angeles with another servant. Rex grew more and more stiff and distant from me: I suppose I drank more and more, though Charon liked me.

---

'A FLEA IN HER EAR' disappointed most of the hopes – marital as well as financial – invested in it. In retrospect, Rex concluded that Feydeau farce was just not filmable. This looked to be the case. Even at its relatively short length of ninety-four minutes, the film dragged: instead of the lightness of clockwork, it moved to the sluggish beat of ship's engines needed to carry the cargo of goings-on in the Paris hotel that specialised in uniting married couples, though never to each other. Excellent as the debonair barrister, Rex floundered as the low-life porter who is his double. (The fact that the 'two' of them never met, even in a trick shot, was an inexplicable disappointment.) Rachel, gowned by Levasseur in marabou, peacock plumes and bird of paradise, looked as if she had allowed an entire exotic aviary to settle on her. But the incidental splendours were nothing if the essentials were missing.

Rex really rated the disintegration of his marriage from this artistic failure. He was not looking forward to the next film in which he and Richard Burton had agreed to appear as a sort of mutual 'dare'. In *Staircase*, both were to play middle-ageing homosexuals: it was extraordinarily ill-chosen for players like this, as well as ill-timed – *La Cage aux Folles* would not open its doors by popular demand for another couple of decades.

Ned Sherrin, who went to Portofino at this time to discuss a new film *for Rachel*, felt Rex would have given a lot to switch movies.

NED SHERRIN: 'I was going to produce a screenplay called *The Vicar's Wife*, by Alan Bennett, who later wrote one of Rachel's greatest comic stage hits, *Habeas Corpus*. She was going to play the local vicar's staid wife who's actually a murderess: we had Cary Grant in mind for the vicar. (Unfortunately, we ran foul of Sam Goldwyn's 1947 film with a similar title, *The Bishop's Wife*, also starring Grant, lost production momentum, and the film never got made.)

'But I went down to Portofino full of high hopes, to find everyone in very low spirits. Rex kept asking, "Why aren't *I* playing the part in your film?" Rachel kept herself busy, keeping Rex and me well fed: she did shepherd's pie to a turn and would start the roast potatoes over again if she missed the exact shade of brown that Rex savoured. He was on edge, I thought. The wig-makers were coming from Rome the next day to fit him with his toupé for *Staircase*. Peter Daubeny, the London impresario, and his wife had asked themselves over, presuming on Rex's casual invitation thrown out when they'd recently met at the Chinese Embassy. Mrs Daubeny said to Rex, "Did you see Paul Scofield in *Staircase* in London?" Rex understandably bridled and snapped back, "No – why should I see Paul? Aren't I doing it myself?" As I recall, Mrs Daubeny either didn't notice the thin ice she was on, or ignored it, and gave us a rather interesting interpretation of the play: "About two men living together, absolutely no servants, so they can't give dinner parties." I enjoyed the week-end. Few others did.'

Rex struggled through *Staircase* in Paris – the making of it he later described as 'ghastly', the end result was 'more so'. But there were welcome respites: he and Rachel, accompanied by her mother and niece Jackie, flew to Portofino, again by private jet, for the merriment of the grape harvest. But in spite of efforts to busy herself in Paris, Rachel returned to her erratic life-style and, perhaps to steady herself as once she had tried to do by marrying Alan Dobie, she grabbed at a film offer – to star opposite Nicol Williamson in *The Reckoning*. Williamson played a ruthless self-made man who returns to his working-class roots in Liverpool and vital contact with physical life – which was incarnated by Rachel's randy housewife with poker-work eyebrows. At first sight, the sort of role that had been her making – but that had been eight years earlier and now it was likely only to revive Rex's distaste for its earthy slovenliness. But now, as she talked to a reporter from the *Evening Standard*, en route via London to Merseyside, Rachel was frank in admitting the error whose magnitude she was just now grasping:

'I tried to give up work completely, to be just a wife to Rex . . . but I came increasingly to miss it. I've been away an awfully long time. It's been largely my own fault. I did really make a superhuman effort to give up the desire to act. To just completely forget about it. But I could not. It's in your blood and that's that.'

By 1969, their marriage was being maintained for appearance' sake only. Rachel was being sustained by drugs – drugs and work. She barely got through a TV film, *The Gaunt Woman*, which she made in London with Lorne Greene in the late spring of 1969. While making it, she took a small apartment in Eaton Square – in her own name. This was enough to ignite the smouldering rumours of a separation. Already the American papers were printing stories about Rex being seen in the company of Richard Harris's wife, Elizabeth. Elizabeth Harris and her three small boys had been the Harrisons' Easter guests at Portofino.

Sheilah Graham, the Hollywood columnist, made a date to see Rachel in London that June. Rachel entered the Connaught – London's most exclusive hotel and one that grew surprisingly tolerant of Rachel's 'behaviour' over the years – wearing 'waist-high chocolate brown suede leg-hugging panty hose', as Mrs Graham reported breathlessly.

JEAN MARSH: 'Rachel never went shopping to buy anything she needed. She looked at the things that caught her eye – daft things, for the most part. You wondered where on earth she could possibly wear this or that. Twin-sets they certainly weren't.'

SYBIL CHRISTOPHER: 'She did tend to overkill, even in her dress sense. I recall that outfit well. It became notorious. She saw it at Yves St Laurent. It was sueded boots and trousers all in one piece. She didn't buy just one set, but *four*! All different colours. When she'd on the green set, she'd draw calls of "There goes Robin Hood!" from people she passed on the street, she looked as if she'd just come out of the Christmas pantomime. Dear Rachel!'

When Mrs Graham had recovered from the shock of St Laurent, she obliquely quizzed Rachel about the upcoming ninth anniversary of her marriage – 'What do you give your husband when he has everything?' she asked. But Rachel had an answer ready. She had written out in longhand and on expensive parchment paper – twenty pages and then eight more of illustrations – a story-essay called *An Odyssey to Homer*, about Rex's beloved basset hound. She had then had it bound in elegant high-grade calf at a cost of $350, with six slightly cheaper copies run off for friends. This would be Rex's present from her for their 1971 wedding anniversary.

'To get back to these rumours,' Mrs Graham ended her column. 'A woman who has left, or been left by her husband, would hardly go to all this trouble, now would she?'

It was a pay-off paragraph that did not fool her readers one bit.

For someone 'under suspicion' by the celebrity watchers of the international press, Rachel did a surprising thing that late summer of 1969: she passed some of it with her first husband, Alan Dobie. They acted together, in a play in whose domestic turmoil one could easily catch the self-destructive reverberations of her own shaky present marriage. *Who's Afraid of Virginia Woolf?* was staged at the Theatre Royal, Bath. Rachel held open day for the press, who dutifully noted the silver-framed photo of

Rex inscribed 'To my own dearest Rachel' and the two-dozen long-stemmed red roses next to it.

'I'm not such a bitch as Martha in *Virginia Woolf*' Rachel said, though she owned up to being a 'gregarious Celt'. Alan Dobie's 'marvellous qualities of strength and kindness' had matured since their marriage was dissolved, she said. 'The first thing I did when I got to England . . . was grab the Rolls-Royce that Rex keeps in London and go down to have lunch with Alan and Maureen [Scott, an actress whom Dobie married in 1963] in Kent. They've got three beautiful children who all call me Aunty Rachel . . . I think that being able to work with my ex-husband like this is a sign that our marriages are as steady as a rock.'

One wonders if the play she was about to do re-activated one of Rachel's abiding fantasies. *Virginia Woolf*'s depth of pathos is measured – if at all – by the revelation of a child in the past history of the perpetually obstreperous couple, a child which may have indeed died, or else has been 'born' only in Martha's wishful thinking. The high spot of Rachel's play-acting in the West Country was a visit, accompanied by Alan Dobie, to a Church of England children's home. 'Even the tiniest ones were clustering around her,' said the matron. 'She has a wonderful way with children.' Rachel did not leave before she had obtained the office address of the religious adoption society. She later said, '[Rex and I] may decide on [adopting] an Italian child, because our home is in Portofino. One thing is certain: it will be a girl. One man is enough for any woman to handle.'

Now Rachel's mention of adopting a child was a recurring concern: not entirely self-indulgent whimsy, either. She reverted to it whenever she reached a crisis-point in life: she had already passed one such point, when the Easter cruise with their friends had reconciled Rex and herself. But she was well aware he was seeing Elizabeth Harris. So the gesture she made towards the act of adoption was akin to a not-too-distant early warning signal of a disintegrating life, rather than any realistic prospect of a more fortified future that might be implied by bringing a child into the home. Her preference for an *Italian* child is worth noting, too. Though not impossible, such a child would be an unlikely find in a Church of England adoption home. But the insistence on a Latin infant, as well as a girl, suggests the strength of Rachel's need to preserve the Portofino dream-world in all its exotic local colour, and at the same time temper the male chauvinist character of the San Genesio household with an ally, albeit an immature one, of her own gender.

From the end of autumn, 1969, this second crisis fairly rushed towards her. Rex returned to England from the *Staircase* film and made a singularly unlucky choice among the plays on offer to him to mark his return to the West End stage after seven years. Feeling, as he said (in advance of the reviews), 'a little philanthropic', he went into *The Lionel Touch*, a lightweight piece by an untested author about a rebellious artist battling the bureaucracy. The generally dismissive reviews, though not as derisive as those greeting Rex and Richard Burton playing homosexuals in their film *Staircase* a few weeks earlier, created a mood of edginess at the party after the first night – which exploded publicly into hot-tempered words. There was no use pretending any longer, for Rex anyhow. An indisposition took him temporarily out of the play in mid-December: at the same time he withdrew from a commitment to make a musical version of *A Christmas Carol*; he was replaced by Albert Finney.

Rachel went into rehearsals for a light-hearted Christmas entertainment based on *The Three Musketeers* which Eleanor Fazan had earlier directed with a comedy-juggling act as its pantomime centre-piece.

ELEANOR FAZAN: 'The show had gone down well when I'd first done it. Then Lindsay Anderson rang me up at the end of 1969. "You should re-stage it at the Royal Court for their Christmas show," he said, "and use Rachel." – "Would *she* want to be in this kind of show?" – "Go and talk to her and ask her: I think she needs to be kept busy." We met at the Connaught: she was wearing her usual exotic get-up of tiger-skin coat and thigh-length boots: Rex had provided her with an opportunity to be a rebel and also lead a languorous life. Then just as we started rehearsals, her marriage fell down round her.'

On 19 December, 1969, Rex's London lawyer issued a statement: 'In view of certain rumours that have begun to circulate about his marriage to Rachel Roberts, Rex Harrison has authorised me to announce that he and his wife are living separately and apart.'

The delayed shock that Rachel suffered transmitted a pain that did not cripple her for some years yet: but her response indicated how stunned she was by the bluntness of the judgment that had been read out publicly. She was unwilling to accept it, emotionally unable even to take it in. 'I am sure we are going to be reconciled,' she claimed the next day. 'I spoke to Rex on the telephone . . . he told me the whole thing had been blown up out of all proportion. There is no question of a divorce or legal separation, or anything like that.' Her protests then became nearly incoherent: 'We are adult people . . . what is happening now is only a little thing really. The Sixties are over and the Seventies are here – let's all be friends. That's what Rex would want. I will see him soon – Ask me what I want for 1970, and I will say Rex. I love him with all my heart, but I have known the end was near for two months.

'Rex is upset because the announcement had to be made in legalistic terms.' And with a wink and a grin, she added to a reporter, 'We are just taking a breather, love.'

Rex, advised by lawyers, said only: 'I issued a statement . . . and I stand by this statement.'

ELEANOR FAZAN: 'Our rehearsals for *The Three Musketeers Ride Again* were going on all through this terrible turmoil, in a cold, depressing church hall in King's Cross, with us literally barricaded inside by the press. Rachel was in a great and continuous state of anger, which occasionally erupted, and then she would begin to throw things about. She simply couldn't accept what was happening to her.

'Part of the time when we were rehearsing the rest of the cast she had nothing to do, so I told Valentine Dyall, who was in the cast, to smuggle her out and give her a drink in a pub. No sooner was she in the bar than she lined up one glass of port after another, then suddenly chucked them into the pub's open fireplace where they made a great splutter and belched clouds of green smoke into the room – it didn't say much for the quality of the port!'

But when the show opened just before Christmas, she looked as if she was thoroughly enjoying herself as wicked Milady de Winter. She played her straight – which shows Rachel had learned a lot about comedy. But it was clear she was tensing herself for some kind of explosion; congenial company was the only thing holding her back.

ELEANOR FAZAN: 'She was so good in the opening performances that I took her out to dinner – let her choose the restaurant. Of course, she chose the "in" place of the moment. As we entered with Nicol Williamson, a waiter whispered, "Mr Harrison is here tonight." I asked Rachel if she wanted to leave, but she said No – the rebel in her again. Rex left shortly afterwards without meeting her: then Rachel excused herself, to go to the loo. I thought she'd been gone a suspicious length of time. So I went downstairs. In the basement cloakroom stood a line of pay phones, and there Rachel was – hurling the receivers, one by one, against the wall with all her force.'

Anthony Page had been artistic director at the Royal Court Theatre where he had won acclaim for his productions of *Inadmissible Evidence*, *A Patriot for Me* and other plays. It was there, in 1958, that he had first met Rachel.

ANTHONY PAGE: 'The play was John Arden's *Live Like Pigs*, about culture-clash on a housing estate. Rachel didn't get the part – a mistake, in retrospect. She was a most variable person: one day she would give a reading that was just genius: the next, she could be absolutely awful. The trouble this time was she seemed urbane and glamorous on that particular day, and we were looking for someone with gypsy-like attributes.

'But I didn't really get to know her till things were going badly wrong between her and Rex. She was staying at the Connaught, and most unhappy. She needed to act, she kept saying. I got the impression that she felt cut off from something that would have been fruitful to her. But Rex hated what were called "political plays". She kept bringing up one thing after another about a marriage that had obviously gone very wrong: she looked disturbed. Just listening to her made one feel a "shrink". Then I met her in the foyer of the Royal Court Hotel that Christmas in 1969, when she and Rex had formally separated. She looked simply terrible. "Are you all right?" I said to her, anxiously. "Yes, I've just swallowed fifty aspirin," she said gaily, and she went up to the desk to check in. "Do you want a doctor, Rachel?" I asked. "No, no, I'm all right." Later on that night, I got an urgent telephone call. It was Lindsay Anderson. "Get over to St George's Hospital quickly," he said, "Rachel's there, with a stomach pump down her!"'

SYBIL CHRISTOPHER: 'She told me she'd simply swallowed all the pills she had, went to sleep, and woke up at St George's to find her stomach being pumped out and "Jingle Bells" and other carols ringing in her ears. For a minute, she thought she'd died and gone to heaven. She survived. Rachel had the constitution of an ox. She was capable of inflicting great punishment on herself, then pulling herself together again in half the time it would have taken most people to recuperate. I never remember her missing a performance through illness.'

Rachel took her massive overdose on Christmas Eve – and was back in *The Three Musketeers Ride Again* the day after Boxing Day. By some miracle, or maybe because few newspaper staff are at their desks over these three days, news of the second suicide attempt she had made in her lifetime was only vaguely reported in the press: she insisted she had spent the time at her rented apartment in nearby Lowndes Square. The hospital maintained she had been in their care, but refused to say why.

After this, there was no way for Rex and Rachel to get together again. When the short Christmas season ended at the Royal Court, Rachel went to America: Rex stayed on in London to finish the disappointing run of *The Lionel Touch* and was now seen openly enjoying the company of Elizabeth Harris. They left by private jet on the play's closing night for a 'suprise destination', arranged by Rex. It turned out to be Tangier, where a yacht was waiting to take them both cruising along the Moroccan coast. Rex confessed to being sublimely happy. Once more, he said, it had been proved to him that there was a tomorrow.

In the following years, Rachel never seems to have resented Elizabeth Harrison – as she became – because she was the one Rex now turned to. Perhaps, given the man that Rex was, she sensed the inevitability of it. In Elizabeth's autobiography, *Love, Honour and Dismay*, published in 1976, soon after her own marriage to Rex was dissolved, she recalls Rachel, then officially separated from her husband, putting it to her point blank in a telephone call whether she and Rex were lovers. When Rachel got the answer she anticipated, there was a long silence: then Rachel said simply, 'It happens.' A tenser encounter occurred, according to Elizabeth Harrison, when Rachel suddenly appeared at her home, when Rex happened to be there, and demanded he chose between them – 'Now'. Which of the women would he take? Rex extricated himself by falling back on very much the sort of matinée-comedy line which accounted for the success of one or two of his own favourite playwrights. He pointed to Elizabeth's pet dog, which had fortuitously made an entrance at this dramatic point, and said he would take *it* – then made his own exit.

On a later occasion, after her marriage to Rex, Elizabeth says she locked him and Rachel in the library of her country home, where Rachel had unexpectedly dropped in to see them and reminisce over old times. It was soon apparent to her, as Rachel's invective reached a crescendo, that 'the recalled pleasures of yesteryear already had palled'.

But, generally, no recrimination was harboured by Rachel; and her journals, as well as their friends' recollections, testify to occasions when Rachel (sometimes with Darren) got on well over dinner with Rex and Elizabeth, or, later, with Elizabeth and her next husband, financier Peter Aitken. Perhaps Rachel detected early warning signs of the cooling relations between Rex and Elizabeth Harrison – as the latter put it, 'I fell in love with the man only to see him disappear into the actor' – and believed, whether on good grounds or not, that a free Rex would gravitate back to a woman like herself for the kick she could put into life.

The sadness of disenchantment with her marriage, which Elizabeth Harrison describes so acutely in her book (written with the assistance of Peter Evans), was matched by the misfortunes that befell the lovely Villa San Genesio, which Rex had come to see as the only true home he had ever known and Rachel as a bit of paradise she would ever after hanker for. The local *mafiosi* appear to have staged a graduated *coup* on the privileged estates in the neighbourhood whose owners were unaccommodating to their demands; and as servants left and the villas became vulnerable to burglary or worse eventuality, retaining them became an unacceptable risk rather than a prized asset. Rex Harrison, never a man to negotiate under duress, decided to sell up and get out. Rachel's reveries for the life she led at Portofino make those days seem irrecoverable: but there was also a good sound reason why this was actually so.

Then came the real end – the film *Staircase*, which Rex made in Paris with Richard Burton. I was locked into the Plaza-Athenée hotel watching Richard and his wife Elizabeth 'living'. My spirit was really dying now. Half-heartedly, I went to a Berlitz school to learn to speak Italian properly, then to a Cordon-Bleu cooking class. Tears in the morning – and Oh! the change of life was coming on, the physical aspect of it anyway. My 'Anna Petrovna' had long ago gone down the drain.

Nevertheless, I did a film with Nicol Williamson – *The Reckoning*. I used to walk around the Plaza-Athenée suite with Rex, asking him to hear my 'Plain Duff' lines. He hated the part I was to play. I went to London, stayed at the Connaught, saw Elizabeth Taylor and did a drunken one-night stand with a film actor – 'without passion', as he said. I told Rex, in desperation. His comment was that he couldn't imagine two uglier people together. I went out of control – gave a Champagne party in the Connaught for all my friends. Lindsay Anderson came, was affronted more than shocked by what met his eyes. I fell into the plane back to Paris and went to Fouquet's with Rex, still sobbing.

We went to New York via Milan in a snow-storm. We stayed at the Carlyle. When I woke up in the morning, I found Rex turned in on himself, reading the *New York Times*. I wept. I went to have my hair done downstairs. The hairdresser talked of Kay Kendall.

There was a party for Alan Jay Lerner that night. Rex functioned. Lindsay came to have a drink with Aaron Frosch and asked me to have breakfast with him the next day at Hampshire House. He advised me to seek professional help. I rejected the idea. I still didn't think I needed it.

Finally the evening of Maggie Smith's film *The Prime of Miss Jean Brodie* in London. I went. I didn't think I'd be able to walk down the ramp at the Leicester Square Theatre to the tune of 'Maggie May'. But I did.

Dr Glyn Davies gave me Seconal (two) and told me that I was in such a state of tension that it would be the only thing to bring me down. I sat next to Rex after my successful negotiation of the steps. He was silent. So I left and went to the bar and drank gin with Michael Redgrave all evening. Then I went into the clinic for a 'sleep' treatment. For the last eight years, it had been drink and pills in order to sleep. I was given the 'truth drug' and the first thing I said was, 'I want to fucking kill him.' So started the end of my marriage. Then came the separation from Rex.

I took an apartment in Eaton Square, was on twelve–fourteen tablets a day, and started to 'function' again. I did a lousy TV film – but *did* it – with Lorne Greene.

They were shapeless, those years with Rex. At 6.00 in the evening, having slept off lunch, I used to ask myself (to turn a cliché), 'Is this all it's ever going to be?' I'd walk up from the Port past the Splendido hotel with the trees dripping wet, up the mule track to the house that was now so dead and the 'husband' who gave me no nourishment at all. My simple and ordinary needs were never bothered about. No pats on the back at all. I tried to play chess, fixed up the games room with a dart-board, intervened if Rex was tempted to snap at anyone, encouraged him in his work, neglected my own, got seriously ill. I kept on trying; I didn't make a life of my own; I lived entirely through him. I flung myself at him when he made his decision to go to Elizabeth Harris. Reading the book that Elizabeth eventually wrote, *Love, Honour and Dismay*, I can well understand Rex going to see her. He was lonely. As for Portofino, Elizabeth put it well when she wrote about its selfishness and its ominous quality of self-containment – they got to me in the end, too.

This morning I thought of what O'Toole and Burton and I had in common. We've all come croppers in the eyes of the 'world' we three wanted not only to impress, but to dominate. They, why? Possibly because, rumour hath it, they are insecure men cursed with feelings of inadequacy. I, too, am riddled with feelings of utter inadequacy – no matter whether inherited, or learned, or because of early conditioning, or just because I'm me – or (more likely) all of it. So I, too, went into acting to take it all on at once with one fell blow to assert my tremendous adequacy, my great gifts, my uniqueness – underneath, the uncertainties and the instabilities bubbled away.

---

BACK IN CALIFORNIA at the start of 1970, Rachel sought distraction in work. It is pathetically ironic that someone in her still emotionally stunned and confused condition should have opted for a film like *Doctors' Wives*. This Columbia Pictures melodrama resembled a series of overlapping traumas. It was as if a dozen *Ben Casey* segments had been cannibalised into one monster number involving drink, drugs, sterility and female homosexuality among a high-living group of medicos, their wives and mistresses. For Rachel, it was to be a case of the sick playing the sick. She took the part of a wife who confesses a lesbian relationship to her husband and is nobly forgiven. In the pre-Women's Lib era, this passed for an enlightened ending.

Rachel threw herself into the thick of things with an energy which did not suggest a healthy balance, but only a neurotic lack of direction. She dyed her hair blonde and took up the social life of Beverly Hills like a refugee anxious to assume a foreign identity. She was sometimes heavily tranquillised and in the company of a nurse.

Occasionally, an old friend passing through Hollywood took the pressure off her, let her relax back into the congenial companionship of people who summoned up a happier past. One such was Felix Barker, film and theatre critic of the London *Evening News*, in Hollywood in 1970 to report on the film industry crisis which then loomed so huge that the movie capital's very survival looked in doubt.

FELIX BARKER: 'One of the first people I looked up was Rachel. I'd previously met her when she was happily married to Rex and we had a comic, Molnar-type lunch in the Grill Room of the Café Royal with Rachel and her friend Brenda Houston at one table and Rex (who wanted to discuss what he should do if he came back to the theatre) and me at another. Over coffee and brandy, we ogled the women and discussed whether we fancied them and should ask them over to join us!

'I think Rachel was doing her best in Hollywood to get over an upset . . . We went dancing in nightclubs and spent one wild evening at Disneyland. She found the one place there where drink is served to VIPs and, after a great deal of whisky, I remember we went on a scenic railway very late, shouting to a few remaining and astonished visitors, "Kill Nixon! Shoot the man." Somehow we got back to Beverly Hills and bathed in her pool as the sun came up. All very Fitzgerald!

'She said she didn't think she would ever accept the kind of blind offer sometimes made by a director however much she admired him. She'd want to see a finished script. "Not even for Antonioni?" I asked. "No, I couldn't. I'd want to read the part. There's just one person for whom I might, because I so admire his integrity and self-discipline, and that's Lindsay Anderson."

'Lindsay's influence and her reliance on him were repeated over and over again . . . She had a telephone by the pool, and in the middle of the night, once, she suddenly, without any warning, got out of the water while we were swimming and rang through to Lindsay in London. They just talked friendly nothings and she sent him my regards. It was something she needed to do every few days.'

But life in this community had some compensations. One occurred when she met the young man who, off and on (but mostly 'on'), was to be her closest companion, confidant and lover over the rest of the decade: Darren Ramirez.

DARREN RAMIREZ: 'I was about twenty-three then, and living in Los Angeles after my divorce from a New York model, a girl who'd occasionally appeared on *Vogue* covers. I was feeling very lonely. I'd been upset by the way my marriage had ended. I had few friends, though a lot of acquaintance. I was working at the Beverly Wilshire Hotel, and it was there I first saw Rachel, with her nurse. Helen Chaplin, the hotel's public relations lady, told me who she was. I'd been fascinated by her five or six years earlier when I saw *This Sporting Life* at the Lido, a fine-art theatre in Los Angeles – I prefer to go to foreign films. I thought her so wonderful, I returned to see the movie several times. Now here she was.

'She was behaving very oddly, doing anything and everything to attract attention, especially from men. She was very slim then, wearing semi-transparent tops, the shortest in miniskirts, often with sandals, wigs that came down to her waist, and boots that came up to her thighs – she imagined this enhanced her legs. She was very, very blonde. I didn't know she was attracted to me till our second or third meeting. That was at Pamela Mason's – she was throwing a party for her daughter, Portland. Elizabeth Taylor was there, too, and Rachel, wearing a high-waisted chamois dress – she always liked outfits that flattered her waist. I thought she was like the heroine of Muriel Spark's novel *The Driver's Seat* that had just been published – about the woman who just ups and leaves her job and

86

flies off in search of some obsessional experience and ends up dead with stab wounds in a park somewhere abroad. Elizabeth Taylor later played the part in a movie. Like the girl in the book, Rachel had got herself up in the most outrageous outfit so as to attract the men. But this day, she looked in a daze: she wasn't even aware of what people around were saying about her. She was just out to get the "Hellos". Then she said to me, "Come along for a drink." She was living in 904 North Bedford, which she and Rex had when he was making *Dr Dolittle*. It was costing $4,000 a month to rent, but I gathered Rex was paying. Ruby, their black maid, was working for her. Rachel had no idea how to do things about the house, or even, in the state she was in, how to look after herself properly. One minute she'd be noisy and animated, the next as dead-faced as a walking zombie.'

PAMELA MASON: 'That piano down there [pointing to a grand piano in the huge pillared split-level living-area of her Beverly Hills home where cats pace silently and interminably about, maybe looking with surprise at themselves pictured in a dozen different media in the pictures on the walls], we had to move it way down the room, for every time Rachel came to a party here, or when there were guests present, she'd sit down and play with the loud pedal on and bellow away at some song – people couldn't hear themselves speak.'

DARREN RAMIREZ: 'At this time she was having an affair with one of the co-stars of her film: but she'd also fallen for a character who worried me, for *this* liaison wasn't your conventional Beverly Hills affair. He was a professional black hustler, in it for the money. Dangerous too, I thought, though Rachel didn't see it that way: he simply amused her. He encouraged her to gamble – she had the money, which he used – and took her to the Santa Anita racetrack: she was there the day I called round, she'd completely forgotten me.

'At this time I was young, a bit inexperienced, but even I was surprised when I asked her out to dinner and she said, "Can Ruby come, too?" Ruby – the maid! She liked Ruby, though, and seemed genuinely amused by the black friends Ruby introduced to her, forgave her when she didn't show for work, spent money on buying Ruby's husband bottles of Scotch, clothes for their kids, and so on.

'One of my friends is Verita Thompson. She'd been Humphrey Bogart's lover, was now married to a well-known film editor, and had opened a Mexican restaurant, Verita's Sa Cantina. Rachel had actually taken her hustler friend there, the two of them eating upstairs where you're not so visible – just as well, since Rachel stripped off to the buff for a dare, the Mexican boys were shocked, and Verita had to come running upstairs to sort things out. So before I met Rachel, I knew how perverse she could be – I'd no illusions. But when her spirits were high, she was great fun to be with and she and Ruby and I enjoyed dinner at Sa Cantina. All the same, I was getting more and more worried. She was sleepwalking much of the time, couldn't drive a car (a blessing, probably, for other motorists), depended on a rented limousine to take her everywhere, had no notion of housekeeping budgets and couldn't keep track where the money was going to. I believed Ruby kept in touch with Aaron Frosch, Rex's lawyer who was working out their divorce, and he told Rex what was going on – and I couldn't believe Rex was happy about the odd crowd of underworld hangers-on Rachel was entertaining. They were trying to get her into hard drugs. Luckily, she had no stomach for these. But when I saw her hustler cutting cocaine in the living room one night, I said to Rachel, "This guy is dangerous." He was cunning as well. I believe he faked an attempt on his life, then tried to make out that Rex had taken a contract out on him!'

PAMELA MASON: 'Rachel had this absurd notion that Rex was going to kill her black lover. "Nonsense," I told her cynically, "if anyone's in Rex's bad books, it's you – you're going to cost him alimony!"'

DARREN RAMIREZ: 'At this time, Rachel was in such a state of subdued shock that you couldn't talk sense to her. She was acting more and more irresponsibly. She bought a Cadillac for her hustler, another car for Ruby. I could see, though, that the strain was starting to tell on Ruby, what with Rachel inviting fourteen people on impulse to come to dinner, or locking herself up in her room for days on end. Throughout these months she was so high on a variety of things that she simply couldn't go to sleep till she passed out on her feet. Eventually, she passed into a state resembling comatosis and I took the initiative and called up Rex Kennamer, the one they call "the doctor to the stars", and he sent over an assistant to examine Rachel. He found her undernourished and gave her a vitamin shot to pep her up. But no sooner did she improve than the cycle recommenced. Eventually, there was only one thing for it, and she was admitted for rest and observation to the Cedars of Lebanon Hospital in Beverly Hills. She was in the clinic for a week, drying out and taking the sleep cure.'

Some of the best performances that Rachel gave during this chaotic time were for the benefit of the media. For someone so flamboyant, it is odd to find her so anxious about the rectitude of her image in the media: but she was . . .

Friends attributed it to 'the Welsh' in her, that small-town, closed-community feeling that 'people will talk . . .' if you don't behave yourself. She did all in her still considerable power to play this scene by conventional rules, fostering the impression that where her marriage was concerned all was not lost and, indeed, if it were, it might have been all for the best.

'Rex and I just took a little domestic breather,' she told Earl Wilson, when he interviewed her in April, 1970, in the Negulesco house. 'You have to recognise that this is the time to rest and recharge your batteries, hoping that it will all start over again, and, if it doesn't, it is ended.'

To an English newspaperman, William Hall of London's *Evening News*, she sounded even more fatalistic: 'I believe in life taking its course. This kind of thing happens to most human beings, especially if you've lived close together for a long time and if you're passionate and warm-hearted rather than clear-sighted and cold.' Hollywood, she added, was 'less frightening' than she had imagined. 'It's wiser to go on living life normally. And it's been much easier for me to remain calm.'

It is doubtful if many of the seasoned show-business reporters in whom she confided were deceived. But it is one of the peculiar conventions of Hollywood life that those who are granted 'access' to celebrities rarely question their veracity. The 'privilege' of conferring with the famous, giving an impression of intimacy with them and conveying what they say to readers, implies a collusion that both parties connive at – till it is in neither party's interest to conceal the truth, whereupon a similarly un-embarrassed *volte face* takes place.

If Rachel manipulated the media, it was simply what the media expected her to do: they played along, for the moment.

By this time, she and Darren were keeping constant company.

DARREN RAMIREZ: 'I was mesmerised by Rachel, though at first a lot of it was concern for her . . . the thought that I couldn't let this talented woman destroy herself. In time, of course, I began seeing aspects of Rachel that I hadn't suspected. She had a mean side to her, and a vindictive streak when she was out of control. I remember Pamela Mason and her discussing the upcoming divorce and Rachel being advised to hold out for more money. She was in two minds about this: if she gave in peaceably and didn't demand too much, Rex might not think so badly of her. Rachel always valued people's good opinion of her, even that of ex-husbands! On the other hand, there was the money to be considered . . . She saw a series of lawyers about this time: one man in New York advised her to break off her friendship with me. She heeded him and for a time we had quarrels. She could become quite vicious: it was like a walk-out on me. I realised later that this was to be the pattern of our relationship. Rachel would fly into a rage, which could be very upsetting, then an hour later apologise for it and we'd make up.'

PAMELA MASON: 'Rex and Rachel, you see, were both very combative personalities: when they fought, they went at each other like champions. Darren wasn't that way at all: we used to call him "Fluffy", because you could thump him and you wouldn't hit anything hard. Rachel, I'm sure, often wanted to drag him into a good row in order to relieve herself, but "Fluffy" wouldn't respond – and that just enraged her more.'

When Diane Negulesco returned to Beverly Hills to reclaim her North Bedford house, Rachel had to move elsewhere and at first rented a place on Rodeo Drive. Everyone found it very depressing.

RONNIE CASS: 'I went to see her at this time, when I was in Hollywood working with the singer Tom Jones. I went to dinner with her. It was a bad experience: like being in a mausoleum, everything atrophied. I remember, appropriately enough, the cold mashed potatoes.'

Evie Bricusse, the wife of composer Leslie Bricusse, advised her to move: so did another of her closest friends, actress and singer Marti Stevens, the daughter of one of Hollywood's founder moguls, Nicholas Schenck.

DARREN RAMIREZ: 'I added my voice to Marti's and at last we got Rachel out of the place and into the guest house owned by a doctor on North Kanter Drive – Leslie Caron had been living there. Which is odd, in retrospect, since Rachel would later buy Leslie Caron's London house from her. I moved in with Rachel, and did my best to look after her. By this time, she'd got rid of the rented limousine: now she gave me the down payment on a Mercedes. She certainly didn't *buy* me the car, as she sometimes claimed. I sold my Jag to Portland Mason. At Kanter, life started to function a little more calmly and independently. We'd plan week-end country drives, up to Carmel and other places on the coast, often staying overnight. When I was seeing Rachel, I felt like a nurse – I often felt something disastrous would happen, if I weren't there to prevent it. I had a home of my own on Mulholland Drive, which I'd enjoyed furnishing: but all this time I saw very little of it.

'Rachel received two special presents that Christmas – 1970. One was the biggest poinsettia I'd ever seen, with Rex's name on the label. The other was a basket of American cheeses from Aaron Frosch. Rachel threw the poinsettia bodily out of the back door and followed it with the cheeses. The plant made her suspect that Rex's secretary had simply ordered it from the florist's and there was nothing personal in it – no loving thought at all behind such a gift. Whether that was true or not, I don't know. The cheeses she thought vulgar and pretentious. She then threw a hysterical fit and locked herself up in the bedroom. It really was a case of *any* excuse to assert herself violently.

'But other times were good times. Rachel recovered some of her good spirits. We'd cook and read or go over to Marti Stevens' at the Palisades. Marti always called Rachel her "Pied Piper", since some days Rachel would explore downtown areas of Los Angeles – she was absolutely fearless where she went – and discover out-of-the-way restaurants, then rush over to Marti's with the news, lead her to the place and the two of them would be like schoolkids, Rachel leading Marti on "a treat" the way the Pied Piper used to lead the children of Hamelin!

'One night Rachel and I went over to Westwood for a special screening of Carl Reiner's black comedy with George Segal, *Where's Poppa?* A lurking newsman snapped a photo of Rachel and me and it found its way into the papers in England. Rachel received a clipping of herself saying: "Rachel Roberts steps out with a young man of twenty-three." It upset Rachel terribly. She believed that calling attention to the difference in our ages – there was twenty years between us – would start people talking. She was strange that way! So she sat down right away and wrote a sarcastic letter to the *Daily Express* . . .'

The *Express* files still hold Rachel's original letter which was taken seriously enough to be marked with a 'Caveat', warning anyone making future references to the parties named in it not to trust the self-perpetuating 'facts' of this particular report. The letter, dated December 29, 1970, reads:

'Dear Sir – I read with interest on Page 9 of the *Daily Express* of Saturday, December 12, that my "constant escort" in Hollywood was Darren Ramirez, aged 23. Darren is actually 18. His brother Martin is 28 and I have indeed been to the cinema with Martin on several occasions. I am of course very old. I am 43, but don't feel it. My husband, Rex, I keep reading, is 62, but doesn't look it. Elizabeth, whom he is going to marry next, is in her thirties. My mother is 76, but neither feels it, looks it or will admit to it. If there is anyone else remotely concerned with me whose chronological ages you think might be of interest to your readers, I will gladly forward the information. Meanwhile, a Happy New Year to all – Rachel Roberts.'

In thus adjusting the ages, and switching escorts from Darren to Martin, Rachel was manifesting her anxiety about being seen publicly in the company of men who were visibly much younger-looking than she was. It is odd to reflect on this now, when the 'Toy Boy', as such a youthful escort came to be called, is much in fashion – and demand. But in sickness and in health – increasingly in sickness – Rachel remained highly conscious of her image: good publicity was an essential part of it.

At this time, early 1971, she made the professional acquaintance of Jeffrey Lane, then a publicist in Columbia Pictures' London office which was handling Rachel's film *Doctors' Wives*. Lane, nicknamed 'The Egg', was a bald, pocket-sized cone of energy – he threw off energy even more tirelessly when he joined Rogers and Cowan, a leading Anglo-American PR agency, and began handling the 'A'-List accounts of show-business. He became one of Rachel's intimate friends, valued for his talent at 'placing' stories and pictures, but also for the total coloration he had absorbed from his job and the way he set his mind on some far-from-obscure object of desire and went out to get it. Rachel admired this resolution and let it influence her decisively at at least one crucial stage of her life.

JEFFREY LANE: 'I met her when she was starting her romance with Darren Ramirez and trying to keep it quiet. Publicity about having a "young lover" would hurt her, she thought: it might also remind people of her own "unsatisfactory" relationship with Rex. I tried telling her that having a younger lover was chic, and advised her to make no secret of it. But she went to extraordinary lengths to deflect attention from Darren, even when she'd been after me to arrange publicity for her in situations where he certainly couldn't be ignored. Partly, too, I suspect, she was conscious of her physical looks and didn't want comparisons made with the younger features beside her. When they returned to New York, on the *Queen Elizabeth*, in 1971, I laid on a shipboard photo-session and Rachel wore a maxicoat which she let swing open to expose glittering black hot-pants which she believed would draw attention to her legs and divert it from Darren.'

Letter from Rachel to Jeffrey Lane, written from the *Queen Elizabeth*:

'My Dear Jeffrey – I don't quite know what to make of the QE2. It is a beautiful ship, and that nice young man, Garry, took us all over it (let's face it, the first class is more luxurious!) – the cabins are very comfortable, beds very sleepable in. The food is good despite the canteen atmosphere. There's a delicious sauna-room and a sea-water pool. The cinema is *very* comfortable (I *adored Waterloo*). I really think it's the slightly and vaguely army-trained attitude of the staff that gives me the impression that one is mentally retarded and living in a floating nursing home.

'All the staff from the old *Queens* are all here. A typical example is when you go down to have a massage and a *huge* lady, in charge, says, "No, dear, I don't think it's a good idea today. You look a bit green." Pleasantly said, of course, but one gets the impression that she'd rather die than work! However, we're enjoying it and it is a *marvellous* place to work.

'I can't thank you enough for seeing us off so splendidly with that delicious cat, and all those photographers. Thank you, and Columbia, for all the beautiful flowers I found in my cabin.

'I thoroughly enjoyed all the interviews. I could hope that they will edit the last TV one where I said "Do you understand?" to the interviewer forty-four times. Do you suppose you could ask them to delete a bit of that? Perhaps they intend to, anyway.

'I hear the hot-pants made the *Evening Standard* and the *News of the World*. I hope *Doctors' Wives* was mentioned somewhere along the line. If there were any more pictures in the other papers, do you think I could see them? While I belong to Durrant's I will automatically get the press clippings the agency provides – but *if* it's not too much trouble. When I have an address where you could send them, do you think I could have the *News of the World* and the *Evening Standard* whole, so to speak? By that I mean a copy of each.

'I thoroughly enjoyed meeting you, and have every intention of looking you up, if I may, on my return to London. Meanwhile, thank you very much again. L. – Rachel.'

The American actors' union, Equity, had put a stop to Rachel's hope of appearing in a new play, *Rosebloom*, by Harvey Perr, which was set to open in mid-1970.

She had already applied for 'resident alien' status. But the quota was full. This meant that the obligatory 'green card', allowing aliens to qualify for work under Equity rules, could not be issued. This temporarily blocked one way she could have used up her dangerously surplus energy.

Instead, she went straight into another film, *The Wild Rovers*, with Ryan O'Neal.

Now movies, and the whole promotional set-up surrounding them during and after shooting, give stars insidious opportunities for displaying their ego that stage plays do not usually serve so well. Exposure only increased Rachel's fever. She appeared on David Frost's Show in New York, babbling almost incoherently about herself, and was scarcely more coherent about the movie. She was on a heady ego trip. Though separated from Rex, she had caught the infection of his stardom and now wanted some of the glory for herself. The symptoms are already present in the letter, and others, which she wrote to Jeffrey Lane.

PAMELA MASON: 'Circumstances now made Rachel star-conscious: she wasn't naturally so – not at first, anyhow. She didn't really want the trappings of stardom. Stars thrive on the audience gratification they give, actresses depend upon the natural rewards of self-achievement. From now on, the one fatally got mixed up with the other, as far as Rachel was concerned.'

DARREN RAMIREZ: 'She broke with her agent Paul Kohner around this time. She was offered a part in a segment in a TV series. "It's not prestigious enough," she was told. "Send the script over," she ordered, and she did it, and, of course, suffered for it. But she was paid $75,000 for it. One of her reasons for doing *The Wild Rovers* was the ambition she said she'd always had to play a saloon-bar madam! She moved over to International Creative Management: its London head, Laurie Evans, handled Rex. It was odd, going to this of all agencies, just as her divorce from Rex was coming through. It was as if she was entering into competition with him.'

Rachel filed for divorce in the Santa Monica courts in February, 1971.

She claimed 'irreconcilable differences'. The action, unsurprisingly, was not contested and simply amounted to the lawyers for both parties announcing an agreed settlement. Under this, Rachel got a farewell sum of $35,000 (about £15,000 at that time), plus $10,000 (£4,200) annually while she lived – though this was to be halved if she should remarry. Rex was further ordered to pay for the purchase of a home costing up to $100,000 (£42,000) for his ex-wife: the choice of where it was to be was left to Rachel. By some, this was considered an expensive way of buying freedom. Wilfrid Hyde-White, who had played Col Pickering in *My Fair Lady*, said, 'Frankly, I am absolutely amazed at the amount Rex is going to pay Rachel . . . I don't see how any man can be as generous as this.' But Hollywood lawyers thought it lenient and Rex 'very lucky' to have got away with 'so little in the land of the million-dollar settlement'.

Asked to comment, Rachel simply said, 'I am quite satisfied . . . Nobody ever promised me a glass slipper.'

JEAN MARSH: 'She used to say to me in her excited Welsh voice, "I've just got my alimony, let's go out and blow it!" '

Rex Harrison and Elizabeth Harris were married at Alan Jay Lerner's Long Island home on August 26, 1971. It was what Rex called 'a festive occasion', though right up to the time of the judge's arrival to conduct the ceremony he was engaged in rapping out professional instructions over the telephone to BBC TV in London regarding the final cut of a play he had filmed for American showing. The play was *Platonov*, the one in which he and Rachel had had their fatal meeting. His memoirs do not record that he was struck by the irony of this.

DARREN RAMIREZ: 'Rachel and I had been together long enough now to find our life falling into a pattern. It was a disturbing one of ups and downs, infectious "highs" and despondent "lows" coupled with withering abuse on her part and passive forebearance on mine. Sometimes I was tempted to break away and make my own life, then Rachel would feel abandoned and guilt would bring me back.

'But when we were travelling, then it was all right – she got attention, experienced new places, was treated like a star, and all this removed her from the necessity to face reality. When there was distraction in Rachel's life, it was fine: as soon as she and I tried to settle down by ourselves, it was chaos. The making of a home created a self-destructive feeling in her: she didn't want to see herself as a suburban housewife, she was scared of anything that gave her life a constricting pattern, such as "settling down".'

PAMELA MASON: 'They stayed with me for a time in a house on the estate. She was no problem then. But then I was very down-to-earth. I'd tick her off, a bit schoolmarm-y. She had one most annoying habit which only got worse with the years. She used to call people at 3.00 am or 4.00 am, oblivious to their sleeping arrangements.'

JEAN MARSH: 'When the phone rang at an odd hour, usually in the early morning, you could nearly always bet it was Rachel and be right. She loved having long chats. But she always had difficulty working out the time difference between Los Angeles and New York, and as for anywhere outside America . . . ! '

PAMELA MASON: 'She never really troubled me that way at all, but then I use an answering service nearly all the time. I do recall she once telephoned an old flame she'd met in Australia and she called him at 3.00 am, his time – simply to tell him that she'd been thinking how inadequate his performance was in bed. I suppose telling a man that would have been inopportune *any* time.

'Though Rachel was sometimes a slob, she behaved very well while she was here. She'd spread all her make-up out on a little towel in the guest-house here, keep it excessively neat, and do an elaborate job on her face, which she called "pug-like". She was always having things done to her face. She went to the most fashionable cosmetic surgeon around here. She had her nose done again, her eyes lifted, a little bit off her chin. She was constantly fretting and fiddling. She used to return from surgery looking black and blue, but not caring. Rachel's trouble, though, wasn't ageing. However she altered herself physically, it didn't seem to make any difference to the way she felt inside.'

DARREN RAMIREZ: 'When we left Pamela's guest-house, we flew down to Mexico and stayed in the lovely house that Leslie and Evie Bricusse own in Las Brisas, a suburb of Acapulco. I'd never seen Rachel so relaxed. We spent a week there, catching up on our reading – both of us devoured the new books – and considering the film scripts that ICM sent out for Rachel's scrutiny. Then, in April, 1971, we flew to London. By this time, Rachel was getting less self-conscious about being seen with me in public.'

Rachel was now almost aggressively asserting her own identity. 'I should never have let myself get better known as Mrs Rex Harrison of Portofino than Rachel Roberts from Llanelli, Wales,' she said on landing at Heathrow. She took Darren down to Swansea, to meet her mother, and laughed when she reported the old lady saying, 'This is the third one you've brought here. People will think you're promiscuous.' At the same time, she was careful not to let the dam waters of old grievances break through her public gesture of independence. She denied that she and Rex had made each other unhappy in their ten years together: 'It makes me look a fool and a liar, considering how happy most of our marriage was.' She was asked what she thought Rex admired in his present wife Elizabeth. Rachel never played the coward: she jumped at that daunting hurdle. 'Well, for a start, she's much more in the Kay Kendall mould than I am. She's *very* beautiful, in that gorgeous soft-skinned limpid way that men seem to find so attractive. Also, she's a "fun" person, her father is a Lord [Elizabeth's father was Baron Ogmore] and she's a *much* better hostess than I could ever be. And to Rex, things like that are important.' The media went away well pleased: in such moments, Rachel's apparent candour concealed a multitude of inner conflicts.

Her theatrical luck stayed with her when she and Darren returned to Los Angeles at the end of May. She went straight into her first American play, *The Effect of Gamma Rays on Man-in-the-Moon Marigolds*, staged at the Huntington Hartford Theater with two of the three mainstays of the original cast, Pamela Payton-Wright and Amy Levitt. As these two had been doing the play for months and 'had it cold', Rachel learned her lines going back on the *Queen Elizabeth* and went into rehearsals 'letter-perfect', something she always resisted, preferring the part to take her over and using the lines only as a way of 'fixing' her reading.

*Gamma Rays* was a play in the William Inge–Tennessee Williams tradition, both a celebration and an exorcism of an earth-mother figure whose inspirational energy can produce beautiful mutations in some and reduce others to struggling emotional cripples. When Rachel talked of Beatrice to Winfred Blevins, entertainment editor of the *Los Angeles Herald-Examiner*, it was obvious she was projecting much of her present mood into the character: 'I like [her] very much. She's not a defeatist. She's lost everything she wanted and found herself somewhere she never expected to be . . . What I like about her is that she faces things. She acts. She meets situations . . . She probably will be played sometimes as a more passive woman, but I like her struggling.'

This interpretation divided the American critics who saw her; and their remarks are (not for the last time), in retrospect, like an oblique, unconscious commentary on the way Rachel's struggle from now on for health and sanity – never mind success – would force her, in Charles Faber's words reviewing her performance, 'to play the character, a loser, as if she were a winner . . . The interpretation is bold and right, because the whole point . . . is that of a dynamic, aspiring human being, frustrated by circumstances and tortured by self-doubt [who] must still create something, even if that something is evil. Her final negation – "I hate the world" – is so positive that we weep for what the world has lost in her.'

Dan Sullivan, the *Los Angeles Times*'s critic, objected to Rachel's technical proficiency: yet even his remarks, considering the confident public image Rachel set such store by, have a somewhat premonitory resonance: they advertise the desperation she was striving to present as creative energy, and somewhat overdoing it:

'The first problem,' Sullivan wrote, 'involves her accent which starts out as a hybrid Brooklyn-Midlands and soon pretty much dispenses with Brooklyn. Certainly the mother could be British-born. But her Britishness would then be a part of the story. For instance, it would be one of the things the older daughter taunts her about in a climactic scene where the girl tells her that everybody at high school thinks she's crazy. Let that pass, however. The basic objection to Miss Roberts' approach to the part is that she is so damned healthy . . . . [She] makes the play almost a romp, moving with gusto, showing us a face radiant with cheer, and, in general, behaving like a mother that most girls would be delighted to have around. So much fun! The lines say despair, the performer says buck-up!' The play, Sullivan concluded, was about one of life's victims, not its victors. Rachel, he felt, fell into the wrong category.

Despite Rachel's protestations of nostalgia for her Welsh background and birthplace, Darren noticed she retained a lot of the 'Mrs Rex Harrison' characteristics when travel took them abroad. She was still without a permanent home, though her alimony settlement encouraged her to choose one quickly, as Rex would be paying most of the bill. She had to go back to Portofino to get her belongings out of the villa.

DARREN RAMIREZ: 'All she really "owned" there were her books, a Welsh dresser and a Victorian desk she had bought for herself. We decided to

95

combine collecting these things with a visit to Rachel's married niece, Jackie. She had a soft place for Jackie, who lived in Cervinia, in Italy, with her Italian husband Marco. When one of the Portofino "characters" had opened a disco in Cervinia, Rex had got young Jackie a job there, which was where she'd met her husband. Marco's father owned three small hotels in Cervinia and they were given one of them to manage. Rachel invited Lord and Lady Royston to join us on the trip – that was part of the "Rex" bit of her. "Pips" Royston and his wife had gone cruising with Rachel and Rex when they were married: she always was a bit snobbish about such aristocratic bits and pieces as remained from that marriage, though they were nice people and we were glad of the loan of their London flat the following year – though that was to have its dramas, too.

'We drove over to Portofino from Cervinia: Rachel was only permitted to enter the villa she loved in the company of her ex-husband's lawyer. She stayed at the Hotel Splendido: I took a room in a different hotel – appearance again, you see. We spent a week in Florence, then stored Rachel's things.'

Postcard from Rachel to Jeffrey Lane, datelined Cervinia: 'Too much pasta and *vino rosso*! It's very hot, and altogether I'm having a splendid time – thinking very little about my next job, which starts all too soon.'

DARREN RAMIREZ: 'Rachel's "job" just seemed to be more proof that someone was watching over her. We'd stopped over in London and, as it was a Saturday, there was no bank open to cash a cheque. Rachel had an idea – "Let's try a theatre: they should have plenty of money and they all know me." The Royal Court wasn't far away and on the way there we ran into Anthony Page, the theatre director. "We've got Albert Finney cast in *Alpha Beta*, but we haven't got a female lead," he said. "It's a new play – just a two-hander – about a marriage over the years. The wife has to age from her late twenties to her early forties. Rachel, I know you could do the later age all right, but would you agree to read the part and see if you're okay for the younger age?" Because it was Tony, Rachel said yes . . . Three hours later, she and Tony and Albert Finney breezed into the flat we were staying in with three bottles of Champagne. She'd got the part!'

However, it wasn't quite as clear-cut as that, though probably neither Rachel nor Darren Ramirez realised it at that time.

ALBERT FINNEY: 'After Rachel agreed to audition for *Alpha Beta* we played a few scenes together at the Royal Court – to Tony's approval. But he is a perfectionist, you know, and a few days later it got into his head that he should be *absolutely* sure – so he told me he intended to test her again! I said, "Tony, you simply *can't* do that to Rachel. I won't do it with her. In fact, I won't do the play unless she does it with me!"

'Frankly, I didn't think she'd changed much since *Saturday Night and Sunday Morning*, though now we were both more experienced, so it was a much more *open* professional relationship, both of us working generously together, suggesting ideas to each other unselfishly – though we didn't see much of each other between performances. After all, when you spend a lot of the play hurling abuse, and even cups and saucers, at each other, anything off stage seems low-powered. But I'll say this: there are very few people whom it's *extending* to work with. Rachel fitted that category.'

ANTHONY PAGE: 'It was a bit cheeky, really, considering her established reputation, to treat her like a beginner at an audition. But she agreed without a second's hesitation. You see, we badly needed a "female heavyweight" able to hold the stage and slug it out with Albert – who better than Rachel? Her great *forte* on stage and screen was to make so much of the passionate women she played – sometimes more than the parts contained.

'*Alpha Beta* began with Rachel wallpapering a room on stage, laying on the paste, hanging the paper straight, quite a complicated bit of business. She said it stopped her eating, having so much to attend to – but she was marvellous! I'd say to her sometimes, "You were acting tonight, it wasn't real." She'd get angry. But usually she had to agree. We later filmed the stage play for television. When we did, she wanted to keep a lot of dialogue, but Albert said, "Put it into looks, don't write any words." Which is how we did it: Rachel and Albert were well-matched and brought each other up to pitch. There was one scene in the play where the woman threatened suicide and this she thought was totally unreal. So when we came to do it, she improvised it – and it was terrific! She really felt that she connected with that play.'

E. A. Whitehead's *Alpha Beta*, which opened at the Royal Court on January 26, 1972, drew near-capacity crowds to watch a modern working-class marriage self-destruct over a period of twelve years. Rachel and Albert Finney chewed each other up with cannibalistic relish, though some critics noted that the man had the choicer cuts to masticate. Irving Wardle in the London *Times* wrote: '[Finney] may tear the paper off the walls and stamp on the presents from his children, but you are taken inside his head, asked to sympathise with his fantasies and his sense of injustice. He gets all the best arguments; all the reason is on his side. The good will comes from him, the malevolence from his wife. What [Rachel Roberts] contributes is a blank assertion of her marital rights and a view of his extra-marital life that rises from contemptuous indifference to murderous jealousy and threats of suicide when he leaves her.'

But Herbert Kretzmer, the *Daily Express* theatre critic, predicted that Rachel would carry off 'a fistful of Best Actress awards at the end of '72'. And she did, though it was a near-run thing. Her competition for the *Evening Standard* Best Actress Award – the same prize as *Platonov* had won her twelve years earlier – included Deborah Kerr and Julia Foster (*The Day After the Fair*), Lauren Bacall (*Applause*) and Diana Rigg (*Macbeth*) The *Standard* editor, Charles Wintour, broke a tied vote and Bernard Levin, presenting the award, said that Rachel had 'the realism of the woman in a disintegrating marriage, trapped behind the bars of her own devising, contrasted with the haunting quality of Miss Kerr spinning herself into a web of imaginary love'.

The nightly rows on stage with Finney, spitting out painful truths that (she was well aware) applied to her own emotional troubles, took a heavy toll of Rachel – 'Every night I would go and play this wild and bitter and terribly sad woman: then Darren would be there to pick up the pieces and put them together again as a happy and peaceful woman.' It was a comment that concealed more than anyone could have guessed.

When the play closed at the Royal Court after its limited thirty-two-performance season and awaited a transfer to the West End, it was decided to film it for television – Anthony Page again directing. Rachel and Darren took what was supposed to be a rest.

DARREN RAMIREZ: 'We went to the house that Leslie and Evie Bricusse owned in the South of France. A lovely modern villa at the top of a hill, near Vence. They'd lent it to us. But Rachel was in a highly neurotic state – perhaps affected by the power of the play and also keyed up to make the film version when we got back. It was a pattern that preceded any new play or film she was due to start: she got depressive and self-destructive. I knew we were in for trouble when we arrived. The very first day, she took a whole box of Supporenyl. She resented the life-style that success enabled Leslie Bricusse and his wife to enjoy. Rachel always hungered after that kind of life for herself, yet something drove her to take the opposite attitude to it. Instead of appreciating the luxury home we were in, enjoying the scenery, getting some rest, she went into a deep depression because it was something she couldn't herself possess.

'She wouldn't come out of her bedroom for three days – which shocked Leslie's secretary. We eventually called the paramedics who arrived from Nice, along with a doctor. We found Rachel had completely passed out, she simply wouldn't react to treatment. She was dehydrated. We had to feed her intravenously. But the odd thing about such depressive states was the speed with which she pulled out of them. She was very strong. She recuperated very quickly. And after she came out of it, the guilt feeling took over and she couldn't be nicer to everyone. She made up her mind to enjoy the rest of the holiday: it was as if this crisis had never happened. I just couldn't believe it was the same woman we'd found when we broke into the bedroom, unable to move, help herself or even recognise us.

'But then we returned to London via Paris, it was the black pit again. I'd hoped we'd have a couple of romantic days there, but all the visit did was remind Rachel of the glamorous times she'd spent with Rex in that city.'

The life that consists of living in other people's houses, using other people's transportation – Albert Finney put his limousine at Rachel's disposal during the play's run – and envying other people's lives was one that Rachel wished to end: she knew she had to regain some solid ground. Like others in this disoriented state, she tended at first to sink her roots into her memories. Memories of home became precious to her: her mother's health was ailing and, in fact, Mrs Roberts was to die shortly. Rachel took to visiting her in Swansea, sometimes looking as if she had stepped out of one world without fully adjusting to the other. She was seen in a full-length mink coat riding on the top of a Swansea-bound double-decker bus from the railway station in nearby Cardiff. Instead of taking a taxi for the sentimental journey, she chose to spend nineteen pence for the ten-mile trip while cocooned in the £11,000 fur.

But Darren, who hankered after some sort of permanent domicile, kept at her to make use of Rex's obligation to provide his ex-wife with a suitable home of her own.

DARREN RAMIREZ: 'The time came for us to move out of the Roystons' flat in Egerton Place – I never liked it, anyway, it was a rather gloomy, Victorian apartment at the back door of Harrod's. Rachel mentioned that Genevieve Bujold had a house to rent – 'in fact,' she said, 'she wants rid of it. Why don't we buy it?' That was Rachel all over! She never looked around to see if there was anything better, something else she preferred. She just impulsively bought the thing! It was a terrace house in Cambridge Street, Pimlico, behind Victoria Station. Not the most fashionable area: but then Rachel had this double standard, part of her snobbishly wanting to live with "the best people", part of her identifying with the "genuine" working class.

'Genevieve had decorated the house with props from the film *Anne of the Thousand Days*, in which she'd played Anne Boleyn, in 1969. To visit it was a sort of schizoid experience. Outside, it looked like a normal London house in a row, with basement area, steps up to a solid front door, and rooms decreasing in size and pretentiousness until you got up to the old servants' quarters under the tile roof. But inside, you stepped back into the sixteenth century with Tudor chairs and Elizabethan four-posters! Moreover, it was decorated in purple and orange – orange in two shades! – with purple velour on the walls. Can you imagine?

'We moved into a service apartment in Hill Street, Mayfair, until Genevieve vacated the place. Rachel had Rex's $100,000 settlement to buy the house, and other money from their separation to furnish it: she had to acquire a place within three years of the divorce and if she died before Rex, it reverted to him.

'At the first opportunity, she went to 42 Cambridge Street and spent a night in the hideous place. She called me the next day in hysterics – she hated the place, she could never live there! She couldn't even bring herself to look for new furnishings for it.

'I told her, "Why don't you go and stay with your mother in Wales for a couple of weeks and while you're away I'll have the house cleaned up." I didn't realise how long these refurbishments take in London! At least I tore the two-tone orange fabric out of the bedroom and I got her another essential part of any house Rachel lived in – two Angora kittens, which were named Max and Carlotta. She returned with her mother, fell in love with the kittens, and pronounced it all "liveable". Her nephew came by and moved into the downstairs flat. Throughout her life, Rachel was always putting on an act, trying to please the members of her family: but their ways weren't hers, and she often felt unappreciated and invariably I got the worst of it! For instance, she didn't want her nephew to witness her when she was in one of her screaming moods, so after a time I was given the job of asking him to move out: which soured relations between Rachel's sister and myself. I'm afraid I was cast as the "bad guy". You couldn't win!'

Rachel spent Christmas, 1972, with her family in Swansea; for once, all went well and she returned happy. But one of her stormiest and – in retrospect – most bitterly self-reproachful experiences arrived at the same time as her triumph, winning the *Evening Standard* Best Actress Award for *Alpha Beta*. It was presented at the *Standard*'s luncheon, along with awards to Olivier (for *Long Day's Journey into Night*) and Tom Stoppard (for *Jumpers*, the Best Play), at the Dorchester on January 22, 1973. The next evening, she was scheduled to bask in her glory as one of the guests on the prime-time television chat show hosted by Russell Harty: it was to be recorded, for transmission later in the week. That was fortunate, as things turned out . . .

DARREN RAMIREZ: 'After the awards, we were all due to go and see Olivier and Michael Caine in the film version of *Sleuth*. Nicol Williamson was in the party, with Jill Bennett, who was married to John Osborne at the time. But Rachel said, "We don't want to go and see a *film* – let's go and celebrate!" She sent her mother (who'd come to London for the occasion) off on a bus and told *her* to see the film. Then the rest of us, with John Mills and his wife Mary in tow, went off to Nicol's house and started drinking and singing. We were in *very* good spirits when Johnny Mills said, "Let's go on to our flat. We've got a piano: we can have a real sing-song round it." Everybody got smashed. People began to pass out. Nicol said, "let's go on to my favourite restaurant," so we staggered over to it – I can't remember which it is: is it any wonder! Nicol ordered a whole pitcher of Pimm's and drank it in one go. Rachel got rowdy. Someone objected. Somebody else tried to pick a fight with Nicol. I said to Jill, "Let me take you home" – and we fled.

'The next day Rachel had to appear for the recording of the chat show. She couldn't get up and spent most of the day in bed with a colossal hangover. We took her mother to lunch at Mimo's. When we got back, Rachel was still in bed with the sheets over her head. I was to stay at home with her mother while Rachel went along with her publicist, Jeffrey Lane, to the theatre where they were recording the show. Half an hour before Jeffrey came, Rachel was still in bed, her hair not done, her face unmade-up. In walked Jeffrey – with a bottle of Champagne! We managed to get Rachel up and dressed somehow and she set off with Jeffrey.'

JEFFREY LANE: 'At that time, Rachel really wasn't a big drinker – she could go for months without a drink. But she was taking all kinds of pills, and they didn't mix with alcohol. Despite the award, she was still very unsure of herself and needed constant reassuring. Every time a role came to an end, she thought she'd never be employed again – of course, she never missed a beat! Darren had bought her an Yves Saint-Laurent dress for the TV show: he always wanted her to look glamorous, and he had very good taste – Rachel had no dress sense at all, and once when she attended her friend Ethel Merman's opening at the Palladium, she was wearing a long white dress, and a Marlene Dietrich-length white boa – and she lifted her dress all the way up to show me she still had those famous thigh boots on underneath!

'We'd hardly got into the reception room for the TV taping when one of the greeters was pouring a drink down Rachel's throat. What with her pills and her nervous excitement, one drink set her off – and she passed from sober to drunk in a few seconds! Then all hell broke out.

'She'd previously told Russell Harty what she would talk about and what she wouldn't – among the latter *verboten* subjects was anything about married life with Rex.

'She walked down the steps on to the stage with her glass still in her hand, sat down beside Russell and immediately said, "Darren wanted me to come in looking like Lauren Bacall." Then she plunged into details about her marriage to Rex and their love life. She called Russell "a silly cunt". He didn't know what to do. Then she spoke her mind about Women's Lib. And after that she walked down into the audience and cried out, "This is what you all want to know about me, isn't it?" She told them she had two cats, Maximilian and Carlotta. "All the cats want to do is screw," she said to the astonished audience.'

DARREN RAMIREZ: 'After Jeffrey had left for the taping, some instinct told me I should have gone with Rachel. So I rushed over to the theatre. Peter Hall was there, and Elton John and Barbara Cartland: they were the other guests, and when I dashed in they were sitting there stunned. Ronnie Cowan, the publicist, was working for Russell Harty at this time, and she dashed up to me and screamed, "You must do something – *get her off the stage!*" There was a TV monitor in the greenroom and on it I could see this wild apparition. Every other word she uttered was a four-letter one. Then she started insulting Russell Harty. Ronnie Cowan rushed out and Rachel turned on her and called her names. "Get her off! Get her off!" everyone was now shouting – whereupon Rachel started to sing "The Lady Is a Tramp".

JEFFREY LANE: 'We eventually dragged her off, got her into Darren's car and drove at high speed back to Pimlico.'

DARREN RAMIREZ: 'I was so angry, I was crying. I was shouting at her, "I try all the time to help you. I try to help you in your work. I try to help you keep your reputation. How can you dare do this!" By now she was in a state of utter shock.'

JEFFREY LANE: 'Immediately she was indoors, Rachel shut herself in the lavatory, started crying hysterically and said she was going to kill herself. Meanwhile I called the TV people, told them to wipe the tape and threatened them with all kinds of retribution if they didn't. They said they were only too glad to do so. Much later, we were all to laugh at that night and I remember lying on the floor at a party with her and Jill Bennett and Rachel recalling, "Then I said this . . . then I said that . . ." And when she appeared on the other chat show hosted by Michael Parkinson, she was so well behaved she was almost boring. But at the time, it was a traumatic experience she never really got over, I think.'

DARREN RAMIREZ: 'I called Lindsay Anderson that night: we always turned to Lindsay when things went badly. And Ned Sherrin came over to comfort her. She was almost comatose. The next day we called Glyn Davies, the psychiatrist and psychotherapist, who had treated her at the time of her break-up with Rex. He said we had to put her into a clinic immediately, so she was admitted to Bowden House to dry out – and in what seemed no time at all, she was on her feet again!'

When Rachel returned from Bowden House, a private hospital in Harrow, near London, Lindsay Anderson decided in his unsentimental Scots way that what she needed first and foremost was – work. He immediately recruited her for the cast of *O! Lucky Man*, his satirical film comedy which set out to chastise a contemporary Vanity Fair world and bend the reality of a specific, though not exclusively English society just far enough to show its essential madness. The film cast some of its leading players in multiple roles: for though life changes, Anderson said, one keeps on meeting the same kind of people in it. Thus Rachel played a PR lady who seduces the Candide-type hero, Malcolm McDowell; the slinky Asian mistress of a Third World bigshot; and a houseproud Welshwoman who feels defeated by life and commits suicide after carefully doing the chores.

In tragic retrospect, of course, this last characterisation hardly bears thinking about: but at the time, it was intended (and accepted) as a bit of self-mockery from the director of *This Sporting Life* who had guided Rachel through the life-denying role of the repressed and houseproud widow in that earlier film.

When *O! Lucky Man* opened in America, the suicide sequence had disappeared: but this was due to the need to shorten its running time, for although it had aroused fierce critical controversy (as its successor *Britannia Hospital* was to do ten years later), it had proved disappointing box-office.

But the Cannes Film Festival chose it to represent Britain; and, after filming an undistinguished TV play in Bristol, Rachel accompanied by Darren, both of them having nothing better to do, went down to Cannes for the festival in May.

DARREN RAMIREZ: 'It was the fiftieth anniversary of Warner Bros, who were Lindsay's distributors, and they were coupling it with the opening of a new motel, the Mas d'Artigny, in the hilly hinterland behind Cannes, and also presenting several of their latest Hollywood films, sight unseen for the most part, which, as it turned out, were disastrously received by the world's press and cast a funereal gloom over everyone: it was more like a wake than a birthday.

'We were soon moved out of the Mas by the arrival of the Warner executives and went to a much nicer place opposite, the Colombe d'Or. Every day we were there, though, Rachel was drunk and either I or actor Michael Medwin would sober her up and pull her out of her depression. And then, suddenly, she got one of the biggest breaks of her entire career. When you think back on it, it was amazing the way fate found its way to her every time she needed it, whereas other deserving talents go through life always missing things just by a minute or a mile.

'We were sitting having dinner, when in walked Rex Reed, then a star columnist for the New York *Daily News*. "Rachel," he said, stopping by our table, "do you know there's been a letter addressed to you waiting at the Carlton Hotel in Cannes for two days now? I saw it next to my own mail. It's from Hal Prince, and when I told him you were up in the hills, not at the Carlton, and I might see you, he asked me to give it to you. Here it is."

'Rex gave her the letter – Hal Prince is one of the most successful-ever Broadway directors. He'd written to Rachel, asking her if she'd be interested in appearing in two plays that were going to be done that fall! "Rachel," said Rex, "there's your passport to Broadway."'

Very shortly afterwards, Harold Prince himself came up to the Colombe d'Or.

DARREN RAMIREZ: 'He'd been in Cannes for the premiere of *The Last of Sheila*, which had been written by his friend Stephen Sondheim, and had been panned (or was just about to be) by critics who'd had a field-day slaughtering all the other new Warner films, most of which never recovered from their execution at Cannes. "We're presenting two plays in repertory," Hal told Rachel, "Durrenmatt's *The Visit* and a Feydeau farce, *Chemin de Fer*. We want you to appear in each – in totally different roles. Can you come?" I mean ". . . can you come?"!! But Rachel was dithering:

she always got into a panic when opportunity knocked on the door. She kept saying she'd agreed to play the part of Miriam in Lew Grade's religious spectacular *Moses – The Lawgiver*. Lindsay was at our table, too, and he said furiously, "Rachel, don't be a fool! Take Harold's offer. It's the stage, it's Broadway – you *must* go to America." So she said yes – and that, incidentally, is how Ingrid Thulin became Miriam in *Moses!*'

LINDSAY ANDERSON: 'She was scared by Hal's offer. For one thing, it would mean her doing the plays "on her own", far from friends like myself. And although it's hard to believe, I suspect she wasn't too thrilled by the idea of Broadway. By this time, Rachel was bent on being "A Star". Being a respected "actress" wasn't really as glamorous an enterprise as she'd have liked. However, she said yes.'

This settled, Darren Ramirez left for a week or so's holiday in Paris, by himself. He felt in need of a little time alone. He had a yearning to work for himself, not always be dancing attendance on Rachel: but when she called the tune, he was amazed how quickly he responded.

KAREL REISZ: 'Darren was totally loyal to Rachel, really sweet and nice, but certainly not the formidable and strong-willed character she might have benefited from having by her side. At times Darren would be kicked out and have to sit in the waiting room till told to come back. Rachel couldn't cope with the feeling that Darren was in a filial position, so she would both alternately adore him and give him a terrible time.'

PAMELA MASON: 'I continually ask myself why she didn't go into hospital and have herself constrained to stay there until she was cured – as might have been possible at this time. If "Fluffy" had been strong enough he'd have played the same role to Rachel as Sid Luft did to Judy Garland – backing up his affection for her with enough force to head her off from the self-destructive course she was set on. She was taking far more pills at this time than she needed. Pills give one that over-emotional slant. They put you out of touch with the real world other people have to inhabit. In that world, to the addict, everything goes on as if he or she hadn't done a thing to disturb it or provoke any retributive consequences. When the rebound comes, it's an inexplicable shock. It can't be coped with.'

Darren had not been long in Paris before the phone went, as usual well after midnight.

DARREN RAMIREZ: 'She was hysterical. She'd gone down to the country to see Rex and his wife. She wanted to see what sort of life they were living: Rachel was a glutton for punishment! She'd also had more to drink than was good for her. Elizabeth had put her and Rex into the library together, to talk things over – Elizabeth always had her head screwed on the right way. But it hadn't helped calm Rachel; she sounded out of control. I told her, as quietly as I could, "Rachel, I simply can't take any more rows."
'Well, I stayed on in Paris for about two weeks when, suddenly, she called again. Her mother had had a stroke. Mrs Roberts was staying with her other daughter, Hazel, but proving, I gathered, too much for Hazel with her other family responsibilities to cope with satisfactorily. So the mother was

coming to Rachel's house in Pimlico and now she rang me in a panic. She'd no idea what to do.

'This time I couldn't refuse. I got over there on the next available plane. And I found Rachel had stowed her mother away in the basement! I don't think she consciously realised how she was punishing her parent: Rachel had a need, you see, when she herself was insecure, to behave very badly to people in order to test the strength of their love or concern for her. I said, "Rachel, bring your mother upstairs immediately!" She did, and put her into the main bedroom.'

Not long after this, Mrs Richard Rees Roberts died in hospital. Rachel had already left for America to rehearse the two plays, *The Visit* and *Chemin de Fer*, which were being staged 'back to back' by the New Phoenix Company and directed, respectively, by Harold Prince and Stephen Porter.

After Rex and I separated, I left for California in the care of a nurse. I did a movie no one remembers – I can't even remember its name. I got drunk. I got lower and lower, though still coasting along on the strength of old memories, staying in the Château Marmont, living in our Bedford Drive house, ordering cases of Château-Margaux, giving parties, having Leslie and Evie Bricusse round for Champagne – whooping it up, in fact, keeping the mad whirligig.

I wasn't facing life realistically. I was running from it in a mad, 'exciting' disguise. Everyone else was more or less tackling it properly, but not me. *Not quietly thinking what I should do about my future* – nor yet making any attempt to get my husband back. I was doing the reverse, telling him over the phone at Harvey Perr's first-night party that I'd slept with at least ten men then, every Tom, Dick and Harry. It even got back to him that I was living with a black man. What I ought to have been doing was going quietly to my home in Portofino to see to my things, my dog, my cats, ordering the boat to take me out – I couldn't drive it: at least, I could, but I was too scared: Armando could have taken it out for me – and generally asserting myself. But no, I stayed in Los Angeles, dressed up, dolled up, screwed around, drank. 'You're either depressed or drunk,' Rex said, 'you were always in bed.' An element of truth in both statements.

Oh, if only I could wipe the slate clean. I remember the positive joy of holding an audience, both in comedy and tragedy. I used to be able to sing, too, in a husky sort of way. And I once had great love for and faith in my acting abilities. No loneliness then, no fear of the audience. A sense of command and a great love for it.

I've just read that Lilli Palmer is to do a one-woman play on the life of Sarah Bernhardt; and that Rex is going out on tour with his chosen cast of *My Fair Lady*. And what of me? I'm in a pitiable mess.

'You'll be left alone,' my Mother said, and I am. I am so bewildered and so frightened and getting older and used up by life.

Did I indeed repress for so many years the shock of losing Rex and all he represented for me – protection, escape and privilege? Yes, I suppose so.

When he left, I just couldn't relax at all in the flat near Sloane Street – just walked up and down, couldn't eat or sleep. I 'escaped' to California and did *Doctors' Wives* – *that* was the name of the film I couldn't remember – and I got through it by keeping up the all-powerful Mrs Rex Harrison pretence. Otherwise, I went completely off the rails. What *did* I think I was doing with Paul and his black friends – being 'sexy'? That September, when Rex said he loved me but didn't want to live with me any more, I collapsed. It was Darren Ramirez who saved me – and then saved my face. Darren gently led me to a clinic. Darren gently picked me up when, dead drunk, I lifted up my skirts and peed off Sunset Boulevard.

I tried to ignore the handbag, that we weren't lovers. He was peaceful and gentle and lovely to look at and *there*.

I sheltered under Pamela Mason's protection, staying in her guest-house and buying Darren a Mercedes – 'A dream come true,' he said, and why not? For me, though, it was all still an 'escape' from reality. Going back to London involved me in more pretence. I tipped off Jeffrey Lane, my publicist at Rogers and Cowan, and arrived in a blaze of publicity and photographs in the papers. Rachel the 'beautiful', always 'attractive', returning to London with an unusually handsome 'younger' man – 'proving' to the world what a sexy, glamorous cat I was. 'Rachel without Rex.' As he'd flown off with a young woman, I flew in with a younger man. 'Look, Rex, I've got a handsome young man.' I used Darren subconsciously – I lied about our relationship. I gave dinner parties for my English upper-class friends, flew them to Cervinia, being 'vital' and 'funny' and 'charming'. I collected my 'things' from the villa at Portofino, full of wine and drugs, left them with my niece Jackie and her husband Marco at Cervinia, returned to London and checked into 49 Hill Street – all the time, I expect, in a state of shock. Then back I went on the *Queen Elizabeth*, photographed of course, to stay with Pam Mason again, not one bit aware of the unreality of it all. I acted in repertory in Los Angeles, not very well – but my cover still hadn't been smashed. I used Darren who was content to be used – he was using me, too. Shuttling back to London, for $15,000 I played the fourth or fifth lead in a film for television, still thinking or pretending to myself that I was someone special. Then at the end of 1971 came my lucky break, the play *Alpha Beta*.

Darren threw me a party at San Lorenzo, inviting all my 'friends', Joan Collins and Sean Connery included. Who can blame him? Sick with fear, I shoved a whole lot of Supporenyl up my backside in Leslie's house in the South of France. A doctor had to be called. I was found to be dehydrated. The fear before I undertook *Alpha Beta* was out of all proportion to my actual ability to do it. My ability earned me the applause – and the *Evening Standard* Best Actress Award. Albert Finney starred in the play with me, but the Best Actor that year, 1972, was Laurence Olivier. Me and Olivier – *that* was my talent. Mine and mine alone. And no sooner was the moment mine than I had to go and ruin it.

At the awards ceremony, I felt awkward, unworthy – I spoke goofishly. And *then* . . . I lost all control. My behaviour on *The Russell Harty Show* on television! It was of someone who if not mad – and Lindsay Anderson insists I'm not – then of a creature with sealed eyes. I completely sabotaged what should have been my moment of triumph with clips from my two award-winning films, *Saturday Night and Sunday Morning* and *This Sporting Life*. That I was drunk at the time is of less importance than *why* I got drunk and behaved so maniacally. I'm no longer feeling guilty from a moral point of view, but I'm questioning what was in my head to be so out of control. Why did I want to – or *did* I want to? – make such an inordinate *disgrace* of myself? Where was the pride of achievement, the self-assurance and personal dignity that others less talented than I would have presented?

As the Actress of the Year, what was – or is – in me that couldn't be composed enough, drunk or not, to answer 'What do you think of Women's Lib?' with a conventional or even a witty reply? Why did I have to answer, 'All they need is a cock up their cunt or their arse'? What was – or is – in me that made me want to sing 'The Lady Is a Tramp' before a dumb-struck Russell Harty and a live audience? What was – or is – in me that thought I was being a riot? Smiling away, I was, and embarrassing everyone. Was it all those years of repression, now unleashed and out of control? I can't really answer the question any more than I can explain my present state.

This is not self-recrimination. It is painful self-knowledge. I am, as they say, up against it. Predictable, I suppose, all predictable. But I'm not going to be so hard on myself. It helped me today to read Joyce Cary in *To Be a Pilgrim*:

'Conclusion, that though I am not a good man, I need not fall into the vanity of supposing myself a monster. I have lived a futile and foolish life and done many things of which I have cause to be ashamed; but I must not allow myself the luxury of these romantic ecstasies by which an Alfred de Musset makes of his common and vulgar sins a special glory. That would be out of place in a retired English lawyer of seventy-one, suffering from a diseased head.'

The latter part does not apply to me, but I am a fifty-two-year-old divorcee, at the moment homeless and out of work, who is ill, has been very ill, but who is fighting.

While I was doing *Alpha Beta* I rented Lady Royston's flat in Knightsbridge and was driven home nightly in Albie's car. I moved the twin beds together, but to no avail. Occasionally the lie that was the relationship between Darren and me erupted, but it was repressed most of the time.

It's preposterous that I kept on lying to myself about the reality of the situation. I went down to Bristol to do a BBC TV play and slept with this one and that, got drunk, and lashed out in the restaurant at 'the fucking English'. Darren came down to Bristol and left after our miserable Sunday in Bath. Then we went to the Cannes Film Festival, in May, to do publicity for Lindsay's film *O! Lucky Man*. Drunk, I spent the afternoon at the hotel. I wasn't staying at the Colombe d'Or. I was as anchorless then as now, but repressed it. I tried so hard with my 'see-through' dress to be the 'star' I was never destined to be. I don't have Rex's charisma or drive, and I'm so unbelievably lazy. 'The play' was never 'the thing' for me as, through himself, it was for Rex.

For me, there just doesn't seem to be a way out. Lindsay Anderson has done his best for me, but I'm just beginning to believe that no psychiatrist in the world can get at my malaise – at the disappointment and frustration and emptiness in this, my one and only life. Without being masochistic, I can believe that I've brought a lot of it on myself. Lindsay's got his world, his cottage, mainly his work which brings friends with it. He settles down and works. His secretary comes in, his life is in order, not pieces. Joan Plowright set her teeth and made up her mind and succeeded with Larry Olivier, whatever the problems. She doggedly lived through the memories of Vivien Leigh. She had three children, a son and two girls; the boy is studying in California. She didn't get drunk. She got on with her career, survived the pre-eminence that Larry gave to Maggie Smith when he was director of the National Theatre, survived the fact that Larry got cancer . . . She always was a brilliant comedienne. I'm quite sure that in her compactness she's never screwed around. So today she wakes up fulfilled, successful, secure in herself. Not for her the pathetic traipsing to see Laurie Evans and find out if there's any work for her to do. Yet her cottage that I visited was by no means comfortable, though she's got a pool and a jacuzzi. She doesn't accompany her husband to the awards ceremonies. Joan, as they say, has her head screwed on the right way. If she did go to Los Angeles as 'Lady Olivier', Ben [concierge] would take care of her at L'Hermitage. On her own bat, she can call up Tony Richardson to play tennis or learn to play it – *and learn she will*. It is *not* self-pity when I dread what I have to face. I've tried it all – my pathetic, lonely tennis lessons and trying to build up a relationship with Darren. I very much doubt, however, that I had Joan's talent. When she was working with the director John Dexter in the Arnold Wesker play *Roots*, she was radiantly good all those years ago. I was playing in a limp farce at the Arts.

I'm sitting here in London having my hair done, preparing to go off to Los Angeles tomorrow – because there's nowhere else to go. But what my mind's on is the emotional havoc I have made of everything. I remember rushing off to Swansea in a large rented car to get comfort from the family, only to find the house shut up. Rex had called, saying he was feeling low and, grudgingly, missed me. I let my frustrations out on the phone. When I came back to London to have my hair done, I called him – he'd changed. Didn't want to see me. I took some books and a hydrangea plant round to the Connaught. I had to ask permission to see him in his suite. He was at his most unforthcoming. I left – he lying on the bed talking on the phone to 'Darling'. In the general emotional furore, I left my photograph of me as a child behind, had to knock on the door to regain entry – was met with ice. That was ten years ago.

---

DARREN RAMIREZ: 'Rachel begged me to come and stay with her in New York while she rehearsed and did a tour before the Broadway opening. I was glad to be in New York. I had a chance to do a bit of designing, my Manhattan home had been rented, but Rachel leased Sir John Gielgud's apartment on Central Park West, with a lovely view from the terrace, overlooking the reservoir.'

JEFFREY LANE: 'It was there she gave me the first glass of *chilled* red wine I'd ever had, which she mixed with port, if you please! She was wonderful at mixing drinks, though when Rachel herself began ordering vodka Martinis, that was "nervous time". Then look out! Anything might happen. With the plays to do, she was in a high state of nervous excitement. I remember she went to a party for me which my uncle, Lionel Larner, gave the day I was leaving New York for London and Rachel persuaded Ethel Merman –

whom she adored, and who didn't need much persuading, because they were of a similar boisterous temperament – and the other guests to escort me in a flying column to Kennedy Airport, where they jumped queues – I was travelling "economy" – and pulled rank to get me the VIP treatment. I was dreadfully embarrassed, wishing the earth would open up! Even worse, they demanded a wheel-chair for me and I was steered out to the aircraft with Rachel and Ethel Merman in hysterics – and when I got to London, I found they'd ordered an ambulance to stand by at the foot of the aircraft steps and take me the whole way home. Rachel wrote later that she'd soon sobered up and was hoping I'd see the joke – but how could you do otherwise!?

'While she was rehearsing in New York, she and Darren and I went to dinner at a Chinese restaurant. Darren thought it squalid. But there was a side of Rachel that was at home in a back street, or at the best table in "21". As we walked back to Central Park West, a total stranger, a man, stopped us. "Are you Rachel Roberts?" – "Yes." – "Oh, you're so much prettier than you are on the screen." That backhanded compliment pleased her a lot.

'She sent for one of the black maids she'd had in California to come over and look after her in New York. She enjoyed this woman's company. She was very independent-minded about her household duties, but Rachel always thought it very funny when she'd arrive in the morning and decide she'd had a rough night and was too tired to tackle the housework. She answered Rachel back, which amused her, too, and told Rachel how black women handled their men. The black stud whom Rachel had known in Los Angeles caught up with her again in New York. He took her to a wedding in Harlem. She had just had her hair re-dyed, a bleached blonde tint, and was wearing a white linen dress and pale stockings and white gloves – she was the Superwhite in that congrega⸝ ı and loved it when the service began swinging into gospel music and song.'

Rachel was the subject of an interview by Judy Klemesrud of the *Times*, to whom she presented 'her upturned nose and Dick Tracy jaw . . . unlike many women in her profession she has not starved herself into a bony skeleton . . . she has an honest-to-goodness noticeable stomach, not some concave pit.'

Rachel, as was her way, gave a clearer and more cogent view of herself while talking to the media. Sitting there in the Gielgud apartment, which Ms Klemesrud described as 'of the drop dead/House Beautiful genre . . . with several paintings on the walls that all say "LOVE",' she sounded saner and better balanced than her recent conduct warranted.

On giving up acting when married to Rex Harrison: 'It was my own choice, my own stupidity, and I've only myself to blame . . . In my frustration I became a clown rather than a shrew. I apologised for myself by overfriendliness and clowning around and lacking reserve. But my energy went into compulsive talk and chatter . . . [But] I could never have played Ophelia, anyway.'

On her religious upbringing: 'If I were to be anything today, I'd be a Catholic. Whenever I go to church I go to St Patrick's. I really do think there's a great peace there, don't you?'

On a family: 'Sometimes I think about adoption, but it only enters my head, no more.'

JEFFREY LANE: 'About this time she said to me, "Do you like children?" "I'm not crazy," I said. "Me, neither," she said, "I don't regret not having any."'

Rachel began rehearsing the two plays in the autumn of 1973. But her temperament swiftly introduced tensions into her work, which became apparent when Darren threw a surprise party for her on her birthday, September 20.

DARREN RAMIREZ: 'I think she'd begun to alienate Harold Prince, who, after all, was responsible for her being there at all, by very obviously befriending Stephen Porter, who was directing the other play, *Chemin de Fer*, and who hadn't Hal Prince's Broadway reputation. Everyone from the company arrived earlier, including Hal Prince. We all sat around waiting . . . and waiting. Finally Rachel arrived two hours late, absolutely stoned, with Stephen Porter in tow. All her friends were there, including Ethel Merman who'd brought along six friends of *hers* just to meet Rachel. But Rachel only stayed five minutes, then took off again. "The stage managers are having a get-together," was all the explanation she gave for leaving her guests in the lurch. The truth was, Rachel's choice of company was often based on her need to feel superior to it – hence she would snub the star to take up with the understudy. I felt dreadful about it, particularly for the way Hal Prince had been treated, though I suppose he was used to such behaviour."

'A hellion,' said Hal Prince, smiling sadly and almost sympathetically, 'that's the best word for her. I had a begrudging affection for Rachel. She was, at the very least, consistently outrageous.'

Prince, a wiry, compact, energetic man, springing up with apologies now and then to take personal calls from Lew Wasserman, head of Universal, in Hollywood, works from a silver-wallpapered office on The Avenue of the Americas, posters for *Follies*, *Evita* and others of his multitude of hits packing every foot of it, large square tables of heavy glass, brown suede and tubular chrome chairs with bamboo fold-away seats for impromptu conferences, art-deco bookshelving, a polished walnut drinks cabinet in the same style, tall spiky, carnivorous-looking plants . . . He did not look a man whom anything could offend. 'Offence' was the sort of *petit-bourgeois* emotion Hal Prince wouldn't have permitted himself to feel.

HAL PRINCE: 'Rachel was a displaced and splendid figure. On stage, she was tremendously disciplined and what I afterwards saw, or heard about, seemed to me to make no sense at all. For instance, I remember my stage-director colleague John Dexter telephoning me to say he had been in Sardi's after the curtain had fallen on *The Visit*. Suddenly, out of the corner of his eye, he saw something moving. He looked round. What he witnessed was Rachel crawling towards him *over the tops* of the intervening tables, and when she got near enough to him she hissed, "That Hal Prince is the coldest son of a bitch I've ever seen in my life."'

Judy Klemesrud asked Rachel if she wasn't intimidated by the memory that Alfred Lunt and Lynn Fontanne had left when they had first performed Durrenmatt's play *The Visit* in the 1950s. Rachel replied, 'In my country, so many actors play Hamlet, and you aren't always thinking of how Olivier played the part.'

HAL PRINCE: 'The Visit, as I directed it, was very unlike the version the Lunts did. I never did feel theirs was what Durrenmatt had in mind, so I flew to Switzerland and told him I'd do the play if I could adapt it freely to my view of it, which was much more Expressionist. He confirmed the Lunts' version wasn't his conception either and gave me permission. Rachel was superb in it – and all I wanted. You should have seen her entry with the coffin she destines for the old flame who jilted her in the days she was a peasant girl, before she became the much-married millionairess vengeance-figure. The coffin became all kinds of things on stage – a bar counter, a police-chief's desk, and finally a coffin once again. Likewise, every bit of luggage in Rachel's retinue turned into some kind of stage furniture. She was surrounded by mirrored glass – "distressed" glass as a background to the villagers' own moral confusion and anxiety at the choice of ritual execution which Rachel forces on them – then, when they'd made the decision, a highly-polished mirror background to replicate their hard-edged self-interest.

'Rachel looked spectacular, just as I'd hoped, a marvellous animal in the cage we devised for her.

'Then in the Feydeau farce, Chemin de Fer, as an empty-headed, gig-gling blonde having her first extra-marital fling, she seemed a creature of totally different weight and appearance. It was a terrific transformation.'

Generally, the New York critics echoed this satisfaction. Clive Barnes in the Times described Rachel as playing Clara Zachanassian 'with hard-bitten worldliness and yet also with a driven need to expiate love. She finds layer after layer of meaning in the role.' Richards Watts Jr, in the Post, wrote, 'Miss Roberts, an interesting actress, is excellent even to those of us who also remember Lynn Fontanne.' Even to those of us who may not have remembered Lynn Fontanne, or even liked Hal Prince's or Rachel's re-interpretation, the critical response signified a basic disagreement rather than disappointment. As John Simon put it: 'Rachel Roberts has been misdirected as interpreting the heroine as if she were Richard Crookback under a dose of Novocaine. Hunching her back and moodily surveying the floorboards, she balefully drags out her funniest lines as if they were a defeated political candidate's good wishes to the winner. She settles on the play like a blight, instead of being the waggish cynical demon and accusingly plain flesh-and-blood woman the author has written.'

The Visit had its first night on November 25, 1973: a week later, Chemin de Fer brought Rachel unanimous praise. Richard Watts Jr called her a 'superb farceuse'. Walter Kerr wrote in the Times, 'Rachel Roberts . . . is so alarmed to wake in her lover's bed and discover it is six o'clock in the morning that her voice drops from a Marilyn Monroe high frequency to a Barnacle Bill basso without apparent transition.' Rex Reed, in the News, contrasted the 'delicious air of menace' she made in The Visit as 'a wooden-legged, cigar-smoking monster, her face a tight mask of cruelty, her mouth a scarlet scar', with the revelation of a 'totally different facet of her talent as a dim-witted blonde coquette . . . all bubbles and wide eyes and chattering nonsense'.

Rachel spoke to the London Times's Michael Leech about how she achieved the contrast: 'Francine in *Chemin de Fer* came to me very easily. She's a bubbly id-iot . . . Maybe I'm a bubbly id-iot myself, but I found I was much closer to Francine than to Clara in the Durrenmatt play. I remember we rehearsed the plays at the American Theater Club and there was a cat there called Jack who was a tremendous personality, a very bright cat. Always around. He must have had an effect, because when we did the photos of Francine, I looked like Jack.' Leech commented, 'In her *fin de siecle* costume, crowned with an oval black hat shaped like a half-opened oyster, she did indeed look like a cat in a cumulo-nimbus cloud.'

'It took me a long time to get to Clara,' Rachel continued, unconsciously citing an analogy the very opposite of her model for Francine, 'I worked like a small dog during rehearsals. She was a bit tight to begin with and, for better or worse, I'm a reasonably warm-hearted human being – and Clara *isn't*. At first I found it very hard to get the *right* level of fanaticism. I won't be *histrionic*, if I can possibly avoid it . . . Inevitably it takes time . . . and I'm not always finished at dress rehearsal. I find that the chemistry between audience and actor is bound to affect that third person which is the character.'

In early 1974, Rachel received a Tony nomination for each characterisation: the first time in the history of the theatre award that such a 'double' had been brought off.

But she had not achieved such success without damage to herself – the kind that an audience did *not* perceive. She was overdosing herself with pills, and during the out-of-town openings her behaviour became flagrantly unconventional.

HAL PRINCE: 'We opened *The Visit* at Annenberg, Philadelphia, in a theatre which has strong links with the college campus. There were always lots of kids whom we welcomed to rehearsals and who performed minor functions behind the scenes. And of course that was just when Rachel would take it into her head to walk out of her dressing room on some errand that took her down the corridor and back again past all these kids. What was wrong with that? Nothing, except that she was stark bare-assed naked!'

DARREN RAMIREZ: 'I went down to Boston, along with Milton Goldman, who headed ICM in New York and was now her agent, to see her do the plays there. I found her very broody and, to my surprise, quite unkempt looking. She kept on asking how she should have her hair done. I arranged with a Vidal Sassoon colorist I knew to have it attended to – I wanted to perk her up. I thought it would help. I thought this was her way of letting me see how much I had been neglecting her. Not a bit of it. Instead we had a big, big row. You see, she had met Val Mayer on this tour and they had fallen for each other.

'For me, I decided this *has* to be the end – I simply couldn't go on living that sort of life. I went back to New York. I was angry with myself for putting up with things as long as I did.'

Some of their friends received the news more laconically. Sir John Gielgud, according to Rachel, telephoned the New York apartment with some enquiry and courteously asked how Darren Ramirez was. 'We'd just had a row, I told him,' said Rachel. '"Ah, *Private Lives*," was all he said.'

And some, to be truthful, did not even notice that Rachel had changed affections and taken up with a different man. Clive Hirschhorn, arriving at the Central Park West apartment to do an interview, saw 'a good-looking young man' materialise in the living room. 'It had to be Darren Ramirez, I said. "My darling," said Rachel, "that's not Darren, that's Val. Valentine Mayer. He's a producer." I apologised for my *faux pas*, but Rachel just threw her head back and guffawed. "Never mind, sweetheart," she said. "They're both very attractive specimens, aren't they? I can see how you made the mistake."'

Valentine Mayer was indeed as good-looking as Darren, about the same build, wore his hair in much the same mop-topped way and was also at least ten years younger than Rachel. He worked as one of the stage managers during the run of the two plays. Rachel and he were instantly attracted; his Irish-American charm answering her own Celtic forwardness flash for flash. Rachel called him a 'chum', but their way of expressing affection was much more passionately conceived and, in this talented young man who shared her own appreciation of life and determination not to let a minute of it pass by unfilled with experience, whatever the painful aftermath, she found for a time the sort of robust satisfaction she had not hitherto known with the steadfast but less demonstrative Darren Ramirez. Darren took his banishment hard.

DARREN RAMIREZ: 'I suffered withdrawal symptoms and, to my surprise, felt quite depressed for a time. Although Rachel called me on average about twice a week – she never let go! – it just wasn't the same. Fortunately for me, Ned Sherrin came along. He was then – this was 1974 – getting into films with his partner Terry Glinwood – they produced several British comedies with Frankie Howerd. "Could I do anything?" I asked. "Come back to England," he said. And I did and stayed there, working, off and on, for the next year.'

Meanwhile, Rachel and what she called her 'new fella' lived the foot-loose, tempt-fate life much as she and Darren had done. She did *not* win a Tony for either of her Broadway roles – 'maybe the two cancelled each other out' – but, like Jack the cat, she dropped on her feet without any difficulty.

MILTON GOLDMAN: 'Rachel kept ringing me up, asking if all the producers and directors who might give her employment had seen *The Visit* and *Chemin de Fer*. Then she happened to read an article by Sidney Lumet in the Sunday edition of the *Times* in which he described his childhood days when he had been a boy actor. It obviously connected with Rachel. "He sounds a lovely man," she said. "How about him? Has he seen . . . etc., etc.?" I knew Sidney well and said I'd call him. Ten minutes later I was on the phone again to Rachel, asking her, "Can you do a German accent?" That's how she got to be among the all-star passengers in *Murder on the Orient Express*, the film that Sidney was set to direct in England in 1974.'

Rachel had decided that Agatha Christie's tale of murder in the locked *wagons-lits*, with its all-star cast of suspects whom Albert Finney's pocket detective Hercule Poirot worked over, scarcely needed her to go out and enrol again in a Berlitz course simply to be Dame Wendy Hiller's Teutonic travelling companion. There and then she devised a crash course in

German – and gave herself full marks. She simply remembered how Marlon Brando had sounded in *The Young Lions*, copied his accent, and tried it out on a tape recorder. Her 'Choiman' gutturals were beyond suspicion – and she took the accent over, unimpaired, to London and joined the cast a few weeks later at Easter-time, 1974.

It was twenty years since an attack of mumps had laid Wendy Hiller low when she was playing Emilia to Richard Burton's Othello – and her understudy, Rachel Roberts, had taken over. Now they were playing side by side.

It was the first time Rachel had worked with Vanessa Redgrave, an actress who combined a distinction worthy of the theatrical Establishment with, some of her critics said, a hard line in revolutionary politics somewhat tougher than the Bolsheviks. Rachel was never a 'politicised' performer: but she admired Vanessa's guts. Had Rachel been a Trotskyite, one gets the impression from what she told Clive Hirschhorn, she might have behaved like Vanessa.

'One day a group of us, including Sean Connery, Albie Finney, Richard Widmark, Michael York and Lauren Bacall, were rehearsing at the Carlton Tower Hotel – this being a big, expensive production, they'd taken the ballroom, if you please, for the rehearsals that Sidney Lumet always goes in for before we go before the cameras. On the dot of one o'clock, Vanessa told us all to stop work and take a full hour off for lunch. It was an Equity rule, had been fought for, and must be obeyed, she said. Well, Sean was most indignant. "We're not down a bloody salt mine," he said. "We don't need an hour for lunch." And Albie, in that North Country way of his, said, "Well, I don't know. I don't like having lunch when I'm working." But Vanessa was adamant. She asked me what I thought. I told her that if I wanted lunch, I'd have it – but that nobody could *order* me to have it, if I didn't want to. Anyway ... the point is, Vanessa displayed guts and courage. Some people might see it as sheer bloody stupidity, but I don't ... It's a typically English sort of courage. Foolhardy, maybe, but you have to admire it. It's the sort of determination that conquers nations.'

Sidney Lumet moved this glittering cast into the set at Elstree Studios. He was amused at the way Rachel would send her Teutonic character up rotten between takes, but always play for real and sink herself into the character the second he called for action. Only once did Rachel's guard drop, though Lumet was to recall it with embarrassment ten years later.

SIDNEY LUMET: 'It was 5.30 pm, and I'd dismissed the stars for the day – when suddenly I remembered a close-up of Rachel's we hadn't picked up. I desperately wanted it there and then: it was only a reaction shot – she wouldn't even be out of her make-up, I thought, as I had her called back ... Well, when she appeared, it was obvious we couldn't possibly shoot on her that day. She couldn't have had time for more than one drink at the bar, but she was already pretty hung-over. What was worse, she was deeply ashamed of having it revealed to me. What could I do, except pretend I didn't notice a thing wrong with her, apologise for a false alarm and arrange to pick up the close-up first thing next morning – when she was look- and letter-perfect.'

Darren was staying in Ned Sherrin's house – though he tactfully found a reason for leaving for the South of France when Rachel and Val arrived in London; and as she had let her Cambridge Street home to Bishop Muzorewa, whom the British Government was (vainly, as it turned out) backing to head a new Zimbabwe–Rhodesia Government, Rachel moved into the old block of service apartments in Hill Street, Mayfair. She and Val now virtually repeated the round of jet-set entertainment she had enjoyed a few years earlier with Darren. She plunged into a couple of plays that Harlech TV taped in Cardiff, playing a Welsh 'character', Old Olwen, in *Back of Beyond*, and then, in *Graceless Go I*, a psychiatrist's wife (her husband was Stanley Baker) who is crushed by sex, drugs and drink. She considered applying for American citizenship: but did nothing about it. And again she took the *Queen Elizabeth* back to New York, again first-class, again accompanied by her 'young man', and again writing to Jeffrey Lane a letter that, save for her now unblushing attitude to being seen in public with the youthful Val, might have been a carbon copy of her star-struck trip with youthful Darren a few years earlier:

'Dearest Jeffrey – It's absolutely SMASHING. It has been from the beginning. As we swept out of our Daimler (!) – on time, and looking lovely (I hope) – not one, but THREE people took expert charge of us, and we were whisked aboard . . . We had a mini-press conference with the assistant editor of the *Daily Express*, a very attractive man, except he *did* look as if it was a bit early for him! A rather serious young man (*Evening Standard*). The BBC (sound). Southern Television (a local station). And the show-business columnist from the local paper!

'Of course they were mainly interested in whether I was emigrating, marrying, and what age Val was!! He was very good, and said, "Old enough," and when asked to elaborate, said, "Oh, old enough for just about everything." And he got a laugh! What the result was, and if indeed we made the papers, I don't know, there being no Jeffrey the other end to check up! I always fear that I'll come out looking like the back of a bus – and sounding immoral or something – but that's just my guilt complex that I promised myself I would conquer when I finished reading *Portnoy's Complaint*.

'Henry Weinstein, the head cook and bottle-washer of the American Film Theater, came over and introduced himself to us at the Captain's party, and we had dinner with him last night. Afterwards, we went to the casino, and I felt sleepy, so went and had an early-ish night. Meanwhile, some time later, Val came back flushed with success, having just won $200!! How about that!

'I'm doing my desperate best not to eat and drink everything in sight and we've both gone to the sauna and the swimming pool and walked around the deck to keep trim, so we won't let you down in New York – but it's tough! You get such an enormous appetite at sea.

'Val sends great love. His tuxedo is stunning – and Great Love from me – Rachel.'

It sounded just like the old times, with a different travelling companion: but there was now a hyper-tenseness in Rachel's everyday attitude that made her friends uneasy. It communicated itself even to those who did not know her well. They admired her professionalism, but . . .

MICHAEL YORK: 'I played a fiery Hungarian count in *Murder on the Orient Express* – Jacqueline Bisset was my svelte countess. We never saw Rachel do a thing wrong – she was wonderful as the German travelling companion, precision-lipped, diligently pretending to read Goethe, never trying to dominate what was essentially an ensemble set-up. But the odd thing was, I never felt drawn to her. Quite the reverse. I can't pin it down, but some actor's instinct in me said, "Don't get too close to this woman, she's dangerous." It was just a feeling – no *reason* for it, except the wariness one learns from meeting certain types in life. God knows, though, she was generous to me and some months later called me to tell me that Peter Weir, the Australian who'd directed her in *Picnic at Hanging Rock*, was preparing a new film, an eerie apocalyptic piece set in modern Sydney but dealing with an aboriginal foreboding about a twentieth-century apocalypse. "Michael," she said on the phone, "the leading character's a young lawyer, *perfect* for you." But no one had heard of Australian cinema then, my agent pooh-poohed the notion – it became *The Last Wave* with Richard Chamberlain. Rachel's professional instinct for other people was so right – but so, I think, was mine about her.'

The fondness that Val Mayer and Rachel felt for each other was sometimes rowdily dissipated: both were headstrong people and, unlike Darren, Val could give as good as he got.

SYBIL CHRISTOPHER: 'There's a line in the film *Petulia* that comes into my mind when I think of them: "I took these beautiful hands and turned them into fists."Val adored Rachel, but he'd say to her when she gave him expensive presents, "Rachel, you're unmanning me."'

ANTHONY PAGE: 'Val and I gave her a party for her forty-seventh birthday, in September, 1974. It was a disaster. Rachel succeeded in saying something bitchy about almost everyone present, who included actors like John Guare and even friends like Marti Stevens and Sybil Christopher – she had to bring up Elizabeth Taylor in front of Sybil, who took it very well, I'm relieved to say – Karel Reisz she called something awful . . .'

KAREL REISZ: 'She'd had a bit too much to drink. One was prepared to humour her, but we had a tiff. But do you know, until I was reminded of it now, I had completely forgotten she called me "My little Jewish refugee from the gas chambers." I was very angry at the time: but later, I could see the state she was in. The party had been an attempt to bring together a very disparate set of people. Rachel had to hold them all together, misjudged it and, I'm afraid, made a fool of herself.'

ANTHONY PAGE: 'I wrote her a very long, reproving letter saying how worried I was at her carrying on like this. She took it to heart at first, I think, but soon she was turning the whole incident into a joke – that was Rachel's way of dealing with bad memories.'

JEFFREY LANE: 'She was always outspoken, and never really considered the effect her language might have. She'd say to me, "You little Jew – what do you know?" But it was in much the same way as she'd refer to herself as "a Welsh cow". She did get more impulsive than ever at this time. She was going through Los Angeles Customs on one of her trips back from England – as you know, they're pretty tough sometimes at that airport – and she intervened off her own bat when she thought a Customs officer was being officious towards a woman carrying a baby. "Let her through, she's had a long flight," Rachel ordered. "Lady," said the Customs man, who was a black, "we do things differently in this country and she doesn't belong here." Whereupon Rachel snapped back, "From the look of you, it isn't exactly your country, either!" Well, you know, when you're dependent on good will to earn your living, that isn't the most sensible way to treat authorities who can make things difficult for you. But that was the other side of Rachel's often impossible impulsiveness – springing to the defence of a total stranger, regardless of consequences to herself.'

Nineteen-seventy-four was the year of 'big money' for Rachel: in addition to *Murder on the Orient Express* and the two British TV plays, she crammed in a cameo as Miss Havisham in a *Great Expectations* special for an American network. All in all, she probably made the better part of $300,000. This, plus her alimony and the rent of £250–£300 a week she obtained from the Pimlico house (even though, when she got it back, it looked as if the furniture had been jumped on) allowed Rachel to indulge herself and buy the Central Park West apartment. When things were good between Val and herself, they were very good indeed.

JEFFREY LANE: 'She insisted on buying Val very expensive clothes; in return, he wrote poetry to her and she composed verses in praise of him. They spent money as fast as it came in, and it came in fast. They'd go off on adventures across town to places I'd never dare venture into alone – like the Bowery, where the two of them played a trick on me, taking off in the taxi, leaving me standing there with the sun going down and all kinds of terrors coming out of the shadows. I thought the end of my life had come. To them, it was a big joke. A way of living a heightened existence. When they turned on each other, as they sometimes did, being both high-tempered and passionate people, I felt it was Rachel's way of bringing down punishment on herself. Of course, she kept in touch with Darren, who, generally, took a benign view of it all once he'd got over his hurt feelings.'

Rachel wrote to Jeffrey Lane from Central Park West in mid-November, 1974:

'Dearest Jeffrey – Thanks to you, Paramount gave me a splendid private screening for *Murder on the Orient Express* for *sixty-nine* people, with drinks and *hors d'oeuvres* before AND after. Not even Sidney Lumet got that . . . Darren tells me you are in excellent form and he sounds pretty good himself, curls and all. *Great Expectations* is being networked next week and I find I've got billing though I didn't ask for it!! David Merrick is still interested in me for that play, but I'm more anxious to get Val's TV mystery on . . . They have approached me about starring in Pirandello's *Rules of the Game* – but I'm undecided . . . Lindsay Anderson and Tony Page will be coming to N.Y. early next month, so if I *don't* do *Rules of the Game*, those two, who are my favourite directors, will push me in the direction I should go, professionally speaking. I'm quite enjoying the sabbatical (if that's the right word).

'Val had to go to Boston last week-end, so Louis invited me to drive with him to Connecticut, to have dinner with Sandy Dennis, who is divine and has *twenty* cats. Her mother, who lives up the road from her, has *twenty-seven* cats!! I've seen a wonderful, self-contained, brownish-blackish-tortoiseshell lady-kitten called Valerie who, I think, I have to adopt. She is so poised and rather self-satisfied, with gold eyes. The sort of kitten who should wear spectacles!

'I've got to re-read *Rules of the Game* now and make up my mind. (What a bore! Wish we were all having a party!) – Rachel.'

Rachel drew back from doing the Pirandello play, but yet again her fear of being out of work proved groundless. A cable arrived from the playwright John Osborne. 'Come on, Rachel. Join us gypsies – we need you at Greenwich.'

The idea of appearing in Osborne's new play, *The End of Me Old Cigar*, which was to run for three-and-a-half weeks at Greenwich, on the River Thames, in early 1975, put the wind up Rachel. 'I went into a state of *terror*,' she told Michael Leech of the London *Times*, speaking 'with a wash of Welsh accents'.

'Osborne is so well read, a brilliant man, and I found myself terrified at all his knowledge . . . then I thought, "Come on, girl, get a little Welsh backbone; and whether I turn out to be good, bad or indifferent – at least it's been *fascinating*.' Because she was Welsh, she confessed, she liked a play, a non-political plea for women's liberation; it had *four* important female roles. One of them was played by Osborne's then wife, Jill Bennett.

JILL BENNETT: 'Rachel arrived a day late and a bit scared. That she liked being looked after was obvious. "Don't you miss the chauffeur-driven car?" I once asked her. "No," she said, "I miss the chauffeur." She quickly became one of my closest friends. She nicknamed me "Jello", because inside I was a wall-to-wall quivering mass. My name for her was "Palanca", which is Yiddish for "guts". When we first met, she said to me, "I'm Rachel Roberts." I didn't dare say, "I'm Jill Bennett," in case she said, "Who?" We were made for each other, as you can see. She read beautifully at the rehearsal, even though quaking inside: afterwards, we'd tea at the Dorchester – we both loved the best places! Before we'd finished tea I was accusing her of being like Hedda Gabler, parading her men in the last act.

'Although Rachel would accuse herself of not being domestic, she had a great capacity for putting everything in order. "I'm a clean middle-class slut," was how she'd describe herself. I'd give her the key of my little house off the King's Road, Chelsea, and when I'd come back everything would have been re-arranged, only much, much tidier.

'I'd say to her, "Rachel, you only half love yourself. You don't have to work all the time. You can be devoted to someone without being absorbed by them." But she had another thing in common with me. Though she worked hard, she was very dependent on a good director. She needed guidance. She fell in love with her director – almost a crush, it was. If she wasn't getting it, there was trouble. Lindsay Anderson, when we worked with him, was always making us go over our lines: which Rachel liked – the tender loving care thing, you see. She wasn't good at handling life on her own: I'm more adaptable. I'm more of a gypsy, but Rachel liked things to have a shape to them, she liked the menu written out.

'Of course we had our upsets – one famous one in particular. We were out on the town together. It was a dodgy evening from the start: for some reason we were both a bit on edge. We were in this nightclub place, Maunskberry's, in Jermyn Street. I had a friend with me who was black – "Black Eric", I called him. At one point, for no reason, probably just a joke on her part, Rachel called him a "black motherfucker", and before I knew what I was doing, I'd hit her a real hard clout. She pretended to burst into tears, but I could see no water coming from her eyes. Then we each abruptly left the table – Rachel, I think, fled into the kitchen – and exited the nightclub by separate taxis. Eric comforted me, as I think he felt he had to, though I could see he was taken by Rachel!'

JEFFREY LANE: 'Of course, no sooner had someone witnessed the scene than the papers were on to it. Rachel called me up in panic and tried to get me to stop it appearing. I said, "Rachel, if it's true and you behaved that way in public, you can't complain if it gets reported." But the next day I persuaded her to make her peace with Jill.'

JILL BENNETT: 'We all met up in the Dorchester for a reconciliation dinner. I took Lindsay Anderson. Rachel, loaded down with Bulgari jewellery, was with Darren. And Lindsay, to show his disapproval, made Rachel and all her bejewelled grandeur ride home in a bus.'

Darren Ramirez had planned to spend Christmas 1974 in Acapulco, in order to avoid running into Rachel in London. But a few days before her arrival, he fell on the stairs in Ned Sherrin's house where he was living and broke his left leg. This 'lucky' accident re-united them, though Rachel kept up her transatlantic calls to Val and returned to him in New York once the Osborne play was over in mid-February, 1975. But she had barely unpacked at Central Park West before another cable arrived. This one was from Australia.

'I'm going to Australia, Thursday, for two weeks,' Rachel wrote to Jeffrey Lane at the end of February, 'to do a movie called *Picnic at Hanging Rock*. Money's good and "Mrs Appleby" is a good part – so why not?'

A year or so later, the movie finished and exhibited at the Cannes Film Festival, Rachel could have added a third reason, not so obvious in 1975: *Picnic at Hanging Rock* was the film that put Australian movies on the international map. An eerie, 'atmospheric' piece, set in the State of Victoria, in 1900, it mysteriously crystallised the unseen apprehensions and latent longings of a group of politely reared, unusually refined schoolgirls, three of whom inexplicably disappear on a nature expedition to the ominously beckoning Hanging Rock. Peter Weir proved himself an Antipodean Antonioni in suggesting the fateful interlocking of people and particular places. Mrs Appleyard was the school's headmistress whose physical and spiritual disintegration seems to be triggered by the powers of primitive Australia that challenge her imported European sophistication. The executive producer of this film, a landmark in more than its title, was a successful and forceful Australian woman, Patricia (or Pat) Lovell:

PAT LOVELL: 'Rachel was an eleventh-hour, last-minute, SOS choice for the part. We'd cast Vivien Merchant just as her marriage to Harold Pinter started coming apart and only two weeks before shooting began, with all

An auburn-haired Rachel, starring in *Oh! My Papa!* in 1956, visits the fortune teller on Brighton Pier during the pre-London run of the musical to discover what her future holds.

Love scene with Albert Finney in the 1960 film *Saturday Night and Sunday Morning*: the straps of her slip provided 'a useful hint of modesty' in the censor's eyes.

Rachel in 1961, on the night she won the British Film Academy's 'Best Actress' award for *Saturday Night and Sunday Morning*.

As Anna Petrovna, with Rex, in *Platonov*. In the years to come, she would re-play their scenes in memory.

Fatal casting: Rachel and Rex Harrison (with Elvi Hale) meet to read the script of Chekhov's *Platonov* at the Royal Court in September 1960: 'His vitality energised me.'

Portofino, 1961: not yet married to each other, but (as the tactful news caption put it) 'firm friends'. Rachel wrote: 'We were together all the time. Ease entered my life.'

Rome, 1962. Already tasting life as 'the future Mrs Rex Harrison,' Rachel arrives with her husband-to-be, then playing Julius Caesar in *Cleopatra*, at their rented Roman villa.

Genoa City Hall, March 21, 1962.
After a 'closed door' marriage, the
newly-weds manage a smile for their
*paparazzi* persecutors . . .

. . . then it was a race back to
Portofino (*above right*) and a
scramble into the wedding
'limousine', Rex's battered Jeep, for
the last lap up the mule track to the
Villa San Genesio.

Walking through the Port with
Homer the basset hound, outwardly
happy, but inwardly 'groping for an
idealised form of life and riddled
with self-doubts.'

London, 1964, as Lionel Bart's 'monumental whore', Maggie May

A hug and congratulations for 'Maggie May' from a first-night celebrity: Judy Garland had less than five years left of her own life.

Italian Riviera, circa 1965: idyllic landscape with figures and limousine, but the 'feeling of being stifled' had started, soon would follow a suicide attempt.

Paris, 1967. Rachel and Rex (disguised as a low-life hotel porter) filming *A Flea in Her Ear* and trying to hold together a disintegrating marriage.

contracts signed, investments firmed and reputations on the line, Vivien withdrew – too distressed, she told us, to come and play the part. Hal and Jim McElroy, the producers, mentioned Rachel. "An utterly different kind of actress," I told them, "but I've never seen her give a bad performance." We couriered the script to her: within days, she'd made up her mind. I welcomed her at the airport. "What does she look like?" Jim McElroy asked on the line. "She looks like she eats little boys for breakfast," I told him.

'Talk about a shock for Peter Weir! I mean, Vivien and Rachel couldn't have been more different. Peter had seen Vivien as dark and withdrawn and mysterious, her very Englishness an evil factor in the mysterious happenings. And here was this great Welsh pouter pigeon turning up. She'd even brought along her own wig, a huge creation which was absolutely all wrong!'

PETER WEIR: 'I can understand the wig "thing". Actors are a superstitious tribe. And one of the well-known "curses" is wearing a wig intended for someone else, especially if the original wearer's suffered some misfortune. But Rachel's notion of a Victorian headmistress's wig was a bit outrageous all the same.'

A history could be written of Rachel's different wigs at various times in her life. On one occasion, when she was preparing herself to appear on *The David Frost Show*, Lindsay Anderson caught her wearing a wig hanging down round her like a blonde octopus. 'I'd be frightened to go on without it,' she protested. 'Has it ever struck you,' Anderson said severely, 'that you might frighten *them* even more with it?'

PETER WEIR: 'We managed to reduce the wig's dimensions, but there still remained the problem of characterisation. I had to wrench my concept of the part from that of a woman entrenched in her cultural vanity, which was to be Vivien, round to that of a woman destroyed by inebriation and failure of will.'

PAT LOVELL: 'Peter was white by the end of the first day's shooting. The McElroys felt Rachel was wildly overacting, treating the schoolgirls' disappearance like the death of Little Nell in *The Old Curiosity Shop*. But Peter assured them it would cut together. Film is a funny thing – at the end, it looked a very good and original performance.

'I found her presence growing on me as Vivien Merchant faded out of mind. But I didn't know from one day to the next what she'd be like. The only constant thing about her was the attention she needed – like her drinking, attention was essential. When she was around, you knew it. She stayed at a motel near Adelaide, in the bridal suite. Don Dunstan, the Premier of Southern Australia, gave a party for the film and Rachel insistently called him "Mr President" in a very loud voice. She went on and on about her Celtic origins. "Rachel, dear," I'd say, "no need to tell us where *you've* come from – it's obvious." She knew she was being outrageous, and enjoyed it. She appeared at the door of the motel one night, stark naked, calling "Goodnight" to everyone across the courtyard. She always insisted on a first-class ticket and on air trips would order gins, even though it was only an hour's flight to location. She looked a million dollars even if it was a slightly incongruous ensemble that carried that price tag, like a halter-neck top worn with slacks and a huge and luxurious fur coat on top. She certainly stood out from the rest of us in our dirty jeans, denim tops and clip-boards. Her sexual mischievousness was a way of drawing attention to herself. One time I called a wardrobe girl up to sit beside me while we went over some point or other. As soon as she sat down, and she was a very pretty girl, Rachel across the aisle started winking at her and beckoning to her and saying, "Hello, sweetheart . . . Hello, darling." At work, though, an utter pro.'

PETER WEIR: 'An odd thing happened one day. We were having a drink in a bar after work. Suddenly this man comes in. Rachel takes one look at him and then they both run at each other and fall into their arms, Rachel babbling in Welsh. The guy was an old flame of hers she'd known at Stratford-upon-Avon, who'd once asked her to marry him. Now he was a doctor in Melbourne.'

PAT LOVELL: 'Once when the plane was taking off and we were tightening our seat belts, she looked at me and said, "You need a young lover, Pat. We've both been married to older men. Take my tip, the twenty-six-year-olds are the best." I thought of myself at my age, with my children nearly grown up, and said I couldn't visualise throwing myself casually on to a twenty-six-year-old. She said, "You're a very determined woman, Pat, like someone else I know – Pamela Mason." Shortly afterwards we had lunch at Peter Weir's place beside the ocean, at Palm Beach, and she turned up – with a twenty-six-year-old! An actor: I've forgotten his name.

'She'd become much quieter. In fact, she seemed very sad, perhaps because she'd enjoyed our company – she never treated us as "colonials", and, in retrospect, I think our outward-giving ways helped stabilise something in her. But even at that time there was a sense of wishful mortality about her.

'She took her money – she was paid about US$9,500 for two weeks' work – and left us just as she'd come. I said to my daughter, "Something tells me I'm not going to see Rachel again."'


After the debacle on *The Russell Harty Show*, my luck and illusion still held and off to Broadway I went, renting Sir John Gielgud's apartment on Central Park West. Darren had the choice of remaining in London or accompanying me – and chose New York. But no sooner was I there than I called maniacally for Paul [former lover from Los Angeles] – through the black maid we had. Paul – whom I saw in the supermarket recently and thought him now to be a ridiculous, conceited, swaggering, rather cheap man. I was to do two plays on Broadway, *The Visit* and *Chemin de Fer* – this was at the end of 1973. I worked hard on the role of Clara Zachanassian in the first, on Francine in the other, but queened it in the bar with Stephen Porter [stage director of *Chemin de Fer*], ate up flattery – and then saw Val. Wanted him.

I didn't go to Sardi's after the opening night but, after the dressing room crowd had left me, traipsed down to the Lower East Side. Excitement at all costs! I loved the Lower East Side. I loved having sex and drinking. I loved Valentine. Ungovernable and out of control, I railed against the director whose name right now I can't remember, so poisoned is my mind – poisoned with the memories of my own self-destructive path. Sybil, in control, telephoned me – to tell me to pull myself together. I loved Val, out on the town, both of us in high spirits, coming home to Central Park West and his sexiness, was actually proud of him. I called Milton Goldman, who headed my agency in New York, and got a job in *Murder on the Orient Express* which Sidney Lumet was directing in London. Drunken times over there, and worse...I was still not seeing where I was going. Little intimations came, like not being invited to Sidney Lumet's party—or not seeing that beautiful and controlled Jacqueline Bisset and I were very removed from each other.

Val and I lived in about four or five different apartments. Several times he flew off, after a riotous spree, back to New York, but came back. I got a part in the television play *Back of Beyond*. I was still caught up in my own fiction – I was the 'star' playing Old Olwen, asking Desmond Davis [film and TV director] if Val could assist. He was as caught up, I thought then, as I was in the fiction. We sailed back first-class in the *Queen Elizabeth*, dining by the port-hole. I remained in my own mind the seductive, gifted actress able to attract men – he was nearly twenty years younger than I.

The helpful Nina Cameron saw that we were off the liner very nearly first. Friends were there to greet us. We had Champagne on the terrace at Central Park West. After a bit, reality struck and I went back to London to do the John Osborne play *The End of Me Old Cigar* – this must have been at the end of 1974. But no sooner in rehearsals at Greenwich than I tried getting one of the actors into bed, and failed. I quarrelled with Val over transatlantic telephone calls – really lost my temper with him. Yet when we went to '21' to drink vodka and dine and I saw Rex with his new wife Elizabeth at the VIP table, we joined them – I bright and smiling with a handsome young man in tow. *I didn't want Rex* – was what I was saying. I flew off as a replacement for the suffering Vivien Merchant in the Australian film *Picnic at Hanging Rock* and met up with an old flame, but flew back to Val. Had I seen it, reality was coming closer – but I didn't see it.

---

RACHEL RETURNED TO NEW YORK in mid-March, 1975, still elated by filming in unfamiliar Australia. Val was impatiently awaiting her and delighted to see her look so 'vital'. But soon enough, an opposite reaction set in. She became tired, bored and restless. There was talk of taking a place for the summer on one of the islands off Maine: Val thought the sea air was what she needed.

From time to time, Rex came to town. By then, his marriage to Elizabeth Harris was nearing its end and he, too, was restless, fretting over what to do next.

ANTHONY PAGE: 'He and Rachel would meet for lunch. Rex was disturbed to see how much she was drinking and did his best to discourage her. But her habit led to a "typical Rachel" situation. She'd been up to see Rex in his hotel and he was leaving for somewhere or other. Feeling sleepy after lunch, she lay down in the bedroom after Rex had gone, and went to sleep. The next thing she heard, was someone opening the door of the suite. The maid! Rachel suddenly took it into her head that she must on no account be seen in the bedroom. It would look bad with Rex in the middle of a divorce. It might get into the papers. All her Welsh "correctness" overcame her and she managed to slip out somehow, charged down the hotel's back stairs – the suite was only on the fifth floor – and when she opened a side door to get out, it was the wrong one – and off went the alarm bell! She gabbled something about there being a fire – and fled down the street.'

Such Feydeau-esque exits were always good for a laugh but by-play like this did not fill the day. Rachel hankered after work, partly to stretch her talent, partly to maintain her public profile. She heard that Harold Prince was toying with staging some of the playlets which Noël Coward had written under the umbrella title *Tonight at 8.30.*

HAL PRINCE: 'Rachel wanted a singing role in some of them. The trouble was, she was not quite good enough. She could bark all right, but she couldn't sing. She was taken by *We Were Dancing*, *Red Peppers* and *Shadow Play*, but these playlets require much more *precise* singing than she could manage. The sound had to be expressive of the period in which they were set.

'But she *was* very fixed on a singing role at this time. Indeed I remember one evening in which three female stars, Stephen Sondheim and myself were in my apartment, and each woman wanted what the other was doing. Glynis Johns was in the Broadway production of *A Little Night Music*, Jean Simmons was in the touring production, and nothing would satisfy Rachel Roberts until she sang "Send in the Clowns" in front of Stephen Sondheim, who'd written it, and the other two ladies, who were performing it. Now to do that, you have to have *chutzpah*, or be drunk.'

DARREN RAMIREZ: 'In the fall of 1975, I was still living in London, designing some of the costumes for Ned Sherrin's film productions. Suddenly, one morning at 4.00 am, the phone rings: it couldn't be anyone else but Rachel at that time. She was crying and in need of help. She was just starting a tour of the play *Habeas Corpus*, and in a jangle of nerves. I got the next possible flight to New York: I'm still amazed at the control she had over me – she was alone again, as she and Val had had a bust-up. I didn't even stop over in New York, but caught the Amtrak train to Boston and spent the next two days with her. She was staying at the Ritz-Carlton – she always considered it her due as a star to live like a rich woman. But there was a change in her I hadn't seen before – she was neurotically worried about money. "Rachel," I said, "your trouble is not making money. You've plenty. Your trouble is knowing what to do with what you have!" Good heavens, the money was rolling in – every *Habeas Corpus* performance was a sell-out.'

*Habeas Corpus*, written by the English satirist Alan Bennett and directed by Frank Dunlop, was a surrealist comedy – the Magritte-like theatre curtain displaying a typical English gent in bowler hat and mackintosh, but wearing a bra, was emblematic of the absurd goings-on in a very 'correct' English doctor's South Coast surgery where sex was forever rearing its funny head.

Rachel played the doctor's well-endowed wife; Jean Marsh was a flat-chested spinster who had sent off for a pair of mail-order 'falsies'; Richard Gere was the salesman who arrived to adjust them and, of course, mistook the naturally bosomy Rachel for the after-treatment Jean.

JEAN MARSH: 'We had a great time together on *Habeas Corpus*. Rachel's work was immaculate, scrupulous, detailed. She took endless pains – I remember her saying two or three times, "Am I taking up too much rehearsal time?" Once she'd got it, she repeated it perfectly, every performance. Her "precision", that's the quality I'd put my finger on. There was one Noël Coward-like scene between Rachel and her husband, played by Donald Sinden. Instead of doing it naturalistically – her usual way – Rachel played it full-face to the audience, laying down the rules for a successful marriage with a vibrant command of *"You will . . ."* to Sinden, drinking tea at the same time, with cup poised and little finger elevated in exceedingly genteel contrast to the dragon-like edicts issuing from her lips.

'Actors have an "in group" habit of picking up lines from scenes that play memorably well in a show and repeating them to each other in off-stage situations. *Habeas Corpus* had several things like this, in every instance they were lines of Rachel's – *she* had made them memorable.

'Her scene with Richard Gere, as the man from the "falsies" company who follows up sales, was one of the best in the play and the most intimate. I'm actually the purchaser, but when Richard enters and sees full-bosomed Rachel he advances with yelps of delight at the effect he attributes to the product, and starts feeling her boobs – "Oh, wonderful!" It was very physical and flirtatious, which is why Rachel liked it so much. But it had to be carefully done, otherwise the audience might feel itself being manipulated as indecorously as the falsies. Rachel's reaction is to be thrilled by this handsome man feeling her so intimately and boldly – then I come downstairs with my falsies on back to front and he realises his mistake.'

RICHARD GERE: 'I think of Rachel like a child. She never hurt anyone. She had no sense of consequence. And though she suffered for it, everything to her was "drama". Crazy though she was, she stayed within the bounds of loveableness. She'd try anything – that was another endearing aspect of her.'

'She was all too briefly a comedienne, but our incredibly farcical scene in *Habeas Corpus* gave her a real comic kick, just arranging those tits. She was giggling all the time.

'I was just a kid then, and she was extremely generous to me in terms of stage technique. We'd kid about beforehand, discuss what we intended doing on stage, then Rachel would always have these good little ideas for varying and improving our performance together. As for her habit of stripping her clothes off in order to "make" a man, my God, I know plenty of actresses who exist on that level *only*. With Rachel, that kind of sexy by-play was all part and parcel of the drama she made around her. She liked being outrageous and stripping off is as good a short-cut as any. She was a real drama queen, tough as they come, and yet I always sensed something fragile about her, tensed up, ready to snap.'

*Habeas Corpus* opened at the Martin Beck Theater, New York, on November 24, 1975, and had a hugely successful run. Almost every one of the cast collected bouquets of notices: Rachel, in particular.

'She is the very essence of Thurberian Woman,' Howard Kissel wrote in *The Christian Science Monitor*, 'that ominous presence looming over the house, a fearful specter to her husband nervously making his way home from work.'

Walter Kerr, in the *Times*, relished her 'fancying herself as lithe as a panther . . . while advancing like an armored tank'. To Clive Barnes, in the same newspaper, she was a comic delight, 'weighing her words like hand grenades . . . her glances like searchlights . . . sailing full-scud through the menopause'. 'The cast act as if they are on speed,' said Gina Mallet in *Time*. 'Rachel Roberts' impression of [the wife's] well-bred façade to exigent desire fills the stage with the cheery sensuality of old-time British music-hall.'

They were the best notices Rachel ever got; and it may be that their universal and rarely qualified praise propelled her even more purposefully along that deceptive path that seems to be a continuation of the road to success, but, in fact, proves to be a detour (a fatal one in Rachel's case) into the state of self-delusion that goes by the name of celebrity.

V al was working: I wasn't. I saw Rex and got drunk in his suite at the Regency Hotel and had to leave by the back stairs and ring the alarm bell in order to save my face – luckily they bought my unlikely story of a fire on the fifth floor.

I got so drunk at the birthday party which Tony and Val gave for me at Angelo's that I don't remember it. Don't remember calling Karel Reisz 'my little refugee from the gas chamber'. Don't remember bringing up Elizabeth Taylor and Burton flauntingly to Sybil and her husband Jordan. But I remember the other party years before when Taylor and Burton were making *Cleopatra* – I couldn't go near the set until I'd finished *This Sporting Life*, so inferior did I feel, or even to one of their parties. But when I did go, I basked a lot, spoke in a Welsh-ified way to an offended Burton and told Sybil that she looked more like his mistress than his wife – it didn't go down too well, I recall. But I was then with Rex the all-powerful. I could be all-powerful, too.

After my birthday party, Val said he wasn't coming back – though he wanted to – and I woke up alone. Sybil called up for 'our friendship's sake', and I downed several brandies and did an interview with the *Village Voice*.

I did the play *Habeas Corpus* and tried to make Richard Gere by the simple expedient of, drunk, taking off my clothes and lying on his bed. But I was good on stage in the play.

Whenever I act well, my head clears. Always a bit frail I was personally, but never professionally. Acting well helps to exorcise the things that, unconsciously, were done to me after my meeting with Rex and my introduction to that nonsensical, cold and insane world of big 'stars' and false values. I remember how instinct screamed within me that my film *This Sporting Life* was superior to any of the razzmatazz going on in Rome, but surrounded as I was with the 'World's Favourites', among them my own husband, it was hard to believe my solitary instincts, outnumbered as I was – although I will always treasure the memory of Rex's forlorn longing to be in 'Eric's boots' and not the leading participant in 'Reggie's Triumphal Entry into Rome'.

---

DARREN RAMIREZ: 'While Rachel was doing *Habeas Corpus*, I was back in Los Angeles – and deciding to make a break with my California life-style. I'd sold my Mulholland Drive house and invested in units in an apartment block. But I decided I could never live in an apartment. So I brought a house, 2620 Hutton Drive. It was unpretentious, but comfortable. There was a front garden and a back yard, space for a dog, secluded yet neighbourly, not too far from work in Beverly Hills, but not too close to be caught up in a life-style that was attractive but sometimes "too much". It was a home and a refuge.

'One day Rachel called from the Carlyle in New York. Great excitement! She told me Tony Randall had caught her performance in *Habeas Corpus* and offered her the leading-lady part in a sit-com series on TV after they'd successfully sold the pilot in New York. Now she told me that she'd never really believed in her earlier film and stage achievements. She didn't any longer want to be "Rachel Roberts – distinguished actress". She wanted to be "Rachel Roberts – celebrity". *The Tony Randall Show* was to be filmed in California and as soon as she could get out of the play she was coming there, too. I knew she was still seeing Val in New York, though I heard they were having rows. Now she would have me. Two young loves on different coasts: it was like a film scenario!'

TONY RANDALL: '*The Tony Randall Show* was a situation comedy: each segment was set in the household and the courtroom of a judge. I played His Honour. We showed the judge with his shoes off, his relations with his children (he's a widower) and his fusspot housekeeper: then we showed the man with the robes of authority on him. It took months to work it all out and get Tom Patchett and Jay Tarses to write it: then when Rachel's name was proposed by Milton Goldman, and I'd caught her play, and she'd indicated she was willing and would be available, we had to rewrite it again as we hadn't thought of an *English* housekeeper!

'I'd first met Rachel some years before, at a party at Woburn Abbey, in England, given by the Duke and Duchess of Bedford. She was quiet then, even subdued. She talked about her first marriage to Alan Dobie, whom she called very sweet, and then to Rex, which I gathered was a bit more stormy and, she said, had once resulted in a row early on in it, with her exiting and her new husband rushing after her crying, "Wait a minute, Ruth ... er, Rita ... Oh hell! What *is* it!" Rather like a sitcom scene!

'I was delighted to get her for the show. She was now a big name. But I could see what was in her mind when she said she wanted to do it. She was saying to herself, "It'll do a lot for my career. It'll be seen by millions. It'll be a big hit." It's the way every player does who begins a television series. "Here is security and money and exposure – what can be bad about that?"

And well rewarded Rachel certainly was. She was to get $5,000 a week for a twenty-two-week show in the first year; in the second, she was up to over $9,000 a week. A lot of money then. As for the rest, it wasn't her fault if it didn't work out the way she imagined – though she certainly got fair warning from me and the writers.'

TOM PATCHETT: 'Jay Tarses and I were very surprised when Rachel said she wanted to be in the show we were writing for Tony. We had our doubts. I mean, a distinguished stage actress, a screen star, twice a Tony nominee taking a supporting role in a TV sitcom show . . . ? We didn't want any unhappiness manifesting itself in Rachel at doing a part that was beneath her customary challenge or by reason of the show's repetitive format. Indeed when we met, we tried to discourage her by spelling out the downside of the job. To be frank with you, we didn't feel she would be satisfied for long.'

DARREN RAMIREZ: '*The Tony Randall Show* was a Grant Tinker–Mary Tyler Moore production filmed in the Valley, at Studio City. When Rachel arrived in California, I'd found an apartment on Sunset Boulevard and furnished it with sheets, plants, china, pictures, etc., and she started filming. We'd meet after filming and have dinner. But as time went on, she began hating her apartment and spending more and more time in my house on Hutton Drive. She'd stay overnight. In the morning I'd drive her to the set at Studio City. Very soon she was referring to the apartment as "that hole in a cement block". To all intents, she was back with me. So I said to her it would be nice if she pitched in and shared expense. I'd invested $60–70,000 in the house: she put in a tax rebate she'd got of $10,000 and undertook to meet the mortgage payments, which came to round about what she'd been paying to rent her apartment. All went well on the TV show, for a time.'

TOM PATCHETT: 'When we got to know Rachel and see how she fitted into the format, we co-opted some of her characteristics into the character she played. We gave the judge's housekeeper more authority, made her more of an adversary-figure for Tony.'

TONY RANDALL: 'She often spoke about Rex. It seemed to me that they talked frequently, every day if one believed Rachel. They seemed great pals.
'Rex came to see the show recorded one day and expressed amazement that we could do a segment in five days (four days, really, to get it together, a fifth to record it). We used a live audience and as we didn't use tape in those days, the cameras had only eight or nine minutes of film at a time and it means the action was always coming to a halt. "How *do* you keep your concentration, old man?" Rex would ask. Just before we recorded the show, we'd all line up in front of the studio audience and take a bow and I'd do a spiel with them for about ten minutes. That shocked Rex. "How *can* you do it?" he kept asking. I said it was good for me: it got rid of my nerves. It worked Rachel up to pitch, too. She and I would joke and horse around often very ribaldly just before we went on in front of the audience and the cameras – I'd rib her, she'd goose me. Rex was left rubbing his eyes.'

TOM PATCHETT: 'I was surprised at Rachel's lack of self-confidence off the set. She said to me on one occasion, "You're one of the most intimidating people I've ever met. You come down on stage when we're shooting the show and I feel you're looking straight through me." The truth was, I was in awe of her and her capacities: she was frightened of me and my talents! I concluded she wasn't a very secure person, possibly an unhappy one, too – not that I saw much of her socially. On the days when Rex or Lindsay Anderson or her other friends came on the set, she'd perk up. But there was a deep dissatisfaction in her somewhere, showing itself in irritability, especially at American things. The way we made tea, for instance. "Don't you know the water has to be boiling hot, you asshole?" she'd say.'

TONY RANDALL: 'I can honestly say I never saw her "other" side. People in New York would say to me, "Is she behaving herself?" And I'd say "Yes", and wonder what they were getting at. If anyone had told me she was wild and ungovernable and hooked on alcohol, I simply wouldn't have been able to reconcile that with the woman who played in the show with me for two years.

'But looking back, I can see some things made me uneasy. For example, I could never have a conversation with Rachel. You would say that you admired, say, an actor like Paul Rogers and hope she would tell you something of interest about him. But every time, whatever the subject, she'd always bring the conversation back to herself.

'Another thing that made me uneasy – she covered every inch of her dressing-room walls with drawings, and all of them were of *cats*. Everywhere you looked, nothing but *cats*!

'Another odd thing. I kept a diary of the show and I recall that one day I wrote down, without now being able to recall why, "Rachel Roberts is *crazy!*"

'We began *The Tony Randall Show* with the ABC network. They dropped it at the end of its first year; although we had gotten good notices, we didn't get good ratings. Then, to my surprise, CBS picked it up – it's most rare for one network to pick up what another's dropped – and we began a second year.

'It's my experience you don't really know what you've got in such a show until the second year. We found out, and it didn't turn out to Rachel's advantage.'

TOM PATCHETT: 'We were already finding in the first series that we couldn't use her to full advantage. A lot of the action took place in the judge's chambers, where Allyn McLerie played his secretary. We found it hard to get Rachel's character out of the judge's home and into another location or area of comic activity.'

TONY RANDALL: 'Slowly it dawned on Rachel that the episodes in the judge's home were not as effective or funny as the ones elsewhere, and there was simply nothing she could do about it. She got angrier and angrier.'

TOM PATCHETT: 'The only alterations she attempted in the script were those that any intelligent actress might make. You know, "My character wouldn't do this. My character wouldn't say that." We listened and we adjusted it where we could: we never actually came to loggerheads. But she couldn't any longer hide her disappointment with the finite nature of the role she was playing.'

TONY RANDALL: 'I don't blame her: anyone would be depressed. At the end of the first year, she could practically have telephoned her part in. She got to be less co-operative in the second year and more peremptory. Again, I don't blame her: I could understand – it wasn't the first time I'd seen things get that way.

'I will say this, though, never at any time while rehearsing or recording the show did I see her less than stone cold sober. In two years and forty-four segments, I don't recall her blowing a line. Everyone else did, at least once. I thought I was pretty good, I seldom blew one. Rachel never did. However, occasionally, when work was over she'd have a glass of wine and this would have a *terrible* effect on her. It was obvious to everyone that she couldn't drink. One glass altered her personality: she'd become angry and even abusive. Not that such a reaction was a surprise to me – I've seen it in other players, particularly women. But as a professional, Rachel was wonderful, just wonderful!'

TOM PATCHETT: 'After the show came to an end in 1977, she went into a film, *Foul Play*, with Chevy Chase and Goldie Hawn. I saw her having what looked like quite a few tough scraps in it with Burgess Meredith, and I said to myself, "This lady could have been a lot of trouble to us."'

*Foul Play*, a comedy-melodrama more half-cock than Hitchcock, written and directed by Colin Higgins, did nothing for Rachel, except fill up empty time in a well-paid, dramatically unrewarding way as a German-accented 'hit' lady involved in a plot to assassinate the Pope at a performance of *The Mikado* in San Francisco. She confessed that she enjoyed letting loose her 'pent-up feelings': that was about all she can have enjoyed.

TOM PATCHETT: 'I didn't see her again more than once – but that occasion was one I'll never forget. It was in New York. She was standing on a corner with a woman companion waiting to cross on the lights. She looked different. She looked like a zombie, or a woman waiting for the fog to clear and let her take a step ahead. I felt compelled to re-introduce myself. To make her feel more comfortable. For there was a flash of non-recognition in her eye, a signal that said, "My God, I ought to know this person!" I liked her as a person and always felt she wanted to get closer to me when we worked together. But when I saw her in New York, it was like looking into a well – My God, this thing is bottomless!'

Jean Marsh felt that *The Tony Randall Show*, despite its limitations, restored to Rachel the feeling of being part of 'a family'.

JEAN MARSH: 'She liked the family feeling that came with official feast days like Thanksgiving, etc. when she could cook up a banquet and so bring her friends together. Even getting up in the morning and having Darren take her to work was, for her, like returning to a family – I think that's why she stuck it so long.'

JEFFREY LANE: 'Even when she had no home of her own, she'd behave as if she had. One Christmas, I remember, she was staying at the Beverly Wilshire Hotel – it was when she and Darren had temporarily split up and he was in New York. She couldn't drive then and I didn't dare trust myself to Los Angeles traffic. So we hired a cab, drove to Hughes Supermarket, facing Chasen's, and in spite of the bright sun and hot weather started buying all the traditional goodies we could find to go with Christmas dinner – the turkey, brussels sprouts, mincemeat, sausages, and so on. Then we went to the Daisy on Rodeo Drive for a drink or two, back to the Bev Wilsh for a few more drinks in El Padrino, and finally wound up standing on the corner at Wilshire and Rodeo with a hat at our feet, singing Christmas carols to passing motorists as the sun went down.'

Re-creating family life was one thing: living in a domestic set-up was quite another – it did not bring out the same sentimental hankering to belong. Throughout 1977, Rachel's behaviour established an increasingly worrying pattern.

DARREN RAMIREZ: 'She didn't want to stay put in Hutton Drive, even though she now looked on it as home. She'd take a notion into her head to fly off to New York, find she couldn't stick it there after two or three days, fly back and get drunk and start taking the house apart.'

JEFFREY LANE: 'Darren had put together the Hutton Place house and it reflected his tastes. Rachel could be a very perverse lady and sometimes do things simply to annoy or aggravate, like changing all the light bulbs in the house so as to ruin Darren's well thought-out lighting plan.'

DARREN RAMIREZ: 'We'd have blazing rows. In the middle of one, a call came from my sister in Mexico. My father was dying. Rachel calmed down at once. She so wanted to be part of everything that she said, "Don't go to Mexico tonight, go tomorrow and then I can come with you." Other people's suffering seemed to trigger off her compassionate urge. We went down to my hometown, Morelia, and spent about five days there and Rachel was wonderful, sitting alongside my father as he died. Her own mother had died while she was in the Hal Prince play in New York and this had added to the guilt she felt. Probably the death of one of my parents was a kind of catharsis – now she could be of help. She got on well with all my family.
'I was glad when people came to stay. They had a soothing effect on Rachel. Lindsay Anderson came as a house guest. But Rachel's neurosis was now so strong that he saw her in her "true colours" for the first time. Her "good manners" faltered after a couple of days and on the third day we had another of our blazing rows. Rachel was as appalled as Lindsay was by what had been revealed. You see, she went in awe of him, for he *judged* her.'

After *Habeas Corpus*, another lucky break – or so it seemed. Actually it turned out my most hateful and humiliating job, degrading and upsetting. I was signed for *The Tony Randall Show* on television. I had my eyes done, stayed at the Cavalier Motel, saw Darren again – was on a high. I really thought I'd be another Lucille Ball and become a household name. Reality came creeping ever closer, but unnoticed or repressed by me. I began to discern that Tom Patchett who was one of the two writers, didn't see me as sexy Rachel at all. I was fat then. Next I got drunk at my birthday party and told Tony Randall he didn't faze me one bit, that I'd lived with a man like him – i.e. Rex – except that the man was a better actor and taller. I bounded on to the set the next day and called out, 'Good morning – Rex.' Still oblivious of the reality of the situation. When Rex came to visit me on the set, I glowed. I maniacally drew puss-cats on my dressing-room walls – left them covered in cat-graffiti. I flew back and forth to New York and furnished my apartment with the help of Jack Stark [New York interior designer]. I was seen by an ever increasingly hostile Val. I always travelled first-class. Why not? – I was earning big money, wasn't I? At Los Angeles, I was always met by Darren. I liked my little apartment off the Strip, without a television, taking the celebrity cabs that the company sent round daily to bring me to work, seeing Darren. Rex stayed the night once. We went to have a bloody Mary at the Cock and Bull and walked down Sunset Strip – Rex was then making his advertisement for automobiles. I got drunk with him and walked in floods of tears back to my apartment. I called him the next morning to apologise and asked him to stay over one night more. He agreed.

His chauffeur came to collect me and together we drove to Venice on the California coast and looked at the cats. I stayed the night. I remember the expression on his face very well when he drove off the next morning and Darren and I waved him good-bye. There was superficial talk of going back to each other. That Christmas, 1976, I spent with him – back to trees and cooking a turkey and walks, and calves' liver for Rosie the cat and tending to Rex. Then I went back to Los Angeles and *The Tony Randall Show*.

I still clung on to Val. But the day I called him to end it, I called Rex. By then, though, he had met Mercia and the icy voice said, 'Tell her we're not at home,' but the operator mistook the advice and put him on the line. I reminded him about his invitation to go to the South of France – as I recall it, he said something about there being room in the attic. I told him my days of staying in other people's attics were over. It was understandable, Rex's attitude, I suppose. By then he'd met the woman who was to become his future wife.

I phoned Darren in Los Angeles and told him I'd come in on the house he wanted to buy. I'd just had a $10,000 tax rebate. Into a little house on Hutton Drive it went.

That year, 1977, was to be awful for me. By now I hated *The Tony Randall Show*. I got drunk more and more, and my part in the show got smaller and smaller. I had to be brought home on several occasions. I was warned by Lindsay Anderson that drinking could only lead to more drastic unhappiness – in so many words – but that I also still had the wherewithal to make something of my life.

RACHEL SPENT CHRISTMAS, 1977, in Los Angeles, feeling increasingly and desperately frustrated. But once again, Lindsay Anderson came to the (temporary) rescue by offering her a role in Alan Bennett's new TV film, *The Old Crowd*, which he was to direct in February, 1978, in London. To her pleasure, it meant acting with Jill Bennett again.

JILL BENNETT: 'She did *The Old Crowd* without knowing anything about it except that Alan had written it and Lindsay was directing it. We all liked Lindsay so much – I turned down a West End play in order to do the film with him. None of us read the script much in advance – Rachel only when she was coming over in the plane. But that was Lindsay all over. He had confidence in himself, so we had confidence in him. It's when some director *pleads* with you to "Trust me" that I know I'm in the shit – that was Rachel's view of things, too.'

' "Look at those two. They're like a married couple. I feel like a distraught mistress from the Midlands." Miss Jill Bennett . . . was referring to Rachel Roberts and Lindsay Anderson having a cosy argument in a corner of a cavernous drill hall in Bloomsbury.' Thus Sydney Edwards, of London's *Evening Standard*, witnessed the reunion during rehearsals of *The Old Crowd*. His account nicely encapsulated the affinity between Rachel and the woman who stood by her to the end among the dwindling number of really close friends she trusted.

'Miss Roberts has returned after a long absence in America. She remains as cooing Welsh as ever. "Darling, I've been making this sitcom television series with Tony Randall. It's been well paid full stop. Nothing else to say about it."

'. . . I said how different they were – Miss Roberts warm and friendly, Miss Bennett a stylish sufferer in silence.

' "Oh, no. We're both the same in the middle," said Miss Bennett. "Passionate, violent women. Just different exteriors." – "Oh, no, darling," said Miss Roberts, shocked. – "We are ironical about ourselves and our so-called successful lives," said Miss Bennett. – "She's out every night," said Miss Roberts. "She's an uppercrust Scot. I'm indoors talking my head off. Neither of us is really violent. She's only saying that. She's like a very cultivated pussy-cat. When we are reincarnated, I want to come back like my own contented pussy-cat. You remember my cat, Rosie Roberts, don't you?" I remembered in time.

' "What do you want to come back as, Jill?" asked Rachel.

' "I don't want to come here again," said Miss Bennett. "I made a mistake the first time." '

JILL BENNETT: 'We had plans of appearing together in *Duel of Angels*. I talked about it with Michael Medwin, with whom Albert Finney set up Memorial Productions, and for a time Rachel was as excited as I was and it looked as if it would come off. We wanted Lindsay to direct it. But in the end we decided against it on the grounds that the third act wasn't really very good. So *The Old Crowd* was our last appearance together.'

*The Old Crowd* was one of six television scripts that Bennett had written for London Weekend TV – and proved by far the most controversial, being alternately praised and acerbically derided by the critics. Its 'sin' was to present an English dinner-party in terms of Bunuel-esque absurdism.

A group of guests gathered for a house-warming party held in an old Edwardian mansion in Islington, then coming into its own as the trendiest part of London, an area much favoured by the media people whose likeness Alan Bennett's play caught most wittily. The house also happens to be almost entirely empty, because the furniture sent up from Horsham has been taken by the driver several hundreds of miles north, to Carlisle, in order to earn him overtime. The scenario – or else Anderson, whose first TV film it was – seems to have recruited a few of Rachel's better-known public mannerisms, like her penchant when tipsy of crawling under the table to bite a guest on the ankle. Not surprisingly, idiosyncratic touches like this increased some critics' bafflement at the play and consequent fury in their response to it. For all its unpretentious satire of the bourgeoisie, the play sparked press reviews that made it appear deeply subversive. All of which was manna to Anderson.

After the filming, Rachel returned to New York, seeking a new play, telephoning Rex Harrison and hating being cooped up in the Central Park West apartment she had once adored possessing – where Rex's 'house-warming' present to her, an ice-bucket with a tiger motif, cooled the white wine which numbed her rational functions after the first glass or two.

JEAN MARSH: 'I felt she made a great mistake hanging around waiting for something to turn up for her on Broadway. At the best of times, Broadway's a very small self-centred world. For an English actress, it's particularly tough – and Rachel was always thought of as that. You're not likely to get a leading role in the latest American play and the ones that come over from Shaftesbury Avenue have usually had the star roles cast back in London. On the other hand, America has a much better cross-country theatre than England: the audiences are more appreciative, the pay is good, the casting opportunities are much wider, and, let's face it, the hotels are infinitely better. I kept telling Rachel she should do more of that. The sort of companionship she'd have found in a touring company would have helped her to feel more fulfilled.'

But then John Schlesinger asked her to be in *Yanks*, a wistful but painstakingly exact re-creating of what life and love were like for the GIs stationed near a Lancashire village in wartime England.

Rachel's was not one of the star parts – they went to Vanessa Redgrave, Richard Gere, Lisa Eichhorn and William Devane. But her role was a good one: she played Lisa Eichhorn's mother, a feet-on-the-ground North Country woman, whose illness and death shadow her daughter's love affair with Gere.

JOHN SCHLESINGER: 'She was very subdued when she came to England for *Yanks* in the middle of 1978. I think she felt the edge in the air that was perceptible to those of us, myself included, who felt we were resented because we had pursued our careers in the United States.

'For *Yanks*, she had about two weeks of rehearsals, some of them in a room at the Kensington Palace Hotel. One day Alan Dobie dropped in to watch. Rachel suddenly stopped and said to me, "Oh Christ, I wish I'd never made that terrible mistake and left Alan for Rex." To help the cast fit into the mood of wartime England, I showed Humphrey Jennings's film *A Diary for Timothy* to the leading players. When it was over, there was a silence I took as signifying how thoughtful and impressed they were. Then Rachel's voice broke it, "Oh, luv, it's all about the stiff upper cunt, isn't it?"

'Several of Rachel's scenes were with Richard Gere. One especially I remember, when she was dying of cancer – she played it in a very low key and moved all of us who were on the set watching her. Nothing flamboyant: she gave it the emphasis and projection it demanded, judging both very skilfully. She'd always a good ear for the vocal weight a part needed and let us see the emotions as if her skin were transparent.'

RICHARD GERE: 'I enjoyed working with Rachel again after *Habeas Corpus*. She was still incredibly concerned about her appearance: she always wanted to present herself younger than she was and more attractive than she believed herself to be. It led to a conflict within some of the roles she played. In *Yanks*, she was the mother of my English girlfriend and we had a quiet and tender final scene when Rachel is dying of cancer. But she came out of her dressing room to do the scene looking aged twenty-two, she'd plastered her face with so much make-up and mascara – the very opposite of what the part demanded!

'John tactfully suggested she go back into the dressing room and do her make-up all over again, and she got the point – and this time, wearing very little, she began to look like a worn-down mother at death's door and not like the Lady of the Camelias.'

JOHN SCHLESINGER: 'After the filming, I remember her telling everyone how she was going to win an Oscar with the role she had in the film. This was at my house and she'd had a bit too much to drink. My cleaning woman was leaving me at the time to emigrate to Canada – she was Welsh, too. Rachel soon discovered this and raced off to comfort the woman with her arms round her neck and a great outpouring of Welsh emotions – that might indeed have won her an Oscar nomination! I must admit I knew of Rachel's drinking habits at the time of shooting: but I needn't have worried. When she was working, no one was more professional.

'But when she hadn't any work, well, it was a different and a sad story. I remember a party I gave at the Russian Tea Room a year or so later to launch *Honky Tonk Freeway* – which, of course, she wasn't in. She came along and, really, was a shocking sight.'

Rachel very rarely gave press interviews revealing her true state of mind. This is not to say that she lied. But she set out to create an 'effect'. She *acted* the part the interviewer expected her to be playing. It seems she is often talking herself into believing what she would like to think and, sometimes, convincing herself by her own performance that things were just so . . . when frequently, as her journals reveal, things were very sadly otherwise. Occasionally, though, a sceptical, though not unfriendly interviewer saw *round* her act, rather than *through* it, noting some of the features of herself and the environment of the moment which did not add up to the conventional picture of energetic, hoydenish talent whipping up a merry mess that would be reported as the sort of thing a 'larger than life-size' personality was expected to do. One such interviewer came to see her in London at this increasingly fraught time in her life and fortunes when she was preparing to play her role in *Yanks*. She had borrowed the

Knightsbridge apartment owned by the Broadway impresario Alexander Cohen. Gordon Burn's report in *The Sunday Times* of April 9, 1978, reads as if the writer had called unexpectedly early on Rachel, before she could completely arrange the scene, or herself.

'She said she'd bought the gin. I said I'd brought these flowers, a bit battered. Her "Hello, luvvy" had been a touch cautious, though. Later, she'd confess that, waiting to keep this appointment, she'd had her doubts. I'd hesitated on that doorstep long enough to hear her talking on the telephone in a twang that didn't sound half so strong as it was going to. The flat overlooking the park in Knightsbridge was rented. It was a big place to be rattling around in alone. The chicness of the foyer, I suppose you'd call it – the only thing missing was a ticket kiosk – was dented by a big Welsh rugby rosette pinned to the back of one of the designer-designed chairs. A candle was burning on a low table and she led the way with it on to the main set, a rug-rolled lounge decorated with books and a burgundy suede three-piece. She said she loved candle-light, *loved* it. And the sound of traffic splashing in the rain that you could hear through the double-glazing that she'd shoved back. Instead of nuts, she handed me a typed "biog", a habit she's picked up in America, and went to the drinks. For *Picnic at Hanging Rock*, it said, she'd received the Gold Crown Plague (*sic*).
    'She'd tried to make a fire in the grate, but it hadn't taken. She'd used old newspapers scrunched and tied into knots which had reminded her of Llanelli and the manse . . . She'd been playing and singing to herself at the piano, songs like "The Old Folks at Home" . . . She sang a snatch of the song she used to perform in fishnet stockings at Churchill's Club in the very early days. She settled herself on the sofa with a sensible-looking mug. Something for her cold. Her feet were slipped into a pair of nothing-there high heels and she drew them up beside her. She had Huntcoat Red Creme on her toe-nails and she looked like an ad for panty-hose in the subway. Her legs have always been her strong point. She looked great. She says she stopped counting when she got to forty-seven, about four years ago. She's enjoying growing older, she says, because she's got nothing to lose. Her face looked soft. Perhaps it was the light . . . She had to admit, though, that she was busy trying to lose five pounds. For her next part, in John Schlesinger's film *Yanks*, she's supposed to look "fragile". Some hope . . .
    'She apologised for the umpteenth time for her sniffles. This cold. But, of course, it hadn't kept her in. "I think she could enjoy the fleshpots as much as I, but felt a deep need to earn them," Rex Harrison wrote of his ex-wife in his autobiography. She agreed about the big broad puritan streak running through her, but said she's not a great one for the fleshpots. She had been hitting the hot spots a bit lately, though, with her pal Jill Bennett. Being able to have a night on the tiles with a girlfriend is a new-found freedom. And being able to turn up at dinner parties unescorted without even caring if the looks say, "Poor thing" . . . She didn't want to dwell on the subject of Rex Harrison though: it wasn't fair to the women in his life, past and present, or to the men in hers. "I'm divorced," she said, "but I'm not without men." In London? She was looking for a light. "I'm not going to tell you."'

It is the sense of loneliness, despite denials, that impregnates this interview. Even Rachel's 'men' were, like her, lonely souls; and one, a

London critic, a passionate and intelligent man who met her in a club and returned to the Knightsbridge apartment with her, found that the two days they spent there together became terminally desperate as well as physically satisfying. 'Each morning, when we woke, there was the biggest vodka bottle in the world . . . we'd try and race each other to it.' Their affair was intense and quickly consumed: but the carnal satisfaction they mutually if briefly found in each other's company could invoke a tender melancholy in the man years later.

*Yanks* opened in New York in September, 1979, and did not fare well. At a time when hard-edged revisionism on the subject of war was critically in fashion, its soft-focused nostalgia was deemed by its detractors as sentimental, at best, or at worst musty; possibly the controversy surrounding Vanessa Redgrave's pro-Arab stance in her public life harmed its box-office. Rachel's part, by its nature, was not likely to feature large even in the reviews – and there were some substantial ones – which appreciated the picture: but critics who liked it noted her performance with pleasure, and sometimes more. Charles Champlin, in the *Los Angeles Times*, wrote: 'Ms Roberts, scolding and accusing out of a mother's worry and a serious illness, contributes one of her best characterisations for some time.' And Stephen Farber, in *New West*, said, 'Rachel Roberts gives an incisive, memorable performance as an English shopkeeper trying to shield her daughter from the trauma of a liaison with an American: we can understand her concern even as we deplore her narrow-mindedness.'

It fared much better, commercially and critically, when it opened in London a month later: but Rachel did not get her anticipated Oscar nomination as Best Supporting Actress, though the British Academy of Film and Television Arts (the renamed British Film Academy) gave her its award early in 1980, in circumstances – as later journal passages reveal – already darkened by her self-destructive breakdown.

She flew back to New York after filming *Yanks*, found herself unable to settle, could not face returning to Los Angeles, and, on an impulse, flew off alone to the Caribbean.

She seemed to need to keep travelling – in that continuum, at least no problems collected. It was like playtime: nothing mattered: one could assume the irresponsibility of a child: everything was novelty, everyone was exotic, nothing need be taken seriously, not for long . . .


N ineteen-seventy-eight saved me from myself a little. Not only did John Schlesinger unexpectedly turn up trumps and offer me a part in *Yanks*, but Lindsay offered me a part in the film he was making for television based on the Alan Bennett script – *The Old Crowd*. But the old disease hit. Back rushed unreality. I rented Alex Cohen's flat overlooking Hyde Park in Knightsbridge, gave a party, pretended . . . Full of 'Palanca', my merry old self had a rare old time. We started rehearsals for *Yanks* and I got drunk in the theatrical club. A critic happened to be there. We went home. He stayed two days and nights, getting out of bed in the morning and going straight for the vodka. I was enthralled. Love at last! I was very late for my make-up test for the film and kept poor Tony Melody, who was playing my husband, waiting in the car that was to take me to Twickenham Studios. I nearly missed the test.

Once shooting had begun on *Yanks*, I miraculously sobered up and was happy. Back in New York again, I saw Val and cooked a chicken, he didn't stay to eat. I asked him if our life together was all over and remember with some abhorrence the way he said, 'What do you think?' In this mood, I took myself off, all alone, to St Thomas and the Virgin Islands. First-class seemed to have been booked *entirely* by babies under two, both black and white, and a very nice dachshund who kicked up a row when its besotted master was ordered to put him in his box. The dachshund won, was brought back out and behaved impeccably.

The stewardess unfortunately recognised me. I was deep into a paperback entitled *Rape: Statistics of . . .* She wouldn't stop talking, but she did pass on an interesting theory about the Chappaquiddick case, said to have been let slip by Kennedy's priest – and that was that Mary-Jo Kopechne, not being a party girl, went to relax and sleep in the back of the car and that Ted and his party friend literally did not know she was there till it was too late.

When I arrived at St Thomas, I took a taxi or, rather, a mini-bus to Rock Point Landing and, from there, a water-taxi to the plantation. We wound through funny little streets in blazing sun for about two minutes and then *straight* into a tropical thunderstorm. There was an hour-and-a-half wait for the public boat till I realised after ten minutes there were such things to be had as taxis. However, in that time I saw a beautiful pelican and lots of tiger-striped fishes the size of large sardines. Then a white American boy, nice with no brain, ferried me over to the Plantation Hotel.

I was met by one of that strange breed of blond young Americans who look as if they should be playing baseball on Mars, and was instantly 'programmed'. In fact, the hotel is for all the world like a *very* hot Cunard liner and your day is planned for you. It looks like 150 acres of the Beverly Hills Hotel, except surrounded by sea. I unpacked. I know I should have plunged straight into the sea lapping at my cabaña, but I didn't. I cautiously paddled.

I got lost on the way to the dining room since my room is at least a mile-and-a-half from the restaurant. Also, on my way there, there was another unbelievable electric storm. A bus picks you up at a quarter-to-and-after the hour, but I decided to walk, sheet lightning or no sheet lightning. Fortunately a gigantic black guard shone his torch on me and whistled for the bus.

I dined with a sweet insect who had the same tiger-striped markings as the little fish I'd seen earlier. He sat quietly on my napkin until he plunged to his death in the storm lantern that covered the lighted candle.

I had the local fish which was excellent and refrained from wine, which is a bore.

On the dining table was Thursday's brochure informing me that at 9.00 pm an 'enjoyable and informative presentation for all ages' entitled 'National Park Presentation' was to be held in the 'Activities Pavilion'. I decided to give that the proverbial miss and, instead, skimmed through *Alistair Cooke's America*. I find him rather simple. Then I started reading Kenneth Clark's autobiography *Another Part of the Wood*, which is wonderful – especially the section about the pony that sat down!

To me, the place appeared as if it still *was* a plantation, only modernised. All the blacks do the work, some mutinously, and the whites sit around aimlessly snorkelling or drinking or eating, or all three. I don't know what tribe of Africans was imported here by the Dutch, but they are all very large men.

The water was lovely and I swam a lot the next morning.

I had an extraordinary dream which, when I awoke, flooded me with tears – of relief? I dreamed of Hollywood and the parties and Merle Oberon and me snarling that I don't 'do' Hollywood movies, and feeling inadequate, and of Alan's white face, confused and hurt. My strange memories of Kate at the London Clinic, my exorcism. The fact that usually my inner life is so much more important to me than my external life. Cathartic, to say the least!

I swam out of my depth for the first time and made friends with a dog.

It took me a few days to return to some facsimile of level-headedness in this tropical sanitarium. Since I hunger after love in all its miraculous and unrealistic aspects, more than anything in what I imagine to be life, I fought to suppress melancholic thoughts of how much I'd really prefer to be in a roach-ridden apartment on the Lower East Side with Val. Life based on such fantasy is like a house built on shifting sand. I reminded myself of little David Fletcher's [unidentified – perhaps a character in fiction] remark. 'He feels poorly.' – 'Why, David?' – 'Whenever he sees me do something, he feels poorly.' Whoever David's little friend was, I know how he feels. I hope he grows out of his fears and inferiorities, too, and will be able to enjoy *himself*.

---

SHE FLEW BACK to Los Angeles from her Caribbean 'sabattical'. Things immediately became so fraught between her and Darren that the latter, seeking to distract her, proposed another vacation, this time in his native Mexico.

They were not long back in Hutton Drive – Rachel instantly feeling depressed, fractious, desperate and violent as soon as she had been back a few hours –when Lindsay Anderson came on a visit.

DARREN RAMIREZ: 'Lindsay was appalled by Rachel's deterioration. He thought work was the best cure for her. He thought doing a play would help and proposed a run of the comedy *The Bed Before Yesterday* in Australia – which would keep Rachel busy *and* give her a change of scene. But before he left, he wrote her a very stiff letter. He admonished her very firmly about her conduct and told her that the sooner she faced up to things, the better she would be. He always felt that when she was acting, she was fine. The truth, though, was that she continued drinking after the show, but her constitution was so strong she could fool people, even Lindsay. But anything Lindsay said, she would do – so it was settled. Lindsay called her from Australia and promised to meet her when she arrived in Sydney.

'It was during Lindsay's stay that Rachel took to going to the Los Angeles Public Library and writing her journals.'

SYBIL CHRISTOPHER: 'She found peace in writing. She recalled the past very easily, perhaps because she lived so much in it. Dates, for example, she could always remember – for the same reason. She'd been trying her hand at short stories, barely fictionalised versions of her mood of the moment and what was happening to her. She'd never show me the journals she'd been writing, though.'

DARREN RAMIREZ: 'She kept them very close to herself, locking them up, taking them with her whenever she left Hutton Drive. She talked of publishing what she wrote. She'd been calling Rex pretty constantly, maybe hopeful he would come back to her; but in 1978 he married Mercia Tinker, his sixth wife. Maybe it was a reaction to this that started Rachel's interest in putting some record of her life and career into print the way Rex had done four years earlier while still married to Elizabeth . . . Anyway, who knows . . . ? The important thing is, writing it down gave her temporary peace of mind.'

SYBIL CHRISTOPHER: 'I'd go down to the L.A. public library and meet her for lunch. Usually, we'd walk from the library to a terrible place that we called "The Vietnam Coffee Shop" – with Rachel, it was either a "Greasy Spoon" or Ma Maison. We'd eat bacon, lettuce and tomato sandwiches and French fries over cups of tea! Then I'd walk her back to the library.'

Rachel flew off to Australia in early January, 1979, to begin rehearsals for the comedy *The Bed Before Yesterday*.

DARREN RAMIREZ: 'I believed all was going well – then she called. Very angry and upset. Lindsay had had to leave after the play opened and he had put things in the care of an Australian assistant director. That was the end for Rachel. "How dare Lindsay leave!" "How dare his assistant tell Rachel Roberts what to do!" – so unfair. She was going on with the play in Sydney, but poor advances had cancelled the Melbourne opening. She implored me to come and join her; so I flew out to Sydney the day before the last performance and stayed about a week.'

Rachel's letter to her agent, Milton Goldman, dated February 6, 1979, sounded considerably more even-tempered than, according to Darren, was the case. Though Milton Goldman was a man well experienced in the traumas and temperaments of agency work, Rachel was not anxious to expose to him her growing inadequacy in coping with the daily realities of life – and her letter, paradoxically, shows a concern with the future that suggests a managerial acumen wildly at odds with the gathering disarray of her life.

'My Darling Milton – It was a most up-beat feeling to receive your lively letter and the cuttings, especially Rex Reed's *Yanks* article where he said *twice* "that fine actress R.R."!!
'I've enclosed a photograph that recently appeared in Sydney, as I rather fancy myself in it!
'I've had a wonderful time in Sydney. The company is composed of not only talented, but extraordinarily sweet people, I'm spoilt rotten at the Boulevard Hotel, and have a view of Sydney Harbour and the Opera House that fights 295 Central Park West for glamour – well, not quite!! Funny place, Australia. It's basically far too British for me to really like it, and I'm not sure the Australians like it much, either! They do an immense amount

of drinking, and almost all the men over thirty have decidedly large pot-bellies! But I'm in love with America, so I expect I'm prejudiced.

'Darren flies out to join me later in the month, and we are returning to the States via Singapore, Bangkok, Hong Kong and Tokyo, taking two weeks to do so. I'm very excited about the trip, never having been to the East, and I long to see Darren. I've missed him more this trip than ever before. He is so 100-per-cent *for* me, and ever has been, through thick and thin, and I've known him nine years now. Margot McDowell [Malcolm McDowell's estranged wife] will be staying in our house in Beverly Hills and looking after Rosie and Bessie, the cats, and Boosie, Darren's glamorous (wouldn't you know!) dog.

'We won't be going to Melbourne with the play, and finish here on February 26. I'm not sorry. It's been wonderful, but enough's enough.

'Now down to serious matters. Time has come to think hard about Broadway. I'd like to do something dramatic. I enjoyed so much playing Clara in Hal Prince's production of *The Visit*, and I believe my kind of dramatic power works well with American audiences, much as I enjoy comedy. It was interesting that my predecessor at the Theatre Royal was Liv Ullmann, and the four weeks of that show, the advance wasn't good. This surprised me. I always tend to undervalue myself (which is a vice) but my reception here has given me a great shot in the arm as far as my confidence is concerned.

'So, darling, there it is, as of February 26, I'm free and available. Well, not quite. First comes the vacation, and then I have some looping to do for John Schlesinger in L.A. on *Yanks* – but after that, by mid-March, I'm up for grabs!!

'My love to you. Rachel.'

Either Rachel did not record in her journals the South Seas holiday that she and Darren took when the Australian engagement ended, or else she did and the pages have not survived. Unlike their other recent vacations abroad, it was not a refreshing experience.

DARREN RAMIREZ: 'It was all part of the deal she made before leaving Los Angeles for Australia, that she'd get two first-class return tickets. One was hers, the other mine – she was always devising ways to get me to escort her here and there, and I was generally weak enough to do it. When Rachel was travelling, she was usually at peace with the world. But on this occasion, it was ominous that she didn't show much interest in the marvellous round of places we visited. A pattern formed early on. She would stay in her bed till midday, then laze around the pool, reading, or writing letters, not trusting herself to find out about the exotic world outside. She hated Tokyo the minute she arrived there, and, two days after hitting Hong Kong, she hated it, too. All that Singapore meant to her was a chance to stay at the fabled Raffles Hotel.

'It was when we returned to Los Angeles in March, 1979, that things really began to fall irreparably apart.'

Rachel began what she describes as 'this spiral of suicidal depression' within days of their arriving home.

DARREN RAMIREZ: 'Sybil had invited us over for a lunch of "bangers and mash". Besides us, there were Roddy MacDowall and Gavin Lambert. Rachel got quickly and disastrously drunk at lunch. Her worst bout yet. Everyone was shocked, especially Gavin – he hadn't realised the gravity of the problem till then. He gave Rachel the address of a psychologist and said he'd help. I think Rachel was so frightened by her conduct in front of her closest friends that she acted on the advice and started going to him.'

Rachel calls the analyst 'Phil' in her journals. She was introduced by a well-known movie actress to a local branch of Alcoholics Anonymous and she took up increasingly fitful attendance, though, for her, the meetings came to be regarded as a place where she could meet men – and men who were not necessarily the best ones to help her cope with that particular problem.

Reading her journal entries from now on, one has the strange impression of a woman increasingly unable to control her life except on the paper where she is writing about it. There, her recollections of the distant and recent past have a vividness and an internal coherence that was belied in her daily efforts, valiant but desperate, to find her direction and put together again a complete sense of identity and self-confidence. Although the journals develop a somewhat unnerving trick of swerving between past and present, as some associative curve of incident or reflection takes Rachel off course, one's first impression is that of a woman writing from the vantage point of an imminent cure, so controlled is the insight into herself, and not plunging deeper and deeper, as she actually was, into the circular descent to self-destruction.

I returned to Los Angeles and Darren – who almost instantly got his car stolen. Happily, it was found. But it showed how helpless I was, so I started taking driving lessons. Endless expense and endless fear – but I discovered that I can drive. Drunkenly, though, I tried to take a short-cut and slammed into his boss's car. It cost $1,000 to repair.

What I was doing, really, wasn't adjusting – but simply filling in time – until 'it' would hit me.

I saw that Rex had re-married for the sixth time – to Mercia.

Darren suggested we take a break. We went to Mexico, to Cancun. Our room, 832, had two naked light bulbs, one of which did not work. A large quantity of dark pubic hair decorated the bathroom, the ceiling of which had not yet been finished. It had a mottled appearance with a few holes round the edges. The 'terrace' looked over what would one day be a new road, but as of now was a squat block of cement. On the terrace was one good upright chair, and another with a broken leg. The manager and his assistant were nowhere to be found. In the hotel foyer there was a large notice chalked on a blackboard announcing that the pool would not be in use on the 7th, 8th, 9th or 10th – *travajadores* would be cleaning it. These were the four days we were to be staying at the hotel.

However, the lagoon was beautiful. Blue and oval, and protected fish seemed to acknowledge our presence courteously before swimming unhurriedly away. One extra-large rock-coloured lizard scuttled away nervously when he saw we'd uncovered his act. The Mayan ruins with their temples and descending Gods and, presumably, their sacrificial altars were an unpleasant testimony to the sheer stupidity of men. The sea and shore were incredibly beautiful, surrounded by jungle, red hibiscus flowers, yellow sand crabs, palm trees, coconut trees and an alarming tree that seemed to grow buzzards.

The Woman's Island, reached by an uncomfortable local boat which chugged along for forty-five minutes, was enchanting. Pretty little streets interwove amongst each other and we saw the most beautiful child imaginable. Very dark-skinned with incredible eyes, a wicked expression, faultless teeth – Cleopatra in fact.

We dined at a thatched-roof restaurant, alongside a shy but indulged Husky and a tough little semi-sandy, semi-tabby cat. We were served a marvellous *ceviche* and then lobsters *con achos* and a palatable wine. The pretty hanging conch shells I so admired turned out to come from Miami! The young man at the next table looked Irish and shifty, with a fine nose.

Our beach place seemed devised exclusively for hustlers of both sexes. A nasty, pretentious, cemented vulgar place, with a lot of blond young men tackling sail boards. A great deal of thigh- and calf-flexing went on. Chocos was a noisy, friendly, easy-going restaurant which served marvellous octopus soup and very strong margaritas. Darren observed that I was either boring when on a philosophical binge, or on the other kind! Quite accurate!

The Hotel Camino Real had the most magnificent pool and looked a delightful place to stay in. We decided to give it a try sometime. The mariachis came on very strongly indeed. The beauty of the palm fronds and an aquamarine-coloured sea, tropical breezes, hot sun, fish cooked deliciously and cold, sweetish, mildly alcoholic drinks really was pleasurable, except that, occasionally, I wished that the Spanish colonists had not banned the Mayan custom of human sacrifice, though I felt their Gods would not accept the offerings of great numbers of human debris lolling by the pool, not all of them 'los Americanos', either. For example, the spoilt-looking Jewish boy who yawned and scratched his stomach incessantly under his yellow hotel towel, stretched alongside his blonde, discontented but quite pretty girlfriend who was as over-eager and over-anxious with him as the American 'good-family' girl had been with the young Mexican boy at Concho's the previous evening. The latter blonde was affecting to be a photographer, training her expensive camera on the nice-looking but vapid Mexican boy. Both women, one felt, were doomed to believe that their deficiencies were to blame for the uneasy inattention afforded them by their rather tepid male partners. Mismatching and its consequences are no doubt as daily an occurrence in a tropical paradise resort as they are on a University campus.

Darren and I went on an idyllic holiday to Bali and Bangkok and Singapore and Hong Kong and then home. Three days into Los Angeles, it hit. I drank a bottle of wine, cut my toe and started this spiral of suicidal depression. I went to Phil the psychologist recommended to me by Gavin Lambert and started Alcoholics Anonymous. I turned desperately to books for help in recognising my own state. Quote from *Sleepless Nights* by Elizabeth Hardwick:

'Herman was shifty, idle, a wandering isolate with a morose and needy nature that could, when the need was upon him, attach itself somewhere. He had the soul and body of a convict. But the parole spirit was on him, and dull schemes began to enter his mind once more.'

'Juanita, who represented the fallen state too vividly and fortuitously to be endured . . . She developed a refusal to meet your glance. She drank, she aged, she suffered terribly from her dissipations, and all had to be paid for by Juanita, every penny of the cost.'

In the beginning, I wouldn't meet anyone's eyes. I remember Tony Richardson saying I was very attractive. But knowing myself, I knew that I didn't go towards men of my own calibre, instead chased a safe bet . . . This morning, I remember Rex saying, 'I couldn't' – after my attempting suicide at the time of our public separation in London and the return from St George's Hospital – when I suggested, 'Let's start married life all over again.' It was a lie on my part. His 'I couldn't' meant much more than a return to our marriage. I understand it. I share it – the pain of reality. Rex supports it so much better than I do.

My idealisation of early marriage and having babies may have been just that – an idealisation. Anyway, it didn't happen for me. Now I'd like to replace childlessness with something. It is too empty, certainly, as it is. I long for the peaceful and structured week-ends I spent at Quogue . . . how good to talk to Bobby Frosch and share a sense of humour. My inability to concentrate on the minutiae of daily living – everyone has to – I'm beginning to put down to the feverish, chaotic life I led with Rex – but that's only partly true. My mind is in a constant whirl and I live each moment in a jumble of past, present and future. The present, therefore, takes an agonising beating; and the result is frayed nerves. So much I understand now that I didn't. My rough friendship with my Mother at the end had a warmth – but no real knowledge of her fears and loneliness . . . too late to rectify that, Mum dear, I wish I could . . .

When I get to feel like that, I remember 1960 and *my* dash to escapism, and my stomach lurches, and I wish, again, that I was neatly and hypocritically under that amphibian tail . . . I am in limbo anyway. Why not have chosen, if choice there was, protected limbo. Poor Richard Jenkins – snap!

It seems I have been experimenting with life-styles – finding out how to live, or what it is in this life that will make mine fit properly. There have been moments of impulsive pleasure and periods of deep despondency. Some days the migraine in my vitals eased, winning the driving compulsion to drown the scream inside myself with just that little drink – which only compounds the issue. To drive the actor I met at Alcoholics Anonymous to Paramount Studios, to drive back, to be sitting in the peaceful, cool Los Angeles Public Library, writing these lines, fortified by $2.60-cents' worth of excellent toasted wholewheat eggs-and-bacon sandwich served by the friendly Vietnam gives me the happiness that goes away at lunches in the Beverly Hills Hotel's Polo Lounge – lunches spent dissecting other actors and actresses with a lonely woman totally dependent on the chance remarks of her fellow human beings who have by talent, or luck, or determination, or marriage, achieved an ephemeral 'name'. The smallness and narcissism of both the theatre and film world is getting more than my insides can bear.

RACHEL'S CONDITION WORSENED during the late spring and summer months of 1979. She was unable to settle at anything. She felt her incompetence in handling even her minor daily needs. A visit to a friend's was now an anguishing business of seeing someone else 'perform' the commonplace things that routinely defeated her. One technique she did master, in a rough and ready way: driving a car. But it took two instructors, supporting her simultaneously, before she got the hang of it!

As her nerves got worse, the rows with Darren grew more frequent, more wildly irrational. The incident she mentions, of the 'grilled lamb', was a symptom of this inner dissatisfaction settling on any 'offence'. They had both been to London to catch the Tim Rice – Andrew Lloyd Webber musical, *Joseph and his Amazing Technicolor Dreamcoat*, at the Round House. Binkie Beaumont, the impresario, had impulsively invited them to lunch. Noël Coward was to be there. Darren was in high heaven at the prospect. Maybe because of this, Rachel woke up on the day screaming she wasn't going to eat 'with those faggots'. A disconsolate Darren, hungry as well as out of sorts, found a leg of lamb in the fridge and rather than cook the whole joint for their own uncertain meal, cut off a few slices for himself and grilled them. Result: an intemperate accusation of 'selfishness'. It was as if he had cut off the lamb to spite his loved one!

Rachel seized on anything for the sake of distraction. In April, she went to New York to promote a film, *The Belstone Fox*, which she had made in England in 1973. After faring poorly at the box-office, this outdoor story of a sort of super-fox which outwitted the local hunt was disposed of by the disgruntled Rank Organisation to a minor American distributor. The latter instantly eliminated the death of the chief huntsman, played by Eric Porter, as being unsuitable for family audiences, but left Nature otherwise dripping red in tooth and claw, and got Rachel to 'voice over' a new ending.

Despite this and a more upbeat title-change to *A Free Spirit*, the film proved unsalvageable. And Rachel returned home with a nagging sense of having lent herself to a depressing occasion.

F renetic and harsh though the world is when seen through the eyes of some of my lovers – I'd still not completely opened my own when I met them – it was nevertheless less alarming than attempting to imitate a cockatoo on a Sunday afternoon in a smart rented house in Beverly Hills just to fill the empty days.

Now a decade later after the hell of Paris in '68, the convalescence of '69, the desperation of that Christmas, the new decade has at least been colourful and my eyes have opened. The return from Australia has been shattering. I am frightened and feel empty and alone again, and long for love and life and am finding myself forced to face the reality of my affairs and friendships. The blissful escapes from reality are over: days of sunning by a pool in Bangkok, staying in comfort in first-class hotels, with only Darren and myself to pamper, no cares, no responsibilities other than getting to the airport lounge in time, to be ushered into a first-class seat, Champagne and book in hand. When the ugly reality of bills and facing facts obtrudes, it seems we just cannot do it. I do not want to think this, but in not doing so I'm not facing facts and matters can only get worse. There is so little warmth in the house. The pattern is repeating itself.

The episode in London, when we were staying in Pimlico, cutting a slice of meat off a leg of lamb to grill it is nothing in itself, but on another level it is a clear indication of how little we really have in common. I wanted a day of warmth and intimacy and talk and laughter, and I'm entitled to that. He wanted his own grilled meat – he's entitled to that. But how can we live together? Why am I so pathetically grateful for crumbs? Is my sense of self-worth really so low or am I indeed unworthy? (Which is what I suspect.) His selfishness is finally too blatant to ignore. That every nook and cranny of the house should be filled with his silks and satins is not just laughably selfish, but indicative of his inability to sense even the most simple needs of others. He pulls away from me at every step and I feel starved for simple communication.

Even what my actor lover in Australia gave, when we were making the film, was heart-warming in comparison. He needed the lavatory – we both did, and laughed! He joined in with the preparation for dinner and it was harmonious. I enjoyed the drive to Union Station and the memories of those days of railway travel that the film conjured up. I didn't feel lost and finished and alone.

After those driving instructors, the 'two Phils', had left they took some warmth away with them. Something must be wrong when my eyes fill with tears at losing driving instructors.

The awful summer of 1979 came to an end. Lindsay Anderson left for London and I got ready to go away, too. I didn't ever want to come back to Los Angeles. It is dead and dull and boring and there is nothing to do.

I constantly thresh about, trying this one and that one to lean on. Maybe I do have 'idées au-dessus de sa gare', maybe I am a nobody-trying-to-be-a-somebody. I certainly find it difficult to be in control of myself by myself and seem to look on the bleak and black side of things, and seem to be hopeless at dealing with everyday living. I thrive on compliments. Would love to go to Paris, for instance, to promote myself and my book, would love to have won an award – I didn't get the Oscar nomination for Yanks, Jane Alexander did [as Best Supporting Actress for Kramer vs. Kramer, though Meryl Streep won]. I must straighten myself out before it's too late – and that means now. I seem to enjoy only extremes and don't want to join the crowd, but I must stop this morbid self-dislike and self-distrust and at least get outside myself – otherwise my fate will be unhappiness.

Imagination is the prelude to behaviour.

Poor Darren, I feel a tenderness for him, but it was a terrible strain to be with him. I thought earlier – all my loves end after vacations and a move into a home: Alan and Sitges and Lancaster Gate's flat. Rex and Corsica and the villa. Now the Orient and Darren's house and mine on Hutton Drive. Such a longing for love, intelligent talk, cuddling up in bed. If only the little house and the pretty garden room could have been filled with love and talk and breakfast and reading the papers and contented animals, and not my tears, the sound of the hair dryer . . . all those clothes, the cringing dog (my fault, I fear), the total uninterest I felt in a little defenceless kitten. Oh, poor Darren! I know you're lonely, too, and you're sweet, but I can't live with you again. I can't go into that empty little house which you did try hard and bravely, but also pathetically, to turn into a 'Beverly Hills' home. You *are* sweet and you *are* good, but those attempts to 'crash' society were pathetic – be it dinner for John Mills and his wife and Laurie Evans and Mary, or my 'surprise' birthday parties, or the week-end in the villa in the South of France with Tommy Kyle [film producer], or the embarrassing parties with Ricky and Leonard [fashionable London hair stylist]. I remember the smiling and hugging that went on to get invited out, often to no avail. And yet it was better to go to this or that party with you than to stay at 'home'.

Oh, little Darren, I'm going to be so lonely. We both are, and we've held on so long because of this mutual need.

I did not have the 'comfort' of Val any longer. The year before, 1978, we had split up. I felt it deeply enough to write a poem:

'No longer could I play the
    role
Of Mother Confessor to one
    man's soul
While others had the best of
    him,
His time, his taste, his
    everything.'

On Val's departure, I wrote more . . . well, prosaically:

'I know the life went out of me, and the laughter turned to howling, and that all my precious and newly shining self-esteem and my dignity dissolved into unbearable confusion and the old "I'll-never-get-it-right" anguish.

'The worst thing about illusion is that apart from its being, obviously, painful to lose, it causes such confusion, not of one's own making. I didn't know about your other love until very recently. Now I do, so much has become clear to me. I thought *I* was triggering off strange responses in you by some frightening and unacceptable streak in me, but couldn't put my finger on it and went to see two psychologists about it. I couldn't fathom your coldness at all, for the very good reason that I didn't know there was someone else . . .'

The AA meetings I attended that summer of 1979 filled me with despair. I found myself jotting down the first names of the people I met, putting them into dramatic order like characters in a stage play or a TV series. Title: *The Address Book*. OPENING SHOT; Camera CLOSES IN on book with this week's number. CUT TO close-up of phone. Over phone is SUPERIMPOSED a number . . . then a name . . . then this week's dilemma. *JOY*, a frightened alcoholic . . . *JANET*, just divorced with two children . . . *JAY*, a balding frightened man . . . *KIM*, a hopeful young girl in love . . . *MAY*, a bright black girl . . . *JOE*, a Chicano trying to go to college . . . *FLO*, giving a party and dying of cancer.

Phil the psychologist, on the other hand, did help. He spoke some truth. 'After all, you're allowed your feelings. Give in to the illness: relax on it.' My feelings were unbearably painful. One day, an unholy dread of renting a car and driving in to Beverly Hills, of not knowing the way, of not being able to read a map. Of not being able to locate the road that would lead to Margot

McDowell's place and then, when I did, the stab of – what? Fear again, I think, when I saw how she'd got Patsy [lawyer, friend of Margot McDowell] staying with her and had taken all her curtains down and was planting flowers and shrubs by the pool – Fear *because I couldn't*. I could act once, understood it, was confident, at ease on the stage. But recently I read that Ernest Hemingway felt that *the worst death for anyone was the loss of what formed the centre of his life and made him what he really was*. Interesting thought. Was Rex the centre of my life – or was acting? I regret missing out on years of practice of my craft and thus not continuing to do something I was used to doing. Nowadays I pick up *Hamlet* with uninterest. But if you're told something over and over again, no matter how nonsensical it is, you get to believe it. Just the repetition of a myth, hammered into your consciousness, stays there and becomes part of it. If I put my wandering mind to it, can I memorise the lines, or have I told myself I can't and therefore won't?

I remember how I barely functioned at the United Artists promotional job for *Yanks*. Everyone else was normal, composed, did their job, in control. As you know, my soul, *I* was maniacally out of control. Was it due to the series of rejections? I came over on the Concorde from New York to London for the Royal performance of *Yanks* – which meant I could at least get away from my New York apartment. I didn't enjoy John Schlesinger's flowers that were waiting for me – I just envied him his house in Victoria Road, his secretary, his new film, his Father . . . I made the presentation, but had to have two Libriums, having madly called Rex and anyone else in London connected past or present with me. The trouble is, the people I want to call are dead. My other friends are getting worn out one by one.

The thought that a man could put all this right just isn't so unless he had the old power of Rex, the intelligence of Karel, the tender gentleness of Darren, could make love like Val, had Lindsay's cool intelligence, John's love of social flair – and even then, it wouldn't be enough.

I found that I went to AA meetings looking at the faces of the men, trying to find one. I always have done so. It was said I was a 'killer'. Yes, I have sweetness and warmth and intelligence and talent, but I have also a devastating psychological flaw that is finally crippling me – and it is.

One of the 'good' days during that terrible summer of 1979 was when Tony Richardson gave a party. It was life-enhancing. Nice people were there, glad to see me – yet I dread it when they say when last they saw me, in case I made a fool of myself on that occasion. Darren looked lonely and out of things – as he did at Pamela Mason's party years ago. I felt pity. Especially since after the meeting with Phil, my psychiatrist, on Friday I'd gone over to his mother's and his sisters'. I saw, this time without any romantic notions, what it was like to be a Mexican-American – I appreciated Darren's attempt to enter into the smart, manicured Anglo-American world, and I didn't blame him in the least. The home very cluttered in the one case, and very Mexican in the other. Children and housework and working-class, with all that means in this world. The party at Tony's had been *my* world. I fitted in. I was very happy and talkative. He was shut out. Another day that was very 'good' was when I took Lindsay Anderson's assistant out to lunch. Amazingly, she turned out to have problems. On to her home. I bought my hostess flowers. There again was a household where life was going on. I delayed getting back to my 'home' and Darren and new anger against the dog. I went to bed and read. When he came in, I couldn't sleep. So on

146

Sunday, I drove -- anywhere – down Sunset Strip, down Hollywood Boulevard, Los Feliz, found myself at Griffith Park and Travel-Town with old trains on display and I wept for the memory of my idyll – those days and nights with Rex, going to Europe . . . I came home. Darren was sitting contentedly sunning himself on the lawn, reading *The World According to Garp* – his kind of music on, his dog, his house – happy without me.

Before I'd left that day, I'd brought up the subject of the house. I was told it was his house . . . that I was ruining his life. I told him he was ruining mine, but that in addition I was paying for it and him. This home-truth made him tell me to go away. He said I could have my $37,000 back, that I was tight and mean. No good explaining to him that even while I was in England last year I paid the monthly mortgage and, in addition, sent him $2,000 for his trip. But it hurt terribly to say such things and I was afraid to be alone. Should I take the pictures and the cushions and start again? I was thinking. Then the phone went and I felt overpowered with relief – but it was a call to say that Darren's father was dying.

I felt close again to Darren on the flight down to Mexico. Staying in his home town, I had vivid dreams. I dreamed of being 'the other half' – sexually fulfilled, no worries, the 'other half'. Then the dream changed into being unable to find Lindsay's address – I needed to contact him because I'd refused him something. Did all those months of depression mean that during that time he and I were in Australia, doing *The Bed Before Yesterday*, I was attracted to him, too? I had a sort of shudder at the total domination it would mean, yet my adolescent fantasies were all of masochistic domination. I woke up happy that morning. Not so the next. I dreamed that Anthony Hopkins, the actor, was showing me a stage trick with his hand – I copied his gesture and accidentally cracked his spectacles into bits. I promised I'd pay. Rex appeared far ahead. I couldn't catch up with him. I was dreaming about what I always used to dream: 'There is someone, there is someone, I know there is.'

Two mornings and I saw Darren lying there and I was happy. Yet I brooded about my situation, sitting with the women, who were knitting, and seemed complete, with their babies and their ordered lives – of course I'm making comparisons . . . the Greek islands and the home of a dying man in a Mexican house above a bakery. The shame of the summer seemed less overwhelming somehow.

Isn't the word 'remember' a rather marvellous one because it, too, belongs to the past?

---

RACHEL WAS ALMOST DAILY IMPLORING her agents to find her work. Anything to get her out of Hutton Drive or Central Park West. An unusual opportunity came up, though perhaps less unusual in the United States (than in Britain) where there is a long, honourable and sometimes lucrative tradition of distinguished stage performers appearing in summer stock. Sometimes a talented new writer is discovered; sometimes a play, so cast, is revealed as potential Broadway material and may, with work on it, actually make it to town.

Rachel was offered a part in *The Sorrows of Gin*, an adaptation of the

John Cheever short story, which was set to tour theatres on the Eastern seaboard during the weeks of high summer. She accepted at once . . .

Not for the last time, there is the feeling of her own condition waiting in ambush for her in the text of the play; for *The Sorrows of Gin* is a funny-pathetic account of people's drinking habits seen through the eyes of an affluent family's small daughter who witnesses the constant hiring-and-firing of tippling cooks by her parents, who are themselves in thrall to the Demon Drink they conjure out of the cocktail shaker. Ironically, Rachel's role was that of Mrs Henlein, the baby-sitter, and the only character with a sober record. It was a good, full-bodied role, with plenty of opportunities for Rachel's attacking line in comic indignation. But she must have felt rather like a poacher turned gamekeeper as she hectored her social betters in the play on their drinking habits.

While rehearsing the play in New York, and touring with it in Connecticut and Massachusetts, she spent relaxing times with Aaron and Bobby Frosch. Aaron Frosch was attorney to Elizabeth Taylor, Richard Burton, her ex-husband Rex Harrison and others of that magnitude. He was now partially paralysed; and Bobby Frosch and Rachel were drawn together by the way they supported their respective burdens. The Frosches had a summer place at Quogue, on Long Island.

It was during that summer that I realised the game of fantasy was up and ran, panic-stricken, from the thought. The strange thing was that it was *after The Bed Before Yesterday*, in Australia, that the neurosis hit me about remembering lines, even on television. I suppose it was living with Darren and getting nothing from him, not even conversation, that I finally realised I *was* on my own and couldn't repress it any more. Darren and I came to a painful full-stop because our mutual need for each other was based on a Walter Mitty fantasy. It wasn't even my world that Darren wanted into – it was Rex's world, a world that *I* wanted to join, and did for a bit.

At this time, the chance of doing summer stock in *The Sorrows of Gin* presented me with an opportunity to get away from Beverly Hills and I took it.

Well, I *did* get through *The Sorrows of Gin* and my role as Mrs Henlein professionally, excellently, but with the irrational fear of not being able to remember a word. (This is not an emotional 'indulgence': it is a real fear that stiffens my wrists and muddles my head and I can't sit still.) Fortunately for me, I had Aaron Frosch and his wife Bobby to fly to at Quogue, on Long Island, when I arrived from Los Angeles and Bobby gave me a Valium to swallow. It was a dreadful time again in New York. The Los Angeles malaise followed me. Darren and I had dined on the eve of my departure at L'Orangerie, and I looked my best. We met Ben Gazzara and Janice Rule and their daughter there – and on the outside, I was pretty, attractive, a little tipsy, but in control. We met Helen Chaplin, the dear lady [and executive assistant manager] from the Beverly Wilshire Hotel, and it passed for an elitist, pleasant social evening – the kind that Darren and millions of others love. He was handsome and sweet. I was met at Los Angeles airport as usual by Hank [airline PR man] – not that those perks work any more. The flight was comfortable; the movie, *Love at First Bite*, was amusing; I drank Champagne and B.B.s – too much. It doesn't work any more, either. Evril [Frosch's chauffeur] met me at JFK and Carlos [porter] greeted me and through Champagne-clouded eyes my New York apartment looked colourful and inviting. I put on a Frank Sinatra record and I phoned Marti [Stevens], with B.B.-induced gaiety. It was all feverish and unstable and Lindsay would have called it disgusting and said, 'Stop playing with yourself.' Later, the emptiness of the New York apartment overwhelmed me.

I went to the Esplanade Hotel on West End Avenue and met the cast and director and read Mrs Henlein well – but inwardly totally alienated, loathing the part, frightened of not remembering the lines. The younger actors depressed me further – everyone seemed 'in control'. Again I remembered Lindsay's comment which frightens me so much: 'It is amazing how someone who seems so in control is so out of control.' I'm right to be frightened – to make my 'flesh crawl', because the path is only downwards if I, and I alone, cannot get myself out of that terrible rut.

Coming out, I met Charlotte [wife of actor John McMartin who had starred with Rachel in *The Visit*] – synchronicity, perhaps! I fell back into the pattern. We went to Sardi's to celebrate the old days. I drank Champagne cocktails and then a stinger with John McMartin – outwardly charming and 'fun'.

I don't remember going to the phone to call Val. An alcoholic blackout again. I don't, except hazily, remember the taxi ride down to 12th Street. Apparently I got there around eleven o'clock, had a beer, talked with that old mad animation to Val – about what? The mortgage; that Darren doesn't really get any pleasure out of our being together; that I intended to go to England . . . I asked him to take me in his arms and kiss me and he did hold me and it was a momentarily good feeling – but he didn't take me in his arms and kiss me. He said that to do so would be to open another can of beans. I was 'charming' enough.

He read a little *Hamlet*. I told him I didn't want to go home. So I spent the night there. Of course, I slept fitfully, looked at him, at the softness in his face . . . I felt ill when I woke. He read me the outline of his screenplay, took me downstairs to get a cab, waved bleakly as I left. We said we'd meet for dinner at Tout-Va-Bien on Monday. I got back to Central Park West and found I'd drunk everything in the apartment the night I arrived. I went and got some brandy to knock back, rinsed my mouth . . . careened through the rehearsal.

I called Gavin [Reid, actor], then poured out my fictitious problems to Marcella, the black girl, as we walked home after rehearsal. Then it was round to Gavin's apartment – neat and orderly – and to dinner at the West Side's Charlie's . . . it was filled with young Americans, all apparently 'in control'. Before this, I'd called Bobby Frosch in desperation, and went to see her and Aaron – by the grace of God and human kindness, they asked me to come and stay with them at Quogue, they were driving down on Saturday. So I didn't drink at Donovan's. We talked about one of my English actor friends who'd just undergone divorce and alcoholism – as wretched as I, poor man, maybe even more so.

The week-end with Bobby and Aaron was a blessed return to normality. Aaron Frosch is incapacitated by multiple sclerosis. Bobby, who not only is highly intelligent, but has a great sense of humour, has no choice but to live a routine life. She believes life is endurance. For her husband, it is a brave struggle to walk, to talk . . . Why, then, do I consider my state of being far worse? It is largely this hell of loneliness. Bobby has her children – they are her achievements. I feel adrift, purposeless, as if now the fixes don't work, now the illusions are gone, and I'm forced back to the centre of my being – and that's frightening.

I didn't drink at Bobby and Aaron's, maybe a glass of wine. Bobby and I talked. We are going to write a play – *Who Jumped First?* Her life is one of dedication – it is reality, though reality sometimes deeply depresses her, too. How I wished I was part of something approaching reality . . . I started to relax again, swam in their pool, went grocery shopping, talked to their pretty daughter, discussed Hunter College and the possibility of my going to lecture.

Doug drove me up to New York, dried out a bit. I called my girl-friends, put on television, got up the next day to get Virginia [Rachel's housekeeper-companion at Central Park West] her money and met the nice young woman writer who had adapted the John Cheever story and we flew in a haphazard fashion to Hartford, Connecticut. Again that old madness gripped me. I had two large vodka Martinis, ate a steak sandwich, had some wine. We talked about the horrors of Los Angeles. Wendy said she drew the drapes against the sunshine. I said it had no feel of life – physical life. The volcanic rock underneath one, the vapours above one: unless one was a pretty, suburban, cemented flower, the place would kill you. I slept for two hours, the vodka taking its effect – then Marcella called. There was a party by the pool at the Sheraton Hotel in Hartford. Unspeakable, unreachable people – a different species from me. I went back with Marcella to her room and we talked over coke and Champagne – she told me of her tough childhood, of the man who was nice to her, how it was time she had a mink coat. I went to bed and didn't work until after lunch.

I was uninterested in everything, including Mrs Henlein – but frightened my mind wouldn't retain the lines. It did – like an old dray-horse used to it.

That night was almost 'normal' – Wendy, Jack [Hofsess, stage director] and the manic hairdresser and I went to have dinner. Peter the producer had bought himself a tuxedo. Dinner was good. My only comment was that my external life was all right, but my internal life troubled, and what a clinger I was to egomaniacal lovers – my own ego being very low. That perhaps is the crux of it. You don't creep downstairs, as I once did, to try on a pair of rollerskates too small for you to see if you can rollerskate. You don't throw a ball into the net – and it goes in *twice*, and you feel good about it. You don't see if you can ride a bike at fifty-one, unless it's all those years of being so hopeless at everything, unless one's whole belief in oneself, one's right to be oneself, has been so punched, so put down, so strangled that one is left with nothing but contempt and fear and no centre, no drive, no hope. Anyway, the evening passed satisfactorily enough. I worked the next day – desperately unhappy – ate a little lunch – played Mrs Henlein like the highly over-emotional, terror-struck but gifted actress I am. Everyone liked me. I hid it all very well indeed.

I went back to the hotel. Jack Hofsess was going to Fire Island, to the house he'd taken with two friends, to the sound of the ocean, to his happy state of being a young and successful director, with his plans for the future to do work he wanted to do. I went and had two glasses of red wine in the bar, talked in my apparently 'controlled' way to the young Irish bar-tender, went upstairs to pack, ordered a sandwich – which was brought by the handsome room-waiter. Recalled him. His name was Omar from Ethiopia, studying psychology. I gave him my name and address in that outwardly charming and warm and assured manner. Then I left with the young student for the airport. The plane was delayed, no air conditioning in the terminal – a gross, fat man attempted conversation. I went out to the passageway where the air was cooler and muttered to myself, play-acting a scene which had Rex in it and we were going to the Plaza to stay in a suite and be met by one of his henchmen. Thus did I escape all form of reality. I was in control enough not to let anyone *see* me muttering – that stage won't happen.

Got on the plane and ordered two Scotch with my ginger ale, arrived home – and couldn't bear it. I went to the Marooney's and asked for another drink. Slept holding the bear and the rabbit and sucking my thumb.

Snoopy came into the room in the early hours of the morning and with profound relief, after I'd woken up and realised that *I* was Snoopy, I saw Virginia asleep in the little room. I relaxed a bit then. I wasn't completely alone.

I didn't sleep, though. I drove down to Quogue with Doug [unidentified friend]. There had been a thunder-storm the night before – the rain was peaceful. My stomach twisted again when I thought of the summer in Los Angeles – the sound of the hair-dryer, all the clothes . . . difficult to live with Darren, but we did have a certain peace and sweetness together and I hate to think of that, too, going out of my life. Difficult to square it with Sybil after probing what she thought.

But Los Angeles is to blame for it, too. Los Angeles belies all that man and womankind have done to minimise the darkness and the inexplicable nature of our very lives. No cockerels crow to announce the day. No cows moo. No reachable birds sing. No church-bells ring on Sunday to remind us of our spirit. We rarely see a funeral procession – no reminder of our mortality is ever present. People don't walk, don't talk, don't really laugh, cry inside or refuse to, and falsity is everywhere. All want to take, not give, and life laughs coldly back.

I got through the play, but it was a bad experience that left me iller than ever. I hated Mrs Henlein and thought her an ugly, old, lonely woman. I tried the old tricks. I always try them. Alcohol induced fantasies, imaginary conversations with Rex. I need to be constantly on a 'high', above reality. It is, of course, killing me: but I, too, have enjoyed life, had euphoric fun, been successful, given love and been loved in turn.

---

RACHEL HARDLY PAUSED between the final curtain on *The Sorrows of Gin* and rehearsals starting in early August, 1979, for *Once a Catholic*. This play by Mary O'Malley, which was still running in London at the time, after two years, at first looked an ideal choice. She was to play Mother Peter, teacher in a Catholic convent school whose bigotry the playwright satirised with ribald wit. Peggy Cass, acclaimed for her stage and film work in *Auntie Mame*, was cast as another nun.

Doris Cole Abrahams produced, in association with Leon Beck. She had attempted to stage the play the previous winter, but met with Equity's resistance to using some of the London cast. Now she had a new director, Mike Ockrent, replacing Frank Dunlop, and a new co-producer, Eddie Kulukundis.

The omens all looked so good . . . In fact, it turned out a disaster – and, for Rachel, something worse. She was now afflicted with fear of an inability to memorise her lines. Among her journals were found sheet after sheet of paper covered with obsessively transcribed dialogue passages from the play. Her nerves were shot to pieces. She could now scarcely stand the sight of her Central Park West apartment. Rehearsals were held above a grimly depressing 42nd Street theatre offering a film called *Queen Hustler*. The weather was unbearably humid. Darren was 3,000 miles away. She turned for comfort to a man she had met at an AA group, an ex-convict out on parole for armed robbery she called John, or 'Knuckles', from his habit of flexing his finger joints. He had a pad in the Bronx and sheer loneliness drove her to stay in it rather than spend a night alone in her own infinitely grander place. Unless she had company, which usually meant a girl called Virginia, a part-time maid-housekeeper in the apartment, she could not bear to spend a night by herself: she gradually abandoned her own place for a room in Bobby Frosch's New York apartment. Sometimes she persuaded Darren to commute to New York: invariably he did so, but no sooner was he at her side than tensions and tantrums separated them and each time he left swearing it was 'the last time'. Of course, it never was . . .

*Once a Catholic* was toured for a few weeks of August, to the accompaniment of mixed reviews, good for her, so-so for the play. Rachel made a few more demoralising self-discoveries, referred to in her journals, and when they returned to New York she felt only loneliness and despair. There were a few weeks to go before the Broadway opening on October 10, 1979, and she impulsively decided to spend a week or two seeking company with her niece and *her* family in Cervinia. From there, on September 10, 1979, she wrote to Milton Goldman, putting a braver face on things than she knew her condition warranted.

'Dearest Milton – I've been here a week now, and rested and read and feasted and fiesta-ed. For the most part, the weather has been brilliant. Until today that is, when Fate struck again. I shall be so glad to see the back of 1979!! [Rachel then refers to the sudden illness of her brother-in-law who had arrived with his wife, Hazel, a few days earlier.] Well, Milton darling, about me. I do hope *Yanks* will be the success we all hope for, because there are two films coming up that I want to be in.

'The first is *Death Trap* that Sidney Lumet is directing, and which we have discussed. The part of the psychic I know I could play humorously, mysteriously, intricately, and well. Perhaps, if Sidney doubts my comedic gifts, he should be invited to *Once a Catholic*.

'The second film is the Jane Fonda one about secretaries [later entitled *Nine to Five*], which I mentioned to you briefly on the phone.

'Regarding *Once a Catholic*, I am so relieved that I got such good notices. I don't know if you saw them. Would you ask Doris Cole Abrahams to send you a copy of all of them – and one for me, too? I left my batch in the theatre by accident. The reason I bring this up is because I had to go my own sweet way to avoid the young director's tendency to ask us to play the characters as caricatures, and this must not happen during the re-rehearsal period prior to the Broadway opening. Fortunately I got such good notices that he probably will have the sense to leave well alone. In case he doesn't, let's get hold of copies of the notices!!!

'I hear that *Yanks* is opening in New York on September 18. Is there any point in my coming back to attend it? If you get this letter before the end of the week, do phone me . . . I shall in any case be back around the 18th September. It's my birthday on the 20th. So let's celebrate! My love to you dear Milton and to Arnold – Rachel.'

*Once a Catholic* closed the week it opened on Broadway. One or two of the critics, notably Walter Kerr, were deeply offended by its anti-Catholic gibes. But one didn't have to be Catholic to dislike it: the rest found that even rated as satirical comedy its tone was erratic; as serious criticism of bigotry and ignorance, it was far too unfocused. Rex Reed called it 'a gorgeous play . . . badly served by its American cast . . . with all sorts of ratchedy-voiced British accents.' But even the one British star, Rachel, did not escape whipping. Walter Kerr singled out her bizarre recital of the Lord's Prayer at a speed 'normally used by five-year-old girls getting past grace and into the meat loaf.'

Rachel viewed the closing with undisguised relief: in her present mood, it was like having a term of life imprisonment commuted to a suspended sentence. But her unexpected freedom was not accompanied by any improvement in her condition. She got steadily worse. Darren had flown back from Los Angeles to be with her on her birthday – 'She had invited my mother to be there,' he said, 'for she got on well with her. She was on her best behaviour.' But he stayed on after *Once a Catholic* closed since he felt Rachel simply could not be left alone.

DARREN RAMIREZ: 'Her condition was very noticeable. Her "outrages" once used to occur every two months: now the periods between them were getting shorter and shorter. She would be crying all the time and unable to get herself out of bed. She had begun receiving Lithium treatment to help calm her and keep her spirits up. She had become alarmed about money, terrified by the fear that she might go broke. I got the impression that she was shocked to have to pay five hundred dollars just for the forty-five minutes she spent consulting a therapist who lived near New York and had a reputation for treating "celebrities". We drove down together to see him. But he said as she was going away very shortly – we were off to the London premiere of *Yanks* at the end of the month – he wouldn't undertake any more rigorous treatment. He just told her not to drink, gave her some pills to keep her calm and said he would treat her later.

'Contrary to what you might expect, pills terrified Rachel – she feared they would affect her memory and she would forget her lines.

'Rachel was always good at devising ways to get me back to her. With the premiere of *Yanks* in London, it was the offer, paid for by United Artists, of a flight over on Concorde and an opening night celebrity-packed party.

'But aboard the Concorde to London, she looked like a zombie. Perhaps it was the pills. Perhaps she was drinking too much on the flight. She could still work wonders at making herself agreeable to people – you'd never have dreamed she was so ill. But on the day of the show for the foreign press, she got drunk, returned to the Intercontinental Hotel, began shouting at me and literally took a door off its hinges. I was desperate. I called Lindsay Anderson, who was in New York, and said, "I can't control her any longer." Lindsay said, she'd just have to exercise self-control. I said, "Lindsay, I don't think she is even capable of working – I think she'll have to be put away, maybe for a year. I'm going to get in touch with Dr Glyn Davies. Please call her, Lindsay, and overcome the resistance I think we're going to get." She was furious at what I'd done and went completely mad on the day of the *Yanks* premiere. One hour before it, she wouldn't even get dressed. Glyn Davies examined her, gave her two tranquillisers and booked a room for her in a nursing home in Harrow and sent her off to the premiere and the party afterwards in an almost comatose state.

'The next day I packed for her and saw her off to the nursing home. Lindsay called again from New York and told me to get in touch with Karel Reisz.'

KAREL REISZ: 'I went down to Bowden House a couple of times. It was always the same: Rachel would be in bed when I arrived, she'd get dressed, we'd take a walk, after two or three hours I'd plead work to get away and then we'd sit in the car for maybe another couple of hours and talk ... Things were circular and we'd finish up as we'd started. I encouraged her to turn to writing. "Look," I'd say, "you're sharp, intelligent, well read and the tone of voice in which you talk about other people is very different from the way you deal with yourself. You can get them into perspective: maybe you could do as much for yourself, if you wrote things down." I remembered how she'd once seen a film of mine – one she wasn't in – and she said, "Oh, that's a dreadful fake bit," and she was right. I felt that maybe if she turned to fiction, she'd help herself.'

But in spite of treatment at Bowden House, in spite of Karel Reisz's friendly ministrations, Rachel realised how badly she needed the help of a professional analyst.

She had committed herself to *The Hostage Tower*, the pilot film of a projected TV series, which was to be shot in Paris in November, 1979. Fears assailed her again: would she be able to remember her lines? Her introspection yielded up such terrifying thoughts to her imagination that she consulted a London psychoanalyst, Dr Amadeo Limentani.

Dr Limentani practises in Upper Wimpole Street, from consulting rooms in one of those fashionably pre-Raphaelite-looking houses whose interiors resemble High Anglican churches which have fallen into disuse for lack of a congregation. But the room where he saw Rachel is cool and relaxing, furnished with a black fabric-covered couch, tawny pillows, a black wing-chair and through the window, from the narrow yard, comes birdsong. As Rachel's journals refer specifically to their sessions together, Dr Limentani agreed to enlarge upon her reasons for consulting him, while continuing to observe his own professional discretion regarding the detailed nature of their conversation.

DR LIMENTANI: 'She came to me complaining about a growing compulsion to look into herself, to become overly introspective. She feared it was paralysing her will to act. She was going to do three or four weeks' filming in Paris and what she wanted to know was, would she be able to make it or not. It was heavy going, indeed.'

KAREL REISZ: 'Knowing that my own son-in-law is an analyst, Rachel kept in touch with me about her treatment. I must admit, I had to smile occasionally. Her analyst was very shrewd in his assessment of her. At the end of her first session, the actress in her said she had had a great time, she felt very encouraged and a weight was already falling off her shoulders. And the analyst said, "Oh, that sounds like a very bad sign to me." He was not going to play along with her "performance".'

DR LIMENTANI: 'She came quite frequently, whenever she could, though she interrupted our encounters twice to put work first. Part of the difficulty was that she was torn between her career as an actress and looking after herself. She was hoping to be able to develop her talents as a writer. By knowing herself, she thought she might improve her writing skills. Personally, I thought she was writing down privately far more than she was telling me.

'My view is that alcoholism is a symptom of a greater disturbance, but it is very difficult to get to this if the patient continues to indulge his or her weakness: there is a physical difficulty, if it is incapacitating. We treat the underlying cause, where we can get to it with the patient's help, and seek a cure for the depression that has led to the drinking. I just would not be prepared to hazard an answer to whether Miss Roberts' fear of not being able to remember her lines was physical or mental. But it seems to me that her mental determination was very strong. She succeeded in filming in France despite her neurosis.'

But if *The Sorrows of Gin* was bad, *Once a Catholic* – the play I did next – was even worse. After a flying visit back to Los Angeles, I came back to New York and started the miserable rehearsals of *Once a Catholic* – young girls 'in love with' the theatre, older second-rate actors, an unhappy playwright and a new director. The reality of hot, humid New York, living alone, no limousine for me, finding the lines hard to memorise, swigging the brandy so that I could get going. I hated the Mother Peter character and I hated summer stock.

One thing of interest emerged from it – I have no desire to taste youth again. Currently, my experience is bitter, but I wouldn't want to return to gaucherie and what I remember of my Bristol Old Vic days.

Cape Cod was stiff and cold and organised in that 'over-organised' American way. We stayed at one inn which was run by dithering dykes and provincial to a suffocating degree. We moved to another where large, florid American vacationers spent their lives lining up for their Boston scrod with a choice of french fries or a baked potato, preceded by salad with a choice of house dressing or Thousand Island. Correct dress had to be worn after six o'clock, so yards of polyester propelled itself into the dining room, yellows and pinks and blues and greens, humidly sticking to over-fleshed white bodies.

Driving to the theatre with Leon [Becker, co-presenter of *Once a Catholic*] – bright, controlled, nice, secretive Leon who looks a little like a fly – we noticed the dense woods. Straight trees growing closely together. Immediately the Indians came to my mind and the beauty of their playful world. While taking notes outside the Falmouth Playhouse, beside the lake, a self-assured rabbit hopped around us and later, two tiny creatures with black stripes down their backs chased each other until one of them saw me, and froze with self-surviving fear, then took off in the opposite direction. In numbing contrast to this was the hard, cold, dirty, cemented squalor of the burnt-out Bronx we drove through on our endless return from Westport at the end of August. A squad of screaming, flashing police cars roared through the murk and the grime. All of it was senseless, dehumanised, wrong. One hunted-looking cat skeetered down the street. Who has a place on this part of the earth?

The Kennedy compound at Hyannis Point suddenly showed just how different American democracy is from its British counterpart. The neat, large, clapboard but expensive houses on their choice pieces of colonial land, with their private beaches and golf clubs, at least four or five belonging to the Camelot Clan, a sort of monarchical amateur dramatic society, brought home to one the uncomfortable divisiveness of American society, and the amazing sense of the importance of manipulation that Joe Kennedy had. His determination not only to belong where Catholic Irishmen like him had not belonged before, but also to become the puppeteer through his sons' mobility. Meanwhile, the other Americans swelter along with the rats and drug themselves into another life, and, if they're caught, are locked up to swelter with more rats. And the police sirens continue to howl.

The tortoiseshell cat and the geese, whose personal habits are unbecoming, but who nevertheless have a certain grace, were soothing influences in Falmouth. I got out of New York on the Saturday. It was raining. I was glad to go, glad to leave the demoralising horror of 42nd Street. The New Amsterdam Theater, which had once housed the beautiful Ziegfeld Follies girls, retained a certain romance, but the hot, humid streets in August and the poor, pathetic, crazed dregs ambling aimlessly along 42nd Street choked one's very compassion. I didn't want to be part of it, but momentarily, was.

Flying down with Leon and Doris [Cole Abrahams, presenter of *Once a Catholic*] and entering someone else's world for a few moments was a relief from the restless, self-disgusted world I've been inhabiting lately. Doris is rich, a little naïve, but very determined. She loses things, her glasses, her watch. She has Leon who attends to her and organises her and who is happy to do so. She's suffered. Life has bored her. Her children don't 'possess' her. The theatre does, and the social aspects of her life. Both give her solace. Leon appears self-possessed, easy in his skin. Tennis satisfies him. He and Doris are good business partners.

The week in Falmouth was messy, amateurish, offensively unskilled. We were not ready to perform, overcome with nerves – an absurd thing to put oneself through.

I told myself it was over – it *wasn't*: the New York opening lay ahead – and not to panic. My God, though, that wasn't acting at Westport – it was sheer rigid torture. I wasn't a professional at all. I had to invent a broken love-affair to explain my state of nerves. I had to see a doctor, the first of many since.

I returned from Falmouth with Peggy Cass [with Rachel, leading player in *Once a Catholic*] through arid American highways, stopping for gas given by unfriendly people, buying coffee at a Howard Johnson's chain, milk at a Puerto Rican store, coming home to a dead, impersonal apartment that I've worked on and that looks outwardly bright and colourful, but gives me so little comfort since there is no one here either to welcome me or with whom I can pass a humorous remark. The four walls do not exclude the void of life. I call desperately people whose lives I infringe on a little, who are, I hope, fond of me, but who are not enclosed in personal loneliness, like I am, with too few resources and interests of my own to fill the hours.

I called Louis [Pulvino, stage manager and close friend], who begged me to nourish myself. I called Bobby Frosch, who has her own family responsibilities and envied me my 'freedom'. I called Sybil, who understood. She is, however, able to have a life with Jordan and her girls. I called Rosemary [Harris, English actress and close friend], who is doing the same with John and Jennifer [her husband and daughter]. I called my sister [Hazel and her husband, family and relatives], enclosed in her world of John and Daniel and Sophie and Christian and Neil and Ye and Jackie and Marco, making ends meet and making dresses for herself and the children and growing tomatoes and lettuce and cooking quiches. I got through the night – then sick with fright, tormented, I saw a doctor and slept at last.

Later, refreshed, I returned to wondering what to do with my life. I wished Darren could be the answer. I was still not entirely sure that it wouldn't be better to be with him than without him. If pride and confidence in acting were ever to come back, perhaps my life would then seem less futile. Into my mind came John, the kind ex-con from the AA meeting: Do I really want him to cook breakfast for? The truth is, I want to feel as though I'm wanted and needed and I want to *give*, as my sister does to her daughter. But I expect I always wanted more than that out of life, and am now at the stage where I have neither the blessed relief of not having to struggle any more, of being able to sink into my age and my life surrounded by the family I brought up who in turn are giving me little treats and a sense of welcome – nor am I the hailed actress in love with the excitement of that world.

I called up my niece Jacqueline, who lives in Italy, to say that I might be coming over to see her the following week before *Once a Catholic* opened on Broadway. The voice at the other end said she had gone to Aosta and would be back the next day. Fear and tearful pain gripped my heart. Jacqueline had gone somewhere with her child, or to the doctor, or with her husband Marco. She had gone somewhere, however, as a whole human being – I got frightened because I felt fractured, because my life seemed to have no form at all.

The problem remains one of – how do I fill my life without a real family? My sister Hazel, I knew, would rather I didn't go to Italy. But my niece's life was so far removed from mine, and I envy it so, that it might give me a little sustenance. If I don't stop these 'lonely woman' phone calls, I shall alienate all my friends, and quite justifiably.

I organised the terrace of the Central Park West apartment so that it would look attractive, then 'scrambled' to Cervinia, still heavy-hearted, but slightly less so for hearing Darren's voice before I left. That he said he loved me was comforting.

Jacqueline accompanied by Marco met me at Milan and we drove through Old Italy. *They* are able to be complete in their 1930s village: she with her blonde children, he never having known anything else. They *live* – do not dream or ache. Memories of my Mother were there. She was to die one year later from the time we were last together in Cervinia. My sense of isolation now was hers then, but I didn't know. I was often brusque, Dear one, forgive me. I should have lavished greater love on you.

I wouldn't ever go to Cervinia to write, but I began to feel better. Memories of sullen Val did not intrude at all. My sister Hazel and her husband and children arrived on the night of 4 September. At heart, I remained fearful. I recalled all too well the restless days and sweating nights of California . . . days of being unable to settle down at all to do anything or see anyone. I despised Darren one minute, longed for his affection the next. Hateful days. I recalled the Sunday afternoon party attended by reformed homosexual alcoholics, still cruising, but now on Perrier water. Who *could* feel life in that world? I recalled driving to my AA meetings, spending the night with a film star friend, crouching in her home the next day reading the book on alcoholism, relating in part to it, but defiantly rejecting much of it. Worst of all was my rejection of Darren, gentle dear good Darren – and my fear that what the psychologist I went to said is true – that Darren just cannot give me what I want. Why do I make it so hard for the two of us? Why do I allow Rosemary to say our relationship is arid and Pamela to say that it's not quite real and Sybil to say that we are staying together for the wrong reasons?

Yes, I get angry when Darren courts the vulgar rich. But do I take it all too seriously? Should I laugh a little more at his vanity and accept him and the tenderness he undeniably has?

I don't know what sick dream I've been living in for years on and off. Part of this time of pain has been awakening from it, I think.

On the plane back to New York from Milan, had Jackie and Marco been with me, it would have been wonderful. The lurch of loneliness I felt when they left the Ambassadors' Lounge was due to fright again – but back they came because 'I looked so lonely' . . . and was . . . and am. Then the world righted itself again as we drove off through the Italian countryside to the *ristorante* where soon the wedding party of the Southern Italians, dressed up in their best, roared in. Wine and good *antipasto* and the sweetness of Jackie and Marco made me happy – and merry on the wine, we parted. She to her *pensione*, her parents, her children, her bar, her 'countrymen' with her husband, who grew up there, in Cervinia, and who knows everyone. Who knows nothing else. Who roars down the valley in his fast car. Who knows every bend. It is his life.

Had Jackie and Marco been with me when I awoke on Sunday after returning to New York, we could have filled the fridge and gone to St Patrick's. I telephoned my friends – Darren, three times. He promised to catch a flight and be with me in an hour or two. I couldn't have gone on much longer, 'alone'. I called John Schlesinger who, I imagine, to be vigorous, satisfied and, because he's busy, unbeset by doubts and fears. Not so. But he's not lonely.

I longed to be fifty-one with a constant husband and girls. I called Lindsay. He told me to stop playing with myself. I chose not to think of Rex and the ravages of time on his face, his loneliness, his needs. 'I can't live your life and you can't live mine,' he said. No, I couldn't live his. I didn't know how – and neither he, nor I, would want to live mine. Even now, I couldn't begin to know how he handles that life of his. He's a sophisticate, what's called 'a man of the world' – with his ease and flair, and the right companions, travels in Europe, eats his *contrefilet*, protects himself with easy assurance. I flounder around in that world, half liking it, half loathing it. I can't handle it, certainly on my own. Rex's wife, Mercia, can.

Darren arrived and we walked arm in arm down Broadway and along 42nd Street where I'd so recently struggled along to work, nervously, with the group of second-rate players, or to learn the part of Mrs Henlein in the ladies' toilet of the Ansonia Hotel because I'd blindly rushed down to the East Side the night before, rather than face the evidence of my life at home in my neat, clean, pretty and empty flat.

A few days after I got back to New York, an invitation arrived. Radio City Music Hall was a complete surprise. Milton Goldman, my agent, called it a black-tie dinner. I went to the apartment that Milton and Arnold Weissberger [New York lawyer, specialising in film and theatre clients] have in Sutton Place. Rachel Gurney was there, slim and sad. So was Patrice Munsel in a red boa-constrictor and ball-gown affair. Milton had been in New Jersey to see his mother. Arnold arrived from the country. The show was in aid of the mentally ill. Gregory Peck was the host. The Rockettes kicked their legs up splendidly. Tiny Lyn Carter was very funny impersonating Dietrich 'falling off the stage again'. Chita Rivera seemed to enjoy herself. At dinner afterwards, Radie Harris [Hollywood columnist] and her escort and John McCallum and I all sat on over our drinks and John talked about himself wanting to be Hamlet.

Another night I went to the re-done King Cole Bar at the St Regis, with old, nice, quaint Sammy Kahn singing his songs, his young wife there with Barbara Sinatra, the photographs in the foyer of the St Regis from 1904 onwards . . . Judy Garland dead, but Bea Lillie alive and not consumed and defeated yet . . . yesterday's socialites . . . my own memories . . . the photograph of yesterday's husband in the London *Daily Express* . . . What a ridiculous fantasy. Portland Mason [daughter of Pamela and James Mason] and her husband Martin, they all harrowingly brought back memories of Los Angeles, those months of depression when an article about the Hotel de Paris in Monte Carlo and Barbara and Frank and Rex and Mercia could throw me into another fit of abject self-pity. The memories were somewhat lightened at the St Regis that night when I saw the evidence on the walls of where fantasy finished up – stale air, stale wine, stale people and a stale spirit next morning.

I went to a psychiatrist soon after that and spent five hundred dollars which shocked me – facing the facts, I suppose! I didn't like such 'facts', or, at least, I didn't until I saw Dr Frere [New York physician specialising in treatment of depression]. Apart from diagnosis and pills, he gave me hope in an entirely unsentimental manner. His reference to *Hamlet* after my reading to him of my own symptoms was euphoric. Hope came back. I came back. Life came back. A surfeit of life?

Later: I'm afraid the hope turned out to be false and alcohol-induced.

I realised I need not spend days alone in a lively-looking apartment that is no longer a home. I could rent office space in New York and use it to write in. The stories I'd begun to set down made the weeks less hard. I wonder: is my fear of forgetting what I have to say on stage yet another example of the blocks I'm putting between me and my own enjoyment? I rather think it is.

I told myself: I want to get out of this hole. I want to nourish myself. I want to enjoy my talent. I want to enjoy my life. I want to live it. It can be done.

I would so love to join hands again with my beloved talent . . . to have faith in it, to have confidence in it, as I did, before *him*. My life would then have meaning, the pain would have been worth it. I can but try.

Writing does seem to alleviate some, if not all of this unfathomable fear.

Of that period after I got back from Cervinia, after *Once a Catholic* had opened and mercifully closed, I remember the magic escape from the world into sleep . . . an evening with Doris . . . real talk with Leon . . . Darren lying quietly in bed beside me, an Antabuse firmly inside me insuring me against the vicious enemy, the call to myself, to Ray, the masochistic dream even – the male wanting me to wear the too tight clothes and the relaxed, sensual pleasure I got from it. My conclusion is that my own form of masochism, having no outlet, has turned in on me, constantly self-punishing, denying me satisfaction of any kind with or without anyone. Having no one to make me suffer, I will make myself suffer intensely. I'll tear myself to shreds, wallow in my lack of self-worth – visit the Sherry Netherland to see a departed source of once-satisfying pain . . . But then again, No! I was just lost and lonely and went to look for Platonov – my illusory Rex.

At the end of October, 1979, I flew over to London with Darren. Elton John's concert in New York gave me pleasure before we left. He was brilliant, the nice Cockney lyricist and his pretty wife were charming and light and happy. I can't remember his name, though. I was only half there, anyhow. I couldn't stand a lot of London. I had dinner with Darren and Jeffrey Lane in Mr Chow's and had to leave them – couldn't stand it. I called Rex. It was a comfort, hearing that familiar voice, a relief to hear that all was not Paradise with him, that he has his problems. A love-hate relationship between him and me, of course. Half of me felt secure and protected talking to him; half of me felt the other side of him. At the lawyer's office, talking about the reduced alimony, his voice was the 'other' voice, but to hear it was a momentary shot in the arm. Over the phone, I read him the short story, 'Five Roses', which I'd written about the days when we were happy in Portofino:

'But five roses would be enough, Reggie, don't you understand?'

He'd built his myth years before. Not before she was born, exactly, but there were twenty of the dangerous years between them. Years in which he'd come to know that world – and what success, position and the accoutrements of wealth meant to it, and what little space there was for warmth, for friendliness, for honesty . . . He, too, had been like she was, once. Carefree, talented he was, charming to a degree . . . but he'd met the blunt face of tragedy, twice. She'd known very little of such harshness, never been exposed to the cold eye of his world. His bloodhound eyes only gazed into chaos: hers weren't even opened yet. He'd been an innocent once. That is what she saw in him and with all the naïveté of sheltered youth supposed she could take on this hooded, self-regarding man and bring him back to the 'chap' he'd been.

It came to an irreversible standstill that day, years later, when, in her own chaos, she tried to face the myth sitting, burgundy-silk dressing-gowned, sipping tea on an Italian terrace of what was not really a villa, served by an Italian peasant girl who was not really a maid. Survival is made of such moments.

'Please try and help me, Reg, I'm not walking in step with life.'

The man behind the myth replied that he couldn't bear it and would take the dog for a walk. If only mimosa trees and escape could be what life is all about, she thought. But it had been *once*, and that 'once' would remain forever among the most magical moments of her life. The feel of the air had been different then, and he had stunned her. It was so improbable, such an incredibly startling bolt from the blue. The past fourteen years for her had been confident ones and determined ones and were beginning to be successful ones. How on earth, then, could she have known what those same years had been for him? It was only now that he was becoming clear to her and that she began to understand. 'If I'd known then what I know now' had been her Father's perennial cry. But was it true? Weren't her precious years made possible only by her very innocence about what he really was or had become? Yet the sensuality of those days would always be with her.

Those close to her wondered why he had such a hold on her still. Of course it wasn't really him at all. Away from that beautiful part of Italy where they spent the marvellous days and nights, they were not really ever at peace with each other. That's what had made it so torturingly bewildering. Together there, it was a voluptuous time, and quiet, too, and very, very elitist. He at once opened wide all those doors. That she entered them was unavoidable; that they could not stay together behind them, inevitable. But the time that they *were* together . . . all was sensation.

It was quiet there in November and quite beautiful. Smells and sounds were as restful as the gentle sun. Good working women dressed sensibly in black and courteous and simple gave her such feelings of steadiness and the sense of the rightness of life. All was harmony in those days. They used to walk up and up the rough mule-track, past the Edwardian villa owned by the old Contessa who still attempted to order it after the fashion of a decade ago. Young girls in blue and white uniforms served the wine from the vineyard while the Contessa discoursed, rather than spoke, the faded picture of Saint Sebastian on the wall. The medieval face of Catholic Italy had a density; you walked in atmosphere; life itself was thick; and he and she felt part of it. He was the *signore*; she, *simpatica* – both labels appealed, and belonged.

There was a sense of good peasant order in the house. The family who lived there tended it well. Maria the cook was small, fat and fierce and good – she, too, respectable in black. Her step-daughter Pina, devout and virginal and sweet-tempered, took great pride in the villa. It was always flower-filled. Giuseppe her Father was shy and getting old now. He loved and cherished his garden, *their* garden, so that mimosa grew and lemon trees and roses and pansies and honeysuckle curled over the gate. They woke up in that nursery every morning. He would open the shutters and in would come the peace, the tradition that surrounded them and blinded them.

The days were cool and sweet. Italy in early autumn, the port rid of its tourists, settled back into simplicity.

At six, the first boats returned and they wandered through a market, lit a candle in the magnificent church that smelled of incense, stopped for a Negroni at the corner café owned by two brothers and their darkly handsome sister. They were not old, but they had old, old Italian faces and again there was that heavy sense of Catholic Italy. The high, steep cobbled mule-track back to the villa they sometimes walked a little drunk, or he drove his Jeep, a little drunk. Giuseppe's fires never winked, not in the living room nor in the bedroom. So they'd brought a tiny English bellows back with them and blew, and laughed, and polished copper pans in front of the smoky wood, and Don Pedro and Don Paco wandered in, feline aristocrats from Spain. They'd bought them when they were in Madrid, tom-cats and brothers, with bushy tails and the elegant coats of their angora breeding.

They played Bessie Smith records and she danced. Pina brought in dinner – the best of Maria's cooking. It was *ucelliniscapati* with the unlikely translation of 'little escaped birds', tid-bits of veal and bacon and bay-leaves on a skewer. Later, she installed a little oven in the serving room and cooked for them. They played chess, made love, went early to bed and read. When it rained, they'd stay there, relight last night's fire, eat fresh boiled eggs from the farm behind the villa where one of the sons bayed like a dog at full moon, get up at noon, and bathe, and drink brandy and wrap up and walk along the cliffs in the rain, alone, together in their special world.

Sometimes on one of their very long walks they met a shy spaniel dog and a one-eyed cat. They belonged to Virginia.

Virginia lived high up in the hills, above the port, with the dog and the cat, a chicken or two, cherry trees, flowers that she dried and took down to the port to sell. It was a hovel, I suppose you could say, but she offered them home-made sour cherry wine and took them to a tumbledown stone ruin close by, where she said she'd been born. It looked out over the blue Mediterranean sea. It had been her Father's house. It was too horrible to contemplate that had toothless, gracious Virginia, eighty years old, been born in some modern monument to progress in the Brave New World, she quite likely would have been an institutionalised, tranquillised, immobilised zombie. Happily, she was dignified, independent, occupied and happy.

They saw Virginia several times on those wonderful walks. There was a tiny inlet where the Italians had buried the Doges of Genoa in the fourteenth century and which now sported a restaurant *a la famiglia* where lobster and wine were served to them when they arrived, contentedly tired, legs trembling, thirsty and hungry and happy. They saw less and less of Virginia as their walks grew fewer and fewer. She surely died as harmoniously as she had lived. But that was to be in the years to come.

Now as November turned to Christmas, and Christmas to spring, their *primavera* days continued with ambitions and that other world of theirs pushed lazily, tranquilly away. It was only much, much later that she realised why those limpid days had been so white-hot – why it was so changed. He brought with him all the sleek sophistication and dazzle of success, all the security of power. No wonder her feet didn't touch the ground. No wonder they became leaden and the fire-flies ceased to dance when the heady concoction of his flattering attention and Italy began to be diluted. But these days, too, were still far away. Now there was everything to do. Paths revisited for him, new to her.

They walked through pines and cypress groves, drove to the villa where Max Beerbohm had lived his last days in quiet culture, far from the changed London that he'd loved, and where he'd remembered a goat, some forgotten regimental mascot, being walked down Piccadilly. And they were always together. They wanted each other. They excited each other. They calmed each other.

When did the crackle of pine needles and darkening afternoons become melancholy? When did those blessedly simple people who lived their family lives, hour, day, month and year in and out, lose their power to give peace and, instead, served only to throw up in stark relief the deadness that was growing? The deadness that he and she dreaded so much that they went on together for too many years, hoping, and then flailing out at each other as every corner became a dead end and every feeling grew cold and curdled. As silence grew, they retreated from each other in different ways. Inertia immobilised her; a forced and sad activity gripped him; and between was a void and ashy chaos that the noise of the busy cicadas and the far away cries of the *contadini* and the voice of the cow mooing in the dark barn could no longer enter.

She stayed there once without him. The last time.

It was soon to be her birthday, nine years later. Autumn again. They were living apart now. She flew to London, saw him in his hotel suite. There was a bulky packet on his bed. He'd got a furrier to bring round a dark, expensive mink coat. He knew she wouldn't want it. 'Five roses would have been enough, Reggie,' she said.

It was over.

I feel that I don't belong to life – but I did once, didn't I? Did only eight years with Rex do this to me? No – I was *ready* for it to be done. I've been screaming out for emotional support all year, internal reassurance of some kind. My mind is turning away from acting, so that my memory is being affected. I used acting to attract men – that was *part* of it. So did the great tragic neurotics, Judy [Garland] and Marilyn [Monroe]. In *Chemin de Fer*, I played Francine, especially in the bedroom scene, for Val in the wings. I have no family support, now no artistic ambition, and am crumbling daily inside. No wonder I am torn with anxiety and fear and am immobilised.

I had a wonderful, surprisingly wonderful time last night. I woke this morning with a clear head and the familiar lurch in my stomach that cleared my head. I've lost the thought, but it felt as though my dichotomy was moving closer together. The lurch in the stomach seemed to have to do with my masochism and fear, and for an instant I understood and recognised it. I'd dreamed of New York and rain and someone resembling Knuckles, who was the 'find' of the AA meetings, and holding my white bra, about to go to Germany with a voucher for a dictionary that had to be cashed in over there. Trivia. But to return to that lurch for a moment – it seemed that if it and my head could join together, I'd be all right. So I *am* disturbed, and ever have been, haven't I? I remembered one of the analysts I went to saying, 'You can't work because you're thinking of your life,' and that if your head was doing one thing, and your body another, you'd be bound to be disturbed. A cautious little urge to act entered me – I immediately countered the hope with a million excuses. a) I've not really *worked* at my trade, and b) I don't stick at anything. Then I remembered the awards I'd won, and the performances I've given, and how they don't nurture me. I know how amazed I was when I won them, how I don't always take my talent seriously. I wanted, like Burton and O'Toole, to use my talent for power – to be noticed.

I was far too impulsive and impetuous to think of consequences, and was so dazzled by Rex, that when a few uncomfortable glimpses that didn't fit in with my day-dreams pierced through, I ignored them. There were three or four quite early on. First in Vivien Leigh's kitchen, after the show, when I looked at Rex and thought he's everything I want, but maybe not that intelligent. Then again at the Lancaster Hotel in Paris, when he was resting on the bed, and looking very careworn. I flung myself on him and banished the thought. Again I remember feeling resentment when he said he couldn't equate the girl he went to bed with with the girl on the screen in *Saturday Night and Sunday Morning*. I thought it was grudging. I never saw Rex quite as I see him now. I never really saw the creature of habit that Rex is, an animal that really takes care of itself, likes being sleek and well-fed. Rex is much more conservative and conventional than I'd expected: the social mores were, and are, important to him. On our wedding day, we both drank a considerable amount – Rex whisky, me Fernet-Branca. I was frightened. He was, too. But being married to Rex the all-powerful, I felt all-powerful, too. After years of being nothing, it was heady stuff . . . Dr Goldman had told me that Rex was a very lonely man. I didn't know what he was talking about.

Before I left London to return to California, where it had all surfaced almost a year ago, I called the analyst, three times. He said I'd lost everything I'd dreamed and hoped for, and had behaved with dignity through it all, and that I'd been punishing myself for years – the world hadn't been punishing me, *I* had. He quoted Marcus Aurelius: 'Deal yourself a happy lot and portion.'

Once back in California, I called the doctor I used to go to: he put me on anti-depressant pills.

As I passed by, I heard someone say, 'She's a dead ringer for Rita.' Remembered the time I saw Rita Hayworth in the supermarket, utterly lost, letting her companion do the shopping for her.

In November, it was back again to London. I told myself I was physically healthy, able, attractive, intelligent and talented – and nice. And yet more and more I realised, through my terrible depression, that I was emotionally crippled, too.

I wonder if my new thought about my sister is what it's all about – I really do. Darren reminds me of the hard struggle my sister has had, and how she has succeeded so well where I have failed in rearing a family, making a home for herself – and also how much she would love to fly in the Concorde, stay in a suite, drive in a limousine. Do I feel guilt at having what she doesn't? If not, why do I hate the things I've done?

I don't know, unless it's all part and parcel of the same thing – those early years, when it was instilled into me that everything I did was wrong.

Yet what is the point in continuing my mourning over my lack of love in the family? I dined with my sister, with John [her husband], with Neil [their son] and with Darren at Langan's Brasserie when I got to London. The comment that hurt most was the one about Burton ('He had everything' – head-nod indicating me –'but he drank') and it just plain isn't true.

Things got so bad in London that I had to enter Bowden House clinic. I sensed that I almost wouldn't make the premiere of the film I'd come over for, and nearly didn't. Then I over-reacted again when it came to doing a TV interview for France, where I was about to make a TV film. I'd drunk too much. At lunch that day, everyone but me seemed normal, going about their business. I felt choked with angst and guilt. Before, when I was first in Bowden House, there was hope and a husband. Now, except for Darren, I was alone. I never realised I was quite so ill. I so want to be in a happy home with an intelligent man to love, and my children, and their children coming to stay. To be able to give out love and warmth! I thought of writing my life-story, beginning each chapter with, for example, '1931: Aged Four', but my will-power deserted me, my appetite for life was gone. I seemed to have collapsed inside. When it all began, after that wonderful Oriental trip, I had thought it was *because Rex had finally remarried happily*. But I'm even deeper into despair. I know that an attitude of mind can change all this – and it *must* change, or I shall end up hopeless or dead.

I know there have been, will be and *are* others like me – like me as I lay in the clinic – who are shaking inside themselves. I watched the BBC television programme about the Earls Court suicides, the woman whose husband left her, the young man whose wife went off with his boyfriend, the diabetic married to the alcoholic who killed himself. Dr Limentani, my London analyst, came closest, I think, to diagnosing me. Sadistic to myself as well as masochistic. The clever doctor said that the trouble with self-analysis such as I indulge in is that there is no one around to referee the blows. What on earth, though, do I *really* think of myself? What I'm currently thinking is almost too appalling to live with. I say 'almost', because I'm still here, but barely. Around me, wherever it is, be it California where the birds twittering at dawn now get on my nerves, or New York where the sound of the clip-clopping horses trotting into Central Park gets on my nerves, or London where, a moment ago, there were human voices enjoying life, people having a quiet drink, living a life that seems to be ebbing away from inside *me* at ever increasing rate. I literally didn't know what tomorrow would bring.

I was absolutely terrified at the thought of making that film, *The Hostage Tower*, for television. I doubted I'd be able to drag my carcass over to Paris to do it. I didn't know what to do about it all – and, worse, I really did not believe now that it was due to 'me', not to 'them'.

I didn't want to read a newspaper, or have a bath, or even to eat. Dr Limentani suggested there was no one around this time to 'share' or 'suffer with me' my 'nervous breakdown'. He suggested I'd never got over the fact that my Mother didn't want children and that my sister was unhappy that I'd arrived ten years after she did.

---

'THE HOSTAGE TOWER', a telefeature for a series that never eventualised, was hardly likely to raise Rachel's spirits, much less her reputation. She was doing it strictly for the money, protected – rather than encouraged – by the reputable names associated with the cast, though few of *them* could have had many illusions, either.

It was based on Alistair MacLean's first scenario written directly for television and was described in merciless terms by *Hollywood Reporter* as a 'far-fetched, unamusing outing ... a trivial exercise in international conspiracy that seems tasteless and ill-timed in light of recent headlines ... Who wants to see an American president's mother being held hostage in the Eiffel Tower, for heaven's sake?'

Celia Johnson played the indignant hostage and was at least credited with investing the role with 'compelling energy'. Others involved included Keir Dullea as the criminal mastermind, Britt Ekland, Peter Fonda, Billy Dee Williams and Maud Adams. Rachel was fortunate in that many of her scenes were shared with an actor of great sympathy who took a mild, gentlemanly, amused attitude to the goings-on – Douglas Fairbanks Jr. He and Rachel headed a UN anti-crime group and, according to the *Reporter*'s Gail Williams, 'weathered the film by adopting bemused, laid-back attitudes'.

DOUGLAS FAIRBANKS JR: 'Rachel was, let's say, "neurotic", but then we have a lot of people like that in the acting profession. I didn't take it too seriously. She appeared fixated about Rex Harrison, always bringing him back into the conversation. I was tempted to write to Rex about it, but then decided against it. What could I tell him he probably didn't know?

'I was a sort of super-Intelligence chief in the film, Rachel was my assistant. It took about ten to twelve weeks to shoot: I was in Paris most of the schedule, since I was one of the names on whom the money was riding. Rachel got off with about three or four weeks. I tried to keep our relationship friendly, but impersonal, telling silly jokes, keeping things as normal as possible to balance her overstrung emotions. When she was worried about not getting her lines right in the film, I'd say, "Rachel, it's really unimportant in the scheme of things, this film. Even remembering your lines is hardly a thing of great magnitude. Five years from now, the chances are no one will remember this particular film has ever been made – it might not even get shown! Have you thought of that?" That brought a smile to her face and calmed her down a bit.

'As far as I could see, Rachel was a well-disciplined technician – which is about all that such a farrago allowed one to be. I must say she worked harder at her particular character than I did at mine. Even when she simply said "Yes" or "No", it came out better than most people's dialogue on that job. My wife wasn't too well at the time and Rachel was most attentive to her – other people's upsets seemed to touch a very caring side of her nature. My wife said she thought she had a drinking problem at the time. But I must confess, I didn't notice it. To my eyes, Rachel was a first-rate professional.'

Somehow, by filling myself up with pills, I got over to Paris. I travelled elegantly and first-class, and was met at Charles de Gaulle airport. The Sheraton wasn't to my liking, so I switched to the Cecilia, a pretty *pension* off the Champs-Elysées. For two days I was driven around and fitted with attractive clothes which I could buy at the end of the film. I even made an effort one night and went to L'Entrecôte with Darren. Afterwards we watched a film, *The Eyes of Laura Mars*, with Faye Dunaway thinking she was going mad – but in fact being *driven* mad [it was actually *St Jack* with Ben Gazzara: the confusion is interesting].

I thought all the release of tension I managed in the sobbing bout I had at the end of it would do me good. But next morning I woke up with cold feet. I had a dream, too. I dreamed of seeing Rex's recent play *The Kingfisher* – people coming in and out of the theatre while he performed, charming, smiling at first, then bloated looking. Claudette Colbert [his co-star] looked like a French working woman, forgot her lines except when her speech concerned Lindsay Anderson – and then real feeling crept into her delivery and she was good. Lindsay appeared in my dream, but an angry and insecure Lindsay with a voice not his own – one belonging to the English upper class. Then I dreamed of being in Darren's car in Los Angeles and woke overcome with fear again. We had coffee and Perrier in the restaurant opposite the Cecilia – and then I don't remember any more, except that I talked 'at' Darren, told him how much I needed to be made love to and talked to. I really don't know any longer if it *is* me, or if psychologists do muck up your mind – if it is simply due to frustration on all levels and homelessness and having no family. As gentle John from the AA meeting said to me, 'Perhaps you need a cat.'

A long time ago, whenever I behaved impulsively or recklessly I thought I was 'different', because I had such a 'personality', such vitality, such talent. Now my extraordinary and chaotic behaviour is frightening me, so much so that I *really* have no inner core to even tell me what to do. There was really nothing intrinsically wrong in calling Alan, comforting even, momentarily anyhow, knowing that all is not over-the-rainbow land with him either, any more than it had seemed with Rex. Nothing intrinsically wrong in drinking Champagne. Nothing intrinsically wrong in calling Dr Limentani: *He sees so many people who make themselves suffer, he says.*

Paris set me recalling my first honeymoon there with Alan. I wasn't happy. We fought in silence. I wanted 'men'. I was turned inwards – not for me the joy and beauty of Paris or the first real glimpse of France. While Alan tried to paint, watch the river and the fish, I behaved like a sick greedy baby. I blamed *him* for me not being happy. Alan is morose by nature, perhaps, but I now know I demanded of him more, it seemed, than anyone can demand, to give ME, ME, ME contentment. The Ritz in Paris with Rex and Homer was a bitter period, too, and the house in Malmaison a series of tearful binges. My Mother was there, too, and Jacqueline, an unmarried Jacqueline who loved me. My cat came and Ruby arrived from America and Pina from Portofino. I cried with unhappiness whenever Pina and I went to the French supermarket – the same feeling of desolation I get today when I drive to the Beverly Glen store for liver for Rosie my cat – or for some half-heartedly chosen food for myself.

But I've allowed all this to happen, just as I'm allowing it to happen now. When I think, as I did then in beautiful Paris, 'What do you really want?' – to my horror I say, 'To be in a bar getting high as a prelude to getting sex. Talking animatedly, not to get or give knowledge, but to turn him on, so that I can be entombed or enwombed, taken over, looked after, petted, pampered, cuddled and, as a result, not have any responsibilities at all.'

I devoted a lot of time in Paris to writing this journal. I recall stopping one moment and 'knowing' that the footstep in the hall was Darren's – that he'd come smiling in and make it all right for ME. I really 'knew' it was Darren's footstep. But of course it wasn't . . . It was the footstep of a relatively composed looking Frenchman, and his wife, both of whom can soberly sit side by side and read the evening newspapers.

---

ALTHOUGH SHEER 'PROFESSIONALISM' got Rachel through *The Hostage Tower*, it was no help in steadying her personal life. With her return to London at the beginning of December, 1979, this began to totter alarmingly. Try as he did to give her support, Darren felt increasingly powerless.

DARREN RAMIREZ: 'Rachel's preoccupation with money had now reached a neurotic pitch. She was always saying she was broke, that she could no longer earn enough, that maybe the day would come when she couldn't earn *any*. She really had no cause to worry: but she was deaf to any reassurances I gave her. Although she could well afford the best suite in a first-class hotel, she called Milton Goldman in New York to ask his help in finding a place to stay in London and he said, "You can use Leon Becker's London apartment, just behind Harrods."

'Leon was in his apartment when we arrived, but made us welcome. The very first day there, Rachel disappeared – simply didn't return home from shopping. And she was completely "lost" for two days – we were at our wits' end! Then I had an idea . . .

'I went round to her house in Cambridge Street, which was empty now after the messy Rhodesian tenants had moved out. And there I found her, completely naked, drunk on Champagne, crying and shouting. She was incapable of rational thought or action. I had to make the bed she'd slept in and help her on with her clothes. She kept ordering me to sell the house we had back on Hutton Drive. "I need the money," she kept shouting. If I didn't, she threatened she'd sue me: she'd already told her nephew, who was a lawyer, she said. I called her London doctor. But all he said was, "Miss Roberts has a drinking problem. There is nothing I can do. Contact Dr Glyn Davies." I said that a visit from Dr Davies might frighten her into thinking she was going to be "put away" again. I felt wretched – angry with Rachel for her behaviour, desperately sorry for her in the state she was in, incapable of knowing what to do next. Fortunately, her doctor at last agreed to send over his assistant to give Rachel a shot to calm her. Would you believe it, as soon as the assistant walked in, Rachel switched moods, became very composed, refused to take the shot, said there was nothing wrong with her!

'I blew up at that. I yelled, "Rachel, you left me in a terrible position. You haven't been seen around for forty-eight hours. I'm sick and tired of it all. I'm going back to New York."

'That calmed her a little and we went back to Leon's apartment. But once there, she became abusive again and I walked out. Poor Leon! he was really in the centre of it all. The next day I went back to pack my things and found her packing hers. She'd run into an old friend, Judy Tarlo, a publicist she liked – when Judy had gotten married, Rachel gave her a tiny stone cat as a wedding present. Judy had fixed Rachel a special deal at the Athenaeum Hotel in Piccadilly. Rachel said to me now, as if we'd never exchanged a harsh word, "Meet me at Harrods. I want to buy Leon a scarf to make up for all the trouble I've caused him." When I got round to Harrods, a bit apprehensive, I found she hadn't bought a scarf at all – she'd bought herself a tiny angora kitten, which she called "Doug", after Douglas Fairbanks Jr, and she took it back with her to the Athenaeum.

'The next day there was a rather grand children's party held at Regine's club which was on the roof-top of the store that used to be Derry and Toms, in Kensington High Street. All the celebrities took their children. Rachel had made friends with Jane Seymour, the actress, and Jane invited Rachel – so Rachel went out on a shopping spree, to buy presents *for other people's* children, people she didn't even know. In her mood, it was the worst thing she could have done. The next day, she was incapable.'

ELEANOR FAZAN: 'If Rachel's spirits were low, which they were frequently in the last year or so, it always depressed her even more to see other people enjoying themselves, seemingly secure and happy. I remember both of us were at one big summer fête held for a show-business charity and filled with celebrities – and it depressed Rachel just to hear some well-dressed woman, a complete stranger, saying she'd got to be off, get the Rolls-Royce, pick up her daughter from some go-go disco and do the shopping at Fortnum and Mason's – that was what Rachel hankered after, if you can believe it, *that* kind of busy-busy social life!'

DARREN RAMIREZ: 'She managed to call me up and say, "Will you help me get ready?" We succeeded in getting to the plane, along with Doug the kitten, and took off for New York. We arrived there on December 23 and the next night, Christmas Eve, Rachel went out to an Alcoholics Anonymous meeting in some old church on the West Side and came back in the depths of despair.'

PAMELA MASON: 'Part of the trouble, I suspect, was that Rachel was a very "fast" character and the AA meetings she'd go to in New York were probably ill-chosen ones: the people at them were not of her set, or out of her world, or moving at her pace. She'd have done better to stick to the AA meetings in Hollywood – instead of those New York folk who can be like "the poor, the huddled masses", no stars among them.'

DARREN RAMIREZ: 'We spent Christmas, 1979, with Elizabeth Aitken, formerly Elizabeth Harrison who had married Rex after he and Rachel were divorced. Elizabeth is a marvellous hostess, very well organised, and has a beautiful duplex on the East Side. All of which made Rachel feel positively suicidal. I left for Los Angeles and she moved into Bobby Frosch's, since she couldn't stand the Central Park West apartment any longer.'

Well, I did the TV movie in Paris. It was a terrible time. Whether it was due to my withdrawal from that massive dose of pills or Darren's passivity, I don't know; but I shook and trembled and shuddered and sobbed, going over and over and over the lines. Douglas Fairbanks Jr was happily and outwardly composed. He wasn't troubled by the nonsense, so that took the edge off me. But I couldn't get up in the morning, railed at Darren, then left for London and stayed with Leon, went to see Brenda and got drunk. I railed at Darren again, then moved to the Athenaeum Hotel and bought Douglas – not the actor, but a kitten. It was so

169

obviously my attempt to live the old life, or what I imagined to be the old life, but it didn't work anyway.

It was a relief to see Jill Bennett and Jeffrey Lane at the Dorchester, to laugh a bit, and to try to make light of my handshake. 'Hit my fist into my palm, cower, and repeat.' But it is *not* funny.

Things got so bad in London that I wanted to stay with Brenda, with Sian Phillips [actress, ex-wife of Peter O'Toole], with that pretty young actress Jane Seymour. I went to a children's party and ached to be a mother. I went to the house I had bought and furnished, 42 Cambridge Street, to try and sort out the mess that the Rhodesian tenants had left. Couldn't face it. I succumbed to drink. The next day, Darren packed for me and we rushed off to the airport – the aircraft crew were fortunately late, so we got on the plane with Doug.

---

IN THE DYING DAYS of December, 1979, Rachel turned for professional help to a distinguished psycho-analyst, Ferruccio A. di Cori, who practised on New York's East 60s, from two large houses, converted into one mansion, a listed building, which had belonged to Gypsy Rose Lee – a suitable place for stripping one's soul bare.

Dr di Cori had emigrated from Italy (and the University of Rome) before the war. He was now many things besides a successful and fashionable analyst with a talent for unravelling the problems of stage and screen people. He was director of psychodrama at a Brooklyn hospital; he worked with psychotics there in ways that earned him the attention of stage directors; he wrote clever plays of psychotherapeutic value which his sometimes famous patients read or acted in and which were performed in Little Theaters in New York and elsewhere to praise from a director like Peter Brook or a critic like Harold Clurman.

Rachel's London analyst, Dr Limentani, a compatriot and colleague of Dr di Cori, had recommended her to the New York practitioner.

DR LIMENTANI: 'She was most determined in getting help. She used to leave very urgent messages that would have got past the guard of any protective receptionist. She didn't allow herself to be kept at a distance. I knew Dr di Cori was very good with professional players, and I gave her his address, wondering if she would go there. She got in touch very quickly.'

DR DI CORI: ' "Patients" is a word I do not like using. The people who come to me should see me as a friend, as Rachel did. I tried at once to establish a supportive connection with Rachel. She totally lacked self-esteem when she arrived. There she was, so elegant, so sophisticated – yet so insecure. I told her that I didn't believe life was a problem to be solved, it was a mystery to be lived. You can only be an accepted friend of the person who's being helped, if he or she sees you that way – and I believe that's how Rachel saw me. I asked her if she'd like to read some of the plays I had written as an extension of my interest in emotional disorders – I've written about fifty-two – and she did so. What kind are they? Well, one she read was called *Beach People*. A woman arrives on a strip of shore. The beach is crowded. She responds aggressively to the presence of the other persons and begins insulting them – but all of them are mannikins, and the theme is the wanton destruction of existence, of life living at the limits. Another play she read had the title of *"Mary"* . . . *"What?"* It featured two adolescents, one of whom calls out "Mary", while the other answers simply, "What?" but treats that monosyllable in fourteen different tones and moods. Another was called *The Blue Mark*. A man and woman are making love and the man finds a blue mark on the beloved's buttocks. He thinks another man has pinched her. She says it is a bruise. Afterwards, alone, the man uses pincers to nip himself on one of his buttocks and attempts to bruise himself on the other, so as to compare the similarity, or dissimilarity of the two contusions and hence test his loved one's fidelity. Rachel read these plays and it was a valuable way of establishing rapport with her.

'Rachel also came to one of my work sessions at King's County Hospital, Brooklyn. My classes with the psychotics there usually comprise twenty to thirty people in a room and she saw me attempting to elicit their reactions to a situation I would create. For instance, I'd say, "I am your father" or "I know nothing" or "There's no air conditioning here" in the hope that by reacting the patient will, through my guidance, gain some helpful catharsis. Peter Brook once asked me what school of psychiatry I represented. I said, "Myself."

'Rachel's sessions lasted the usual fifty minutes, but my acquaintance with her wasn't limited to these "hours" – we'd occasionally go to some of the Little Theaters. We were watching a play in rehearsal at the American Theater Arts Club when she started scribbling little notes about her responses to it – comments on the play – and passing them to me, and I returned them with my remarks. I even wrote a little poem! A very jolly evening. You see, the help I was able to offer Rachel stemmed from my belief in writers, poets and philosophers, not really from classical psychiatry. Freud's genius was that of a poet-visionary: in turn, this created psychiatry. I feel my rapport technique pre-dates psychiatry and connects at deeper and more mysterious levels with people like Rachel who are often themselves attuned by art or craft to benefit from it.

'Rachel had a drinking problem, of course, and had been going to AA meetings. I decided she might find the neighbourhood branch helpful. She attended, introduced herself, explained her problem, made a commitment to help herself and others and, in turn, sought help from them. In a word, she made a pledge. It was at an AA meeting that she met a convict out on parole whom she nicknamed "Knuckles". Their relationship had something of D. H. Lawrence about it: it reminded one of Lady Chatterley and her lower-class lover Mellors. I suppose Rachel attended about fifteen sessions of AA, but I realise now she was doing ten thousand other things at the time which she never told an analyst about. She used to go into very dangerous city neighbourhoods along with Knuckles. I was horrified when eventually I learned she had been to parts of the Bronx. She told me that the aura of danger excited her sexually. It was a response at odds with her treatment.'

Dr di Cori's Manhattan home is the sort of place to which the nearby Metropolitan Museum would consecrate a small wing if it could have it complete with the multitude of *objets d'art* that the doctor has collected over the years. His taste is eclectic, his decor varies from level to level in the house: from an upper-storey study strongly recalling a medieval philosopher's, complete with skull and outsize chess-set, to a dining room hung around with huge surrealist paintings of fruit depicted in the disturbing detail one sometimes sees in the art of the insane. In the cavernous living room, amid many beautiful antiques, is an oil painting of a Mediterranean port scene done in the manner of the English painter L. S. Lowry, though a Lowry transported into exotic Latin latitudes so that while the figures remained populous and stylised they now reflected the hurly-burly of a dockside, not the drab denizens of some North Country conurbation. Rachel must have been disconcerted by one bizarre coincidence: for the doctor's painting is a study of Portofino, where she had lived out her happiest years as Rex's wife.

DR DI CORI: 'Rachel was doing well, relaying her feelings to me, when one day she told me she was going to Yale University – to give lectures! From that minute I felt my support begin to weaken. "How will you keep in touch with me?" I asked. She answered she'd try to come up to New York as often as she could by train or car – it was just under two hours from New Haven by train. I think she did her best. But it really wasn't satisfactory. Her attendance became spasmodic. And then, suddenly! I heard she was out of Yale and off to California and I never saw her again. I often wondered what had happened.'

So it was back to AA meetings and Dr di Cori. 'What a fuss we make of our coitus,' said the doctor, commenting on a remark one of his patients had made. Indeed, and how easy to laugh and agree in the company of an educated, humorous, unfractured man of distinction – but how different when one is alone and helpless and unwanted. How sharp the pang when I encountered a film director friend with whom I started out – and I won the award! Telephones active, busy, preparing another film with a new and talented star, surrounded by his children and grandchildren. I compare what he's done with his life to what I've done with mine. I live in a void.

Yet it wasn't like that at all when I got to the Algonquin Hotel. Karel Reisz is cool and intelligent and composed. He goes home and watches television at night and falls asleep at 10.30 pm. The daughter of Betsy, his wife, has married a man who is sweet and whole – the daughter is just like other people. The children are just like other human beings. No great fanfare of trumpets sounded when they walked into the room. Karel gave them lunch, just like other people. I went to see Pinter's play *Betrayal*. I remain like Kafka's immense and imaginative beetle, thinking life is something else, bemoaning my loneliness, my inability to function, wanting an existence that just plain does not exist for anyone anywhere. Come back little Ray for God's sake and take your place in the world! It hasn't been all that bad. If with Dr di Cori's help I can find out the reasons why I drank so stupidly – and I think I am finding out – then perhaps I can exorcise them and pick up the threads of life again.

But I *must* stop this drinking. It brought on the manic behaviour in London which led to the Bowden House clinic and the news that 'the doctor's giving you up' if you don't stop drinking. I remember going to the house in London and not being able to make the bed. Darren did it for me. Then I stayed in bed the morning after spending the night there in the house and at 11.00 am I went to get Champagne and a horror-story Penguin. I drank the whole bottle. Darren came over to try and help me and I screamed and screamed and he – even he! – pushed me to the floor. My sister knows full well what I'm like. My friends are finding out. Can I get better – and, if so, for what?

I had a nice, sober Christmas Eve with Elizabeth [Aitken, as she now was], a pleasant New Year's Eve with Doris [Cole Abrahams]. I called AA, and went to a meeting, and I met Knuckles there. Madly, he thought he could still be my saviour. The meeting was filled with depressed and depressing people, lonely misfits. I walked through the Village on Sunday, looking for another AA meeting place, and finding them all wrecked. The women's meeting was at 1.00 am (that's in the *morning!*) The Moravian Church was closed. The meeting was held at The Little Church Around the Corner. It was led by a poor, chalk-white-faced old son of an alcoholic undertaker. There were sad black men and mad women – very much the other side of life from what I aspired to. It gave me no happiness. What did was the simplicity of cats and Reg and shopping for our food – *together* – and cuddling. That, I fear, was being a child. Anyhow, it has led me to Dr di Cori, and he's a strength. I need people of strength.

---

IT SEEMS INCREDIBLE, given Rachel's emotionally unbalanced state, that she should have now seen herself as a University lecturer: and scarcely more believable that she could actually have been engaged by a campus. But her illness was well concealed from all but a few friends; the treatment she was undergoing was confidential; those who knew about it genuinely believed that responsibilities of a different kind than appearing in public performances might absorb her restlessness and re-direct her energies.

SYBIL CHRISTOPHER: 'Yale is something I put into her head. I said, "Listen, Rachel, you're so goddam Welsh, you should teach." "What could I teach?" she asked. "What you know all about – drama. What else?" My daughter Kate was at Yale at the time; and their drama school is among the country's best. I knew Rachel was well-read, well-educated, and that she warmed to new acquaintances. I felt it would give her a whole new range of interests.'

MILTON GOLDMAN: 'She approached me of her own accord at ICM and said simply, "I want to teach." I knew *Once a Catholic* had been a disaster, and I thought lecturing for a bit was a good idea – it might get her out of the dumps. So I contacted Lloyd Richards, who's dean of the Yale School of Drama, and made a deal for her – about $300–400 a week, I think.'

Throughout this period and Rachel's time at Yale, Darren was in Los Angeles. The very day Rachel was to meet Lloyd Richards and Earle Gister, the drama school's associate dean, she arranged for herself a brief meeting with Rex Harrison, who was in New York casting *My Fair Lady* for a cross-country tour. The anticipation of seeing Rex again undoubtedly enabled her to sail through her 'audition' with the two Yale academics, who might have been more cautious if they had met her on one of her bad days. She left them to go on to her rendezvous with Rex feeling her forthcoming tenure at Yale was blessed with good omens: in fact, it was to be the most crushing experience she suffered in what was now the last year of her life.

O ne day, towards the end of the first week in January, 1980, I woke up in Bobby Frosch's apartment with the most awful tension and unhappiness. I called Milton Goldman, my agent at ICM, to have lunch with him and, at the lunch, I asked about the possibility of giving some lectures on drama at Yale. This resulted in a meeting which Milton arranged with a wave of his wand with Lloyd Richards and Earle Gister in the former's brownstone at 95th Street and Central Park West and the offer of a 'guest lectureship' on the campus. Coincidentally with that meeting, I learned that Rex was in town. I called Milton to ask him to tell Rex that I needed to see him and get him to call me. At first, the reply was that he was too busy and leaving town that day. Then I called the Drake, where I knew he was staying, and by dint of persevering – after they'd told me he'd 'stepped out' – got virtually an 'appointment' with Rex. He called back and agreed to see me at 5.30 pm. I was instantly galvanised into action. I wore my Paris clothes and did my hair so that I looked like Anna in the play *Platonov*, where I'd met Rex twenty years earlier. Euphoria was in the air and the adrenaline coursed through my veins again – it had started flowing while I was keeping the appointment with the Yale people.

Rex was Rex, caught up in his casting of *My Fair Lady*. I felt more and more like Anna Petrovna. I drank Champagne and told him how 'bereaved' I felt: the depression caused, I felt, by his remarriage and the consequent end that put to my fearful dreams of escape, my having to face up to the reality of living my own life with all its difficulties, my love for him, and the loneliness of it all. I got through to him and we hugged each other, tearfully. I felt like I felt in the old days: it was a good and well-loved and comfortable feeling. He gave me back my confidence. His elegance of living had always made me feel a bit small, I suppose. He was off later on in the week to the Bahamas with his wife Mercia, whom I'd always thought of as formal and a bit bossy. I left Rex determined to stand on my own two feet and enjoy being me – properly!

He took his limousine along with his young director who was going to do *My Fair Lady* and his director's girlfriend on to see *Oklahoma!* and fell asleep. I took the limousine on, intending to see Father Bruce [Ritter, director of Covenant House, a New York charitable foundation working with the young homeless] – we meant to visit the Eighth Avenue Intake Shelter to help the street kids. But Father Bruce had had to cancel the appointment, so I went on to see Ferruccio di Cori's play at one of his Little Theater ventures.

It was euphoric to have met again my fantasy Anna and Platonov. I know I sang a little in the taxi-cab that day . . . and New York looked different. Was I looking at it through the eyes of Rex? Probably. Rex was impressed by my going to Yale. And I saw again the man behind the myth who, as much as I, wants to be looked after. The children in Reg and Ray met emotionally for a minute. I was at my very best, not ravaged, not hysterical, not demanding – the impression I gave was a good one.

Come on, Ray, grow up – hard though it is! I do love Reggie very much. I know him very well . . . and we are temperamentally very alike. Thinking of him while he was in Bermuda, I felt how much I'd love to be lying in the sun, snuggled up next to him, now I know the ropes a bit more. But then I reflect that I'm still not ready. However, whatever anyone says about him – and I know him well – I still love my special, dynamic, silly, crusty, unbearable Rex. The look of him, and the shape of him, his voice, his laugh, his humour and his frailty – but I've nowhere near attempted life on my own yet and I'm not in any way really fit to be someone's other half.

But how am I to cope with the life that remains, infatuated with Rex as I am? I don't care what anyone says, he handles life so much better than I. Three glasses of Champagne last night made me physically sick this morning. I thought of Rex on the plane to Bermuda to sit in the sun or swim. Hurt though I am to think that he's with Mercia, I concluded that it was probably better that way.

I'm quite sure that my excitement over the offer of the Yale job was coloured by my euphoria at the thought of seeing Rex. The only thing that can raise me – try as I will – out of the feeling that life is a tight little ball of strangulating string is Rex. Then it becomes full of sunshine, hope and happiness, and I change into Anna Petrovna. I even sang in the taxi as I went back to Bobby and Aaron's apartment. And yet insight makes me realise that dressed up as I was to look like Anna, fortified by three glasses of Champagne, needing an emotional scene – even using the words, 'Platonov, my own dear love' – it wasn't really Reginald Carey Harrison I was wanting. It was an emotional high that took me back twenty years. Unrealistic to a degree! But I took in the back of Rex going in to see *Oklahoma!* Let the image stay.

---

RACHEL DEVELOPED SOME HESITATIONS of her own about the teaching appointment. They were akin to the nervous tensions she always felt in the count-down period to starting a film or embarking on a play. Before going to Yale, she flew to Los Angeles on a brief stop-over, to get some things she needed from Hutton Drive, and ran into John Schlesinger.

JOHN SCHLESINGER: 'She came up to my house in the Hollywood hills and, over a drink, confessed her misgivings about the lecturing job at Yale. Suddenly she said, "I think I'll kill myself." "Don't be silly," I replied, "you've got far too much to offer – don't be so ridiculous!" She thought this over for a moment, then she said firmly, "I'll do it." And those, as it turned out, were almost the last words I heard her speak.'

The Yale School of Drama, on York Street, New Haven, looks from the outside like a church, all yellowish vellum-coloured bricks, grey roofs, sharp-pointed gables and arched doorways of ecclesiastical appearance. Perhaps the building reminded Rachel of the Welsh chapels of her childhood: not a reassuring feeling for her. But the aura of religious vocation is not inappropriate. The Drama School requires hard work of its students – when Rachel was there, these numbered about 165. The hours of application are long, the timetable is crowded and little social life is available when the term gets under way, or is encouraged. The 'new image' of herself as a campus lecturer had been alluringly burnished in Rachel's mind by all those Hollywood movies she'd seen with campus settings where seductive students and available faculty members pursued passionate extra-curricular relationships: this sort of fantasy left her unprepared for the seriousness of the place. Or, even more onerous for someone in her pitiful condition, for the sheer loneliness of Yale in mid-winter.

Characteristically, though, she arrived well prepared for the new 'role'. Her red loose-leaf notebook is crammed with observations on *King Lear*, the special area of study within the larger brief for her seminars on 'Shakespeare's Verse'.

A typical lecture-note of Rachel's went like this: '*King Lear*: First Scene: It is perfectly possible to perform the first scene of *King Lear* in such a way as to make the motives of the three sisters intelligible – if the scene is seen as a kind of prologue. By making it as short as possible, Shakespeare was able to concentrate on the tragic results of the king's foolishness. His living martyrdom is his progression . . . In our time, the play has been strikingly successful on the stage. No performance of a great play, or of a great piece of music, can be ideal; but a performance, if not too defective, can give us an experience we should not get from a reading of the text.'

But her notebook also, and more ominously, contains a recurring quotation from the play: 'The theme of *Lear*: "Oh, let me not be mad, not mad, sweet heaven! Keep me in temper; I would not be mad."'

Rachel's lectures only skirted theory: they were mainly about the play as seen from the performer's viewpoint: as was appropriate for her second-year class of about fourteen students. She listed their names several times in her notebook, as if trying to commit them to the memory which she now mistrusted: 'Lichtenstein, Sunstedt, Prettie, Natter, Hendrickson, Monk, Borowitz, Gordon, Malamud, and so on . . . To her Anglo-Saxon sensibilities, such a class was a small melting-pot of student America. She rotated the role of Lear, changing the student who played it as scene succeeded scene. Among these Lears was one student whom Rachel singled out with a sure instinct about his talent which shows her own judgment on such matters hadn't been impaired by all her sufferings. He was David Alan Grier, who performed for her one night in a piece entitled *The Place of the Spirit Dance*, written by a fellow student of play-writing and put on at Yale's Afro-American Center. Grier graduated to Broadway and Joseph Papp's Shakespeare-in-the-Park Company and was in the small cast of Robert Altman's film *Streamers* when the Venice Film Festival jury awarded it the collective acting prize in 1983. Rachel was even more moved by what people like Grier could do since she increasingly felt herself losing touch with her own talent.

Cruel confirmation of this came to her unexpectedly at Yale. For although Rachel didn't know it at the time she took it into her head to teach there, Yale was independently getting ready to enlist her for a Drama School project from which the faculty hoped to extract great prestige.

Professor Earle R. Gister, the school's associate dean, remembered the timing of her arrival on campus.

PROF. GISTER: 'At the time we were about to launch into the production of a new play by Athol Fugard. He'd just arrived from South Africa and was playwright-in-residence with us. It was called *A Lesson from Aloes*, and he was going to direct it himself.'

Athol Fugard was then forty-seven. Though a lifelong and obdurate opponent of *apartheid* in his native South Africa, Fugard had learnt the use of tact among the techniques of resistance. As a result, he himself as well as his reputation had travelled widely abroad. He was playwright, actor, and director of works by himself and others on stage and screen. Yale was justly proud of having attracted this small, lean, wiry man with the incredibly hawkish profile and stubby beard, perennially dressed in denims and bush-jacket with a pipe going and a satchel slung over one shoulder as if he was just about to embark on another trek into his sundered country's physical and moral wasteland.

*A Lesson from Aloes*, his latest play, owed its curious title to the cactus-like aloe plant's ability to survive a drought. It was clearly a metaphor for the husband in it, a former anti-*apartheid* fighter who now spends his time tending his collection of this twisted and misshapen species of plant. He is visited by a one-time political comrade, a warm and boisterous figure bubbling with hearty laughter but overtaken by sudden thunderous rages. The third character in the play is the aloe-collector's wife, a woman named Gladys.

ATHOL FUGARD: 'I arrived at Yale shortly after New Year's Day, 1980. We were due to start rehearsals of *A Lesson from Aloes* in a few weeks. I'd already cast James Earl Jones in it, as the visiting comrade, when Lloyd Richards called me. He was in his first year as Dean of the Drama School. "Don't let me raise your hopes," he said, "but Rachel Roberts is coming here to teach. As I read your play, Athol, I kept thinking she'd be perfect for Gladys." Well, I knew Rachel's work and I couldn't have agreed more. It looked like a real stroke of luck.'

PROF. GISTER: 'It's unusual for a play to begin life at Yale and move on to Broadway, as *A Lesson from Aloes* eventually did. But then it's unusual for us to engage someone like Rachel as a lecturer. Usually, it's directors we pick to teach on campus and also do plays there. The reason is, the teaching schedule comprises two three-hour periods a week, or else three two-hour ones, and actor-teachers on daily rehearsal call don't have much time to prepare for class. If Rachel did take the role in the play, she'd have a hell of a lot on her plate: rehearsals, production schedules, preparation for her seminars, and personal tutoring for the students she'd agreed to teach from January through May.

'My first impression of her was of a bright, warm personality. One thing about her was odd – here was a fifty-two-year-old woman who confessed as soon as she arrived that she couldn't drive an automobile. She said she'd had driving lessons, but had forgotten how . . . So she rented a Vega and two students undertook to instruct her, in the snow! I think she was very lonely – though, in fairness, it's easy to make this judgment in retrospect.

At the time, we were all just too busy to notice. Yale isn't noted for social life; it's dedicated to hard work; the hours are long; we even snatch meals on the run when staging a play. It's a continuously stretched feeling . . . I imagine Rachel found it hard to adjust.'

DARREN RAMIREZ: 'Actually, she hated it. You could have seen that coming. Yale didn't turn out at all as she expected: she felt it was "beneath" her. She hated the lonely hotel she stayed in on arrival – *then* when she'd moved into a room in a professor's house, she hated *it* because it was like going back to cheap theatrical "digs". It was simply to raise her spirits and find some congenial company that she said she'd do the Athol Fugard play.'

But things were not by any means so simple. Rachel could not have predicted what was lying in wait for her when Athol Fugard gave her the play to read.

ATHOL FUGARD: 'She read the play and said she liked it – very much. But she was uncertain about playing Gladys. I took this at first to be simply professional modesty, though looking back there was a disturbing sense of extreme nervousness about her reaction, rather than a flattering diffidence.

'She was then staying at the Colony Hotel. We started discussing the play cautiously, meeting two or three times a day, examining the role, edging towards Rachel's commitment to it. I explained what a challenge Gladys represented to any actress, a traumatised character scarred by the gross irruption into her life of the South African security police – psychologically raping her, violating the inner recesses of her being. At the end of the play, Gladys realises stoically that maybe she's headed for another spell in a mental institution, possibly with electro-shock treatment. Rachel was very probing, quizzing me about every aspect of Gladys, almost as if she was a living person. This, in retrospect, was also significant: but I didn't recognise how much *then*. She showed such extraordinary understanding of Gladys that I almost asked her if she'd ever undergone any similar experience of breakdown. Finally, she said, "I'll do it. But be very patient with me, lend me your support, give me courage."

'Besides Jimmy Jones and Rachel, I cast Harris Yulin as the husband. But from Day One of rehearsals, it became clear that something was terribly wrong. What I'd taken for nervousness on Rachel's part was something far more overwhelming. She got tenser and tenser. Her hands holding the text of the play went white with tension. I never felt I was getting her to relax and express herself. It was as if she'd caught sight of Gladys's face – and discovered it to be her own.'

This indeed was what had happened. To Rachel, the text she held was like a hand-mirror. In addition to Gladys's history of mental instability, the fictional character and the real-life woman had something else in common which Fugard was certainly not privy to at that time. Gladys has been keeping personal journals which, before the play opened, had been seized in a security raid and used as evidence against her husband's political associates. This, it was suggested, had triggered her mental breakdown. Now Rachel, too, was busy on her own journals, secretly making the lacerating inventory of her feelings which constitutes part of this book. In accepting the role of Gladys, then, she had encountered nothing less than a deeply traumatic part of herself enshrined in the character's guilt and instability. It was like an 'appointment in Samara' – there was no escape from herself. Even in Yale, her self-tortured image was waiting to greet her.

The rehearsal hours took their toll, too: they were long and arduous, from 2.00 pm till 6.00 pm and then from 6.30 pm till 10.00 pm, or even 10.30 pm in a bare room in Crown Street.

ATHOL FUGARD: 'Fairly soon after the start of rehearsals, I became aware that Rachel had another problem – drinking. Not that she drank at work – never! But once it was over, she'd latch on to me and use the social encounter as a licence to go to Kavanagh's bar and get drunk. Then her dominant obsession surfaced – Rex Harrison. She felt things should have turned out otherwise and the two of them ought to be still together. She had a pathetic fear of being alone: which meant that if she couldn't find me, she'd seek the company of my wife and daughter Lisa. We were living in a house in the New Haven suburbs. Thank God we always made her welcome.

'Looking back, the casting of the two male roles was also daunting to her. In filling both roles, I was looking for actors of impressive physicality – almost carnal in quality. She found the players overpowering. Since Gladys had severed her relationship with her husband because of his overweening nature, this was another unhappy parallel that Rachel had to cope with in real life. I tried to turn a problem into an advantage. I told her that if she could get a handle on the play, maybe it would help her deal with reality. But I soon began to realise how serious the battle was going to be and if I'd been sensible, I'd have asked Rachel there and then to reconsider her commitment to us. But she was constantly imploring me to be understanding – and it was very hard to refuse a woman so obviously desperate to win. It might have done more harm than good, or so I felt then.'

PROF. GISTER: 'Athol wouldn't permit anyone from the faculty to attend rehearsals. But we began getting reports that Rachel was rather "unfocused" in her work. At the same time – this was about the first week in February – we were aware her teaching classes were going badly. She'd begun well. A bit nervous: but that's not unusual in novice lecturers. She was developing, we thought, into a forceful teacher until we observed she was having trouble making her seminars fruitful for her students. She seemed distracted by something – and students feel this. Frankly, we were very worried.'

ATHOL FUGARD: 'One night after a particularly anguished rehearsal, Rachel dragged me into Kavanagh's. She was drinking a fearsome amount. Suddenly she rushed out of the bar. I ran after her, very frightened by what might happen to her in her condition and caught up with her at the hotel. She was almost incapable. I got her up to the room she'd moved back into and put her into bed. And then began a pretty desperate three or four hours. All her neuroses burst out. I was afraid that if I left her, she'd do something terrible or, at the very least, run out of the hotel stark naked. I tried everything I could think of to quieten her, including calling all the numbers we could think of, all round the States, to try and locate Rex Harrison – with no luck.

'Eventually she fell asleep. When I went to the bathroom, I found a bottle of sleeping pills and flushed it down the lavatory. A suicide at Yale would have been just unthinkable.'

The next day, Rachel asked to see the Dean, Lloyd Richards, who had engaged her that day in New York when she was buoyed up by the prospect of seeing Rex.

ATHOL FUGARD: 'Lloyd and Jimmy Jones and Harris Yulin and Rachel and myself all met in a corner of Kavanagh's. Rachel didn't go into specifics. She simply asked them if they appreciated she had emotional problems. The play was too close to her, she said. The two actors implored her to *use* the play for therapeutic purposes. But she was adamant. I kept quiet. The irony was that as you listened to Rachel analysing herself, so crisp, so self-assured, so clear-sighted, you'd have sworn that such a woman would have had no difficulty coping with the trauma that the play represented for her. When we left the bar, it had been confirmed – Rachel would be leaving the cast of *A Lesson from Aloes*.

'I had one more meeting with her, over a cup of coffee at a Hickory House café in New York – I was in town to find a replacement for her. We eventually settled on Maria Tucci. To my relief, Rachel was looking less strained, far more in control of things. It looked that way, anyhow. I asked if she'd any plans and she said, quite brightly, Oh yes, she was going out to the Coast to do a Charlie Chan film with Clive Donner. I thought hopefully that maybe she'd sorted things out. I'd my mind on my own work and didn't follow her fortunes and we never subsequently wrote to each other. The events were so painful to both of us that I'm afraid I didn't want to take the initiative of raking them up again.'

PROF. GISTER: 'Soon after all this, Rachel left the campus. That ended her contact with Yale. We never saw or heard from her again.'

I n mid-January, I went to Yale to take up my job as lecturer in the Drama Department. I first stayed at the Colony Hotel, but after an awful all-night party, I made up my mind to look for somewhere else. When I needed to, I drove up and down from New York after trying Grand Central Station and Penn and Amtrak. I tackled *King Lear* in my lectures. I was approached about doing Athol Fugard's new play *A Lesson from Aloes* and met with the author who drank into his beard as we discussed the possibility of my 'keeping an appointment with Gladys' (the character's name). I warned him of my condition – veiled, no doubt. I don't know what I'd hoped for from Athol Fugard. A great deal, I suspect, and, as usual, another hopeless romantic fantasy bit the dust when confronted by his unit – his wife and daughter. I'd tried to push my emotionally starving self into his world. Again, I was half-hoping I could stay with them, a little jilted when I heard Mary [Benson] was. Ridiculous, my sad symptom of loneliness! Mary was there in New Haven to edit his diaries, had known the family for years, shared the same political activism, was South African. I was a woman he'd just met – who he hoped would be in his play.

I went to hear Arthur Miller speak at the Master's House. Miller had mistaken the time, so I was approached to fill the gap. I did. The Master's wife told me she knew of a room to rent in the house of the wife of the Professor of the History of Science. Again I romanticised, being part of the 'academic community' just by taking the little room. I did – and quite predictably, I wasn't.

My lectures started at 9.00 am, and finished at noon. I had nothing to do. I spoke with Rex and told myself, 'Must try harder', but too often I remained lonely and found myself sitting in the Yale Drama Library trying to put together my thoughts and my life . . . writing them both down on paper. I thought of Elizabeth Harrison, Rex's ex-wife and one of my closest friends, and her ability to arrange and give and enjoy parties. Her apartment is always full of guests who are staying there. I thought of how incapable I am of such activity. I remained in the grip of melancholia – a dummy without a ventriloquist. That's what I am. John Schlesinger gave a party at the Russian Tea Room for his new film [*Honky Tonk Freeway*]. I remember the days I hovered in his orbit and felt his aura rub off on me a little. I was amazed at the organised, worldly glitter of the affair, the surface sophistication. I envied him his *living* life.

I spoke with Rex since I was down in the dumps, and I like to talk to him. He's a bit like me, only infinitely more able to cope. Not for him parties and the social whirl. Perhaps again he will be the answer. Yet, there again, I'm unsure. Could I cope with Rex's isolation and ageing? I think, Yes. I was idyllically happy when he and I were alone in Italy. A house and a fire and Rex? I want life to be like an idyll. And it's not.

Staying with Bobby Frosch in New York, I stopped myself just in time from going to Elaine's [the restaurant favoured by film and stage people]. Once too high, in front of Woody Allen and Jack Hofsess, was all right – excusable. I was trying again to thrust myself into their orbit. I'm not the first to have done so. Molière satirises social climbers: I suppose I'm a 'personality climber'. I'm convinced I'm so interesting that all and sundry will clamour for my company. As these days wear on and I see all my friends and family not only quite content in their orbits without me, but actively glad I'm not there with them, then I realise with dismay that in the days gone by when I thought I was, if not essential to their existence, then certainly a shot in their arm – that my excitability cheered them on – it was more often than not the case that, with an unspoken (or maybe spoken!) sigh of relief, they all saw the back of me.

Panic overtook me again at Yale. I found myself with a whole new generation among whom I sat – unremarked and unremarkable. As I looked at the students with young lives before them, I knew I had failed. I couldn't take the endless hours away from class. Even getting to class was an increasing effort. I had moved from the Colony Hotel into a room in a private home with a percolator – and found I didn't belong to either, couldn't live in either. Mike Nichols and Elaine May, who were staying at the Colony, used it all functionally – their respective suites, their room service. I couldn't. All year I had looked at other people's lives and *known* that theirs, which satisfy them, would not satisfy me.

In order to fill the lonely hours, I elected to do the Athol Fugard play, *A Lesson from Aloes*. No sooner had I committed myself than I began to dread the play. If I collapsed under the pressure and strain, there really would be no hope. I desperately wanted someone to wake up to – to help fritter away my frightening thoughts. I fantasised about Rex's wife leaving and letting me move back in.

What do I want? Oh, laughter and warmth and kind faces and laziness and an end to loneliness. What do I dread? Standing before an audience, for one thing. Remember di Cori's words: 'You should be so sure of your craft by now that you don't notice anyone else is there.' Yet I dreaded rehearsing the play. I dreaded manoeuvring the car on the way to rehearsals. But there was no alternative – I *had* to do these things. Like a child, I needed guidance – yet if only anyone would ask for my help, I was sure I'd give it. Now, though, I'm not so sure.

On the days I spent in New York, I found myself drafting letters to Rex in my Yale class notebook:

Darling – I'd had some red wine when we both talked on Saturday night; that was probably obvious. A foolish thing to do, since I had been longing to speak to you genuinely, and from my heart to yours. As it was, the stupid red wine, coursing through my veins, compared James Earl Jones's acting to what Homer's would have been like . . . I'm afraid I played the clown. The pain of the day, and the joy of hearing your voice, became more than I could bear, so (and I expect I'm being puritanical) I tried to ease the misery. Foolhardy, of course! But perhaps to face up squarely to this realisation, as I'm now doing, is better than all the cold analysis in uncaring doctors' offices. Plain and simple, I love you and always have and probably always will. It is something I must live with.

I tried to bury it, stand on my own two feet, lecture at Yale and do the play – denying the loneliness and being frightened that I was going crazy from it. Why should loving bring such agony, I wonder.

I think of you today across Central Park, fighting the battle of hope, and burying the disillusions we all have and not giving in to them, like I do. I remember well what you said, that everyone has to fight. Agonisingly, I don't seem able to suppress my longings to have you as company – to talk to, to laugh with . . . Your incredible guts and fighting spirit used to energise me – and, of course, I don't feel 'up' to you, my dearest Reg, except I know my love was for *you*, not for what I could take from you. However, even that intrudes into my consciousness, and I compare your incredible ability to do the endless tour and organise your life. All I dream about is to be simple and loving and protective and protected . . . It is, as I wrote earlier, perhaps best to finally and completely recognise this and come to terms with it. How, as yet, I don't know, since I look at other faces and hear other voices and they are not yours. Will I really die of this love, Rex? It is not your responsibility, my love, but mine.

Faced with reality at Yale, unaided by a Lindsay Anderson to give me strength, I couldn't go through with it. I couldn't quietly concentrate on the job in hand. I couldn't calmly and objectively assess what the play was trying to say and where my character of Gladys should fit into it. Reading the text on the times I took the train to New York, I'd find myself saying, 'Ah yes, here's a scene where I can draw tremendous and admiring attention to

Doing *Who's Afraid of Virginia Woolf?* at Bath, 1969, with her first husband Alan Dobie. *Inset*: as they had looked at their marriage in Swansea, 1955.

*Right*: Blonde now, and
wearing her famous S[?]
Laurent 'all in one
boots-and-tights, Rache[?]
arrives at Heathrow in
1971 with her new
boy-friend, Darren
Ramirez: 'I was proving to
the world what a sexy
glamorous cat I was.

With stage and film director
Lindsay Anderson in 1969:
'Lindsay has tried so hard to put
some guts into me.'

Rachel (with Valentine Dyall)
rehearses *The Three Musketeers
Ride Again* on December 19,
1969, the day her husband's
lawyer announced that 'Rex
Harrison . . . and his wife are
living separately and apart.' On
Christmas Eve, Rachel
'swallowed all the pills she had.'

*Above*: In *Alpha Beta*, London, 1972: 'Every night I would go and play this wild and bitter and terribly sad woman.' *Below*: In Lindsay Anderson's 1973 film *O! Lucky Man*, teaching Malcolm McDowell about coffee – and life.

*Above left*: On Broadway, 1973, as Clara Zachanassian in *The Visit* and (*left*) Francine in *Chemin de Fer*.

*Above*: With Wendy Hiller in Sidney Lumet's 1974 film *Murder on the Orient Express*: her German accent was borrowed from Marlon Brando

Mid – 1974, leaving on the QE2 with
Valentine Mayer: 'The press were
mainly interested in whether I was
emigrating, marrying and what age
Val was!!'

As Mrs Appleyard (with 'that wig') in
*Picnic at Hanging Rock*, Australia,
1975.

As a 'hit' woman in *Foul Play*, 1978:
'This lady could have been a lot of
trouble to us.'

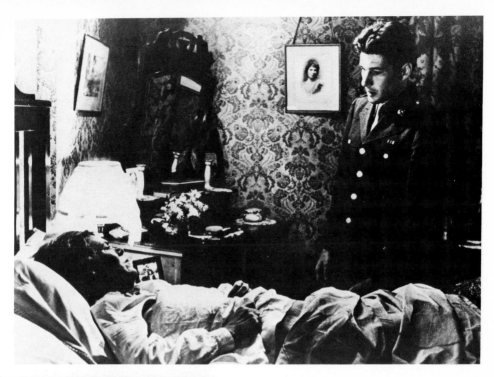

With Richard Gere, her
partner-in-comedy from *Habeas
Corpus*, now at her death-bed in
John Schlesinger's 1979 film *Yanks*.

London, January, 1979, with Darren
Ramirez at the Royal *premiere* of
*Yanks*. 'I barely functioned . . . I was
manically out of control (and) had to
have two Libriums.'

Rachel in her last cinema role, the
comic Mrs Dangers in Clive Donner's
1980 detective parody *Charlie Chan
and the Curse of the Dragon Queen*:
'It was an agitated, lonely ordeal.'

Patrick Garland. If only I could still feel my love for him. Could I? Could I unpack and cook as Maria does. He was glad I was alive he said. He is a scamp. Always was. Impossible I suppose to live with. Woke up at five thinking I am dead. What is there for me? No comfort

_Nov 2020_

I am very ill.

I can't control it anymore and I've been trying with all my failing strength. I'm paralysed. I can't do anything and there seem to be no help, anywhere. What has happened to me. Is it that my dependance on the years on alcohol has so severely debilitated me that now nature it self cannot function at all. Or is it that my nervous system from birth has always been so very frail that life for me is too much to cope with. That I am the hopelessly dependent little girl that found everything too hard to handle so that my intelligence and the ... have been overcome, now I'm in my ... and I can't overcome it. Day after day, night after night I'm in this shell ... why am I so terribly frightened ... life itself I think.

myself – where the raging neurotic in me can be applauded.' Then hearing Rex tell me of his day, the breakfast made for him, the bath, the masseur, the air-conditioned car, the lunch brought in by Roderick, the cast chosen by himself, the star role – it made me ill with envy. No, I don't resent Rex his crutches – I'm just sick that I have none.

I asked to be released from the Fugard play when I found I couldn't retain the lines. I couldn't even remember the name of the hero's dog. The clear talent of James Earl Jones finally made me realise just how far away I am from real acting and real work. It should have been a real relief – and in a way it was. The week-end was to be the test. I drank a bottle of wine at Bobby's, drove up with Athol, and on Monday had to face the fact that I wasn't up to it. I got foolishly drunk and cried about my Rex. Really, no one was *that* disturbed about the decision. It was honest and dignified. Lloyd Richards was far less put out than I'd anticipated. Athol is good and sensitive. I had drunk brandy furiously, then slept, tried to read the play at the Colony, drank some more, came to Kavanagh's, had to be put to bed by Athol. I called Darren at five in the morning in California. He was asleep in his bed with the animals curled around him.

Yes, I was relieved about the play. I didn't want to act again. I want to live. I hate acting and everything connected with it. But I must earn my living somehow. I'd like to be connected to the world of people. I really only want to talk and drink and eat. Perhaps Rex will help me do all these things and then I can feel protected into the bargain.

Outside, I remember, it was snowing in New Haven. Inside, the red wine was abating my pain and fear. I was riddled with guilt and probably a false sense of myself.

Those days of talking to Athol about the play seemed years away and unreal to a degree. I didn't think it was *me* talking to him: it was a 'me' I thought I ought to be. I tell myself, 'I want Rex back'. 'Make a play,' one of my friends said – the last one I would have expected to say such a thing. Rex did make sense to me. What could I give him? He seems to crave sweetness and warmth. Those qualities I have. He doesn't want to be bossed. I want to be guided. There are not many years to go. For me, certainly, very few if things continue to be as they are. Rex kept the void out. And yes, Alan, I do run to acting to meet people. I wanted to do *A Lesson from Aloes* to fill in the empty days at Yale, not because I wanted to create Gladys. I hate facing getting to be an old actress. Good for you, my beloved Rex, you've got the courage, the guts, the narcissism if you like, the arrogance to face it. I know your fears. I know the way you swallow the bitter bile. You lost Kate and I was erratic and inept, naïve and selfish – to minimise it all extravagantly. Given the chance again, I'd love you and cosset you.

Six days after I told Athol I couldn't do the play, I still felt a lost soul. I told myself that if this was a slow descent into suicide, then my prayer and pity go out to all those others who have suffered – or will have to – as I am suffering. It is beyond self-pity.

Pulling out of the play was a 'first'. At other times I had always rallied myself when I had work to do – and did it.

So the next day I called the actor I was playing opposite and went to Kavanagh's and drank brandy to ease the pain. I returned to the hotel and slept it off. I returned to Kavanagh's and met the playwright and drank red wine. Feeling devastated, I couldn't go on to dinner with him and his wife and rushed back to the hotel – without a nightdress, without a toothbrush. What I said, I don't know, other than desperate talk of self-destruction. I took my clothes off – half thinking, madly, that he would look at me and maybe make love to me. Instead, he gently bathed my head – and as the alcohol took full effect, I fell into a sudden sleep. So worried was he that he called Bobby. Then I called Bobby, sobbing that I wanted to get a knife from the hotel kitchen to cut the pain out. And this is not madness?

On the Friday, John came to New Haven and collected me in a rented car – at nine in the morning, he arrived. We went to my 'home', where the painter was painting the bedroom. Denise [friend of Virginia, Rachel's housekeeper-companion] and Virginia were functioning. I drove with him to the Bronx and on red satin slithery sheets we made love. I'd hoped sexual release would still my aching heart. I went back 'home', took Denise out to dinner and spent the night in the little study – dreading the morning when she would get up in the normal way and leave me alone. During the week's madness, I'd called Rex. To do him justice, he had called back but I was no longer in New Haven. He wanted to know if I was in any trouble. Any trouble? I stayed almost comatose all day in bed on Saturday – unable to feed myself. I read a book on addiction – in all its aspects. Addiction to drugs, to alcohol, to love. It made sense. On Sunday, I made frantic efforts to reach Rex in Washington. Left word. Called his assistant director to tell him to call me – but I didn't hear anything. Why should I? How far removed I really am from the Rachel who, prettily coiffed and dressed, had told him I was driving up to Yale, conducting classes, appearing with the distinguished actor James Earl Jones in the Athol Fugard play.

I went to tea on Sunday, an hour late, with Doris and Leon and Linda. Glynis Johns was there. She said how difficult it was to be an actress, divorced, childless, rootless and homeless. She, too, has suffered. I went with her to the Mayflower Hotel for coffee and told her of my dreads. Denise wasn't coming home that night, so the ultimate dread happened. I stayed alone in an unkempt apartment – I who am compulsively fastidious – in the little study, cuddling a teddy-bear, at fifty-two, for comfort.

The next morning, Monday, the painter Tony came. I let him in. I couldn't even make a cup of tea for myself now. For some time I hadn't been able to go into a grocery store to buy food. I couldn't eat it anyway. Then I compulsively called everyone in sight. I'd called Darren for help the night before. He was kind and concerned and gentle and gave some measure of emotional support. I called him again in the morning. I called Sybil. John kept calling – he promised to drive me up to Yale. I kept procrastinating, dreading to go. Finally I left, slightly sedated, and we arrived at nine o'clock. I gave him dinner in the bourgeois, candlelit *maitre d'hotel*'d inn – with the executives and the sales managers wearing (to John) intimidating ties and suits. He handled himself well in unfamiliar and, for him, uncomfortable surroundings. But his face looked at mine with hopelessness – a poor, bereft, neglected, deprived child's face. Mike Nichols and Elaine May were dining there. They were doing *Who's Afraid of Virginia Woolf?* at the Long Wharf. With warmth, they shouted 'Rachel!' across the dining room. I was flummoxed. In the terrible state I was in, I wasn't even sure it was them – and even more surprised that they should recognise me – and still more surprised that they should do so with such warmth. They were quietly dining with their peers before they went to sleep in their respective suites. I was with poor John – miles removed from what I have been given and was in the process of giving up in life.

So, to sum up, it was a hopeless, paralysed, sick week-end. A human being utterly out of step with life, crouching in bed, abandoned, apart from a lost ex-convict on parole who recognises a fellow lost soul and seeks in her some solace. Solace which, except on a superficial level, I haven't got to give.

I made the class that morning. Alienated, of course – yet I enjoyed it. I went to get the yellow legal pad on which I set down my thoughts from my dangerous and cheaply rented car – and there were Nichols and May getting into their Mercedes and going off to a rehearsal. I ate some eggs and went off to the drama library to write, fighting, even through the Valium, my shivering self. I tried to write the pain out.

I awoke at 7.00 am, feeling like a drowning person, reviewing that childhood of mine. It was daylight by then. I didn't have to get up till eight. I let eight o'clock go, and did the only thing I've wanted to do for a year now, snuggled back, eyes closed, into a semblance of oblivion – and remembered how I did the same thing years ago when Rita McCanley called for me to walk to school. She waited in the sitting-room, I cringed in bed. My Father made an omelette that I ate hastily without relish. My Mother was in bed. I went to that high-school and did what I still do – tried to make everyone like me.

With all the good sense I've got, and the intelligence and the talent, how could I have let my demons take control like that?

That I just couldn't be dear Gladys – whom I could have played on my head, movingly, tenderly, bitterly, hopelessly, and had some of New York talking as I need them to talk in order to live – was a terrible blow. Add to it all the other things, ageing, loneliness, a feeling of having thrown away my life. I needed to keep my 'appointment with Gladys'. I needed it more than it needed me. She would have been electrifying.

---

RACHEL RETREATED FROM YALE in a numbing state of guilt, confusion and shock. This was the very first time she had had to withdraw from a play: that was the professional defeat it represented. But as Sybil Christopher later put it, 'leaving the campus and her students in the lurch was also an academic defeat that she felt keenly, for she had been well educated herself and came from a family of preachers and teachers. It seemed like a double betrayal.' She sought some merciful relief before returning to New York or California, places she now detested with equal and irrational vehemence, but which were essential habitations if she was to earn a living. She flew down to North Carolina and spent a short recuperation with one of her oldest and most intimate friends, the English actress Rosemary ('Rosie') Harris, who was married to an American and had a home at Winston-Salem as well as a hideaway cabin in the hills.

$I$ left Yale for good by train – leaving
behind the lecturing, the play, the room with the percolator, the Vega which
I'd run into a fence, Kavanagh's, the whole horrid soulless little town.
Delighted to be doing so.

The week after Yale was predictably traumatic. Denise was leaving the
apartment on Tuesday morning. I couldn't stand the thought of being alone.
So I summoned John to spend a 'virgin' night with me. In the morning, we
both feigned sleep as Denise showered. After she'd left, I shuddered at the
sight of the poor man next to me in the bed – and tried to read 'Crisis of an
Actress' [chapter in Maggie Scarf's book *Unfinished Business*], but couldn't.
John watched television, having cooked his fry-up. I went to Bocusse to
swallow two glasses of red wine, buy cigarettes, visit with Bobby, swallow
the fry-up, vomit. I went to be the 'celebrity' at the wine-and-cheese party
for Channel 13, with John in tow. I drank more wine and evidently passed
out in the cab. I just remember telling the driver, 'Please go', and waking up
in Central Park West, with Virginia, thank God, in attendance.

Somehow I got to darling Rosemary Harris, whose N. Carolina mountain
hideaway is called 'Penland', the brandy and ginger ale at the airport
helping. At Greensboro Airport, Rosie met me and we stopped off for more
brandy (for me). On arrival, I 'gaily' demanded more red wine. Rex called.
On Thursday, I think, Rosie drove me to Old Salem, John had to go to
Washington. I think I stopped drinking on Saturday after we'd driven up to
Penland. I was amid mountain-y people, in an old cabin with an electric
blanket, sitting in the sun and writing – Martha playing with Jennifer. We
visited their friends, a man and a woman who bred sheep and sculpted. We
drove back on Sunday with Pop-Corn's cage, taking it in turn to sit in the
back of the station wagon.

Getting back to Salem, lighting a fire, having supper, watching the
cartoon *Gay Purree* [animated UPA movie made in 1962 about a country cat
going to Paris and getting shanghaied: the cat characters naturally appealed
to Rachel, their human characteristics as well as the plot reminded Rachel of
people in her own life] on television, I felt like the 'me' I *can* be, given half a
chance. It was like coming home. I think Rex called that night. I felt that the
movie *Gay Purree* said it all, with Maiowrice and Robespierre [two cat
characters in *Gay Purree*]. I felt I'd hit the nail on the head there, though it's
much more complicated than that, I fear. Rex on the phone sounded like
Miaowrice and, later, it was a comfort to hear Darren's gentle voice, I
thought.

Rosie's bed was comfy and warm, with Buttercup the cat sitting in it.

My behaviour had been mad and terribly out of control. Once I got back to
Los Angeles, I resolved to change the pattern and go out with Darren, or sit
in the garden.

I was sitting in the woods above the house (surrounded by tiny wild roses),
immersed in the atmosphere of England in 1811, when an agent telephoned
to tell me a friend had been nominated for an Emmy. On being asked what I
was doing, I answered, 'Reading Jane Austen's *Sense and Sensibility*.' He then
asked, seriously, I'm afraid, 'Is there a part in it for you?'

THE BRITISH ACADEMY OF FILM AND TELEVISION ARTS gives its annual awards in March. Rachel was strongly tipped for one of them on the strength of her performance in *Yanks*. The film had done much better in Britain than America. So, hopeful of squeezing some more box-office out of it by the publicity which the televised proceedings would engender, United Artists, the distributors, flew Rachel over to London. She was met by her friend Jeffrey Lane, who was disturbed by the deterioration now distressingly apparent in her.

JEFFREY LANE: 'Although she'd talked to Rex before she left, she arrived in anything but an optimistic mood. She was nervous and looked depressed. I told her that United Artists were unlikely to have flown her all that way and put her up in an expensive suite at the Dorchester if it wasn't true that she had won the Best Supporting Actress award. It didn't cheer her up at all. She was wearing a black dress – she looked in mourning, as if missing the dead rather than getting ready to celebrate a win. "Rachel, you really must change that dress," I said. "It's so dowdy looking." Her hair looked great, long and luxuriant, until she deliberately went and put it up in slides, which increased her haggard appearance. "This is the way I want to look tonight," she said. "No one will think it's you," I said. "Why don't you make yourself glamorous, show them a different Rachel from that plain, repressed woman you play in the film – everyone will think you weren't acting, that it was really *you*."

'As we sat there at the awards ceremony, she told me how unhappy she was. "If I win, I'm not going up to receive the prize," she said. "I feel paralysed." I whispered back, "You're crazy! The award will simply sit there. No one will understand how you're feeling. Pull yourself together, Rachel – *act!*" She whispered back, "I've got cramp. I can't move." Then the announcement came. She'd won! And suddenly she'd sprung up and was rushing forward to get the award throwing smiles of pleasure left, right and centre – the actress all over!'

Her agency, ICM, had got her a character role, as a nutty housekeeper named Mrs Dangers, in a screwball comedy called *Charlie Chan and the Curse of the Dragon Queen*, starring Peter Ustinov, to be directed in Hollywood by Clive Donner. Rachel therefore returned to California at the end of March, or early in April, 1980.

DARREN RAMIREZ: 'She arrived very guilt-ridden and for a time was almost incomprehensible. I was terribly sorry, but felt absolutely helpless. My presence in the house simply seemed to unsettle and anger her even more. Sybil said she could move in with her and then we'd get her a room at the Château Marmont; and when she'd been at Sybil's for a day or so, Rachel called me and said this was the end of things for us, we were destroying each other and it was far better we lived apart. I got the impression she wasn't even listening to what I was saying. A few days later, though, her mood had completely changed. She called me at work – I'd started at I Magnin on Wilshire – and said she felt Sybil disapproved of the way she had misbehaved herself at Yale – what was really gnawing at Rachel was her own remorse, activated by how far short she knew that she'd fallen of the standards imposed by duty and obedience and her Welsh upbringing. Now she desperately wanted to return to me. And again, weakly, I surrendered and cancelled plans I'd made for Easter. Odd, but every time there was a holiday season, Rachel got depressed.

'On Easter Day she woke up, drank a bottle of wine, became obstreperous and kept following me from room to room as I tried to put myself out of her sight so as not to make her angrier still. But it was no good. Every time I settled down, to read the paper or a book, my very presence seemed to offend her. We had a big fight. I threw myself into the car and took off, anywhere, just to escape. When I got back, I found she'd been calling up her friends, Sybil, Pamela, Marti Stevens, looking for help. I tell you, it was I who needed help! I simply didn't know how to cope. The only way I could think of calming Rachel, till she started work on the film, was more medication. But she rushed home from the hospital in Westwood, where she was to be examined, declaring it was a mad-house. She became very depressed.'

Rachel's melancholic mood is apparent in one of the last letters she wrote about this time to her friend and agent Milton Goldman. It shows how low her spirits were, and, not far beneath the businesslike foresight evinced about new films, new parts, how desperate she had grown for the love of the scattered friends she called her 'family'. The letter, written from Hutton Drive, is dated April 23, 1980.

'Dearest Milton – I'm not feeling particularly happy as I sit down to write this letter because, sadly, my dear Milt, I'm taking a temporary leave of absence from ICM at the termination of this year's agency agreement. In all truth it was in my mind to do so last year, but then you went into hospital and I just could not. It just isn't working for me out here, and since I am feeling extremely ambivalent myself about acting these days, and seem to be without any real drive or interest in it, I need more coaxing, more pushing, and perhaps more importantly more interest and encouragement than I'm getting.

'If, of course, my idea of me as the psychic in *Death Trap* meets with Sidney Lumet's enthusiasm, ICM should do the deal, since I mentioned it first to you and to Laurie Evans when he was out here. Did you get any reaction from Sidney, by the way? I know when last we spoke he was out of town.

'I should be coming to New York quite soon, hopefully on my way to Italy via London. I seem to be at some strange sort of cross-roads and need a time of peace and tranquillity to think.

'We're friends, aren't we, Milt? I cannot envisage New York without you, and our enchanting Four Seasons lunches, and our phone calls, and Sutton Place and Arnold. I would be hurt beyond belief, and New York a greyer place, if these precious human things stopped.

'Do write to me soon. I spend most of my days writing in the Public Library, but we have an answering service now, and I can always return your call before leaving in the morning. My love as always – Rachel.'

Sidney Lumet was to add a sad, not unfeeling post-script to this letter a few years later when asked why the idea of casting Rachel as the psychic in the film version of Ira Levin's *Death Trap* had not appealed to him.

SIDNEY LUMET: 'Ah, agents . . . I'm afraid I'd already indicated my preference for Irene Worth. I think someone was probably being kind to Rachel,
not telling her.'

I n March, I flew to London for the
British Film Academy 'Oscar' night – one of the awards was to go to me for
my performance in *Yanks*. But I was depressed and had dinner with Rex the
night before I left in order to try and pick up my spirits. What agony the
award ceremony was! Then there was the dreadful journey back and arrival
in a torrential downpour in New York cancelling all flights to Winston
Salem, where I was to join Rosemary Harris. I rushed back to the apartment
on Central Part West and in desperation tried to find Rex's number that I'd
ripped up before leaving in order to avoid temptation. It would have been
our eighteenth wedding anniversary had we still been together.

I went to Rosie's and stayed with her and wept and called Rex and said *au
revoir*. I waited till he'd left New York and then returned myself. The 'myself'
now without Rex that tried to be the 'myself' that I am with him. This never
worked. I had lunch with Milton Goldman and Jean Marsh at the Four
Seasons, drank Champagne, went off to see yet another analyst, then the
insurance doctor for the film about Charlie Chan that had been offered me.
The insurance doctor's was the wrong address. I panicked, phoned, got the
right address, rushed back to spill my troubles to the analyst, rushed over to
Elizabeth Harris's cocktail party, had more Champagne, cancelled the
theatre with Milton and Arnold Weissberger because there was a 'possible'
man at the party, rushed back upstairs, drank some more, went to
Mortimer's with Elizabeth and her husband Peter and Nancy Holmes and
then back to Central Park West where I put the gas on, brought out the little
white pillow, laid my head on it – and didn't go through with it. I was booked
to fly to Los Angeles the next morning. I woke up, predictably frenzied. I
called Virginia and she recommended her doctor. I was admitted to
hospital overnight, then discharged in his care on the Sunday and flew to
Los Angeles.

Back in Los Angeles, I went with Darren and his dog Boosie to Venice. It was
a glorious day and *I was happy*. We walked on the beach. Boosie had a great
time. Monday was Academy Awards Night. Before we went to lunch at the
Polo Lounge of the Beverly Hills Hotel, I shopped at Hughes supermarket,
filling the basket with yoghourt, strawberries, all sorts of things. When we
got home there was a blazing row based on the fact that Darren hadn't told
me that the Academy Awards had begun. Finally, all his frustrations broke
out and he physically attacked me. I'd goaded and jeered and spoiled his
evening. I was booked for examination into the Westwood Hospital and
drove over there. It was awful: the final degradation: wake-up was at
7.00 am. A torch was shone on one's face during the night. There was a
communal dining room. There were disturbed people. I went home. I toyed
with the idea of moving out to the Château Marmont or the Regency. Gavin
Lambert came on the Sunday and on the Monday I had a wardrobe fitting for
the Charlie Chan movie and went on to see what the Regency was like. I

visited Gavin, a *whole* Gavin, able to live and structure his life. I regained confidence.

I fell asleep on the bed at Hutton Drive and the cat had kittens on the bed alongside me. I didn't want Darren to wash the blood away.

---

TO CLIVE DONNER and Jocelyn Rickards, Rachel Roberts was an old 'Hollywood resident'. Donner, whose nimble, satirical talent had been shown at its best in *What's New, Pussycat?* in 1965, and his costumer-designer wife were the 'newcomers'. It was the first time Donner had worked in Hollywood, though he had directed *Luv* in New York; and it was probably he, as the stranger in town, who reached out for reassurance, and thought he had found it when Rachel visited him and Jocelyn in mid-April to discuss her costumes as Mrs Dangers in *Charlie Chan and the Curse of the Dragon Queen* and say how much she looked forward to working on the picture. It was a romp of the Pink Panther genre trading heavily on period nostalgia for the imperturbable Chinese sleuth whose reincarnation by a Caucasian actor, Peter Ustinov, was to elicit some racial displeasure, though not as much as the critical displeasure that ultimately greeted the picture in spite of its often quite successful passages of comic camp.

CLIVE DONNER: 'Rachel came to me enthusing about working on the picture. That she was highly strung was obvious. But I reminded myself it was a long time since she'd played comedy or farce in a film. She was very, very anxious to do it: that was the main thing at this time. Jocelyn then talked to her about the costumes.'

JOCELYN RICKARDS: 'She came to my studio on North Kings Road, only concerned about one thing – what would the housemaid wear? I said I saw her as a very formal sort of domestic, wearing grey in the mornings, black in the afternoon. She looked at me a bit sadly and said, "Wouldn't I wear anything else?" I said, "Only once, when you go to meet Charlie Chan – you'd wear a coat and a hat." At that, she looked happier: she grasped me close to her. We'd never met, but I was able to say to her, "I remember you from *Platonov*." I'd gone there, to the Royal Court, in 1960, with John Osborne. In the first interval of that very long play – *five acts!* – John turned to me and said, "You and Rachel are so much alike." That kept me thinking for the rest of the play. I wondered if it were still true.'

Rehearsals were set, and a car was due to pick up Rachel at 8.00 am. But the night before began ominously and was to end nearly tragically.

DARREN RAMIREZ: 'Rachel said she wanted a sleeping pill – she was then on Mogadon – and added, "If I don't get one, I'll take these." She waved a nearly full bottle of anti-depressant pills: it turned out she'd been collecting them, in dribs and drabs, from various doctors she'd visited in London and New York during the summer. She then started phoning friends, behaving restlessly and preventing me sleeping – so I went to my room, shut the door, buried my head in the pillow and managed to get some fitful sleep.

'I woke up some time later . . . Not a sound from Rachel's room now. I felt instinctively something bad had happened. I went to the bathroom. The toilet had anti-depressant pills in it: it looked as if she'd tried to flush them away – which is what she generally did even with pills prescribed for her, lest they affected her memory for her lines. I checked on her. I could hear her breathing. But something struck me as not normal. I put the light on. She showed no reaction. I shook her. I slapped her. No reaction – nothing! In a panic, I called the paramedics and they came in five minutes. It was to be touch and go with her for three days.

'I called Clive Donner and stalled. I played for time. For I was afraid to tell him Rachel was in UCLA hospital and might be dead for all one knew. If she wasn't, then I was afraid she'd lose the part in the film if Clive knew what she'd done. "Clive," I said, "it's an extreme reaction to something she ate." Then I called ICM and they managed to keep it quiet, too.'

CLIVE DONNER: 'I began rehearsals thinking, Oh, well, it's a tummy upset: she'll show up tomorrow. But she didn't, and I heard next she'd got a virus infection. Okay, she'll get over that, I told myself. *Then* I heard she was in hospital and having trouble talking . . .'

DARREN RAMIREZ: 'She managed to pull through after about three days, though her throat was raw from the pipe they'd thrust down it to pump out her stomach, and at first they weren't sure she hadn't suffered brain damage. They had called a physician she had seen some time before – he simply didn't want to know about it! The first thing Rachel asked for, however, when she was well enough, was a pen and lots of paper – she was still keeping her journals. *Then* we knew she was all right. She was clever enough, too, to persuade the doctors that the overdose had been an accidental thing. By this time, of course, Clive Donner and the film's producers were anxious and suspicious at Rachel's no-show.'

CLIVE DONNER: 'She had a long letter hand-delivered to me, saying that, on her word as a professional actress she'd be perfectly all right and wouldn't be saying she could play the part if she couldn't. She followed that up with a telephone call – still not telling me what had *really* happened – and said, "You can hear how perfectly all right I am, can't you?" Well, it was sort-of all right: but not the voice I expected to hear from her on the screen.'

DARREN RAMIREZ: 'There was talk of a throat microphone: but you could feel the film people suddenly go very "iffy" about that: they didn't like that at all.'

CLIVE DONNER: 'Finally, she said, "I'll come along on Monday and do a voice test on tape." She was as good as her word. She did the tape and, by some miracle, as I can now appreciate, it was fine. If it hadn't been, she'd have been fired that minute. We couldn't wait any longer – this was a bare two days before shooting. She cut it really fine.'

DARREN RAMIREZ: 'At this very moment, I came across an analyst who seemed willing to help. His name was Richard Rosenthal: he lived on Camden Drive, did work at UCLA, and was highly spoken of. I gave him Rachel's history and warned him to be on his guard when she went to see him. "She'll do her best to get round you," I said. "I think for her own good she should agree to enter an institution where she can be properly treated: but she won't listen to me." At first, Rachel liked Rosenthal. He told me he felt it would do her a lot of good to return to me in Hutton Drive. Rachel said, "It's up to Darren." That was the very first time I'd been given any autonomy in the matter. So she came back. Rosenthal told me, "The first time she takes a drink, call me – we'll arrange treatment in a clinic." '

CLIVE DONNER: 'Once she started filming, she was totally dedicated: but she did want a lot of reassurance. She kept wanting to be assured that the waveband on which she was playing this comic paranoiac was as broad as was right, as truthful as was necessary. She had one running joke with me that throws some light on her character and her insecurity. She would joke about making love in the afternoon – between 3.00 pm and 3.30 pm was the time she preferred, she said. She'd look at me, and I'd shake my head if I was in the middle of a shot, or say "No". When 3.30 pm came and went, she'd say, "Pity, Clive – it's too late now." '

JOCELYN RICKARDS: 'Whatever unhappiness she was nursing alone, she showed nothing but spontaneous gaiety in company. We'd play charades, acting out the syllables of a word – she was great at this. The wardrobe staff adored her – very rare on a film. For she'd always take the trouble to change out of costume when she went to eat so that no harm came to the costume – she was the only one who did this.'

PETER USTINOV: 'I remember thinking she was a lady with some deep social problem – drinking, I thought – though she never let it show on the set. She was a little too determinedly over-cheerful for comfort, though. All her conversation came back to one topic – Rex, Rex, Rex. She asked me what I did between films and when she heard that I did work as a roving ambassador for Unicef, the United Nations organisation that deals with children's welfare, her eyes lit up with interest. "Do you think I could be an ambassador, too?" she asked. I didn't know what to say. It was a little embarrassing: Unicef is more accustomed to the less demonstrative sort of film star, Liv Ullmann say.'

CLIVE DONNER: 'The way she played Mrs Dangers was very odd – it was almost abstract.

'When it was all over, we saw her only once again. Pavla Ustinov, who is Peter's daughter and lives in the Hollywood hills, had the idea of a surprise party for her father, and Jocelyn and I were detailed to delay Peter's return to Pavla's house till all the guests had arrived and been hidden away – to jump out on him when he entered. I mean, surprise parties are just awful!! Never get lumbered with being the decoy! Peter was far too sharp, anyhow, to be fooled for long: so we took him completely into our confidence and told him he'd just have to give a good performance and feign surprise when we eventually made the party. But when we turned up and walked into the house, there wasn't sight or sound of anyone – no great crowd of people suddenly burst out of where they'd all been stashed away. And then we discovered that what had been arranged for "Charlie Chan" was a party at which all the guests were playing dead! As we went in, we gradually came across the "bodies", all the Hollywood partygoers playing murder or suicide victims for Peter to "discover". One fellow had his head in a gas oven – I think that may have been Roddy MacDowall – another was in a pool of "blood" in the kitchen, a third was "drowned" in the bath, and bodies were "hanging" from curtain rails or falling out of cupboards . . . Rachel may have been "strangled". Something terribly mortal had happened to her: what, I don't really remember, but there she was, playing dead . . . I suppose it was one of those things that "seem a good idea at the time".'

I woke up the next day numb and aching and calling everyone I could think of, not knowing what I was saying. I clawed at Darren when he tried to help me and comfort me. Later, I swallowed the pills I'd been given, missed the film reading and awoke in UCLA hospital, not able to speak because of a tube down my throat. I tried frantically to get my voice back in time for the film and wrote to Clive Donner, who was directing it, about having a chest microphone. I nearly lost the job. I did the film, in agony.

Making *Charlie Chan and the Curse of the Dragon Queen* was a nightmare. I could hardly keep still to have my hair done. I couldn't bathe or get up, except five minutes before the car came to collect me. I could have driven to the film location, for I've learnt to drive, but I didn't. I couldn't enjoy eating at Ma Maison because Dudley Moore was there with Susan Anton and Michael Caine – all sane and successful. Champagne kirs only made it worse. I felt utterly alienated from the rest of the cast. I couldn't play backgammon very well and *worried* about it. I hated having the second-fiddle make-up man. I played with a cold Roddy MacDowall, aching all the time. The old, not forgotten obsequiousness was there. I wanted people to ask me to dinner. I flirted almost obscenely with film people. I played up to Clive Donner and Jocelyn Rickards, his wife who was doing the designs. I sucked up to Ustinov, all the time throbbing from the tube that had been stuck down my throat for three days.

It was an agitated, lonely ordeal – horribly caught between what I was feeling inside – lost, bitter, anguished – and the mad antics of Mrs Dangers that I had to register outside.

I read the Alcoholics Anonymous literature again. I am one, I know. I knew the difference between my behaviour and the others on the film set when I had a beer for lunch. Instantly galvanised, I was, into character and vitality.

As I read the book that morning, I thought of eating fresh fish and the accompanying thought was – washed down with white wine. Why must it be always washed down with alcohol? Couldn't I be merry and gay and eat fried fish on its own? For some reason, No.

Rex called one morning in mid-June, but even the thought of running into him at Leslie Bricusse's house did nothing, gave me dread rather than hope. Darren and I went to see a film with Dudley Moore, and I remembered the days when I felt in the same league as Dudley.

I wrote a letter to Rex the other night, when my veins were full of wine. It went:

Dear Rex: It is impossible not to write. Sometimes late at night I remember you. So well. So dearly. So truly. You wanted none of it, my friend. Once you were Reg. No more . . . I tried so hard to love. And I tried so hard not be corrupted by all the things you wanted. I was content with Virginia and Pina, Don Pedro and Paco and Homer. Oh, dear Reg, I was gifted. I gave my gift to you, too. Unfortunately, you weren't secure enough to see it. Rachel.

Drink-induced rubbish, of course!

I have always wanted to be the centre of attention and until now – meaning this year of depressive illness – I genuinely believed myself to be so. And what was I, in fact? A blinkered simpleton, dependent on drink and drugs for years. I drank all the time with Rex, and I loved it. I looked bloated and farted in bed and didn't get up, and was too high really to take in the natural disgust in his eyes. I really went to town in that marriage. There they were, all the important people. I could be their equal, or so I imagined, and I took advantage of it. In Rome, I said to the witty urbane Noël Coward, 'Women can be buggered, too.' Oh, so funny, so delicate, so witty. Terence Rattigan had the measure of it when he wrote about the respective antics of Kay Kendall and myself. Hers had a style, he said. Mine, he didn't say, but I do, were funny to a point, then went too far and could be gross. As that famous writer said to Rex, 'Don't marry her, she'll drag you down.' Poor Rex! I was getting drunk every week-end at David Selznick's – I didn't know you weren't supposed to pee in the pond, or I was too drunk to care. Red-faced, loud-mouthed, unmade-up, 'confident', blithely rushing in where just ordinary mortals feared to tread, I 'patronised' Jane Fonda . . . 'Pretty young girl'. A few comments penetrated my blown-up consciousness: 'You do come on strong', 'She's so loud', 'Your hair's the wrong colour, the wrong length' – the last from Selznick, who liked me. And then when I bought a brown wool dress and had attended to my hair, the people I was 'patronis-ing' appraised *me* and said, 'You do look so nice tonight'. What they must have been saying behind my back is obvious. Dirk Bogarde said, 'If you can look like this, why don't you always?' – all justified. But here was the girl now in the limelight who had once gone to a West End first night in a cheap gold lamé dress, backless, made by the lady-round-the-corner in Padding-ton, and a rented mink stole, and had walked up the dress-circle stairs staring belligerently at Hugh ('Binkie') Beaumont, demanding to be noticed. She wasn't, of course. How could I have thought that I would be?

I got to know all the right people with Rex and behaved like a clown. I felt equal to the rich and the beautiful and I wasn't. When he started to be too embarrassed by it all, I drank more and got louder. I still, unbelievably, thought I was a riot. I barked loudly like a dog at society functions. Drunk, of course. Couldn't I see that my husband was publicly disowning me as he sat with pretty, blonde Elizabeth Harris at one table, leaving me interrupting conversations at another? With my hair dyed black and cut short – to be different – in a mannish black velvet jacket and skirt – what a spectacle I must have made of my poor self! I didn't grasp at all that the two Elizabeths – Taylor and Harris – were being, whatever their faults, women. No secrets did I withhold from the world, no mystery lurked in my eyes, just noisy, manic, uncontrolled behaviour. That's what the glass of wine with the fresh fish did for me, does, and always will do.

This crazy, nonsensical, unfunny behaviour continued with all sorts of persons in all sorts of places, in Hollywood, in Rome, in Paris. If they wouldn't take notice of me, my drinking would soon settle that. I was always smoking, always being affectionately loud, singing Welsh songs with Richard Burton, getting drunk at Maxim's, shouting out loud at Hollywood previews, loudly swearing at the Bistro late into the afternoon, 'smilin' through', like the imbecile I am, and being helped home drunk – and *then*, of course, I was no fun to be with at all!

But there was drunken behaviour of the same kind well before Rex came along, before Alan arrived on the scene. Working in 1952, as a salesgirl at Tom Arnold's circus, I got invited by the dog-trainer to attend an amalgamated Circus Ball at Grosvenor House. It was for him a 'privilege' to escort the 'English girl' who looked like a lady – in a false chignon and a black velvet dress. I got drunk. The salesgirl became the life and soul of the Circus Ball. She left her own table and winningly joined some other table. Winningly and coyly, she said to complete strangers, '*Voulez-vous baiser moi?*' – made, in fact, a complete and utter spectacle of herself and ended up screaming in the ladies' cloakroom and being taken home to the bed-sitter she shared, rather unwantedly, with two other plain girls, by a car-load of Indians who took pity on the 'Queen of the Circus'. She was predictably ill the next day, but the day after when she went back to work *everyone* knew her, recognised her, hardly with respect but with faint amusement. The dog-trainer took her home that week and beat her up.

Years later, Mrs Rex Harrison did something similar at the premiere of her husband's film *Staircase*. Burton and Taylor were then at the height of their fame and present, in the company of Princess Margaret and Lord Snowdon. Rex was away on tour with Elizabeth Harris in tow. I didn't know about that. I was too busy getting incredibly drunk at the Connaught with a woman journalist who'd come to interview me. I'd invited Roger Moore and his wife Luisa to escort me to the premiere. At 5.30 pm, the journalist and myself had nearly passed out and I ordered some Dom Perignon to 'sober me up'. Somehow I got ready – God knows what I must have looked like! – and went to the premiere I did – with all the *creme de la creme* of the British Film Industry present. Totally out of control, I yelled out periodically – what, I don't know – embarrassing my guests and again making a spectacle of myself.

Undeterred, I went to the reception afterwards. And again, 'winningly', I went up to Princess Margaret and in a friendly and familiar manner apologised for my husband's inability to attend the premiere. Of course I caught the cold glint of disgust and disapproval in Her Royal Highness's eye. She had other fish to fry. There were other people present whom she would rather be with. She had no time for Rex Harrison's sloppy-looking, drunken, noisy wife. I had to be up there, though, noticed at last – well, certainly noticeable, bravely smiling 'winningly' at everyone, unkempt and drunk and fooling absolutely no one. They talked about me on the way home, I'm sure, though I didn't think of that at the time. I sent roses, however, to the shocked Luisa Moore. Roger made light of it and said if it had happened a couple of hundred years ago, I'd have been sent to prison at the Tower.

But none of it was funny: it was, in truth, very sick. And there were many more incidents like that. I remember getting drunk in Paris with Jacques Tati, the famous comedy-film director and actor, and advising him what to edit out when we went into the screening room to see his film *Mon Oncle!*

I now face utterly the fact that I had and have serious emotional problems gravely accentuated by alcohol and that I could very well lose my sanity if things go on that way. I have already tried to kill myself. For all of it, I am deeply sorry and deeply ashamed and beg your forgiveness, Almighty God.

---

NO SOONER HAD SHE finished with *Charlie Chan* than Rachel went into a CBS telefilm of John Hersey's novel *The Wall*, which the American critic Annette Insdorf later praised as a 'compelling, well acted and reasonably accurate' story of the victims of the Polish holocaust at Treblinka. It was actually shot on locations in Poland, with Auschwitz doubling for the death camp that had incinerated thousands from the Warsaw ghetto. Tom Conti played a professional 'survivor' pulled into the Polish Underground because of his ability to move in and out of the Aryan sector to acquire arms. Rachel played a minor role as his landlady.

It was a mordant experience for her; and her spirits were low when she stopped off in London – anything to delay returning to Hutton Drive and its screaming sessions. While staying with Lindsay Anderson, she suffered a physical collapse – and from her bed in Hampstead's Royal Free Hospital, she began the 'diary' section of her journals which she kept up, off and on, until almost the very eve of the day she took her life.

Rachel's infatuation with Rex was now affected by a new fantasy. A delusion that came to occupy the centre of her thoughts and ultimately her actions – the belief that she could win her ex-husband back to her, despite Rex's very secure and happy marriage to Mercia Tinker. If he would not come back as her husband, Rachel 'reasoned', then perhaps she could be professionally at his side as his co-star on stage or screen. It was a complete delusion: but a powerfully consuming one and Rachel came to believe it was a practical possibility. Her diary entries lead her, through deepening physical and mental crisis, to the point where she actually made a forlorn and pathetic attempt to bring back the happy past by repossessing at least the affectionate attention of her former husband. Perhaps Richard Burton's remarriage of Elizabeth Taylor in 1975 had kindled Rachel's desire to get Rex back; for although the 'reborn' Burton duo were together for scarcely a year, the imaginative possibility of reliving the romance of earlier times seems to have been growing in Rachel's mind, to judge by what some of her friends felt. She, too, tended to pair off Richard Burton and Rex Harrison in their respective attitude to marriage, to the extent of beginning a short story about them, lightly fictionalised as 'Reg' and 'Rich'. A part of it can be quoted:

'Reg and Rich were handsome. There was no denying that. One was hooded-eyed and tall. He had a beautiful back, a sensuous, weak sort of back, but it was beautiful, swaying down the compartment of the train going to Paris. The other was shorter, bandy, but had a face that Michelangelo would want to sculpt . . . Each married two "sturdy" girls. The one sturdier than the other, in a manner of speaking. Sweet, naïve, rather selfless egotists were these two little people that Reg and Rich sought out . . . Poor things. Ventriloquists, really.'

Rachel's hospital sojourn illustrates in a way that would be comic if it were not so touchingly pathetic the uselessness of trying to treat a woman of her manic-depressive character by 'normal' routines which left her free literally to come and go as and when she wished!

JILL BENNETT: 'It always amused me in a bewildering sort of way how the places where she was supposed to have gone for treatment or a cure would allow her to walk in and out and go and have drinks and even go to parties – it was as if she was using them as a hotel, not a nursing home! I was absolutely astonished when I bumped into her at one of the daily cocktail parties that Arnold Weissberger and Milton Goldman gave in their suite at the Savoy every summer when they came to London to see the new shows. I'd been told she was then undergoing treatment at the Royal Free, in Hampstead, where Lindsay had had her admitted – but there she was, as large as life, a drink in her hand, talking at the top of her voice *and* wearing a new dress she'd bought for the occasion. Funny way of being cured, I thought to myself. But *very* Rachel!'

nything to escape from Los Angeles again . . . so I talked to my agent about doing a film, *The Wall*, for television. I flew to New York to stay in the maid's room at Sharman Douglas's [socialite friend] apartment – drunk most of the time – as Central Park West was up for sale. I went to Sardi's, ordered Champagne and read the screenplay which was to be shot in Europe. Val came round to escort me, still drunk, to the plane. My luggage went on to Frankfurt by mistake. I did the one-page part with Tom Conti while full of Librium, dreading each word. I prayed that my dying heart would at least feel something at Auschwitz, where we were to film a scene. But it didn't. I didn't enjoy Cracow, either, just got the young actor whom I was with to stop off at a bar so that I could drink vodka. Back I flew to London, to stay with Lindsay Anderson, and went to see a doctor. Total collapse followed and a knock-out pill . . . and so I have come here, to the Royal Free Hospital in Hampstead, London, on the 21st day of July, 1980, in the fifty-third year of my life, childless, workless and virtually homeless.

[*Note: From this point on, the entries in Rachel's journals become contemporaneous with the principal events to which they refer.*]

# July 21, 1980

And so it goes on with an endless and macabre horror that seems nothing to do with me – me wherever I've got to. It all seems uncannily predictable – the isolation, the strangeness, the familiar litany of the ill that drones through my head. Word-games with silent, withdrawn young men and hopeless-looking elderly women – feeling momentarily bright, then cascading into inexplicable tears. This English clinic is gentler than its American counterpart – as the English are gentler than the Americans – but the care of the disturbed leaves a whole lot to be desired. There's an unwholesome and false sense of gregariousness, soon dissolved if a patient dissents in any way. It would be better if there was less egalitarianism – if junior nurses wore the badge of junior nurses, senior nurses the same. The place hums with a frenetic sort of activity, footsteps are frantically quick, voices rushed; very little calm reigns – other than chemically induced. My temperament came back to me a little today. I refused to be benumbed and dehumanised.

Using this hospital as a health-farm is ridiculous and mad. Thinking I'm on holiday, making friends with Kitty and her baby, with depressed Zena, wandering around the wards, having 'little drinks' on the open air of Hampstead, dreaming about the houses I pass and eating scones for tea, while all the time I am seriously ill and lost and sick – it's further madness.

Mary [Evans] came to see me – an excuse to sit pathetically outside and sip wine, pretending the chaos doesn't exist. Watching her purr off in her Rolls, while I got drunk and then went to an AA meeting, is painful beyond belief.

I clung to the ghost of Rex. To send the letter or not to send the letter: is that what my peace of mind depends on?

Supposing he and I were to go on tour again in America – at least there'd be money, attention. And he does energise me. But with him at work while I stayed in the hotel suite and did what I did before (and that was, drink) because I didn't know what else to do: that would be suicide. But this seems suicide, too. My other plot is to open a little bar and restaurant in Spain and run it with Darren.

But I must get sobriety first. I've made so many attempts and then returned to drinking. Is this my 'bottom'? I'm in a psychiatric ward in London, my New York apartment rented because I can't emotionally live in it, paying the mortgage on another house I can't live in in Los Angeles and getting rent of a sort for the Pimlico house I can't live in, either . . . Again I fantasise about Rex's life. He'll be working hard at the moment in that horrible New Amsterdam Theater in New York, with the humidity of summer, in preparation for a long tour of America with *My Fair Lady*, eight shows a week, having to sing, memorise, energise in huge auditoriums. Could I do it? No. Would I want to? No.

Perhaps, though I don't know how, stopping drinking will lead me somewhere out of this nowhere I am now. I pray to God, to let this be so.

**July 26, 1980**
At Frank's boy's birthday party. I had a particularly bad time . . . realising that I've missed out entirely on that life, that I wanted to rear a child and see her grow up, give her all the things lacking in me. Though I played with the idea of adoption, I wish I'd taken it more seriously, or that Rex had.

**July 27, 1980**
Went to Stanley Hall's [hair stylist with large theatrical clientele] garden party in the country. It was fun to drive down, fortified by Jill's and Maria

Aitken's [stage actress] Champagne and orange juice. Drank too much there
. . . made Alan Jay Lerner 'laugh' about Rex, talked about so-and-so's
prowess as a lover – with his wife a yard away . . . was told later by Laurie
Evans that I shouldn't have gone, I looked ill.

**July 30, 1980**
Went to Milton's [Goldman] party at the Savoy . . . was bright and animated
and eager and *ill*. Returned to the Royal Free Hospital.

---

SOON AFTER THIS she discharged herself – and went straight out to another
party, at Eleanor Fazan's.

ELEANOR FAZAN: 'All she talked about was Rex. I recommended her to go
and see a friend of mine, Lady de Samaurez, who ran a health clinic in the
country called Shrubland Hall. Julia de Samaurez was also an amateur
but experienced counsellor. I said, "Rachel, you're not looking very well
and you could lose a little weight, too. Take yourself off to Shrublands." She
jumped at it.
  'I think Lindsay was disdainful of the sort of advice he believed Rachel
would get. Anyhow, she certainly didn't profit from it. The girl who was put
in charge of Rachel at Shrublands said that booze alone wasn't her
problem: it was her personality. She had the personality of the alcoholic,
she said. She just didn't respond usefully to an enclosed environment like a
health clinic.'

JILL BENNETT: 'Afterwards, Rachel said she was the only person to have
gone to a health clinic and actually *put on* weight!'

Among the Shrublands guests who had come simply for the tonic effect
of the health treatments was a well-known English journalist, Ann
Leslie.

ANN LESLIE: 'To my mind, there was no mistaking Rachel's intention –
which was to do away with herself. She made no secret of it: in fact, it was
hard to *stop* her talking about death. She hinted she'd written off to Exit to
find out how best to go about it.'

Exit, as it was then known, was a group which had set itself up amidst
considerable public controversy as an advice centre for people who wished
to take leave of life as sanely and responsibly as possible. Of course it did
not *encourage* people to commit suicide; but its pamphlets were available
upon request – and Rachel's London agent, Laurie Evans, intercepted one
or two addressed to Rachel via the ICM organisation in London. Another of
Shrublands' troubled guests was Lady Barnett, well known and loved by
many as a forthright radio 'opinionator'. She was a former court magis-
trate. Lady Barnett suffered periods of great depression and, during one of
these, was arrested and later convicted for shoplifting – her celebrity
magnified her 'sin' and a short time afterwards she committed suicide.
Among Rachel's papers were cuttings from the London *Daily Mail* –

affectionate tributes to the popular public figure which deplored the lack of understanding as well as loss that her suicide represented.

Still, Rachel found compensations among some of Shrublands' fellow guests.

## August 6, 1980
At Eleanor Fazan's party I was told about Shrubland Hall Clinic – where I am writing this – and about Lady de Samaurez who'd helped the unhelpable. Lindsay took me to see her. We talked for two hours about 'dead babies'. I told her of my terrible year. I got into Shrublands quickly.

Lindsay drove down with me: we had a picnic in the car. On arrival, I had a terrible hysterical attack – couldn't relax enough to sit through the massage, the heat treatments . . . I've come to the conclusion that acting must be my salvation and I must accept that I'm in real danger of throwing away my talent.

The following letter to my agent, Laurie Evans:

Dear Laurie, I always have the feeling that you're so busy and I don't want to take up your time. The malaise which I'm overcoming has a lot to do with fear that I'm being left behind. People say I'm a marvellous actress, but the offers lately have been thin and most of the work I've got myself I 'made' it in America, but want to come back home. Miss Marple is a part I could have played well. The British Film Academy award seemed to mean nothing. In the TV film I did with D. Fairbanks Jr, I got the notices. This will probably be true of the last film. It's going to be a struggle to get back into the swim and I need all the help I can get simply to get parts offered to me, on stage or in films. I need your agency ICM in order to work. I realise that in going to New York in '74 I fell between two stools – unlike Sian Phillips, for example, who concentrated on one place, and one place only . . . past history! I'd have loved to have played *Pal Joey*, and was offered Gertrude in *Hamlet* – I need advice badly.

## August 7, 1980
I can't summon back my strength. Where has it gone? Has my spirit been irrevocably broken?
   If you can force your heart
      and nerve and sinew
   To serve your turn long after
      they are gone,
   And so hold on when there is
      nothing in you
   Except the will which says to
      them 'HOLD ON'.

## August 8, 1980
I had four double whiskies last night, the pain was so intolerable and woke up to one of the worst mornings ever. I have just phoned Brenda, busy all week in Sian's pretty little house. Donald working in Wales. I've just phoned Joan Sims, going off to rehearsal, and Jill, too, about to go out. Here at Shrublands, I have made friends with Margaret [not her real name] and

Pam and Kay and met a depressive film producer who wants to take me to see an acupuncturist. Margaret lives not far away with her husband George [not his real name] and she's invited me to stay with them and then to go on to Hazel's to help with the children. I can't read or eat or sleep. I stare at four walls like a prisoner in solitary confinement.

## August 9, 1980
Post-acupuncture. Hope.

## August 11, 1980
I'm staying with Margaret in her lovely house with her attentive accountant husband, her children and grandchildren. The house is well appointed. They have a cosy routine – able to get up every morning at eight, George enjoying the garden, Margaret instructing her little 'Tweenie' house-help. George, an Oxbridge man, well into his thirty-years routine, with a tremendous zest for life, his family, his work, his food, his drink, their villa in Italy – a compleat man, in fact. Their major disaster: his affair, long since ended, with a beautiful woman – enough to cause Margaret very deep distress. One of my other friends at Shrublands was constantly neglected by her husband ('Victor', was it?), endlessly off on his fishing trips or his shooting trips. She was lonely and bewailing the fact of having no grandchildren, living in an awful little market town, just gardening to do and only recently cured of serious (and worrying to her family) drinking bouts.

I succumbed to my depression one day, I'm afraid, and drank brandy surreptitiously, secretly, and then called for more. On my last night with them, I drank Champagne and the next morning had a mild case of the squitters and had to change the sheets.

It's borne in on me that I'm staying with people who, however lonely they may be inside, have lives of some sort . . . I can't even remember or be proud of the undoubted successes I've had, and am genuinely amazed when I'm recognised.

## August 14, 1980
I was driven over to Hazel's home with a few little presents for the children, and crashed into an even worse depression, unable even to get up and dress, the children waking early and screaming or being screamed at. I had to go to the local doctor for tranquillisers. I find things comfortless and contrasted it with Margaret's – George, a born liver, happy with his beautiful home, interested in life, the squash club . . . he enjoyed his lunch, his dinner, he swam, he cleaned the pool, had his sherries, drove off to have lunch with his mother. Thirty years or more they've lived there. Margaret runs the house magnificently and loves her babies. My sister, by contrast, has a rough time. She works in surroundings that are uncomfortable by contrast, cooking and cleaning and gardening and – no wonder – sometimes losing her temper. Despite the anti-depressants I got from the local GP, I found no pleasure in the children. I walked into the nearby town and listlessly bought a woollen skirt and top that I've been wearing ever since. I keep on calling Lindsay and Rex and Darren and succumbing more and more to endless 'telephonitis'.

**August 17, 1980**

Rex just called from America, in control of himself, looking forward to watching *Face the Nation* on television, shaved and bathed, active and interested in things. It's very sweet of him to call me. But no one gets through any more. I'm submerged by it all, not wanting to do anything, see anybody . . . convinced it's just over for me. Simply find the way out. No tears today. My great faults have won over the nice little virtues. I just seek obliteration.

**August 18, 1980**

Blissfully and relievedly back, temporarily, at Lindsay's. I blew my top at my sister's and screamed my frustrations at her and wouldn't accept her attempt to make things up. It was providential that Lindsay called. He's listened to my pleas and found me another hospital to go to.

---

SO RACHEL ENTERED yet another hospital – her third in a month. The Priory had an ancient and disturbing history. Situated in a pleasantly leafy area south of London, it had been a Victorian lunatic asylum, though not all the inmates were certifiably insane and some were simply incarcerated there by unfeeling guardians or by their own mercenary families. (As Elsa Lanchester's autobiography reveals, her own mother was a victim of a family 'vendetta' and her involuntary imprisonment, for it was nothing less, in The Priory led to a famous law suit.) In Rachel's day, it was a private psychiatric hospital, modernised inside and well run.

Rachel, however, appears to have maintained her usual 'come and go as I please' habits. Friends came and went and sometimes there were outings – though one had unhappy consequences.

JILL BENNETT: 'While Rachel was staying at The Priory I took her to see *Juno and the Paycock* which was being done at the Aldwych Theatre in London. She was very quiet, very subdued, not at all herself. Lindsay was with us and we all went along to Joe Allen's after the show. But Rachel got even more depressed and refused anything to eat or even drink. She hired a minicab to take her back to The Priory and we all felt very sad to see her go – but we simply couldn't rouse her from whatever she was thinking.'

It is only speculation, but perhaps she was thinking of the early and intoxicating triumph she had enjoyed, some thirty years before, playing Juno in that very play in her days as a student at the University of Wales. Sometimes, one feels, memory should close the door, not hold it open to let us spy the bursting promise of the past.

# August 23, 1980

The Priory Hospital . . . I've been here now since August 20. I came up to London by train and taxi and must have stayed at his flat that night. I don't remember too clearly. Was it the next day I went to see John Calderon, asked for sherry, had two, went to the Cadogan Club, had another – went back for my clothes at Lindsay's and swigged away at the scotch? I think so. Then I picked up Neil, drove to The Priory, got into bed, was aggressive to the doctor, and, worse, with Lindsay, who'd come all the way down to see me. He was angered and marched out and away to the States. So I must be quite different from what I imagine myself to be like in drink. The minute I was told it would take about a month to get over alcoholism, I rushed off to the pub. I didn't think I could go out to dinner, but after a sleep I made it and enjoyed it – but with complete strangers, and lying about 'bereavement' to get some sympathy.

It's now Saturday. The week-end's upon me, the doctor's away and I'm alone with unhappy thoughts. Today I spoke to a sympathetic Jill, Laurie and Mary and, just now, Hazel. Lindsay has tried so hard to put some guts into me but even he, after the hysteria at Shrublands and the hostility there, is giving up on me. I'm just losing his faith. Maybe it was a wrong faith, anyway.

This August Bank Holiday week-end, normal people are living life. Neil away for the week-end with friends. Hazel and her husband watching television. Rex no doubt out to dinner with Mercia. Milton enjoying life in New York with or without Arnold Weissberger. Mary and Laurie enjoying Horsham, able to garden, or cook, or read, or entertain friends. Brenda looking after Bonare. Donald in his pub. And I'm where I should be, in bed alone in a clinic, a psychiatric clinic, having experienced the worst year of my life so far, and writing to Exit for a way out.

**August 24, 1980**
This really is the pits. I am basically kinder, nicer and more intelligent and talented than these empty, breezy cold nurses. I feel I'm left here to rot – talking to strangers about this utter crack-up of my personality. What do I *really* think? What do I *really* want? To be an acclaimed actress, deservedly so; to enjoy it for its own sake, as I once did. To buy pretty clothes, and wake up each day wanting to live it. To be held, caressed, and made love to. Not endlessly to wake up alone. I tried so hard to make Darren into someone I could wake up to. It couldn't and didn't work, either in New York (worse) or Los Angeles (better for him, madness for me).

Two days of staring into space. Jill Bennett called. She is working at the BBC. Jill takes an interest in her appearance, is game for anything, keeps her dignity, lives her life in her pretty little house with her dogs, her cats, her car, her horse. Good for Jill! It's not easy for her, or, indeed, for anyone. She has tons more pride and backbone than me. I cringe to one and all. What on earth has happened? Could I have controlled it and thus not ended up like this – lying to the other patients about bereavement? Yet, in a sense, not lying. I *have* died. My self-image shattered, right now I think, irretrievably.

I've exposed myself and my miseries to Bobby earlier last year, and was given sanctuary because I couldn't any more live alone in Central Park West. New York, a city I loved, I began to hate. My apartment that I was proud of, I could not live in . . . I hated the West Side, wanted the East Side and a maid, and yet, when I go to parties, I gain no happiness. I'm really left alone now. My 'friends' that I don't cultivate, don't bother. In Los Angeles, I really went mad. I had good sessions with Richard Rosenthal, only to go to the Beverly Wilshire and be so agitated in the chair in the salon that I couldn't keep still enough for my hair to be dried.

Just finished reading Lindsay's concerned and rather admonitory letter. I remain as lost as ever, but pleasantly sedated tonight, looking forward to enjoying *The Ladykillers* [the Ealing comedy starring Alec Guinness] on television.

---

LINDSAY ANDERSON: 'I wrote many a letter to Rachel trying to instil a sense of self-confidence into her. To accept being yourself, to feel whole inside one's *own* personality: if you don't have that in the acting profession, you are lost. But Rachel could never bring herself to be simply herself. No matter how much you said to her, "Rachel, you are marvellous," she'd be frustrated because she wasn't the Hedy Lamarr who'd struck the little Welsh girl as being what stardom was all about. She'd put on those self-consciously "glamorous" clothes, the suede tights, the leopard-skin coats, and I'd say, "Rachel . . . Rachel . . . the little black dress." She could never bring herself to wear that, except in moments of penitence.'

Again Rachel changed hospitals without changing anything else that was material to her illness. She made arrangements to enter Galsworthy House, a private nursing home, specialising in treating alcoholics, at Kingston upon Thames, in Surrey. But before committing herself to treatment there, she had what was to be her last meeting with her immediate family – a trip to see Jackie, her niece, who was holidaying at Ibiza with her husband Marco. Hazel was to join the party in a few days' time.

Before leaving London, Rachel had a typical farewell lunch with Jill Bennett – almost the last time that the two friends met.

JILL BENNETT: 'We lunched at San Lorenzo, where we'd all been to wonderful parties in the years gone by, and I remember Rachel getting up half-way through lunch to ring up her agents and order them to have a hire car come and collect her and take her to London Airport. That was Rachel's *palanca* showing! I'd never have had the nerve to ring *my* agent and demand a hire car. Of course, as was bound to happen, we ate so much and drank so much more and made ourselves so late that the car was kept waiting and waiting expensively as it toured the no-parking streets in the vicinity while Rachel and I finished – in the end she didn't get to the airport in time to catch her plane after all!'

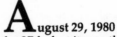

August 29, 1980

I stuck it out at The Priory until the 27th, but it was the worst yet, staring at four walls, sneaking out to get a drink, my memory getting worse. I felt it was doing me no good. I couldn't take it any longer there, so arranged to see Galsworthy House with Peter Coyle – a good recruiting general manager. I thought that perhaps the old, gentle Jacqueline would help, so I sent a wire to Ibiza, where she is now, to tell her of my intending arrival. Then I phoned

Jill, asking if I could spend the night with her in London. She said she'd leave the keys with the stationer next door. I had my hair washed at The Priory, collected some clothes from Lindsay's – part of my clothes are there, part in New York, part with Darren's mother – drove up to town, got in, rushed for Jill's white wine, wanted to post a letter and, while out, double-locked the door, locking us all out. I opened it with a nail file, or some such thing, from the stationer's shop and we all went in again and celebrated with Champagne.

Neil came by and I took him to an expensive dinner at the Meridiana, carefully confining myself to half a carafe of red wine. Came back, went to bed.

### August 30, 1980

Today, I needed some more clothes from Lindsay's. I'd invited Jill for lunch at San Lorenzo's. Driving back I went in error to her house, not the restaurant, so was half an hour late for lunch. We drank some Champagne and at least four Sambuccas. I ordered a car, but I was too late to catch the plane and despite pleading they were adamant. So I gave the 'Mrs Rex Harrison' name at the VIP desk and went to the Iberian lounge and waited two hours for the next plane, fortifying myself with large brandies and sodas.

I arrived late. Marco, Jackie's husband, had had an unnecessary journey to the airport, despite the telex I'd got them to send. I took a taxi to Cale Terida, was found by Marco and went on to their 'villa' where I proceeded to drink *vin rosé* with Jackie.

### September 3, 1980

We drank a lot in Ibiza itself. It was fantasy time again. I talked with Jackie happily. Today was a day like the old days, spent on Marco's boat, nowadays not *risqué* to go bare-breasted, with cold wine (and the rush of joy that I meet it with) and good food. A bad swim, but it felt good – slept well through the wine, with only the occasional cold clutch of madness. At seven o'clock, Jackie awoke, showered and prepared for work – happy and whole, and why not? She told me how shattered she'd been when the avalanche in Cervinia destroyed her apartment and killed four people.

There was a marvellous breeze, a pretty waitress at the restaurant, music and of course drink. Drink which drowned the terror I'm feeling at the chaos my life is in. The apprehension I have about the expensive nursing homes for the really sick – for that's what I'll come to. Next step after Ibiza: Peter Coyle and stopping the denial of my grave alcoholism. The great fear is that it isn't that: that it's insanity without an outlet. I long for a man to turn to in bed, as I saw Marco turn to Jackie. Yes, I want to be told and reassured that my skin is soft, my hands and feet pretty – I also want to be told what to do and how to do it.

How serious Jackie is in her restaurant and her work. My talent was huge, electrifying. I was serious about it: but disillusionment had made me lose my love for it. I used to long for this time of night. To get ready, put on the make-up in my unorthodox way and go out and rivet the audience, even if I was bad – which, looking back, I'm sure I often was. But the force of personality and the pretence and the 'attack' were riveting. When I think of 'waste' and dissipation of talent, I must always remember David Alan Grier doing, electrifyingly, that one-man play about the Negro's position – for three nights only at Yale. And yes, just because I've lost my love, my zest for life, my juices, please let me stop believing that everyone else has – they haven't. Otherwise, people would be dropping like flies, unable to take it as I can't take it.

There's too much fright, too much guilt, too much aloneness, too much blackness of outlook, too much feeling of being 'different' and too much bad luck – or perhaps just a case of too many bad choices. There's been no one but strangers in the New York apartment since Val left me, but better strangers than a Miss Havisham existence. And I can't make Los Angeles work. I told Darren in a way, but 'Accept yourself', I'm told, face the truth and act accordingly – except that acting accordingly really does seem Exit. If acting like I dreamed about last night hadn't died on me, I might not have died on myself. I always had to have it. It was *my* drug really, but more like a massive Vitamin B dose – my *good* drug.

I was born to act.

### September (?), 1980

Hazel arrived in Ibiza with the children. I took an Antabuse and stopped drinking. I was sharing a room with Hazel and an early-waking baby. I longed for love, saw it all around me, but not in my direction. We continued to go out on the boat, but this time it was different. I listened to the 'monitor', went bare-breasted with the young girls, but got no pleasure, only increasing distress. I stayed over the week-end, there were no flights – then took a first-class flight. Hazel took me to the airport. I was forlorn and lonely. I wondered if Hazel wasn't a little lonely too, now that Jackie is a mother of three, absorbed, naturally, in her own children, her work, her friends.

I arrived at London Airport and immediately went into panic. I took a cab to Galsworthy House and entered in tears and was comforted by an Englishman with a title. Faint hope stirred. Prince Charming?

---

ON RETURNING FROM IBIZA in September, Rachel celebrated a bleak fifty-third birthday at the country home, near Horsham, of her agent Lawrence Evans and his wife Mary. The Evanses were understandably nervous about their guest's propensities. To relieve the burden and provide, they hoped, kindred company for Rachel, they'd invited down the Irish-born novelist and screenwriter Edna O'Brien.

EDNA O'BRIEN: 'Rachel looked awful. Puffy – which may have been due to the medication she was getting – and shapeless in a knitted suit. She apologised for looking awful. "No, you don't," I said, hoping maybe to cheer her up. "Listen," she rapped back, "I'm Welsh, so don't try and lie to me." "We all of us look terrible sometimes," was all I could, weakly, think of replying.

'I felt a terrible anger in her. I felt myself trying to placate her. We'd a doleful walk in the garden. I could almost feel her despair gathering round her, it was so dense and overwhelming. To tell the shameful truth, I felt I wanted to escape her. She needed help desperately but she didn't look to me as if any she'd got so far was succeeding. I'm not all that sturdy myself – and the mad pull you in. Over dinner the talk was all of Rex. She wasn't allowed even one drink, so temperance had to be the rule at Laurie's table, which didn't please *me* one bit, I can tell you. After dinner, she asked Mary to go and get the photographs that had been taken years before of her and Rex at Portofino. That was our poor Rachel's birthday treat . . .

'It wasn't the first time I'd seen her. We'd met when she was making *Yanks*. Richard Gere was with us and her mood was far, far brighter. She said she wanted to take an option on a short story I'd written, to see if she could get a producer interested in it for a film. The story was called "Mrs Reinhardt" and it was all about this middle-aged woman shrugging off her last husband and going away on a journey and meeting a much younger man who's a gigolo. In the end, her husband comes back to her.'

'Mrs Reinhardt', included in Edna O'Brien's collection published in America in 1979 under the title *A Rose in the Heart*, contains some premonitory shudders of Rachel's emotional desolation which leave one wondering how consciously she allowed what remained of her life to be infected by the novelist's art. Edna O'Brien had written: 'Mrs Reinhardt had experienced one of those spells that unsettle one forever. The world became black. A blackness permeated her heart. It was like rats scraping at her brain. It was pitiless . . . the few faces of the strange people around her assumed the masks of animals. The world she stood up in, and was about to fall down in, was green and pretty but in a second it would be replaced by a bottomless pit into which Mrs Reinhardt was about to fall for eternity.'

There is also one completely inexplicable coincidence in a story written well before the authoress met Rachel Roberts. Mrs Reinhardt has been called from her restaurant table to take an unexpected phone call – she wonders if it is her husband, 'contrite or drunk'. The story continues:

'She said her "Hello" calmly but pertly. She repeated it. It was a strange voice altogether, a man asking for Rachel. She said who is Rachel.'

The question gets no answer: it is simply a moment of fateful absurdity, such as Antonioni might have been fond of putting into a film during his somnambulistic period of catatonic heroines. Now 'Rachel' appeared discomfortingly present.

EDNA O'BRIEN: 'She was desperately worried about her career, she said; though, if I'd been her, I'd have been more worried about my state of health. She kept talking of Glenda Jackson, asking poor Laurie why Glenda was the one, and not herself, who was flying off to make a film in America. At one point she took up the knife that had carved what we'd had to eat and said quietly, "I think I'll just take this to my room."

'About eleven o'clock, she went to bed. After a bit we couldn't hear any noise coming from her room. So Laurie and Mary and myself crept upstairs, full of anxiety, not knowing what terrible scene we might see when we opened the door. Well, we peeped in, and there she was, in bed, in her Brussels lace nightie, grinning at the three of us.

'No sign of the carving knife, thank God!'

From her bedside in one of the various hospitals and clinics she passed through during her stay in England, Rachel would compulsively keep in touch with Darren, sometimes mistaking the time difference and submitting him to alarming calls in the hours of the morning when resistance is lowest and apprehension greatest. The sheer distance that separated them added to Darren's sense of helplessness. Sometimes he was unsettled by the totally different approach adopted by the English nursing profession to a case like Rachel's – Darren was more familiar with the prompt responses of the paramedics and expensive physicians of Beverly Hills.

DARREN RAMIREZ: 'One time she called and said she was collecting Nembutals in small doses from various doctors who'd seen her. She was going to commit suicide – that very evening, she said. I called the clinic right back and talked to the head nurse. "I've just had a call from Miss Roberts – she's threatening to take her life." – "Oh, I don't think she'd do that," said this terribly detached English voice. "She says she *is* – tonight! She's got Nembutals hidden away." – "Well, we're not authorised to go through patients' private belongings, you know."' Those familiar with English hospital practice will recognise the prudent approach adopted towards an 'outsider': but, of course, distance lent exaggeration to Darren's needless but understandable alarm. Rachel was kept under responsible supervision.

# October 6, 1980

I've written very little lately. The despair remains. 'Paralysis' is nearer the mark. I went to dinner with Ned Sherrin and Caryl Brahms [Ned Sherrin's partner in writing stage shows and revues: Sherrin had rented Rachel's Pimlico house] and 42  Cambridge Street was alive and quite pretty. I didn't want to leave it. Rex is calling, hopefully, tonight from San Francisco suggesting a meeting. I can't think very clearly and am putting off and off the dreaded return to Los Angeles, renting a car, waking up unable to get up and dreading Darren's leaving the house as much as his return. Dreading seeing, or not seeing, Margot, Sybil, Marti and Gavin – and then in November having Rex with Mercia just down the road when *My Fair Lady* opens. Not really interested in *Hamlet*, in which Lindsay wants me to play Gertrude – dreading it really. What on earth *is* the matter? Have I really irredeemably lost interest in life and will nothing and no one revive it? I cannot seem to do it on my own. Rex does seem the only hope. Can Rex resuscitate me?

I've just had a long conversation with Dr Wawman [physician at Galsworthy House] who told me I had a powerful personality – more powerful than I realised. That I was a famous person who could unnerve the staff of this clinic where I'm staying 'in case something happens'. (The bleak reality seems to be, *is*, in fact, that nothing is just going to happen.) If indeed I have this powerful personality, why am I such a shrinking fearful depressed person inside?

## October 9, 1980

Should I throw these Nembutals away and try to live? Rex didn't call, which threw me into another emotional burst . . . and I wept and wept, listened to by the two avid young girls who are patients here, one a hard little Mod, the other a complainer. I was putting off leaving for Los Angeles, based on the prospect of our meeting in San Francisco. When Jeffrey Lane called and, later, Arnold Weissberger, I plunged back into comparisons between other people's lives and my own. Arnold recalled his happy world in New York, his daily routine, pleasing to him, the parties organised by Milton, his photography, Milton's famous talent for 'introductions' at their parties, lunch at the Four Seasons, a party or a play every night. I envy them . . . I, too, want to be able to get up and bathe and walk to work, to work, to be with people, to lunch and drink and return to the office and then to the East Side for more conviviality. No time for morbid thoughts. Jeffrey, too, plunged me back into despair. Tiny Jeffrey living with his brother and his mother, enjoying his life and his work, looking forward to going to Los Angeles to stay with Ruth, to see Warren Cowan [with partner Henry Rogers, half of Rogers and Cowan, top PR agency], to enjoy Ma Maison. Then I thought of Joan Collins who, busy though she is, writes her sex manual and receives a lot of money for it, writes another book on beauty, will soon open in a West End play – never having known the depths I have, or been in a clinic for alcoholism . . . Instead of thinking on the positive side, I plunged into hell again.

## October 10, 1980
My last day here. 'Rock Bottom' pamphlet:

'Alcoholics are perceived by clinicians as heavily maintaining defences of denial and self-deception. *By definition, a defence is a systematic distortion of reality which does not succeed in altering the actual external circumstances.*

'Denial as a defence may be used to diminish the severity of the effects of drinking upon an individual's personal, social, physical, vocational or familial structure. In fact, the alcoholic may not always be lying in the sense of *deliberately* and *consciously* distorting the truth . . . These defences may have been in the process of erosion for some time. What seems to be needed is a dramatic moment or event to pierce the defensive armour, the un-equivocal perception or 'rock bottom', so to speak. The commitment to change begins with a perceptual shift and this perceptual change focuses on the evaluation of the self and, more important, the confrontation *with responsibility for one's own life and one's own actions.*

'This confrontation . . . *forces a choice. Faced with this confrontation, some individuals choose to commit suicide. Others, the 'survivors', begin the slow, laborious road to recovery.*

'We see people who have apparently been suddenly and dramatically stripped of their defence structure. However, retrospection may well have telescoped the time element, so that, in the recounting, the suddenness and dramatic qualities have been highlighted. Their habitual defensive styles, which seem to have served them well for years in developing coping strategies to maintain their 'alcoholic stance', are no longer valid.

'With the defences apparently demolished and the ego apparently help-less, the alcoholic looks for magical sources of external solutions. In some patients we interviewed, their basic adaptation processes, their habitual defensive styles, had not really changed – they were re-directed towards a new goal: sobriety or, in some cases, controlled drinking. One word which came up over and over again was 'bloody-mindedness'. . . The very same 'bloody-mindedness' that kept them drinking while denying the havoc created for themselves and their families is now channelled into the service of keeping them dry. What appears to be the same reported narcissism, the same reported self-absorption which was mobilised to obtain drink, is now used for the preservation of the sober self.'

I have neither a husband like Rex, nor acting, to be my support system. Life must be something else, not just taking clothes to the cleaners or giving 'dinner parties' to suspicious friends. Must change. Tried. Failed. So try again. Have to contribute and *NOT DRINK*.

**October 11, 1980**
Dr Wawman and I discussed the deep distress I'm suffering. I told him what *Rebel Without a Cause* [Rachel may refer to the 1955 film about disordered adolescence or to Robert M. Lindner's 1944 case history of hypno-analysis with the same title but unconnected with the movie] had triggered off – all those wretched childhood feelings. 'Take her away, I don't want to see her.' 'Your father and I never quarrel over anything but you.' 'What you do under your own roof is your business. But here . . . your father has had to go to bed with the shock of what he found in your purse.' I was nineteen and hadn't been screwed. Whether or not this has a bearing on the agony I'm in, I really don't know. I'm beginning to doubt it, too.

---

FIVE WEEKS WERE SPENT in Galsworthy House, drying out and receiving counselling on her drinking problem, and then Rachel returned to what was virtually her only 'refuge', Lindsay Anderson's country cottage. Anderson, continuously anxious about her, resolved that work was still the best remedy and asked her to play Gertrude in the *Hamlet* he was preparing to direct. She was to twist and turn this proposition in her mind, essentially putting off her acceptance or rejection of it, until time decided the matter for her. 'Rachel doesn't want to play Gertrude, she wants to play Hamlet,' one of her friends said tartly at the time. To Jill Bennett, she confided her fears that at fifty-three she was too old for the role. Jill Bennett replied: 'I said to her, "That's a very bourgeois attitude, Rachel – after all, what are numbers?"' To Jeffrey Lane, she said she feared forgetting her lines. He replied: 'I've heard that before, Rachel: *you* are a professional, *you* won't forget – Lindsay won't let you. Do it!'

LINDSAY ANDERSON: 'I offered her the role of Gertrude in *Hamlet* because I thought her problem was creative frustration. She was first and foremost an actress – at her best when working – and she knew it. I'd suggest roles to her when I sensed she 'needed' them. Acting, I'm convinced, would have been her only salvation. Who knows the real reason she hovered and havered over *Hamlet*, or whether there was any *one* reason? In retrospect, I became convinced it was basically because the project simply wasn't glamorous enough. We were to do a provincial tour; then, if things worked out, go into a London theatre – but there was no guarantee of this.
    'She had lunch with myself and Frank Grimes, who was to be Hamlet. I said, "Come on, Rachel . . . commit." She read the part through with Grimes, to lay the ghosts troubling her. She was so good that they

continued through the play – she had an uproarious time playing the Gravedigger. For once, we all relaxed and had a good laugh. I was more than ever convinced that with her emotional strength, her neurotic compulsion and even the fact that she was the right age, she'd be terrific as Gertrude. But when she eventually went back to the States, she was still considering it and I'd a sense that, once on her own again, the idea would count for very little with her: it was only a slender life-line. When Rachel died, I'm afraid the project died with her.'

Within a few days of leaving Galsworthy House, it was evident to her that nothing had changed about her need to drink. As she resumed, another sort of need grew apace in her mind, as if it was indeed the last hope – the need for Rex, whose touring production of *My Fair Lady* was nearing the West Coast. She planned to return to Los Angeles – dreading it – around October 20, 1980, and Jeffrey Lane rearranged his plans so as to accompany her.

JEFFREY LANE: 'A day or two before we were due to catch the plane to LA, we met at the Connaught, the place she adored. I was totally shocked at her appearance. Her eyes were dead flat, no sparkle in them, no shine at all. That may, of course, have been the drugs she was on, but, as if she suspected it revealed more than medication, she asked me, "What do you see in my eyes?" It was hard to tell her, "Nothing, Rachel." We went to a publisher to see about a book of short stories she intended writing – she was scared she might be rejected, but the response was very encouraging and we had a few drinks on it at the Connaught. Before we left for America, she used the phone in my apartment to call Rex and tell him her news.

' "Rachel," I said, when she was through, "what do you really want from Rex?" "I would like to get back with him again," she said. I wasn't sure if she meant "professionally" or not, but I said, "Rachel, you simply can't live your life the way you're doing. You must make up your mind and act on it. If you want to do something, go and do it. Pull yourself together, make yourself attractive, go and see Rex. Go and see him when he gets to San Francisco or Los Angeles." '


# October 13, 1980

It's Monday, I think, in Lindsay's pretty cottage in Rustington. I feel like I did in New Haven – alone, very, very much alone. But I've been brought up sharp to face my present reality.

What is it that overcomes me and causes such mad confusion in my brain? My brain that is sending such destructive messages down into my very being. I've told total strangers that I want, and have the means, to commit suicide.

I remember the Monday morning at Galsworthy House, coming down to the meeting in my dressing-gown, hostile, hating every minute of it. After endless attempts, I went up to Town to see Max Glatt. He's an authority on alcoholism. Immediately I left him, I took a cab from Harley Street to the Connaught and drank in quick succession five gin Martinis and remembered the past . . . I wrote to Rex. I went up to London again to have my hair done, but, before, joined my titled friend from Galsworthy House and his Mother at the Turf Club. Drank gin-and-tonics. I decided we'd go to the Connaught for dinner after more gin-and-tonics. I ordered lobster and wine – frantically pushing my way into the orderly Connaught dining room. Once more that unreal, bright, amusing drunk who made my guests laugh by not under-standing the French menu and ordering 'virgin' lobster.

I stuck the clinic out and beyond it. There was nowhere else to go. I irritated the nurses – was told I wasn't the only pebble on the beach. My mind is still clouded from all the drinking I've been doing. I'm *still* refusing to believe that alcohol has played such a serious part in causing further damage to an already damaged personality.

Lindsay gave me refuge at Rustington and we're about to leave for London. At least I left the clinic and took the car to Victoria and the train to Littlehampton sober . . . Now with the usual dread and panic, I face Los Angeles. The only release seems to be in writing all this sickness down. I hear Lindsay singing, having done a morning's work with David, and I remember when I, too, sang. 'Love yourself, Rachel,' said Peter Coyle. 'Come to terms with the little girl in you and the adult woman,' says Dr Wawman.

### October 16, 1980

The pain was so intense yesterday that despite Antabuse, I took a Scotch and ginger ale, then another. Dragged Jeffrey Lane to the Connaught to have Champagne, then went to the club and had some wine. The beauty of the birds lifted my spirits somewhat. Next it was to Jeffrey's flat to have some sherry. I met his mother, who is very ill, and his brother. Jeffrey so full of life, loving his job, loving life: he doesn't sit and continuously think of himself as I do. If he did, he, too, would go mad – thinking of being so small and bald. No, on the contrary, he's active, is proud of his flat – active and *living*. I met Leonard [fashionable hair stylist] and his new bride, happy in her Porsche. How do they do it, these other human beings?

I talked endlessly of Rex – and he called. He wants to see me. What is it that I dread? The fear that this day-dream of mine would explode, along with the others? . . . I seem to want to be on a permanent 'high' – alcohol-induced, of course. Can't seem to plod along like the rest of the human race. Reading an article about Rex, I bought every bit of the glamour . . . I remain, I believe, in competition with him, amazed that at seventy-two he can so successfully re-work *My Fair Lady* and do it, eight times a week. Albeit frightened of the orchestra, he *does* it! I just want to go to bed all the time or drink myself into oblivion. After five dismal weeks in Galsworthy House, listening to what alcohol does to one, I lasted four days before slipping and swallowed a barbiturate to go to sleep.

Jeffrey says he likes the little house in Los Angeles. He doesn't bewail the non-existence of a pool – doesn't like water! Lindsay's activity only fosters the gloom. I wouldn't want to take the London subway to the National Theatre and talk to Gillian Lynne about casting the play. I don't want to be Gertrude in his *Hamlet*, drearily travelling from one dreary town to another with Frank Grimes playing the lead. The other offer I've had recently, playing Marco Polo's aunt in a TV series!

Jeffrey Lane rings. I put off booking the flight to Los Angeles when Laurence Evans rang for Lindsay, but have just remedied that. I must go. As

Lindsay says, It's No-Man's-Land here. I can't expect of Darren what, with the best intentions in the world, he can't give.

I don't want to swallow these pills and die. I don't want to be a suicide. All and everyone would not be surprised one bit. The alternative is to try and live again – and not through, of all people, Darren . . . I like Jeffrey Lane's attitude – go out and get it for yourself. There is no god, as I understand him. When we die, we die. Supposing I could get Rex back, then what? Would I have the courage to take the back seat?

Back in a day or two to the land of *Little Miss McGuire*, the story I wrote – *Little Miss McGuire*, or *Part of Things*:

It was a perfect day, blue and antiseptic, but the sun shone, the cars were neatly parked across the street from the public library, the fountain splashed in an ordinary fashion into the aquamarine-coloured water. Occasionally a police siren howled, alerting little Miss McGuire to the incontestable fact that there was a living, screaming, laughing, suffering humanity lurking around the well-manicured suburb. Miss McGuire spent a great deal of her time at the public library. Today, she'd selected *Look* magazine for her morning's reading. Not much that was in it meant very much to her, but the photographs were glossy, and she felt less alone and more 'part of things', her favourite phrase, when she was there.

Miss McGuire had been christened Delia. It seemed to her that the fairies at her christening party must have grimly decided to counteract the hope and glamour of that name 'Delia' by wishing upon her a life of amazing and unrelieved gloom. Miss McGuire was not without humour.

By no means plain, neat and dressed trimly within the limits of her means, she'd always tried to make the best of herself, and her overriding ambition was just to be 'part of things'. She often thought that 'Delia' had a lot to do with the curious way she had never been a 'part'. If she'd been Margaret or Janet, or her favourite of all, Elizabeth, might it all have been different? On reflection, she thought, no, better not Elizabeth – after all, not long after she'd arrived into this curious world, England's Elizabeth II and the movie star Elizabeth Taylor had been spawned. She couldn't of course compete with these fortunates. What must it be like? she thought, giving herself up to her favourite day-dream – other people's lives, people who were 'part of things', *Look* magazine . . . Miss McGuire suddenly felt depressed.

Life *was* unfair, she thought . . . It was all very well that she managed to keep her three-roomed apartment with the kitchenette off. That was thirty-dollars a month extra, but seemed less because she rarely used it, thus saving on the electricity. It did look nice and she kept it very clean. She'd often thought of going to the pound to rescue a kitten which could grow into a nice, clean cat and sleep in the kitchenette – but Mrs Myers, the representative of the landlord whom she'd never met, was adamant – 'NO PETS'. Miss McGuire thought in many ways that was just as well. She didn't eat much, was out at the public library such a lot, and it would be awful if her cat had to be infected with that not being 'part of things' feeling.

Miss McGuire pulled herself together. There were many people worse off than she was. She had her little red Datsun. Before she'd decided to raid her savings account and buy it – it was not new, but in excellent condition and she never drove it hard or far – she'd felt very shut in. This metropolis was so vast and distances so great that even if you didn't want to go very far, the fact you couldn't somehow made it larger. The little red Datsun had opened up the world of the public library to her. It had been too far to walk for her and the bus stopped nowhere near it, and she did so enjoy going there. The only thing was that, of course, nobody talked: quite naturally. It was a place for study, after all. You could smile, of course, Miss McGuire did a lot of that, but for some reason never really talked very much, didn't seem to know the places to go where you could.

Once a month, she went to the down-town theatre, but there again you had to be quiet because it was the actors up on stage who were doing the talking, very well, too, some of them, and she enjoyed it. But there was in her that nagging belief that if only she knew where to go to talk, she'd feel 'part of things'. Even in the interval, in the ladies' rest-room, you couldn't talk. There was no time, because there was always a long queue and the interval only fifteen minutes – at the matinées that is. Miss McGuire wasn't fond of night driving, though she'd been to the corner once.

She had a perfectly nice television set, small but adequate, but there again you just had to sit and listen while other people, on all the channels, talked, very interestingly some of them. Miss McGuire had often wondered if her not being 'part of things' was because all her words were kept so firmly and silently in her head. Of course she knew her talking wouldn't be interesting, like the TV people and the actors in the down-town theatre.

Miss McGuire had often wondered whether a little drink in one of the brighter bars she passed while driving to the public library might raise her spirits when she was in one of those moods of hers; but apart from the expense, she'd not been brought up that way, and while she'd quite liked the taste of that sherry at Mrs Myer's niece's wedding reception in Mrs Myer's nice big apartment, drink never appealed to her.

It was beginning to get dark and Miss McGuire thought she ought to be getting ready to go, otherwise she'd be 'night' driving, which made her a little uneasy. But somehow she didn't want to move. Suddenly the unfairness of it all, even including her bright, clean and neat kitchenette, made her feel quite defiant. The library didn't close till nine on Fridays and was closed this Sunday because of Easter. Dammit, thought Delia, I'll stay. You shouldn't, said Miss McGuire, but did.

With a sense of adventure, she returned *Look* neatly to its appointed place on the magazine rack. A young high-school student, a pretty blonde who had been sitting opposite Miss McGuire all afternoon, had left an interesting looking book called *The Last of Ugi* on the table. Miss McGuire picked it up. It was all about the tribal life and customs of a still existing primitive tribe. Every photograph seemed to spell that magic word 'Participation'. The elders were shown in council; the braves, ritualistically adorned, were caught perfectly performing some ritual tribal dance. The girls and women, with their babies and their cooking pots, seemed to fare less interestingly than the men, but they, too, seemed to be so much that longed-for part of a whole.

So immersed was Miss McGuire that she didn't notice for quite a while the unshaven, red-eyed, mad-looking man staring – whether or not directly or into space, she wasn't sure, but it unnerved her. It was also getting very dark. The library lights were on, but at her seat by the window, Miss McGuire could see that outside it looked very dark indeed. She must have been reading about that strange race of people and staring at the wondrous photographs for far longer than she thought – but, oh, it had been worth it, she thought.

Silently, she gathered her bag, her gloves, her spectacle case together, checked that she had her car-keys, tried to avoid glancing up at the strange man. This was the trouble with staying out so late, she thought: lonely, lost people probably came into the library for its warmth and serenity.

It was 8.30 pm. Miss McGuire let herself into the little red Datsun. Carefully, a little worried that she would have to 'night' drive for thirty minutes. But she felt it was an adventure: and had she not stayed, she might never have read about those strange men and women who probably never had felt the feelings of loneliness she had sensed in the alarming-looking man who'd sat opposite her. She really didn't know if he'd been glaring at her directly, or just straight ahead of him.

Far too titillated was she by her sense of daring to notice the lurching delivery van that screeched towards her tremulous little Datsun, far too quick was the sudden collision for her to feel the slightest sensation of pain as Miss McGuire was catapulted rapidly out of all her fond imaginings and became a 'part of things' at last.

### October 20, 1980

Milton tells me that Sybil Christopher is now a literary agent at ICM. So apart from Amy, her days must be filled, while I'm wandering aimlessly around, talking about Rex . . . When I do get out, my one thought is to go and have a drink. With age coming up, of course, I can't 'dance' around any more. I am literally too old. The game is up.

I don't know how to fill the endless hours. It is working as miserably at Lindsay's as it did with everyone else. Just how sick I've become, I sensed yesterday in South Moulton Street, making myself go to Calvin Klein. Life flows on. Young voices with their own lives to lead fill the streets. Everyone I know has his or her niche planned out and are living. I'm flapping terrified wings at life. Discontent with everything. Yes, I envy Mary [Evans] till it hurts. She's not writing out her agony. She's having her hair done and has just come over to talk to me. She's off to buy Kleenex, to shop for the week-end. Her son and the 'children' are coming over. Last week-end, Larry [Olivier, a client of ICM] came to spend a day. I was trying to control myself alone in the clinic, forcing myself to watch television, to eat school food, clutching on to Gerald [fellow patient] and his *Telegraph*. On Wednesday night, I've no idea what I was doing. Came up from the country on Tuesday, saw a doctor to get barbiturates, probably stayed in . . . Yes, I did. I had steak with Lindsay, watched a James Cagney movie without enjoying *any* of it. Ashamed to the point of guilt that I don't want to 'act' any more, that I've grown beyond that. Why can't I congratulate myself? . . . Rex has returned to old triumphs and worked at it. It's what he wants. Jeffrey Lane says, 'You did it once, you can do it again . . .'

My speck of flesh feels gargantuan; my sufferings are immense; my problems insurmountable. Perhaps they are. I'll soon find out now. Anyway, it's been lovely having my hair done. I can't read newspapers or watch television or shop for clothes. I face the week-end in Los Angeles with Darren. It will be no worse than here. But this time I must recognise that it isn't his fault and not rail at him or dread him going to work and leaving me alone. I must rent a car and try and get work done in the library.

And Rex . . . ? Why do my legs go to jelly when I think of San Francisco and our planned visit? Is it because he really is the last resort? That if I feel there is no hope for me with him, then my number is really up?

'I am coming more and more to the conclusion that there is very little to be done about her.' Yes, true, Lindsay – but 'There is so much frailty in her nature and her actions.' Not true, Lindsay. Perhaps I have attempted the impossible. I don't have the face for film stardom. I'm not Lucille Ball. I can't stop the clock. You don't usually have love affairs at fifty-three. You marry a man who is difficult to please. You don't have children. You get divorced in a blaze of publicity. You go into shock. You retaliate or escape into affairs and try to keep up the old life-style. You find a friend who is *tender*. You try to build him into what he isn't, thereby losing what he is. Acting never was to you, perhaps, quite what it was to Joan Plowright and Maggie Smith. It was perhaps more of a means to an end. You want the ease and the luxury you once tasted. All that is true. It does not enable me to rise above it, however.

I read in the paper of Maria Callas who was unhappy and, even with fame and fortune, was a dependent woman who needed a man. She found Ari [Onassis]. When it was over, she desperately and unsuccessfully went back to her art. When love and art both failed her, she died.

Of Lady Barnett whom I followed into Shrublands and who later killed herself, the *Mail* wrote: 'I am sorry for the generation of women among whom Lady Barnett finds herself. Often their lives, without a career and with children gone away from home, go racing downhill into sheer grinding boredom.'

No, Lindsay can't understand. I'm reduced to reading other people's correspondence, rushing into other people's offices, staring at other people in bed, trying to stay in other people's homes, asking other people who they've had to stay . . . What must I do? I don't want to play Gertrude. I'm frightened of the lines, wouldn't know what to do in the dressing room between scenes, don't want to watch the director and his actor – the one concentrating his incredible energy and his submerged emotionalism on an actor, and the actor lapping it up and using it for the glory not of Shakespeare or Lindsay: for his own ambitious self, rather. So what is there? I will try to be pleasant and, affecting a virtue even if I have it not, make things a little easier between Darren and me.

---

LINDSAY ANDERSON: 'Looking back, I don't honestly think that Rachel would have been any more "fulfilled" if she had never met Rex or abandoned her stage ambitions. Rachel hadn't the temperament that took to the English theatrical Establishment. She was Welsh and passionate and both impatient with and unversed in the 'politics' you need to play in order to survive and thrive in places like the National Theatre or the Royal Shakespeare Company. It wasn't her style. All her neuroses needed to be silenced before she could find happiness as a "serious actress". She would have always needed a particular kind of guidance and reassurance. Hers was the star's temperament: it is much easier to succeed in America with such equipment. The English Establishment tends to slap you down. I remember Rachel's once going along to audition and my trying to persuade her not to submit herself to the inspection of the National crowd. I told her, "Rachel, you are not one of them and you are not going to be offered the part." But she persisted. She tried to play the star to them and she was humiliated.'

N ow I feel the marvellous chill of October, my favourite season. I leave for California tomorrow, but today am back at the Connaught and with my treasured memories and a glass of Champagne rushing through the Antabuse in my system – but for a moment away from the hurt and the disappointments and the fear and the awful loneliness. I feel bathed with Rex, just for a moment, the familiar stag staring down at me from the chimney-piece, the lovely bar, the glow (flush-faced though I be) of the Champagne I didn't even have to pay for. Oh, it brings it back! My days of euphoria, more precious than any award, any job . . . Could it happen again? I *must* remember this feeling – when my whole face and being changes, and I feel and love October turning into winter. I can see a pretty dress, which I won't buy now – but would have, if Rex was here . . . Of course, the Champagne helps. I'm back momentarily in my 'milieu', meaning a place that gave my temperament happiness, euphoria, call it what you will, Rachel.

Already it's shifted. I don't care. For a moment, the pain went, and it is my pain . . . It is because I am so bereft of all that made me glow and shine. My Rex, glittering, excitable, high-prancing Rex to whom doors opened. Who is infinitely more sybaritic than Rex, who was and is like Champagne? Glorious days I loved. Crazy happy days. In-love days. I never noticed the world . . . Rex doesn't demand much from me really, except warmth and humour and intelligence and putting him first. I do anyway. Always have. I am so glad to be at the Connaught . . . Grow up, Cinderella! Life isn't the Connaught. No, it isn't. Nor is it your life. But it's a hell of a lot nicer than most of what 'life is about'.

Give San Francisco a whirl, Rachel. Otherwise, the outlook is gloomy.

---

LINDSAY ANDERSON: 'Rachel had stayed with me, off and on and between visits to one clinic or another, during this last visit to England. And at times I'd taken a very stiff attitude to her – otherwise, I felt, there would have been nothing of her left. But by the time she was ready to return to Los Angeles, I knew I had failed to stiffen her resolution. There was nothing left that I could do. And I felt she really didn't want me to do anything more – she had embraced her fate. I said good-bye to her that morning, when she left the flat for the airport. She still hadn't committed herself to playing *Hamlet*. I watched her getting into the limousine that her publicist friend, Jeffrey Lane, had arranged to pick her up. And as I watched, I saw Rachel turn into the "starry" personage I had tried to persuade her not to be ... condescending to the driver, being self-consciously "gracious" to him. Then the car pulled away ... and that was the last time I laid eyes on her.'

JEFFREY LANE: 'We left London on a beautiful autumn day. On the flight, there were some bad moments when she became mentally depressed or physically agitated and talked of jumping out of the plane. Before she left London she had learnt from Milton Goldman that her friend Sybil Christopher was now working as a manuscript reader in ICM's Los Angeles office. Sybil's success at regularising her life and achieving a happy marriage with a family was now underlined by this fresh proof of her ability to do something else Rachel could not – go through a well-ordered and remunerative day's work. It depressed her still more, and she asked her agent if a similar position, perhaps in New York, could be found for herself. Milton understandably demurred.

She arrived in Los Angeles on October 21. Her state had not improved since the last time she had gratefully left what was now, to her, 'that dreadful place'. Indeed, as events soon proved, she was considerably worse.

DARREN RAMIREZ: 'On October 21, I was at work at I Magnin when I received a call from the airport. It was Rachel. Could I come and collect her? I told her pretty shortly I was busy – she could have called in advance to alert me that she was coming. But then the old guilt feeling took over and I put on my jacket and went out to the airport. She'd got off the plane an hour before: now she was drunk. She was with me for a week at Hutton Drive, talking all the time now about going up to San Francisco to see Rex when he opened in *My Fair Lady*, or calling Sybil and "having words" with her.'

SYBIL CHRISTOPHER: 'I had spoken to Richard Rosenthal and told him I felt Rachel was going to do away with herself. "Get her to call me," he said. She didn't at first, of course. When she did get round to it, it was no good. Rachel was an actress – whatever her problems – and such people don't tell their doctors or their analysts anything. They "edit" their analysis sessions. They keep appraising the psychiatrist's reaction to their "performance" – the effect it is having on this expensive one-man audience. In this respect, Rachel was no different, though far more to be pitied.'

PAMELA MASON: 'In my opinion, people who feel like killing themselves and go to analysts for help invariably do end up killing themselves. Analysts make you feel you don't deserve to exist. Though Rachel and I talked on her return to Los Angeles, she didn't dare tell me about all the couches she'd lain on and all the sessions she'd paid for – she knew my views. I used to say to her, "Rachel, write an essay about yourself or put it all down on tape. When you spill everything out to analysts, they always end up asking you, "Well, what do *you* think?" So you might as well give yourself the benefit of your own opinion and not be charged for it.

'I knew she was obsessed with going to see Rex. There had been several years when her infatuation with him had grown quite cool. After all, she'd had a young lover of her own, which proved her attractiveness was potent still. And Rex, in her eyes then, was one of yesterday's stars – he'd hit his peak in *My Fair Lady*, now he was entering his seventies. It was Rex's resurrection as a star as he toured in *My Fair Lady* which, I think, brought it all back again. It was the Third Coming of Rex which fascinated and upset Rachel and called her competitive drive into play again. She loved him, certainly: but it was mixed up with her aggression – a bit like Eliza Dolittle's feelings for her mentor in the musical. It was a case of "Just you wait, 'Enery 'Iggins". Or so I interpreted it.'

# October 21, 1980

Back at 2620 Hutton Drive, Los Angeles, and exactly as I expected it to be. Exactly the same pattern, as though the last three and a half months had never existed.

The day I've dreaded has arrived, although the week-end was much the same as before. I lay awake half the night, knowing I've disgraced and debased myself with everyone I know. The pain remains the same. What is it? A sense of utter failure both in my professional and personal life. But it's fear, isn't it? A terrible belief that I'm really not as others are. I'm frightened of everything – but, worse, don't want to do anything at all except lie in bed and hide and, when I get up, drink.

I made the Daisy for lunch yesterday, after a morning screaming for Darren's non-existent interest and love: a thing I vowed I wouldn't do, but did. Felt some relief, too, at doing it. After my three glasses of wine, I called Ruth to sleep off 'jet-lag' at her place and with the aid of a Valium, did so. I woke up without feeling agony, wanted to stay in bed but, fortunately, was ordered out and walked to a film screening which I enjoyed. Seeing people, being with people, laughing and joking together – I've seen so little of that these last few months. The wine has eased the agony a little – I'm glad Darren's gone.

I think and think of Sybil and how I must have appeared to her . . . I didn't listen to my instinct not to call at all. I just went ahead and spilled the beans to her, drunkenly telling her the secrets of my heart. Left Yale half-way through and 'let the kids down'. She knows nothing of genuine loneliness. I know she's suffered great pain, too. So have I – so that I *couldn't* stay on at Yale and I found I *couldn't* concentrate on the play and was afraid I would not memorise the lines. What else? Getting drunk in the bar the students use . . . But the agony was mine. Talking to her about Rex. I suppose that reminds her of Burton. Complaining about Darren and the mortgage. She advises me to leave him, insisting we are staying together for the wrong reasons. She is probably right. Meantime Darren tells me what Sybil has said about me. I call her up and challenge her about it. Poor Sybil, caught in the middle of Darren and me when she was only trying to help . . .

What's the conclusion of all this? This stupid storm in a teacup. Apart from my complete inertia and apathy, which is dangerous, Darren is growing older, has his house, his dog, his superficial friends, a job, his car, his clothes, his television set. I think he's accepted it, and is really back, except better off, where he was before he met me. In his own narrow world, he's a good-looking likeable young man who goes to screenings, doesn't want to be emotionally disturbed, let alone sexually ruffled, and is content to leave behind the few contacts I've got in the entertainment world. He senses their condescension, which he justifies by attributing it to my complaints to them about him – which may be partly true, had I lived a complete lie with him. In my absence they don't call him. And indeed what are they to me? They were left-over friends from Rex's day.

Sybil's job as a 'literary agent' cuts like a knife into me. I half-heartedly approached Milton about joining his agency. That was only because I wanted something to do with my day, have an office to go to, to get up for, a job that didn't necessitate having to memorise lines on the stage or suffer the indignities, real or imagined, of 'B'-picture film-making.

The wine is having its desired effect. It's eased the pain temporarily. Boosie, 'the little dog I made neurotic' (and I did, too), is on the bed beside me, cuddled up. I appreciate that . . . I just can't go through the routine of driving to Richard Rosenthal's at UCLA hospital, parking the car, telling him about Hazel, etc., etc., feeling better, shuddering in the Beverly Wilshire hairdressing salon, and back home – sigh of relief when it's bedtime, but then wake up to agony. Is there any alternative? Should I do what my nature dictates? Just give in for a bit? Certainly nothing else works. I am extraordinarily tired.

## October 22, 1980

I hear about Lilli Palmer – looking chic, having her hair done, having written her novel, doing her one-woman play, organised, efficient, confident, a survivor of marriage to the man I was married to . . . apart from her looks, far less acting ability than me. It is 10.37 am, in California, with a beautiful day outside. A day I just can't face.

## October 23, 1980

5.56 am. I drank a bottle of red wine yesterday, to get my oblivion. I woke up at 7.30-ish, not sure if it was night or morning. I talked twice to Rex . . . He talks of his shrimps after the matinée and then a snooze before the evening performance, and it's like listening to a world I never knew . . . I dread going to San Francisco.

I find myself thinking of the film *Yanks*, and wonder was my decline during the pre-publicity for it due to my suppressed realisation that the press weren't very interested in me any more. Was it really just the inevitable fact that *all* middle-aged actresses come to face – that the younger, prettier ones will get the craved-for attention? After all, it happened to me years ago at the Bristol Old Vic where I was playing with an Audrey Hepburn look-alike. I couldn't understand it: *I* was the actress. Poor me! With illusions of *grandeur* even then. But I *was* the actress in *Yanks* – the only one in the film to win anything. I'd loved doing it, too. It was the last time I was really happy. Not drinking, in control, not lonely, intending to sleep separately from Darren, reading, watching television, eating taramasalata, yes, writing . . . God, I've called upon you. Am I *so* worthless that other than taking my own life there is no way out?

I can never have youth back, or Rex swaying his shoulders down the corridors of European trains, nor walks to San Fruttuosa, nor cats snuggled on a bed in a room with a fire in it, nor eggs and potatoes in the Delfino, nor drunken lunches at the Connaught, nor the sound of his crackly voice.

I wonder would I ever have played St Joan or Lady Macbeth. Was I ever an 'actress' the way Lilli Palmer is, or, for that matter, Rex is an 'actor', with their dressers and their chauffeured limousines? I 'know' people, that austere psychiatrist said – and I *do*, too! But I suppose I'm not in their camp – I always wanted to be and have even had brief flirtations with it. I miss it powerfully: which is why I expect Lindsay feels a resentment in me. But I do love Harrods and Knightsbridge and a car at my disposal and to be treated as though I *am* someone – not like my 'Mrs Dangers' character from *Charlie Chan*, taking pornographic lip from that dreadful movie executive and fawning upon everyone, so abjectly on the outside, looking in . . .

But if I were with Rex, would I be able to bound up in the morning, fresh and pretty, with *croissants* and coffee, able to live contentedly through the day till he came home from work, drink a little wine, have dinner – in fact, be civilised? No, of course not.

## October 23, 1980

I really am much more disturbed and ill than even I know. I must relax on the illness and not fight it. I've just stopped living, however, and there is no one who brings life to me. No one to live for. It's all getting on top of me in some awful way. It's not right to lie in bed all day behind closed shutters with the heat on, longing to drink. I know I'm not the only one who does it. Others have and others will. But I'm not eating, not moving, not laughing, just hiding out.

I'm now obsessed with Sybil's position as a literary agent . . . imagining that an office to go to every day would rejuvenate me.

I'm just wondering what there is for me to get better for. Rex perhaps. I pray so. That in itself presents a ponderable problem. Could I just tour with him for nine months? Does anyone love someone that much? Without being able to have an interest in anything but my own self and this killing malaise, how could I be for him? There is no magic cure.

I've just talked to Milton about trying the agency side of the business. He says he'll talk to Audrey Wood [ICM executive]. I do so want life back again.

## October 24, 1980

But I drank again. I watched Sophia Loren on television, composed, a mother, in control . . . If I had something to get up for here, I might be able to pull myself out of this ever-increasing downward spiral with no interest in anything.

## October 28, 1980

More agony. Darren is cold and hostile and cannot give anything. The house is hostile. Now I can't entertain my friends here. He brings none of his home. We are totally incompatible. I go to San Francisco tomorrow to see Rex and I'm very frightened. I do want to see him very much and hope, dear God, that he will give me some hope. Yet I await it with terror. If it's not him, there seems no hope at all . . . All I said to Richard Rosenthal, to Darren, to Margot, to Lindsay is true. I hate the increasingly few character parts I play, and I've lost my nerve for the theatre. I don't want to learn to type. Nor do I now want to read books and scripts for ICM. Nor do I want to work with the sick. Rex . . . be the answer for me, as you once were.

Last night at dinner, when again I couldn't eat, couldn't drink, I sat next to Albert Finney with whom I've worked in films and on the stage. He's coarsened, is confident, has a future, a present, a proper relationship, the Bel Air Hotel. I was never a player like him, either. The parts I've played have been of life-defeating and defeated people . . . All my vitality and sense of fun are drowning. Let me be able to live again, God, let me be nourished by tomorrow. I have tried hard, seen coldness, hostility, fear, hopelessness. In the pit of my stomach there is a determination to go on trying, but as Richard Rosenthal said, maybe it's not for Rachel – volunteer work, reading at ICM the play about the woman with the nervous breakdown . . . He says that I'm not dead, that I'm very much alive, that I care too much, that I am oversensitive to feeling, that I am frightened of life – of living – that to wake up in another's atmosphere – and an uncaring atmosphere – leading someone else's life – and what a life! – would be hell for anyone. I've tried driving to the library and writing. I've tried tennis lessons. I've tried Actors' Studio. I've tried so much. All right, then, none of it is for me. What is? Rex? Don't compare yourself with his other wives, says Richard. Don't have such a despicable opinion of yourself. Yes, you are a child, trying things out for yourself for the first time. Don't think of Lilli Palmer doing Sarah Bernhardt on Broadway. Rex's life has had its rough patches, too, if her book is to be believed . . . weekly letters to her, anguished phone calls, keeping the secret of Kay's illness to himself and away from her . . . Please God, don't let the visit to Rex be more pain. Don't let my fear interfere with it. Please God, give us another chance, and give me the strength to love him properly and him love me. Let us energise each other. Let him need me, God, but let me be able to meet his needs. If I can't live for myself, let me be able to make him happy. Give us a miraculous chance, I beg of you.

---

HEAVILY SEDATED BY TRANQUILLISERS and wine, but still trembling at the prospect of a meeting which she regarded as crucial to any happiness that the future held for her, Rachel flew to San Francisco on October 29, 1980, to see Rex play in *My Fair Lady*. It was to be an affectionate meeting for both of them: a sense of 'old time's sake' collected around the pleasures that the two of them took together, simply and, as Rachel's journals suggest, wistfully. But her hope (or delusion) that Rex would somehow 'come back' to her suffered a setback; in spite of the concern that Rex showed her whenever they met, trying to help a sick woman who had been his wife, it was clear that his devotion was to his present wife who was in San Francisco with him, at the Huntington Hotel. When Rachel returned to Los Angeles, she did not go back to the house on Hutton Drive.

# November 1, 1980

Today is Saturday. I'm in bed at Carol's [Carol Scherick, wife of production executive EdgarScherick], a hot-water bottle on my tummy, being nursed by Carol. Rex is in San Francisco, married, in the middle of a matinée to a large audience doing *My Fair Lady*, and very well, with his black dresser, his chauffeured limousine, his two-bedroom suite, well dressed, eating properly, in control, with Mercia preparing his four o'clock meal, and the one after the show, seeing he gets his vitamins. He is independent, goes to the gym, swims, has his hair, his nails, his body 'done'. And now comes the agony part of today's thoughts.

Just to get myself on the plane to San Francisco was a major event. As it was, I got the agency to get my ticket and went to collect it just before Jeffrey's party. I had to have Darren come and collect me and then go to Westwood and back to collect my car. I went to bed glad not to be at Mr Chow's – that I don't blame myself for. Half a bottle of wine and two Valiums were required to pack my bag and get on the plane to San Francisco. At the hotel, I ordered Champagne and fell asleep. Then I went to see Rex and the show and was amazed by it. No one except Rex was really first-class, but he was. Whatever his nerves, he was at ease up there. Immaculate, urbane, graceful, a little removed. Whatever his unhappinesses, he is in control and disciplined, looks well and contains himself – takes, as he says, his distress uncritically. He was wonderful the first night, very moving in 'Accustomed to her Face'. Wine, genuine enjoyment, emotion and relief all contributed to the tears in my eyes. Nostalgia, too.

I saw him afterwards and we drank some wine and talked as we'd planned to do. He'd eaten his steak between shows, was going home to get his dinner – eat on his own and television and bed. His car dropped me off at the hotel. I suppose I slept. Rex came round the next morning and we took a taxi-ride to the beach and went for a long walk. We talked about some of the troubles there had been in our lives. Staring at the sea, peace came, soothing the fright that had possessed me since I had woken up that morning until he came round to the hotel. After our walk, he had to return to rest and eat before the show, and I had to get the aeroplane ticket for the next day. The terror gripped me again. So Rex had to come with me to the United Airline office. I couldn't make my mind up, whether to go at 11.00 am, or 1.00 pm. Decided on the 1.00 pm plane. Rex suggested that I, too, go back to the hotel and 'snooze'. I did so, but I didn't go to sleep. Instead, I went to the bar and had a brandy and ginger ale with the inevitable result – woke up in a panic, wanting to die. I had the grip of screaming fear, I called Margot McDowell – utterly 'bonkers', it would seem from the security and serenity of the bed I'm in now, not having had a drink for nearly a week.

I finally got myself together and went to the theatre and the dressing room. Contained Rex came in. I saw the show. A bad house, and Rex was a little *piano*. But the urbane curtain-call . . . the old-world charm . . . the life-style. Yet I saw Rex 'properly'. I'm admiring, but not adolescently dazzled any more. I see how hard he works, how he can accept prosaic repetitions and a routine, and quite a lot of unhappiness. We reminisced at dinner. I couldn't finish my wine. It was a comfort of sorts. Did it 'lay the ghost of Rex'? Not exactly, however much I recalled the old memories of what had made it so unhappy years before, waiting for him to come home, the enforced idleness, the emptiness inside.

Now what to do? I can get financial help from Rex for the psychiatrist. I can go to the analyst and try and live in my own reality and not through others. I can try and see if Lithium works. It's better to accept the fact that any sort of relationship with Darren is dead and gone, and better to sleep separately. I must try to see reality as it is. Rex included. Sometimes, maybe, Rex is lonely: the difference is, he has his work. It frightens him, but doesn't appal him. And of course he's earned the plaudits of the crowd, is more able to put up with the relentless boredom of eight shows a week. I, too, remember the challenge that a performance used to have . . .

I dozed off on Carol's sofa, nervously exhausted. I tried to enjoy reading Margot Asquith's autobiography and have woken up to this dread again . . . In my mind, I keep going back to the pre-Rex days.

### November 2, 1980
The pain and self-defeat are even more unbearable. I can't go on. I prayed that Rex would be the answer. I've never ever got over my halcyon days with him and however much I try, I can't. I'm utterly immobilised. No longer does he energise me as I hoped he would. Acting doesn't either, even though I've been asked to be in *Hamlet*.

Memo: Buy Acme juice machine. Celery juice or tomato, three times daily. Soups: Lemon, tomato, cucumber, bell pepper (red or green), romaine lettuce (long leaves), celery. Vitamins: B12 and Folic acid, B6, B3. Swami Muktananda [Indian guru, to whom Rachel resorted for curative meditation] on La Cienega, for 8.30 pm.

---

DARREN RAMIREZ: 'She moved in with a friend of hers, Carol Scherick, who had a house not very far from where Rachel and Rex had once rented the old Garbo home on North Bedford. Carol was then separated from her husband, Edgar Scherick, the film and television producer. Carol is a fervent believer in nature cures, health foods, and the like. She refuses to eat anything that might be contaminated by modern farming methods. She prefers to rely on vitamins because she thinks they're the basis of the human metabolism. She liquidises fruit and vegetables and "drinks" her meals. And she has an Indian guru called Baba. Carol felt very moved by Rachel's plight and offered to take her in, care for her, put her on a special diet, make sure she got the right vitamins and generally counsel her. Rachel had her doubts, I think, but she approached it philosophically in a "try anything once" mood and decided to stay with Carol for a month or so.'

PAMELA MASON: 'Sure, Carol was kind to her, but come on . . . ! Rachel's problems couldn't be cured with vitamin-reinforced energy drinks! What I don't think anyone spotted was the calm that comes before the storm. Believe me, that's the danger signal. Suicides become quiet when they've made up their minds to do it. When you see them at peace with themselves, that's the time to look out.'

IT SO HAPPENED THAT in the room next to Rachel's in the Scherick house was staying an old friend and theatrical colleague, the director Anthony Page who had done *Alpha Beta* with her and Finney. Page was one of the very, very few people to whom Rachel vouchsafed a look at parts of the journals which she now spent a lot of her empty days writing up. What she read out to him shocked him scarcely less than the appearance she now presented to the world.

ANTHONY PAGE: 'Carol Scherick acted with the very best intentions: there can be no doubt about that. But Rachel looked terrible. She spent the first week at Carol's in bed. She had hardly any contact with things now. She reminded me of the doomed hero at the end of Evelyn Waugh's novel *A Handful of Dust*, who's come an impossible odyssey from the highlights of Mayfair society and the Bright Young Things to be held captive for the term of his natural life in the jungles of darkest Africa where he is condemned to read to the cannibal chief from the works of Charles Dickens.

'I urged getting Rachel a no-nonsense doctor and finding the right chemical that would knock her out of her self-destructive syndrome before it was too late. I wondered if she had abandoned the pills and the Lithium that had held her together up to now.

'In Carol's home, she was like an invalid. Her attitude was a bit like saying the human race was a club that she didn't want to join. Lindsay

Anderson used to tell her that she was in love with her malaise. But I recall Rachel coming into my room, looking very shaken, and saying, "Lindsay isn't right. I really am fighting this. I am *not* in love with it."

'I last saw her two or three days before I went to New York on some theatrical business. She looked like someone flattened on the floor of the ring, being counted out. She was like a casualty all the time now – no spark of life whatsoever. She kept reading me bits and pieces of her journals, to try and explain what was happening to her.

'She spent a lot of time locked in her room. When we talked, it was frequently about the old days in London and how she should never have left the Royal Court. When she got on a more upbeat theme, she'd mention the Cast Theater, in Hollywood, and say she thought she'd go down there – she knew the director Ted Schmitt – and read plays for them as a kind of distraction from her depression. But mostly she sat in her dressing-gown, not even bothering to get dressed. Where once she'd been a warm, animated person, now she looked weak and diminished. "Vitamins and salads and ashrams, it's not my style, you know," she said to me.'

# November 6, 1980

I am at Carol's now, simply going to the psychiatrist and then back to bed. When I get up, I shake. What has happened to Rachel Roberts? I have no interest in anything, too apathetic and listless to do anything but lie in bed and read. I escaped from the house, but can't stay here for ever . . . I must give my answer today about doing *Hamlet*. Without it, I have nothing in view – but I have no real interest in it, frightened of the lines and my powers of concentration. Seeing Rex gave me (and him) a false return to the old days, but I was desperate in San Francisco, full of Valiums and wine, remembering dully the old privileges that being with him brought. I'm amazed he can still perform so well and with such assurance. But without Rex or acting, I literally have nowhere to go.

I've been thinking back to *The Tony Randall Show* I did on television. It was shrouded with illusions, too. I was on a high when I got the job. I really thought I'd become a 'star'. I thought I'd be 'Muriel' [character played by Rachel in *Tony Randall Show*] every week, and she'd be such a huge success . . . It all seemed so infantile, looking back on it. I suddenly, today, realised that the show probably would have been better if I *had* been 'Muriel'. Far from it being *my* fault, it was *their* fault, and the writers' fault and Randall's fault. I took it out on myself by drinking. No stoicism, it's true, but I'm a better actress than I give myself credit for.

Going up in the elevator to see Richard Rosenthal, for one marvellous moment I felt like Rachel Roberts again. After resting up and deciding to do *Hamlet*, I held my head high in the elevator. I looked out at my fellow human beings who were a poor lot. I came back to myself for a few blessed minutes, the fear inside abated for a bit and I wanted to live and act again. Now it's returned again, so it's difficult to write because I'm shaking with the familiar terror.

**November 7, 1980**
The first preview of *A Lesson from Aloes* was last night in New York.

**November 8, 1980**
Carol is amazing to me. To have reared four children one after the other while being yelled at, to be able to get up and repeat chores day after day, to be so easily content with the least sign of affection, to be so utterly lacking in cynicism . . . I have no way of knowing what it's like to take my teenager son to New York and to show him again the things of childhood and to take him to the Village and the jazz clubs. No idea at all. No idea what it must be like to call my own daughter and hear of her boyfriend trouble. No idea of what it must be like to have her home for Christmas. I imagine it to be lovely. The nearest I've ever come to it was when my niece Jackie was at London University, or stayed with us in Paris or in Portofino or at 42 Cambridge Street. Children grow up, I've noticed that. I noticed Jacqueline with Hazel, immersed in her own children on their arrival. Her mother was taken for granted . . . I hope the stab of pain won't come as I write the next thoughts down. To have a home that had been built up, with memories and people being there; where children can come as a shelter and refuge. Whether or not if the children aren't there the stab of loneliness can be as great, I don't know and won't ever know. My mind starts seizing up in confusion and I try and bring out the deadly fear that's helping to destroy me.

If my confused mind could simply have been in sufficient control of me just quietly and unemotionally to get myself together and board a plane, and check into a San Francisco hotel, and get a cab and go to the theatre. I *did* all those things *and* put myself through the wringer again, terrorising my poor being. Over-dramatic and very masochistic, I know, and I don't want to be like that any more. A vice? Self-indulgence? Exaggerated: that was Rex's word for me. Expects too much: that was Brenda's verdict. I accept all these. It's my nature: but it is a troubled nature. Perhaps it *was* a traumatic experience to go up to see Rex, especially as I'd called him my slender life-line, and already was repressing inward fear that I wouldn't feel that hot pang of love I used to experience with him – and the further repression of the thought that to be re-united with Rex would not solve any problem.

Even as I think about it, my head spins again. The *reality* of the situation was simply that I flew up to San Francisco to see my ex-husband in a musical. I couldn't stay with him because he's remarried. He couldn't have been nicer or gentler and we had supper together the second night and I saw the show twice. That's the *reality* of the situation. Why, then, did I *panic*? In the odd, heady moments in the clinics or the hospitals of the summer, when I felt that Rex and I would be re-united, then the fear retreated and hope replaced it, so that the meeting in San Francisco *was* important. But before I went, there was this defeatist thought that it wasn't going to happen. *Why*? Because the effort to lift myself up from this torpor was too great – I wouldn't be able to function properly. That I wouldn't be able to get Rex's breakfast for him (nor want to), shop at Jurgensen's, cook supper, have my hair done, buy pretty clothes – and that I'd be found out, that I'd want to stay in bed all the time . . . I can't believe it's just a monumental laziness. It has to be an illness that I'm trying so hard to combat. If I could somehow get to the bottom of this panic, control it and relax, I could live. It has always been there, I suppose. Sheer fear. Like taking all those tranquillisers before *Alpha Beta*. When it came to it, I wasn't that scared. Like swallowing those pills in Rome – when I couldn't stand the coldness of our marriage any more, *nor my failure*. I didn't get the part in his movie, nor the TV part in *Stop the World, I Want to Get Off*, nor could I type very well, nor handle the servants, and there were mosquitoes on the bedroom ceiling. All true! But I *panicked* and couldn't bear my *inadequacy*. What *The Russell Harty Show* was all about, I'll never know – drunken impulsive behaviour, I suppose. Likewise, the scene I made at the time of *Staircase*. Likewise, this last major catastrophe when I took the pills after the row with Darren and Sybil and woke up in UCLA . . . blowing everyone's cover, being a general nuisance, in fact, and not obeying the rules of civilised behaviour. Yet Rex often doesn't. Robert Shaw didn't. Burton didn't. O'Toole didn't. I didn't.

Without the bloody panic, I'd be performing well in a good play and going home to my neat apartment every night and, if I was lonely, I could have two little cats on the bed as Rosie once was, tea and toast and the *New York Times* in the morning, a massage, somewhere like the Women's Health Club in the afternoon, a bath and a taxi to the theatre. That's what *should* have happened and be happening. Why is it, then, that not only did I prevent it happening, but that when I describe it, I feel a sort of revulsion and a knowledge that it isn't right for me. Is it too ordinary? Too repetitious? Why do my thoughts instantly turn to wine when I think of the theatre as I've just described it? Do I want heightened reality still? I've done only three Broadway shows in my time, and they were done in conjunction with sex and violence and drink. I don't feel anything other than panicking – with good cause, when I think what my personality has rejected in favour of what I don't have now, but craved then – excitement and sensation and drinking and chatting up 'important' people and being so funny and warm and friendly and bright and, I suppose, basking in their glow and inviting their approval.

Here, I can relax because it's a home, and Carol is extraordinarily kind and mothering and there are other lives going on around me.

### November 9, 1980
Tony's [Page] left for New York, full of books, music, plans, his work, after a busy week of script conferences. He booked into a motel last night with his friend with Champagne. He returned here this morning, bathed and dressed attractively and put on the radio and dressed with composure. He drove himself to the airport and is now on the plane to New York. He's alive. Back rush the memories of my desperate packing – no music, just panic, and so much drink on the plane that I had to be sick . . . I remember Tony years ago at the Royal Court Theatre. I didn't envy him then. I was intact. What do I have to live for now?

'Keep a cool head.' I didn't, Dad.

Oh, to be like Tony with his hours filled, his needs satisfied, his ambitions nourished, his watercolours and his music. I like music, can even paint a little, certainly can write – but I can't direct myself, I just can't . . . Tony *could* live in my apartment on Central Park West alone, just as Ned Sherrin can live in my house in London, just as Darren can cope with Hutton Drive. But they are men – and living.

Rex called, which reduced some of the tension. I could cry. I told him I couldn't hold on. He told me to keep trying, he needed me. Mercia has arranged a dinner for him with some friends after the show – people they'd met in Bermuda. Rex said I wouldn't want Tony's life. The trouble is, I don't want my life.

**November 11, 1980**

I saw the TV *Hamlet* last night. Derek Jacobi was wonderful. I liked Claire Bloom, too. It was secure and pleasant at Carol's. Carol's house is a home. I keep forgetting that she will be selling this and *wants* a small apartment. For some reason, the very address West 44th Street frightens me.

Oh, to be the Rachel I once was! Full of vitality, with appetites and ambitions. No one would live the way I'm living and have been living these past eighteen months. Now writing it down doesn't help, either. I look back and read the stories I used to write in the library – stories like *The Ghost Plant*:

It was a Sunday in May. Hot, scorching, almost. I was sitting in a splendid supermarket. I was among large and important and verdant plants. Alone. I had never had much of an opinion of myself. However, when I glanced down at the label they were tying to me, I confess I felt dashed. It read 'Ghost Plant'. 'Ghost Plant'? *'Ghost Plant'*? But I was me. I wasn't a ghost. I was pale, yes. I wasn't large, important or verdant. But a 'Ghost Plant'? In an exclusive American supermarket, me, a 'Ghost Plant'? It was an unnerving thought.

I looked around to see if my neighbours were staring at me, pityingly, but they didn't seem to be. Apart from the large, important and verdant plants, there were a great many nice ordinary plants, or vegetables as they preferred to be called, around me, and fruits and such like. No labels there. And a lot of them, too, all together, yellow and shining and calm. But then they were allowed to just be naked, unremarked and themselves. I'd been uprooted, pushed into soil, not very comfortable soil, either, and I was pale and not at all important or verdant.

It was hot that day. I felt hopeless. Shoppers came and went. I knew my worth. I was a philosophic plant. But that day, after I'd looked at my label, there was loneliness and yet a defiant sort of hope.

She came by. She'd bought the grapefruits, the tomatoes, the peaches. She looked nice. She saw me. She stopped. She looked at my paleness. She read the dread label. She smiled. She didn't seem to mind. On the contrary, she removed a dying polyp that had been irritating me, and took some money out of her purse. I could not believe it. I was out. Out of the smart supermarket, into a blue Celica car made by the Japanese. I rode down Sunset Boulevard. I was taken into a beautiful and sunny house. I was thirsty. She gave me water. She fussed over me. I was to stay. Her red-headed friend came home. They talked about me. I really was to stay – and in her bedroom.

It didn't seem to matter now that I was not large, or important, or verdant. I was me. A 'Ghost Plant' come to stay.

I 'buried' my talent, according to Lindsay Anderson. Where, I'm not entirely sure. If I was destined to be Irene Worth, I'd be Irene Worth. But I chose Rex. I chose him because of uncertainties in my character and because I wanted some fun, too. But the fear I'm going through is because I haven't got Rex – nor am I sure I want him – and I'm not Irene Worth, either.

Albee wants to interview me for a small part in *Lolita*. Quite right: he doesn't know me. But it's rubbing my nose in the shit, all the same.

Each time I've been in New York trying to work, I've gone to pieces. Same thing during the reading of *The Play About Love* – I couldn't be calm at all, drank crazily and asked Mitch Erickson to try and find Rex in the South of France. I have no hope or faith like Carol – and no children to come home for

228

Christmas. Can I somehow live in Central Park West? I couldn't before. Can I settle for a couple of cats?

---

DARREN RAMIREZ: 'Rachel still got offers, for her terrifying illness was still not generally known. One came from Jack Hofsess who was directing *The Elephant Man* on Broadway and wanted her for the role of the nurse in the Victorian hospital where the Elephant Man is given refuge. Another was Frank Dunlop, who was casting Edward Albee's musical adaptation of *Lolita* and wanted her for the mother's role. Rachel read the script and immediately took against the part, though she later changed her mind – or said she had.

'I felt less and less like going over to Carol's to see her. By the third week of this regime, Rachel thought she was going crazy and started calling up Sybil, who was at ICM now, and begging for help. ICM was honouring a long-time executive of theirs, Ben Benjamin, with a big reception at the Beverly Wilshire. Sybil wanted to go, said Rachel, why couldn't I escort her – she was too shy to ask me herself. Then Sybil herself called me and said, "Rachel's driving me crazy – if you want to go, okay with me. Let's go together. Rachel's certainly not going to go anyhow." But at 4.00 pm on the day of the party, when I get back to Hutton Drive to change, there's Rachel with her hair in curlers, taking a long dress out of the closet and getting ready to press it.

'We're on the way to the ICM party, where we'd now arranged to meet Sybil, when suddenly Rachel gives a shriek. I thought, My God, a heart attack! But what it was, was that she'd forgotten to drink the liquid dinner that Carol Scherick had prepared for her – I think that half the time she flushed it down the loo, which probably helped account for her wasted looks. So we had to go back to Carol's for Rachel to sneak in and drink the stuff – she said she hadn't eaten solid food for weeks now! We get to the ICM reception and Jacqueline Bisset is there. "Rachel," she says, "your eyes – they look funny. They look dead." "Why not?" says Rachel, "I'm going to die anyhow." That set the tone of our evening!

'Sybil was in a corner of the room waiting for Rachel and, I think, pretty shocked by what she saw. I said I'd friends to meet and Sybil promised to take Rachel safely back to Carol's. But when I got back from the supper I'd arranged with friends in the Hollywood Hills, I'm damned if Rachel wasn't sitting in the living room, loaded, and afraid to return to Carol's because in one compulsive binge she's broken every diet rule that'd been laid down for her. Another big row . . . The next day, she went back to Carol's pretending everything's normal.'

At the same ICM reception was the actor who had shared the earliest honours that Rachel's screen career brought her.

ALBERT FINNEY: 'The party was quite a size and there wasn't much chance to say hello to Rachel who was going here, there and everywhere – it was the first time I'd seen her when she had obviously been drinking. Sybil found time to tell me she was going through a bad period . . . I was waiting for the car valet to bring my car round to the door of the Beverly Wilshire's new wing, when I saw them both come out and start to cross the courtyard into the old wing. I had a sense of Sybil helping Rachel along to some extent. I was afflicted with a feeling of sudden sadness, which you sometimes get as you look at people who don't realise they're being watched and are not covering up. Rachel conveyed real womanhood. There was nothing foolishly virginal about her. She was an actress who, I'd felt on the few times we were together, had an enormous supply of power because she felt passionate about life. It was sad now to see her being "assisted", as it were, through life.'

# November 13, 1980

Back at Carol's after the shock of the outing. After Ben Benjamin's party. After seeing Jacqueline Bisset and Albert Finney. I drank, smiled with forced good humour at the agents, the head of M.G.M., David something-or-other. I took Jackie aside and told her of my many troubles. Syb drove me home. I had a mild alcoholic black-out, but went in and registered the scene, candles lit, fire on, Darren sitting on the settee with a male friend of his . . . I had a terrible night. I don't believe that diet or Indian meditation will do anything for me – not with the problems I face. I didn't do *The Elephant Man* – one day's work. Probably for the best. The flight to New York, staying in a hotel and flying to Toronto would have been too exhausting. But this other existence is a nightmare. I don't want endlessly to stay in bed and brood, but, literally, I don't know what else to do. I am sick with envy of the life Jacqueline Bisset leads – and Albert. I really can't bear any of it – Oh, how I wish *something* would happen . . . ! I'll rest now.

## November 14, 1980
Who do I think I'm kidding? I'm in a fucking awful mess. I'm being looked after by Carol and about to go to an intensive bit of Indian meditation with Swami Muktananda because it's preferable to being alone all day in Hutton Drive.

I read about Reagan's friends, Betsy Bloomingdale, the Jurgensens, Mrs William French Smith: how they are disciplined! Getting up at 5.30 am, exercising, breakfast at 6.30 am, working all day, entertaining, dressing well, with children and grandchildren . . . and I wonder that I'm depressed?

I see that Rosie is Madame Arkardina in *The Sea Gull* at the Public Theater. I see Lilli Palmer looking beautiful, having published her book, translated by Carey – and I wonder that I'm depressed? I flung my hand out and smiled my smile at that party of Ben's, desperately wanting to be noticed. Let's face it, I'm a fucking awful failure at living. No wonder Hutton Drive is cold and empty. My pitiful attempts to 'do' something – i.e. taking typing lessons at Beverly High, work as a volunteer with the emotionally ill, sit in a corner at ICM and read scripts and books – are just that – *pitiful!*

I wish I could have lived a proper life. But I was the fourth wife of a difficult and egocentric actor and I drink too much. I never had children and I never grew up. Alan and I had a grim little marriage. Acting was all once, but I was never Rosemary. And now it doesn't feed me at all. Of course I despise myself. My depression is because of what I've become. I've said it over and over again that none of my friends could have put up with New Haven, the snow, that room, the lectures and the loneliness. My bubble burst with the failure of *The Tony Randall Show* . . . What have I been thinking of? It's my life, I know, and looking back there don't seem to have been many alternatives to the path I chose. I wish there had, or that I'd been different. If I had been, I wouldn't have been experiencing this agony, nor have gone through this dreadful summer. Darren's like a red rag to a bull now. But he's absolutely right. I was a drunk – and he did put me to bed. Pretty obvious stuff – middle-aged actress ex-wife of a famous star living in Beverly Hills with a black housekeeper in a rented house and a very nice-looking, younger man who's Mexican, charming and wants to go to the nice restaurants and meet the famous and go to Europe. My situation is monstrous and seemingly hopeless; but even so, it exists and I still exist and I am what I am. But I've stopped living, that's for sure.

Let me day-dream about being one of the Reagan Set wives, with my well-appointed house, my wardrobe full of clothes, my routine, my outside interests, my beautiful car that I can drive, my children and my grandchildren and my successful and familiar husband. I never did envy them when I was with Rex, whooping it up, leading an extraordinary life of rented houses and hotels sandwiched between visits to Portofino. It was really only eight years with Rex, except for my holding on. How about Rex as a possible solution to it all, because there doesn't seem to be any other? (I'm accepting myself tonight – well, it's easy, if boring, to do so here. The little cat, Daisy May, on the bed, again in someone else's home, the day over. See what's happened, Rachel.)

Well, it wasn't for me, marriage to my old love the doctor. I was answering advertisements in a Kensington newspaper for a model and going to keep the appointments for a sexual thrill when Sybil was the good loving bride of Richard's, keeping house, making French fries, ignoring his infidelities, perhaps not even accepting them herself. She wanted babies. I was an actress, living in a bed-sitter. A little wild, perhaps. I did want to be someone, it's true. I went to Churchill's, performed in the nightclub there, abrasively – wasn't ever the quiet, dedicated actress. All right, I've been dissipated and foolish. I've been unaware, rushing in madly like a fool where angels feared to tread. I've not changed. I was the same at Ben's party. But I'm not anyone any more, so it's grotesque now. Why can't I just be me? I could correct the scruffiness. Buy some simple clothes. Get some Calvin Klein expensive ones. Some shoes. Some proper face cream. Have my hair done. Write to my friends, to my friends. Read *Hamlet*. Contact Frank Dunlop. But I *can't* do any of these things. I've been like a lost soul for eighteen months. I'm in this painful depression because inevitability has caught up with me. I made no preparation for my fifties and no one made preparation for me. You don't marry a man twenty years your senior, a temperamental man without a home, much as you loved him – and love him: that's the fact of the matter – and expect serenity. (I wasn't looking for serenity, either.) You don't fail to have children of your own, or by adoption, and expect the joy of them in middle age. You don't divorce when you're forty-two and live first with a gentle, penniless young man and expect stability or emotional satisfaction or with a sexy, emotionally unrestrained young man nearly twenty years your junior and expect to be settled like George and Margaret whom I acquired after the health farm. Hardly preparation for the wives of the Reagan Set!

I *dread* being alone so much. 'You'll be left alone,' Mum said. Just read in the *Los Angeles Times* about the severely retarded women who 'were all dressed appropriately, and obviously felt some pride in their own appearance'. It's about time I started taking pride in mine, too.

---

'A LESSON FROM ALOES' opened in New York on November 17 – to brilliant reviews. Rachel's journals reflect how closely, how enviously she had followed its progress to Broadway success – and how bitterly she regretted not being a part of it. One wonders if she saw the reviews – and half hopes she didn't. Some of them seem not so much to be comments on Maria Tucci's powerful performance as Gladys as diagnostic descriptions of Rachel's own chaotic emotional state. Frank Rich called the characterisation that of '. . . a woman torn by centrifugal forces. In Act One she clings to her last companion, her diaries, as if holding on to the book might prevent her flying apart. In Act Two, Gladys's fluttery nervousness gives way to a horrifying eruption of nihilistic bile.' And Clive Barnes commented, 'she is fantastic at passing through states of sanity and madness in her shrill but cool curse against existence'.

# November 15, 1980

It's 7.15 am, and I'm off to the ashram and Baba. I didn't sleep much last night, but then I knew I wouldn't. I kept wishing I'd been able to do *A Lesson from Aloes* and stunned New York with my torrential emotions. No two ways about it, it's a loss . . . But now . . . enjoy the ashram, for heaven's sake!

## November 19, 1980

I went to hear Baba and meditate and be intensive and got not a moment's peace from it. But it was an accomplishment to shower each day and get into the car. Others around me moaned and laughed and shivered and shook and claimed spiritual uplift. I remained where I'm at, bogged down in hopelessness. On Monday, I read Baba's autobiography. At Tuesday lunchtime, Rex called. He'd been out on a friend's sixty-foot cabin cruiser all day Monday. Monday was the day *A Lesson from Aloes* opened in New York. I swigged back a lot of whisky neat on the Monday and, of course, felt terrible.

I watch Carol, in control, caring for herself, taking her piano lessons, her French lessons, looking after her son – and I look at me, marooned, bed-ridden, shaking, thinking daily of suicide. I am shut off from all my friends now, now even Darren, and the myth of Rex, too, gone. We are worlds apart, Rex and I. We always were. I've written earlier that it wasn't a major mistake for me to go away with him, but, despite the magic days, I think it was. It's too late to do more than speculate, but I had a need to act – have the discipline of that habit and to sublimate all my needs and emotions into the parts I was playing. I wanted to act. Always. But for my first marriage, I would have continued to do so with increasing confidence and flair – my personality and voice and instinct, powerful allies. I would never have sunk into this torpor. Never. Never have had a day like this. Never.

Alone in someone else's house in Los Angeles. Yes, I loved Rex, passionately, and all our good larks. Yes, I adored walking up the Champs-Elysées with him. Yes, I adored Joseph's and the Berkeley and ice-cold, perfectly prepared dry Martinis and beautiful wine and brandy and potage and brains. Yes, I loved going back to the Lancaster and going to bed and making love. Yes, I loved the Rome Express and the adjoining *coupes* and snuggling up to Rex. Yes, I loved our love: it completely tallied with my adolescent fantasies. Yes, I loved the look of Rex's shoulders swaggering down the train corridors. Yes, I loved our walks past the donkey to San Fruttuosa. Yes, I loved the fires, the villa, the books, the cats, Homerino. I loved them passionately. And for all that, I forfeited my birthright inherited from Grandpa – my voice and Welsh emotionalism . . . my acting. It was all I ever knew or understood. Working in the theatre, I was easy with it. Understood it. Liked having my days structured by it. Really preferred rehearsing: I was with people. But I liked stalking the stage, too, I liked being told I was good, I liked controlling an audience *and could do it*!

I wish I could put the clock back. I wouldn't have known such empty days of solitude. I probably wouldn't have known Hollywood or New York. I wonder would I have drunk? Probably – but maybe not so much.

Alan, when I met him last November, was as down-to-earth as ever. Perhaps after all that's what I needed – something downbeat to balance all my emotionalism and steady me. I had affairs all the time we were together – and no children. Would it – could it – have lasted? I don't know for sure, except I don't think I would have left him and he could have controlled me. That I know. I don't think, in a more closed environment, I'd have been so punched about. My failings so highlighted. I don't think Alan would have let me degrade myself to the extent I have. I think, too, I would probably have given him a bad time, because I so wanted to know 'important' people and sophisticated people, and Alan couldn't get on with such people at all. I could and did, and so wanted fun. Nothing turbulent has happened to Alan: he certainly hasn't suffered all I have. Who has?

I did so want to be a great actress. Not being a romantic, nor yet beautiful, it's more than likely I wouldn't have achieved that pinnacle. But I might have plodded along. I might have had a proper home. I might have had familiar Alan to share my bed, so that home really meant home and when it rained I could feel safe with Alan and the cats and books and faith in my craft and pride in Rachel Roberts.

Rex's voice tonight sounded tired. I've read *Aloes* again, and have the same feeling towards it.

**November 21, 1980**
I am getting worse and worse. I can't think of getting out of bed without a shudder of fear and my thoughts are unbearable . . . This morning, Carol's friend came to 'look after me' and I was barely civil – no gratitude at all. My life has completely folded up on me and I find it full of horror. Here I am with a woman I've met maybe three times before, a nutritional zealot, lying comatose in a bed in her house . . . Rex's calls are briefer now. Soon he's coming here for *My Fair Lady*, along with his wife, to stay in Leslie Bricusse's house – Leslie's lending him his Mercedes.

Rosemary Harris is getting up to have some fish prepared by her friend Tricia before going off to play Madame Arkardina in *The Sea Gull*, then sleeping and resting before her performance, which she'll enjoy. Maggie

Smith is going to be Virginia Woolf. And look where I am. *Look where you are, Rachel!* Lying in someone else's bed, being fed with vitamins and resenting every minute of it.

I've tried psychiatrists. I've tried Alcoholics Anonymous. I've tried Indian religion. I've been in and out of homes and clinics and health farms. I've tried sobriety. I've tried prayer. If God is there and would answer my prayer, what would I ask for? To be healed. To be able to live and enjoy life. To be able to act. To be able to give.

Voices on the phone when Carol is out . . . discussing me. 'Carol running around like a chicken, worrying about her . . . That woman's very negative . . . Should get rid of her.' Yes, what indeed am I doing here? The two people that I've phoned today, Rosemary and Tricia, I've told I want to kill myself. Where is my pride?

---

DARREN RAMIREZ: 'Her pain was now terrible to see. Her depression was unliftable. She believed that if she'd been in the play, it would have been the making of her in America. She'd taken to appearing at Hutton Drive without warning – as if checking up on me and what I was doing. She would suddenly *be* there, looking like a ghost. I suggested we take in a movie at the Academy, but on the way there she went into hysteria and threatened to drink a bottle of brandy, then go to a friend's house and jump off the roof – 'People will think I've been blown off,' I remember she said. Even in her state, she was still caring about what other people thought!

'Rex came to town that week to start the previews of *My Fair Lady* at the Pantages. I was at I Magnin when Carol Scherick called. "Rex has just stopped by and picked up Rachel," she warned me. "They've gone to Hutton Drive. I wouldn't go home just now, if I were you." Well, I hung around till I thought they'd have said all they had to say to each other, then went home. As soon as I entered the living room I saw Rex's "Henry Higgins"-style hat on the sofa, and assumed he was still there. So I went back to wait for Rachel at Carol's. She called there and demanded to know why I wasn't coming home. "I thought you wanted to be alone with Rex," I said. "Rex is long gone, he simply forgot his hat. Come back at once." So home I went – and found her smashed.

'The next day, November 25, she was supposed to be leaving for New York to audition the *Lolita* part for Frank Dunlop. But when the time came, she couldn't find her purse. Panic! "I only went out to the liquor store yesterday to get some wine for Rex and me to drink at dinner. I must have left the purse at the store – there's a lot of money in it that I drew for the New York trip from the bank." She'd been drinking and was in no condition to drive to a liquor store, of all places! "Rachel, the cops will be after you," I protested. But she ran off and finally ended up at Carol's, where she found her purse. It was too late by then to catch a plane for New York, so she insisted I take her out for dinner. We went – believe me, it was easier to give in than argue. We ate at Adriano's. One plate of pasta and a glass of wine and she was fine. Another glass of wine, and she passed out. We got home about 9.00 pm. She'd been writing up her diary, but I noticed she'd locked it securely away, as usual. I put her to bed.'

ANTHONY PAGE: 'I was staying at the Mayflower Hotel in New York when something impelled me to put a call through to the Hutton Drive house to see if Rachel was there. Slightly to my surprise, she was. She said she'd had a peaceful dinner with Rex and would be in New York the next day for the *Lolita* try-out. I made her promise to ring me. She said she would, but she also sounded as if she'd drunk a bit too much. I was afraid she mightn't remember the number of the Mayflower, or even where I was staying. We talked about her friends. I told her they loved her and worried about her. She said very calmly, "I wish they wouldn't." Those were the last words of hers I remember. The call I'd asked her to give me never came.'

# November 24, 1980

I never expected this total despair. Even as I look back on it, I remember days of vitality and happiness and hope. And now faced with hopelessness, I can't believe what is happening to me, to Ray, to Rachel Roberts.

Last night I heard Rex say that even if I'd done *A Lesson from Aloes*, I'd still be grumbling about returning to an empty flat after the show, and it was somehow reassuring in that it was the truth. I couldn't do it, night after night.

I never really wanted a real husband. I wanted to act. But I knew I was bad at looking after myself, so I chased after Alan because he was so steady and so good. Rex upset my life, not just because he was so self-centred, not only because he'd lived and loved so much more than I had, but because of something in me that didn't want just to be a man's wife. The loss of my play, *A Lesson from Aloes*, and its subsequent triumph in New York – and the realisation that it was the chance of a lifetime in comparison with what I get offered, and could have been something that could have led somewhere *had I been well and different*, it had its predictable traumatic effect on me.

Rex just called, not liking this place or Leslie's house. Mercia's French maid has flown in. His butler is unpacking for him. He's having a bite at the Beverly Wilshire with Patrick Garland. If only I could still feel my love for him. Could I? Could I unpack and cook as his household does? He was glad I was alive, he said. He is a scamp. Always was. Impossible, I suppose, to live with. Woke up at five o'clock, thinking I was dead. I am very ill.

**November 25, 1980**

I can't control it any more and I've been trying with all my failing strength. I'm paralysed. I can't do anything and there seems to be no help anywhere. What has happened to me? Is it that my dependence over the years on alcohol has so severely debilitated me that now, without it, I just cannot function at all? Or is it that my nervous system from birth has always been so very frail that life for me is too much to cope with? That I was the hopelessly dependent little girl who found everything too hard to handle, so that my intelligence and talent have been overcome now that I'm in my fifties and I can't withstand it? Day after day and night after night, I'm in this shaking fear. What am I so terribly frightened of?

Life itself, I think.

WHEN DARREN AWOKE THE next day, November 26, he knew it was the Wednesday when his Mexican gardener came. The man would find the house empty, he reflected: though this was not unusual. Rachel was due to catch the early afternoon flight to New York. She was still sleeping when he left for the I Magnin store, and he let her sleep in order to get plenty of rest before the flight. He took in that day's issue of the *Los Angeles Times* before he left, but, beyond scanning the news headlines, did not open it further before setting off for Beverly Hills.

DARREN RAMIREZ: 'Some time between 11.00 am and 11.30 am, Rachel called the store to say good-bye to me. She said she intended to be on the 4.00 pm plane. She said she'd also called Rex to say goodbye to him. He was due to open two days later – the day after Thanksgiving – in *My Fair Lady*. I wished her a pleasant flight and told her not to do anything foolish in New York.

'The next time the phone rang, at about 5.00 pm, it was the police asking me did I know a person called Rachel Roberts.'

An actress dying, as Rachel did, in circumstances both unexpected and puzzling, suffers the fate of receiving more attention for the way she has left this life than for what she has achieved during it. It is not usually critics who write or deliver obituaries, but news reporters or rewrite men or simply, as on this occasion, the stand-by staff employed by the media to tide them over the long Thanksgiving holiday which America began the next day until the principal by-line writers get back from vacation. Thus Rachel's death received much attention: her talents, very little. Even the *New York Times*'s seventeen-inch, double column obituary, not published until two days later, was mainly a comprehensive listing of plays, films, roles, marriages and the like, with the summary verdict that here was 'an actress of many facets and great depth'. The British press, uninhibited by public holidays, managed a better coverage of her gifts, though a sense of wasted opportunities echoed through much of what was written.

Michael Billington, theatre critic of the *Guardian*, singled out two of Rachel's appearances in modern plays to confirm his judgment of her as a 'sensational' actress: 'She gave her finest performance in recent years . . . opposite Albert Finney in Ted Whitehead's *Alpha Beta*. She played a vindictive working-class puritan confronting a hopeless marriage with teeth remorselessly gritted; and I well remember the controlled venom with which, speaking of her husband's mistress, she said, "I made you – she's not going to get the benefit." And in John Osborne's *The End of Me Old Cigar* she delivered a long, merciless, anti-masculine harangue with glittering biliousness . . . She was one of those rare actresses who could combine emotional pain with sexual ferocity. What she achieved was considerable. The list of things she might have accomplished, but for her untimely death, is no less considerable.'

She was 'still in her acting prime', wrote Philip French, film critic of the *Observer*, who commented on her 'notable studies of the conflict between reticence and voracity in working-class sexuality', and ended, 'Sadly, the cinema never tapped the comic gifts with which she first impressed London theatregoers in the 1950s.' A few papers, suddenly discovering the liaison with Larry Hagman that went back all of thirty-three years, well before the American actor had risen to international notoriety in *Dallas*, sub-headed their obituaries: 'When Rachel Met J.R.' Truly, death is not the last thing one has to fear.

The bulk of the coverage concentrated on the puzzle – how did Rachel die? At first her death was reported as being due to a heart attack. The fact that she had taken her own life was not confirmed by the Los Angeles county coroner until the following Saturday, November 29. The delay wasn't simply due to public officials being on holiday. There was a mystery in the way Rachel chose to end her life that has not yet been satisfactorily explained.

It was tragically easy to reconstruct most of what had happened from the circumstantial evidence that police officials and, later, Darren Ramirez, discovered when they searched the house and the tangled, overgrown hillside above it.

DARREN RAMIREZ: 'It was evident that Rachel planned everything. Behind the house we had the hill, covered with wild-rose bushes which Rachel loved to sit among because she said it reminded her of English countryside. Up there we found a pillow and a couple of cashmere blankets that had been taken off her bed. It was presumed she took the Nembutals and the other pills she had been hoarding all summer and went up there to lie down and die.'

SYBIL CHRISTOPHER: 'She knew Darren was at work and would be unlikely to come home until it was too late – she had obviously forgotten about the Mexican gardener. Even so, he wouldn't have attended to the dogpatch behind the house. She'd left a letter on the table, about repairs to her car. Everything was deliberately arranged to point to her absence from home. She might have lain undiscovered in the bushes until she was missed by people not being able to find her in New York or not hearing from her back in Los Angeles. God knows how long that might have been!

'My guess is that after swallowing the Nembutals and Mogadons – the way she pronounced the name of that last drug, in her Welsh accent, always made it sound like "Morgan" – she found she wasn't "going under" fast enough – remember, she had a very strong constitution. Also, when the sun leaves that part of the garden – and it did so early on, since it was November – it gets suddenly very cold. I assume she felt chilly and, paradoxically for someone intent on dying, staggered down the little steep flight of hillside steps to get another blanket. Those steps are very narrow – I've had to put my foot sideways on them. In her drugged state, she probably stumbled in and out of the rose bushes on the way down which accounts for all the rips and snags in the nightie she was wearing.'

DARREN RAMIREZ: 'As she entered the house, she probably remembered something that the suicide-counselling pamphlets she sent away for from Exit told her to be sure to do. Suicide attempts are often frustrated because the person vomits up the pills. To avoid this, you should eat something solid. In Rachel's mouth and throat were found bits of an English muffin from a packet in the kitchen – that's why they thought at first she'd choked on a sandwich, had a cardiac and died accidentally.'

SYBIL CHRISTOPHER: 'Whenever she came into anyone's kitchen, being British, she put on the kettle for tea. I guess habit works even when you're on the way out of this world – for they found the kettle boiling with Rachel stretched out on the kitchen floor.'

The inexplicable part of the tragic sequence of events relates to what was probably the immediate and prime cause of death. The *Los Angeles Times*, reporting the official autopsy on November 30, said: 'Actress Rachel Roberts died from swallowing a caustic substance . . . [but] coroner's officials said they could not determine whether it was swallowed intentionally. The substance was described as a lye, alkali, or some deadly acid. The autopsy gave no indication that she had suffered a heart attack or that she could have choked while swallowing food.' A few days later, having apparently pondered the massive dose of barbiturates in the body, the coroner officially listed Rachel's death as one of 'suicide'.

Where the lye came from, no one knows to this day. The substance is the basis of common household disinfectant: it is also used by some people as an insecticide or weedkiller. But no bottle so labelled was ever found. It may be that Rachel had secreted it away, like the pills; it may be that she found it innocently jettisoned by someone in the 'wild wood' tangle which she had destined as her last resting place – perhaps some horticulturist had left it there in an old wine bottle whose later appearance, among the other 'orthodox' bottles of wine in the kitchen, would have caused it to escape attention at the time, especially as such a horrifying agent of sudden death was not suspected until several days after the grim events. At any rate, Rachel drank it and, like Little Miss McGuire, became a 'part of things'.

The related puzzle must remain even more speculative. It is – *Why* did she drink it?

SYBIL CHRISTOPHER: 'She was relying on her overdose of pills. But she'd relied on that before, and survived. She may have thought, "My God, if this doesn't work, I'll wake up in hospital for the Nth time with a stomach pump down my throat. I must finish it for good and all" – so she drank down the lye and then writhed about so violently that she smashed into the little glass kitchen screen and added to the lacerations on her body, though one prays that by then she was numb to the pain.'

PAMELA MASON: 'I think it was related to a deeper disturbance – to do with her infatuation for Rex. Probably it wasn't all love. Hate was part of it, too. A mixture of both. What Rachel could not endure was the apparently effortless success that Rex was rightfully enjoying – and without her. I do believe that the fact she took her own life almost on the eve of his opening night in *My Fair Lady* is not coincidental. The lye was the extra pain she believed she could cause him. I don't think she even remotely remembered what grief and professional harm had been caused to Rex over thirty years before when he was married to Lilli Palmer and his girlfriend Carole Landis had committed suicide in Hollywood. Rachel didn't need precedents. She was much too involved with herself – it was *her* life, *her* death, *her* fate that was uppermost in her mind that day.'

Before Darren left for work on the fatal day, he had taken indoors that day's copy of the *Los Angeles Times*.

Darren hadn't seen one specific article in it: whether Rachel did is, again, totally speculative. But anyone opening the relevant section of the bulky newspaper could not have missed it, so prominently was it displayed across the entire breadth of one page, and two double-sized columns on another. It was written by Sheila Benson, who was shortly to become the paper's film critic in succession to Charles Champlin. It was by-lined 'San Francisco', where she had evidently gone to interview the subject. It was headed: 'Harrison Sculpts His "Fair Lady".'

With many felicitous and perceptive phrases, Ms Benson, who had come prepared for an encounter with 'Shaw's lion with a thorn in its paw', expressed herself impressed by the warmth, 'massive charm and personal kindness which can also radiate from the same regal personage'. Harrison described the *carte blanche* he had been given to re-create a touring production of *My Fair Lady* that would be of the '80s, not of the bygone '50s. He left one in no doubt that the coachwork of a Rolls-Royce concealed the steely chassis of a man who was built to last – and use his unrivalled eminence to get his way. Ms Benson would probably have liked to discuss his 'private life', but she had been warned it was 'off limits'. However, she concluded all was well with it on the strength 'of a small, beautiful collection of poems and prose collected by Harrison', which had so far been published only in England. Its dedication read: 'For Mercia . . . I dedicate this anthology to my beloved wife from whom I have learned the art of living and loving at long last.'

Sheila Benson put her last question to Rex Harrison: Was he a happy man?

' "I don't think that one can honestly say that one is totally happy, no. But then I think that may go with the times of the period in which one lives. I think one has to be a lunatic to be happy. Most lunatics have no lines on their faces at all and no worries. I don't know that I know anybody who'd say they were happy." '

News of Rachel's death spread rapidly among friends and colleagues. The reactions were like the experience she had packed into her lifetime – multitudinous and often diametrically diverse.

RONNIE CASS: 'I never had any presentiment that she would take her own life – quite the reverse, I'd have said. That theatrical type rarely does. But she did need someone of an artistic temperament to keep her alive.'

JEFFREY LANE: 'When I heard that she had taken her own life, I was pleased in an odd way. She had made her choice. The original reports had spoken of a heart attack: I'd thought that was awful, a sneaky way to go.'

DR LIMENTANI: 'When I read about her death in the papers, I experienced a momentary feeling of strong disbelief – not suicide, *surely*, but an accident.'

ELIZABETH JAMES [her school chum]: 'I can understand her end very well. She'd put on weight, had a drinking/love problem, work problems. Oh, yes, I think I'd have taken that way out, too.'

TONY RANDALL: 'Terrible, terrible . . . she was wonderful!'

NED SHERRIN: 'To tell the truth, I think it was all part of the pattern.'

JILL BENNETT: 'When Lindsay Anderson and I heard of her death, we both of us quit whatever we were doing at the time – in my case, it was some lousy movie – and both of us met at the Waldorf Hotel in London and drowned our sorrows. I think Rachel was ill with wanting to die. Lindsay was convinced that she would die. As for me, when people say they want to die, I don't think they're crying wolf.'

SIDNEY LUMET: 'I'm afraid it didn't come as a surprise to me at all, her death . . . A sense of loss, yes, but a surprise . . . No, not at all.'

ALBERT FINNEY: 'I was at the Bel Air Hotel, when I heard – David Lewin woke me with the news. I was appalled and shocked. If he hadn't indicated there was a strong possibility of suicide, I'd have suspected it was murder. I'd never have expected that of Rachel . . . My God, one feels later, if I'd known she was *that* desperate.'

ANTHONY PAGE: 'She had so much talent and appetite for life. I was at the Mayflower when Carol Scherick called from California and broke the news to me. I was in no doubt that it was suicide. At the end, I think she had made her peace with Rex. At least, I hope so.'

KENNETH WILLIAMS: 'I was absolutely amazed when I heard of her death – I just couldn't see any contributory circumstances. As I saw it, she had no problem about getting work. I didn't know she had a drinking problem. I thought to myself, it can't be lack of sex – a person as promiscuous as Rachel could always find someone else.'

BRIAN EVANS: 'I'd the same reaction as I had when I first heard she'd married Rex Harrison – I just couldn't see the sense of it at all.'

ELEANOR FAZAN: 'She was a battler. Even though I wasn't surprised, I was terribly sorry to see the end of her fight.'

PROF. EARLE GISTER: 'She was a warm and loving human being and I was saddened by her death – but, to be honest with you, I was not that surprised. She was volatile.'

JEAN MARSH: 'Her death was a complete surprise to me. I knew she threatened to take her own life: in my wildest dreams, I never thought she'd do it.'

TOM PATCHETT: 'Not a great deal of surprise, I'm afraid.'

PAMELA MASON: 'She wanted to be the floor show as well as the guest.

She was like Tallulah Bankhead in that respect. Great when the power was on: when it was cut off, she fell down. At least, thank God! she died uncaged.'

DR DI CORI: 'Surprised? Yes – and no. What age was she? Fifty-three . . . ? She did not look it. The years dropped away from her when our sessions were working and I believe they would have helped her, given time. Time was what she didn't have. As I used to say to her, "It takes a long time to become young." '

HAL PRINCE: 'Subsequently, I missed her very much, for that big, carnal, sensuous stage personality of hers is damn hard to find nowadays. Godammit, she would have been marvellous as Mrs Lovett in Steve Sondheim's *Sweeney Todd*, and I don't mean any disrespect to Angela Lansbury.'

RICHARD GERE: 'When I heard of her death, I was very much surprised. I knew she was a driven lady, but I never imagined her troubles would drive her to that. She was a lovely lady, and I do miss her.'

SYBIL CHRISTOPHER: 'When she died, I felt she had got what she wanted at last – peace. Every time I hear John Lennon's song "Woman", although I know it expresses the passing of John Lennon, I am weeping for Rachel.'

LIONEL JEFFRIES: 'When I heard of her death, I didn't believe it could possibly be suicide. I thought of Rachel as the last person in the world who would kill herself. When my wife Eileen and I heard the news – from one of our children, who rang us up before we'd hear it on the radio – we didn't speak to each other for the rest of the day, we were so upset. Rachel Roberts dead! It just didn't seem possible to us.'

NANCY HOLMES: 'All of us who really knew Rachel loved her – she was the warmest friend of all. When we heard of her suicide, we had that awful sinking feeling of people who hadn't done enough to help and are being punished for it.'

ATHOL FUGARD: 'I had just arrived at a Thanksgiving party in London given by my agents, William Morris, when a receptionist said to me, "Sad about poor Rachel Roberts, isn't it?" – "What's happened?" – "She's been found dead." I was a wreck . . . I was simply a wreck. I recall saying to someone that it would be nice to speak a few words in memory of her, but I was told, No, better not – it might spoil the party.'

The two men who had been married to Rachel, greeted the news with words that fitted the occasion and, no doubt, restrained and concealed many private feelings. Alan Dobie was quoted as saying, 'Rachel never really took enough care of herself. She would work herself pretty well into the ground. She had enormous vitality and a great heart. She made life exciting.' He uttered these sentiments, of course, before the cause of death had been published. Rex Harrison was simply quoted saying, 'It's a tragedy. Suicide is always a tragedy.' The comments of Rachel's immediate family are not on record.

DARREN RAMIREZ: 'The morgue had taken possession of Rachel's body. Thanksgiving weekend was coming up and I had to wait for the holiday to pass before I could do anything. I thought it would never end. None of Rachel's family came over to Los Angeles. There was only myself to look after things. Fortunately, the morgue official I spoke to after the holiday turned out to be an understanding guy. He saw how upset I was. Perhaps I was also a bit incoherent. Anyhow, he seems to have got the impression that Rachel and I had been married and I wanted to have her body cremated and take her ashes back to Mexico. By this time, the autopsy had established whatever substance it was that Rachel had swallowed, she was an officially listed "suicide", so, really, there was nothing more that could be done with her and, looking at these things practically, which is what these people have to do, I guess they needed the space.

'I arranged the cremation. There was no one except myself present. I wanted it that way. But afterwards, a few of her closest friends, Sybil and Marti Stevens and Gavin Lambert and myself, all had lunch together – we reckoned Rachel would have wanted it that way. She was always fond of quoting that line of Polly Garter's in *Under Milk Wood*: "Oh, isn't life a terrible thing, thank God?" It just seemed right, somehow, that we should remember poor dear departed Rachel in the good company she'd have been the first to enjoy.

'Her Will included me, Lindsay Anderson, Brenda Houston, Virginia, who'd been her maid in New York, her sister Hazel to whom she left her furs and the contents of her house in Cambridge Street, Val Mayer and Louis Pulvino who had been stage director at the Phoenix Theater where she'd met Val and with whom she always kept up a kind of kidding banter whenever they'd met subsequently.

'We had been all set to have her ashes sent home – until we read the Will. This stipulated, in no uncertain terms, that she did not want to be brought home to Wales or have her ashes placed in the chapel. She preferred her ashes to be scattered over water. I wondered if Swansea Bay would satisfy her without being too close to Welsh soil!'

While Darren tried to decide what to do, and pondered it while visiting his family for Christmas, a tribute to Rachel was taking place on the other coast. Arranged by Milton Goldman, at Marymount Manhattan College on 71st Street, it attracted a fair number of those friends who were available in New York. There was an inevitable sense of strain.

JEAN MARSH: 'Milton asked me if I'd speak. I said I was still too shocked to pull my thoughts together. He asked Rosemary Harris, but she excused herself on the same grounds. Sybil couldn't be there, but sent a moving message to be read out. In fact, all the women present said No for one reason or another, so it was an all-male tribute paid to Rachel, which was a bit odd.'

HAL PRINCE: 'To be frank, I've never known what she really thought of me: so I said to Milton, let's just say out loud what we thought of Rachel – and that's what we did. It wasn't a mob scene: it was a respectable, but by no means crowded auditorium. Others there were Ellis Rabb the theatre director, Edward Hambleton, head of the Phoenix Theater, Stephen Porter, Malcolm McDowell and his wife Mary Steenburgen, Nancy Holmes,

Tammy Grimes and Rex's former wife Elizabeth Harris now Mrs Peter Aitken and her husband Peter, and my wife and others who knew Rachel. I spoke first and recalled something of Rachel's hoydenish "outrageousness". Then it was Richard Gere's turn and he said quite simply, "She had good legs. How do I know? Because she was forever throwing her dress up over her head!" Others spoke briefly. Then Dr di Cori went up and delivered a fairly lengthy oration; it took the form of an allegory about a woman who is waiting on a railroad platform to catch a train that never came.

Elizabeth and Peter Aitken invited guests back to their apartment for Champagne toasts to one who was called, in the report appearing in the *Hollywood Reporter*, 'a chum, who will ever be in our hearts'.

After Christmas, Darren consulted some of Rachel's West Coast friends about how he should dispose of her ashes. 'Why not scatter them off Malibu?' someone suggested.

DARREN RAMIREZ: 'Rex called me asking if I wanted to see *My Fair Lady* and I told him about Malibu. He said it sounded a wonderful idea. While I kept holding, Rex consulted his diary to see which day the following week he would be free – the show was closing soon. He said he'd got matinées this day and that day . . .

'I suddenly said, "Rex, to tell you the truth, I haven't completely made up my mind on this. I want to give it some more thought. I'll let you know."

'It struck me that perhaps Rachel's kinfolk might have adjusted to her suicide, now that the shock of it had passed. Maybe they'd welcome her ashes. After all, I told myself, Rachel's spirit might not feel the same way about it as Rachel herself did when she was out of this world. So I consulted Lindsay Anderson and he said in that way of his, not letting you off your responsibilities, "Why not, if that's what you really want?" He advised me to give the ashes to him in the meantime, for safe-keeping. So on my next visit to England, that's what I did. I really don't know what's happened since. And that's how it ended.'

Not quite, though . . . Rachel came home to England in a small box, the size of a couple of house bricks. The box was neatly wrapped in white paper. An official label pasted on the side declared that Darren Ramirez was permitted by the City of Los Angeles to take possession of the ashes of the deceased therein. The box was conveyed to Lindsay Anderson's North London flat in a rather chic shopping bag. A frieze of faces, all of them of handsome young men, runs all the way round the stylishly pleated sides of the bag and at the top is the discreet cachet of Gianni Versace, the Italian designer, whose newest boutique on Rodeo Drive, Beverly Hills, is now run by Darren Ramirez. Lindsay keeps it on the top shelf of a store-room. Somehow the utilitarian box and its contrastingly exotic container seem to fit the nature of the life within far better than any classical funerary urn. Rachel is still in transit.

JILL BENNETT: 'I don't know any other woman like her: I never have and I don't expect I ever will. We could always meet, Rachel and I, no matter how long it had been since we last saw each other, and have a laugh together and go round to the Connaught and eat chicken sandwiches and drink Champagne.

'I know Lindsay still hasn't decided what to do with her ashes. I don't think we should "toss them on the water", so to speak. I think we should take them down to the Connaught and strew them over the bar in memory of the happy times we all had together. It might not have been what Rachel had in mind, but my God, wouldn't she enjoy the joke!'

GAVIN LAMBERT: 'There's always something unreal about suicide, except of course for the person who commits it. Like the act of confession, it's secret and anonymous at the same time. You enter the cubicle, close the curtain, make intimate revelations to a face you cannot see, and then request a kind of absolution. In her last months, Rachel often talked about killing herself, and made a few ineffective attempts before finally succeeding. And yet, however passionately she talked about it, she never made it seem real. Absurd, rather; for she remained completely herself, and if anything more alive than ever.

'Vitality and Rachel always seemed synonymous to me. She had extraordinary energy. I saw her impatient, discouraged, angry, frustrated, but never tired. What kept her going at full speed, maybe, was a conflict between the puritanism she inherited from her family and her own innate, rebellious sense of adventure. She reacted against her background but never freed herself entirely from it. She lived with a constant sense of surprise at being herself, Rachel Roberts, actress, quite famous, from a Welsh village. When I first knew her, she was married to Rex, and it seemed part of the surprise. She was receiving, by association, the full movie star treatment in Hollywood. It amused and excited her, and made her a bit jealous. But there was nothing mean about this jealousy. Rachel was much too open to be mean, and she openly wished to be a movie star. It would have been an adventure, a fantasy to live out. At the same time she knew that she was a "serious" actress, not destined for movie stardom either by temperament or looks. Still, she couldn't quite leave the idea alone. She had a minor face lift, tightening the area around her eyes, smoothing lines on her forehead, which made no difference to her career but gave her pleasure. Fortunately it made no inroads on the character of her face, which remained exactly the same: not beautiful but attractive, individual, strong, with a smile as broad as the world.

'Careful people in Hollywood were rather alarmed by her. Drank too much, they said, and behaved "embarrassingly" at parties. I went to several Hollywood parties with Rachel and was never embarrassed by her: annoyed sometimes, but not for long. At one of them she came over to me and said loudly, "My God, I love you," then ran her forefinger down the ridge of my nose. Her nail was long and sharp, ripped through the skin and made it bleed profusely. She laughed. I went to the bathroom and found a Band-Aid. "Of course, you've scarred me for life," I said when I came back. She laughed again and said, "Well, people have to live with their scars." In fact, she *did* leave me with a very slight scar. Rachel's scar. I'm glad I have it.

'This was not long before the marriage with Rex broke up. Like suicide, fatal passion always seems unreal unless you happen to be struck by it. Around this time Rachel occasionally reminded me of Vivien Leigh after Olivier left her. She began living under the same obsession that a failed

244

love was a personal defeat and cast a permanent shadow over the rest of life, happiness, self-fulfilment, self-respect, friendships, whatever. And there seemed no cure for it. Although she was a remarkable actress, Rachel couldn't reinvent herself as so many people do after a relapse or setback. The sense of surprise at being herself, Rachel Roberts, turned to a sense of disconnection. She kept repeating that her life had lost all savour and purpose and she wanted to die. Useless to argue, although like her other friends I *did* argue, that she had plenty to live for, her talent, her friends, let alone herself. Nothing hit the spot. She went briefly to a couple of analysts, and oddly enough with them she proved too good an actress. One of them told me afterwards that she was such a brilliant performer he could never be sure what she was really feeling.

'On one of the last occasions that I saw her, Rachel turned up unexpectedly at the apartment hotel in Hollywood where I was staying. She was brightly dressed, with an elegant cap. She gave her usual smile and said, "I've lost my will to live." This time I decided to make a joke of it. "Put an ad in the paper," I said. *"Lost, Rachel Roberts' will to live.* And don't forget to say where. Do you remember? Was it at the corner of Fairfax and Fountain, or Rodeo and Santa Monica? You should offer a reward as well." She laughed and changed the subject, asking if I liked Arnold Bennett, saying *The Old Wives' Tale* was one of her favourite novels. Later I read it and saw why, apart from the fact that it's a masterpiece. It describes a woman's attempt to escape a stifling provincial background, documented in brilliant detail. She goes to Paris, has a fatally unhappy love affair, tries and fails to continue an independent life, and ends up back where she started – old and fat, living with a sister who personified (another parallel with Rachel) the existence she tried to escape. Was this perhaps the only third act Rachel could reinvent for herself? I don't know, but wonder now whether during her last months she wasn't giving a great performance for all of us. This is not to suggest she was insincere. But she had made up her mind to turn her face to the wall, and until she managed to do so, she tried very hard to be good company. If she couldn't go gently, she wouldn't go dismally.

'She talked to me directly about the business of suicide only once. On a trip to England she had acquired brochures from Exit, the euthanasia information society, and brought them to my hotel apartment. When she asked what I thought about the organisation and its aims, I told her that I basically supported them. Although I couldn't imagine committing suicide, I respected the right of anyone to do so. Did I think it a cowardly act? No, on the contrary, I thought it very brave. Would I despise someone who killed himself? No, but I would feel very sad about it. At this point Rachel looked rather ferocious. "Why should you be sad if it made them happy?" she asked. "Because I'd wish they could have found something else to make them happy," I said. She laughed. "Yes, I wish that too," she said.

'But when it finally happened I at least felt happy for Rachel, even though sad for myself. She so obviously wanted it. The situation had moved beyond reason or blame or judgment. It had become a mystery and Rachel took the solution with her. After the cremation, Darren asked a few close friends – Sybil and Jordan Christopher, Marti Stevens and myself – to lunch at the Beverly Wilshire hotel. He thought Rachel would have liked the idea. We ordered Champagne, drank toasts to her, and when we talked about her, it was not in the hushed respectful tone that one talks of the recently dead. We refused to make a tragedy of it; we discussed her as if expecting her to join the party at any moment. I feel sure she would have understood this, and understood what I kept thinking: *This time you've really gone too far.* Humour was one of her great attributes, like loyalty and generosity. If only she could have been more generous and less punishing to herself. If only – but now I hear Rachel having the last laugh. For in spite of everything, I still think of her as a force for life, so much more real than her death.'